THOMAS
BALINGER

FOR UKULELE

Other titles by Thomas Balinger:

The Ukulele Songbook – 50 All Time Classics
The Ukulele Songbook – 50 All Time Classics, Vol. II
The Ukulele Songbook – Best of Gospel
The Ukulele Songbook – Hymns and Songs of Worship
The Ukulele Songbook – Christmas carols
The Ukulele Songbook – Shanties and Songs of the sea

Most wanted Ukulele Chords

Thomas Balinger
The Big Book of Children's Songs for Ukulele

thomasbalinger@gmail.com

ISBN: 978-1523763467

Preface

Dear fellow Ukulele players,

This is my big collection of songs to play for (or with) children, arranged for easy Ukulele in standard C tuning (G-C-E-A). There's something here for every age and musical taste and at 150 children's songs, lullabies and nursery rhymes to choose from, it'll take some time before you run out of songs to play. Most of these songs can be played even by the Ukulele beginner and the ones that are somewhat harder to play can be mastered with only a little practice.

To make playing them as easy and straightforward as possible, I've transposed these songs to „easy" Ukulele keys and simplified some rhythmic notations otherwise to difficult to read. Along with chord symbols and lyrics, I included a melody tab to let you play the melody of a song you may not know even if you don't read music at all. Right next to each song you'll also find chord diagrams for the chords needed, so you don't have to turn pages to look up a particular chord - you can even risk a quick glance while playing.

There's also an appendix with a handy compendium of the basic Ukulele chords and a selection of easy strumming and picking patterns you can use to accompany yourself or others (or as a starting point to develop your own patterns).

Wishing you lots of fun,
Thomas Balinger

Contents

Songs (in alphabetical order)

Appendix

A-Hunting we will go

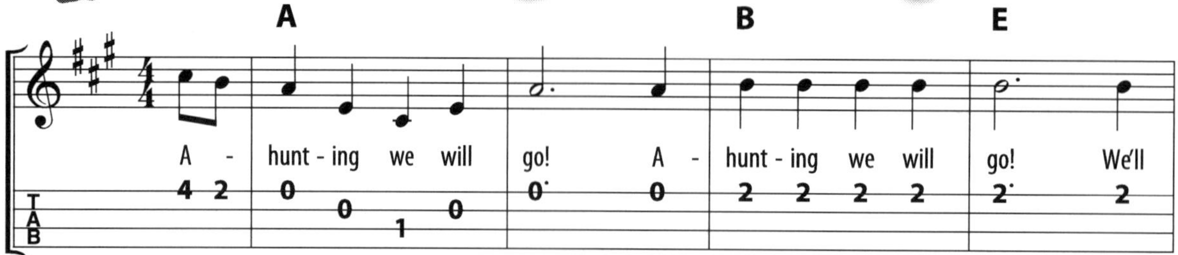

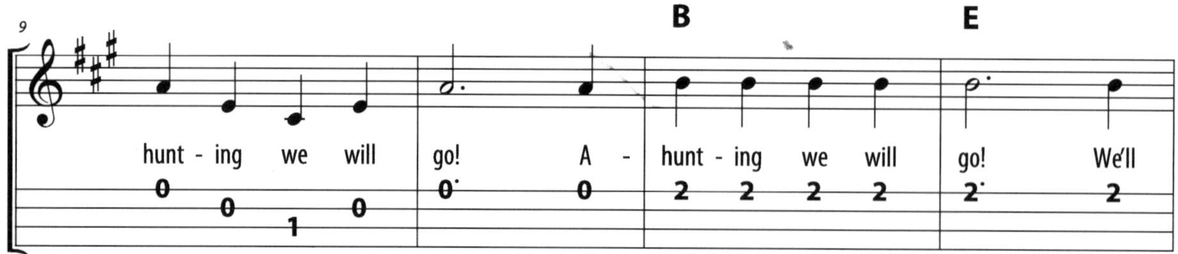

„... a fish and put him on a dish ..."
„... a bear and cut his hair ..."
„... a pig and dance a little jig ..."
„... a giraffe and make him laugh ..."
„... a mouse and put him in a house ..."

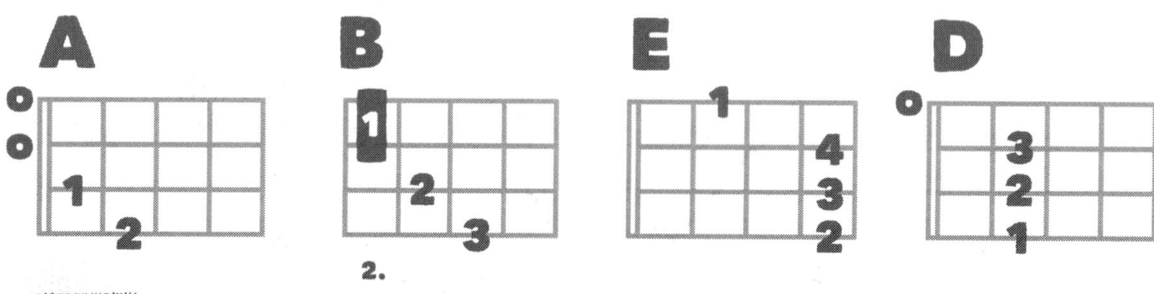

Bill Grogan's goat

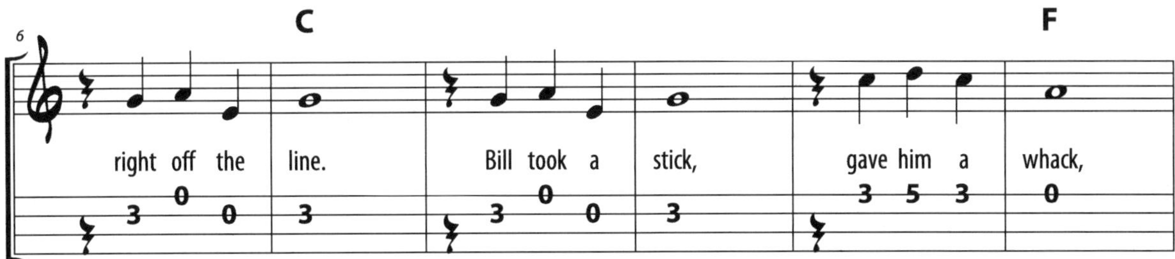

2. *The whistle blew, the train was nigh,*
   Bill Grogan's goat, was doomed to die!
   He gave a cough of mortal pain,
   coughed up those shirts and flagged the train!

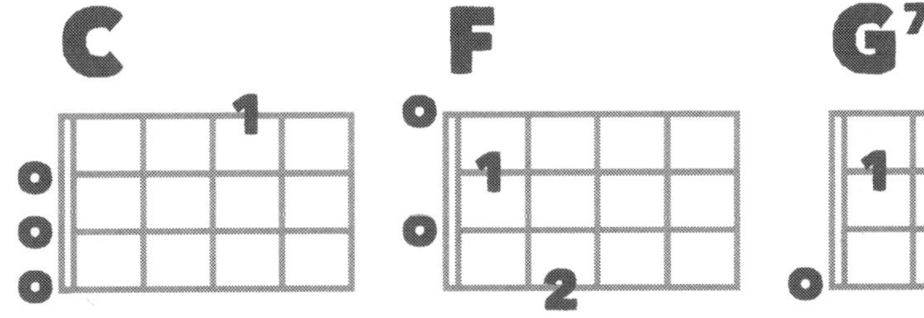

Bobby Shafto

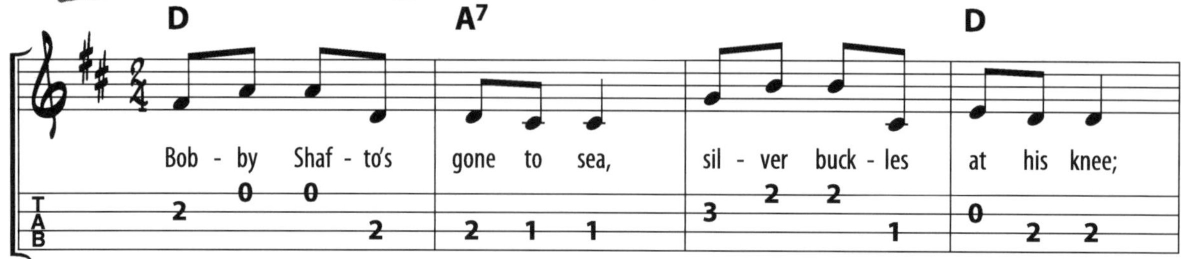

2. *Bobby Shafto's bright and fair,*
   panning out his yellow hair;
   He's my love for evermore,
   Bonny Bobby Shafto!

Bluebird, Bluebird

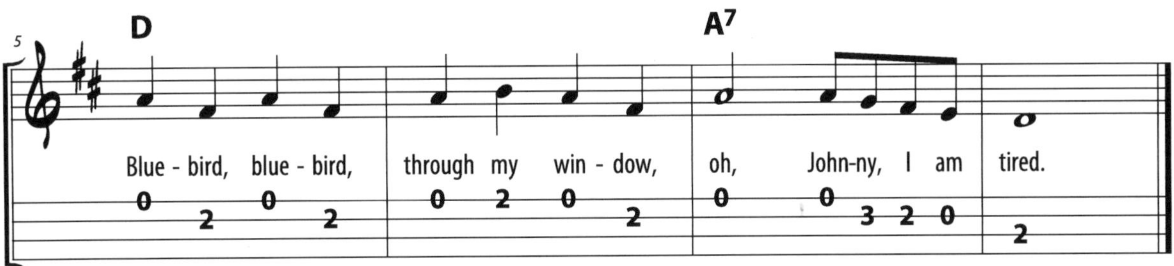

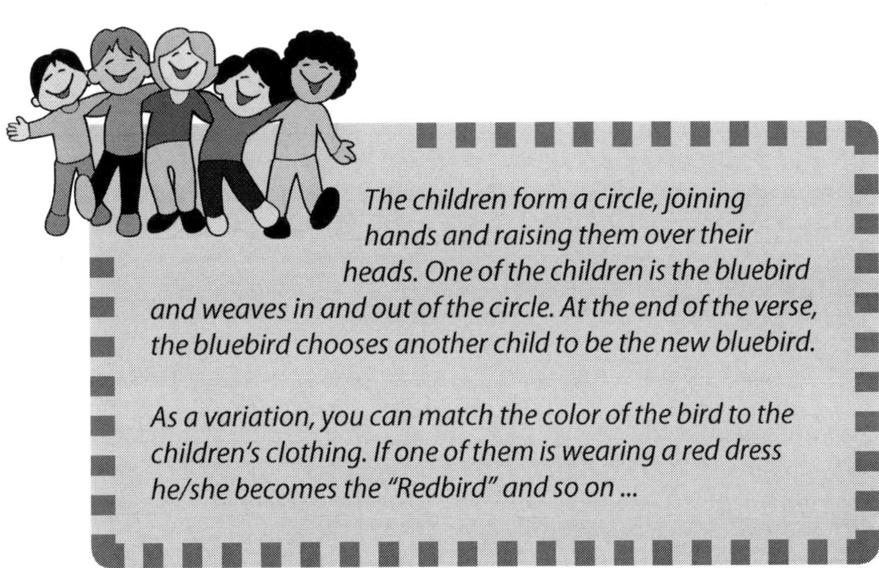

The children form a circle, joining hands and raising them over their heads. One of the children is the bluebird and weaves in and out of the circle. At the end of the verse, the bluebird chooses another child to be the new bluebird.

As a variation, you can match the color of the bird to the children's clothing. If one of them is wearing a red dress he/she becomes the "Redbird" and so on ...

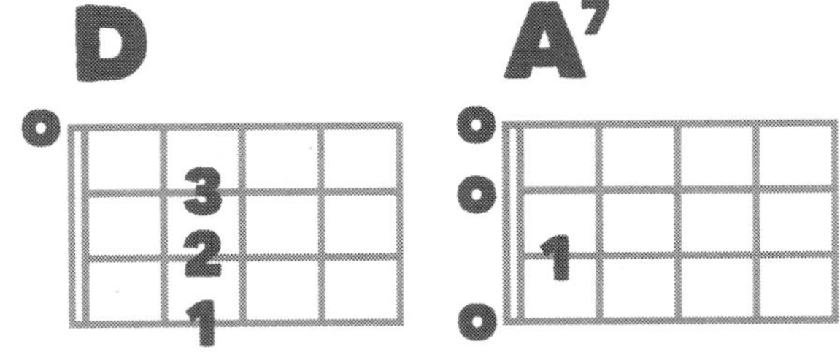

Grandfather's clock

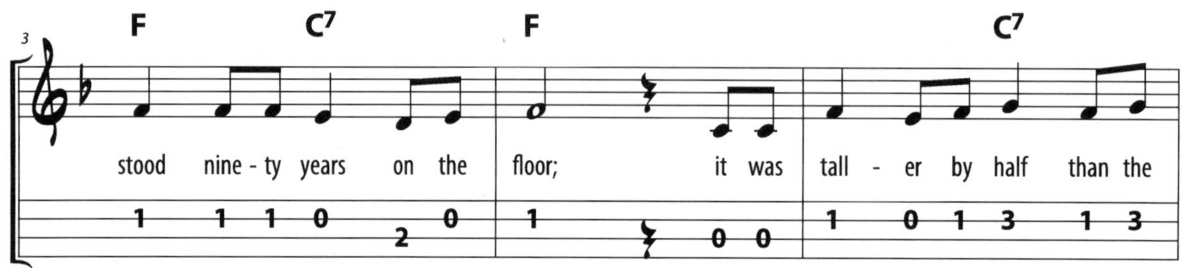

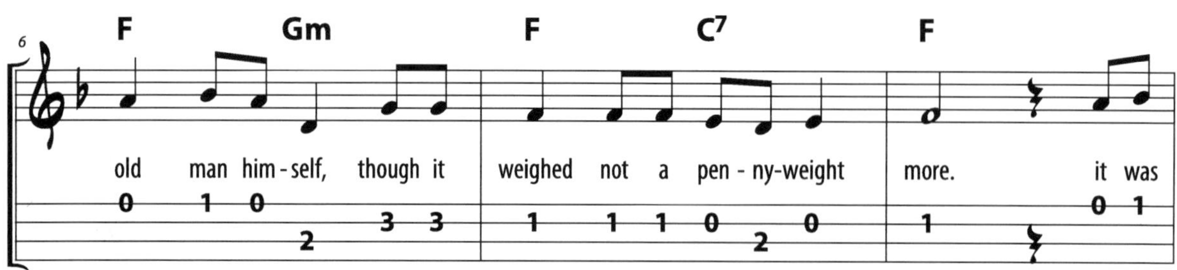

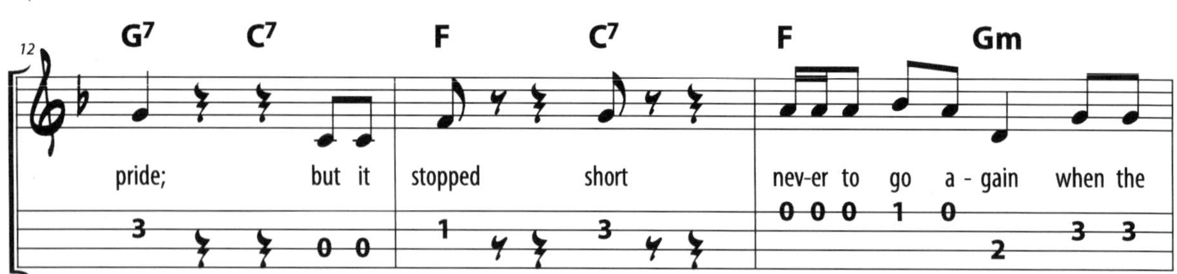

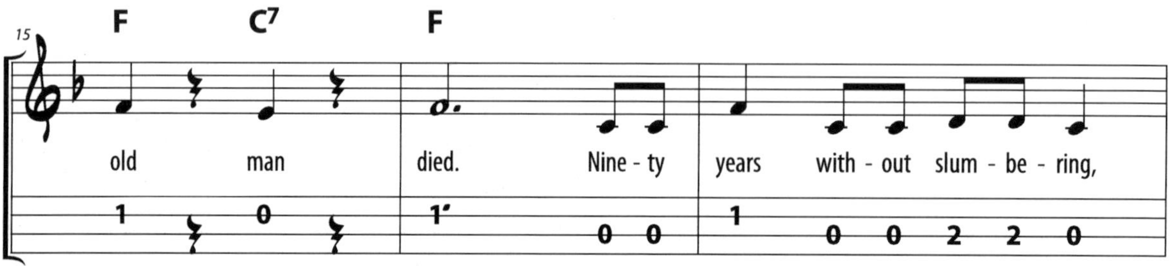

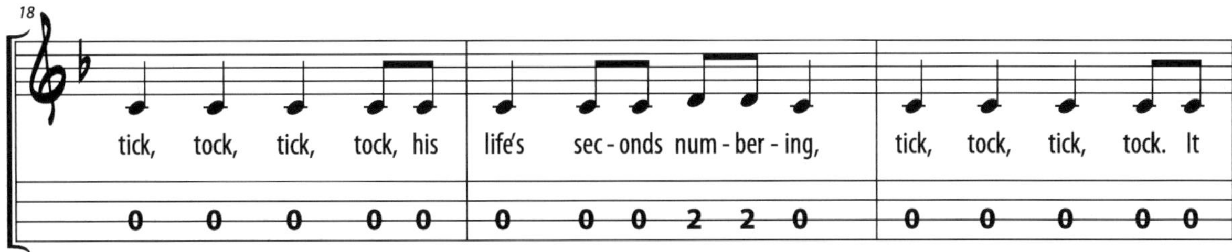

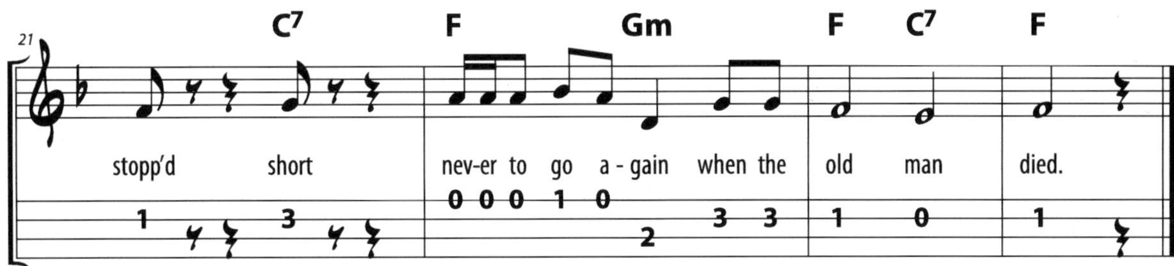

2. *In watching its pendulum swing to and fro,*
   many hours had he spent while a boy;
   and in childhood and manhood the clock seemed to know
   and to share both his grief and his joy.
   For it struck twenty-four when he entered at the door,
   With a blooming and beautiful bride;
   But it stopped short ...
3. *My grandfather said that of those he could hire,*
   not a servant so faithful he found;
   for it wasted no time, and had but one desire,
   at the close of each week to be wound.
   And it kept in its place not a frown upon its face,
   and its hands never hung by its side.
   But it stopped short ...
4. *It rang an alarm in the dead of the night*
   an alarm that for years had been dumb;
   and we knew that his spirit was pluming for flight
   that his hour of departure had come.
   Still the clock kept the time, with a soft and muffled chime,
   as we silently stood by his side;
   But it stopped short ...

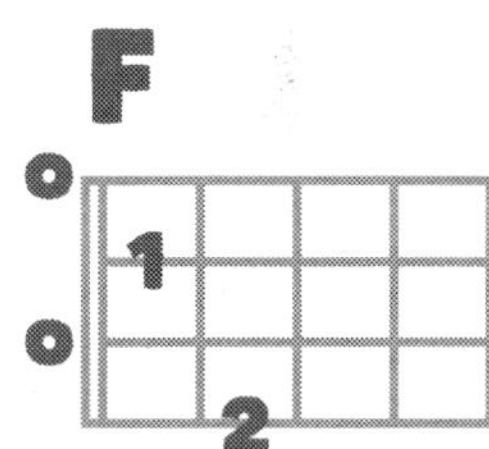

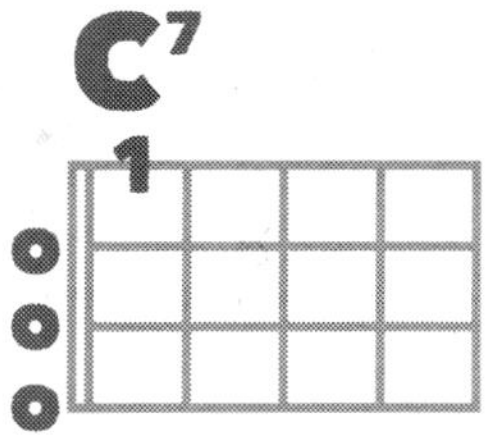

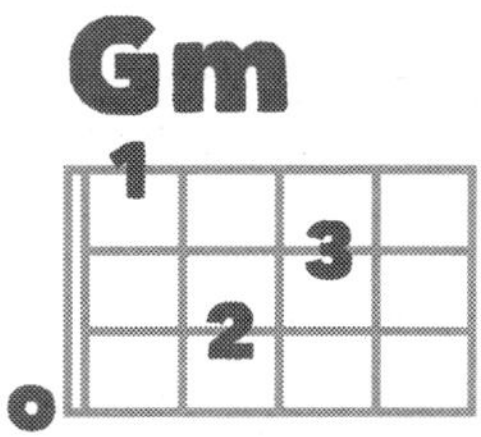

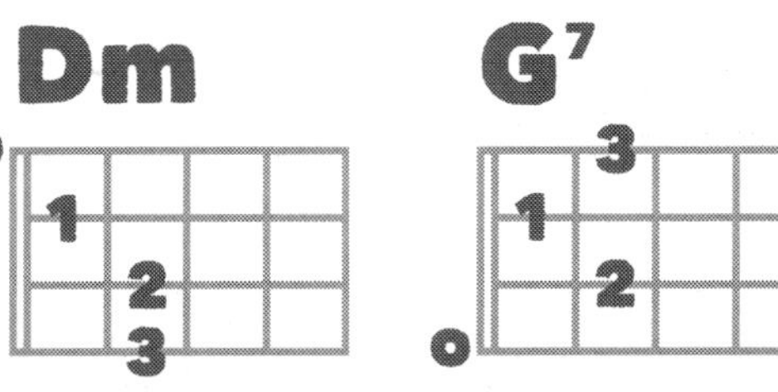

I love little kitty

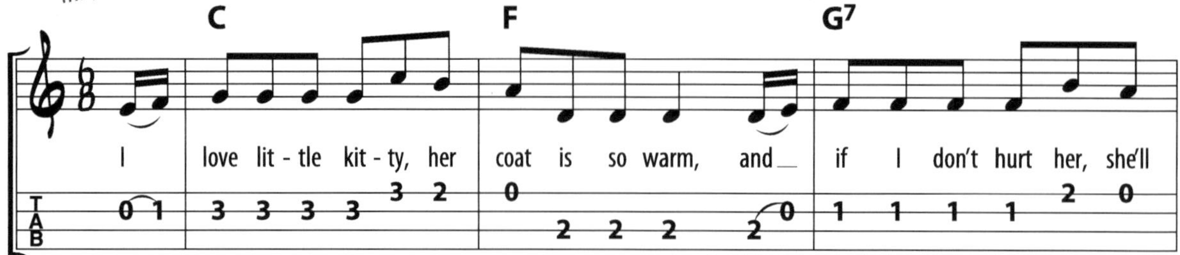

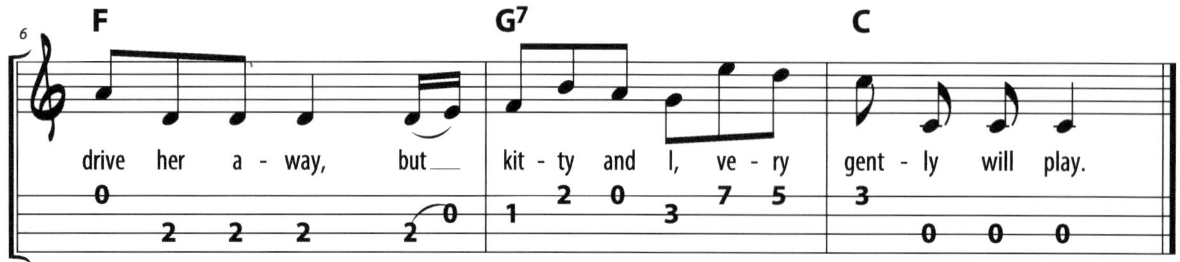

2. *She shall sit by my side and I'll give her some food;*
   And kitty will love me because I am good.
   I'll pat pretty kitty, and then she will purr;
   and thus show her thanks for my kindness to her.

3. *I'll not pinch her ears, nor tread on her paw,*
   lest I should provoke her to use her sharp claw.
   I never will vex her nor make her displeased:
   For kitty don't like to be worried and teased.

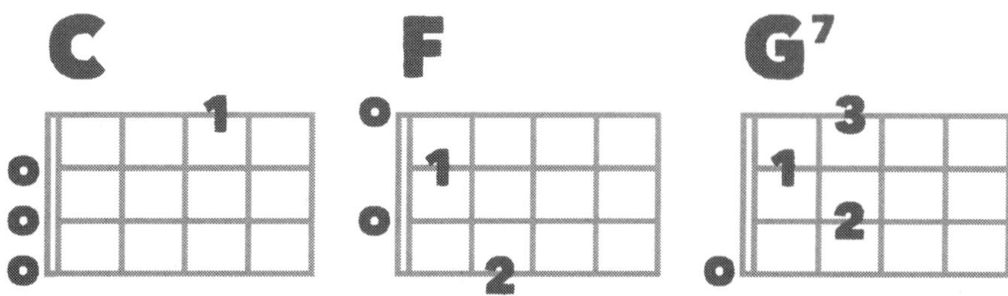

Golden slumbers

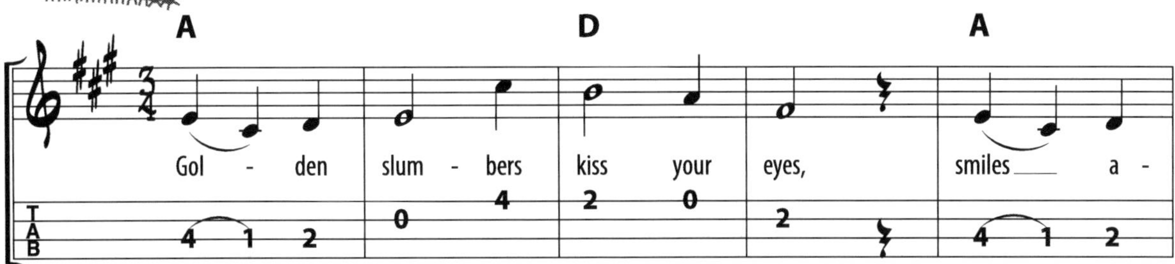

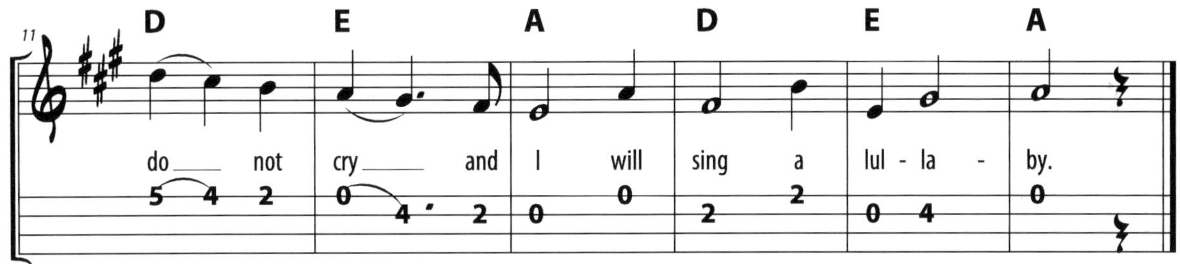

2. *Cares you know not, therefore sleep*
   while over you a watch I'll keep
   Sleep pretty darling, do not cry
   and I will sing a lullaby.

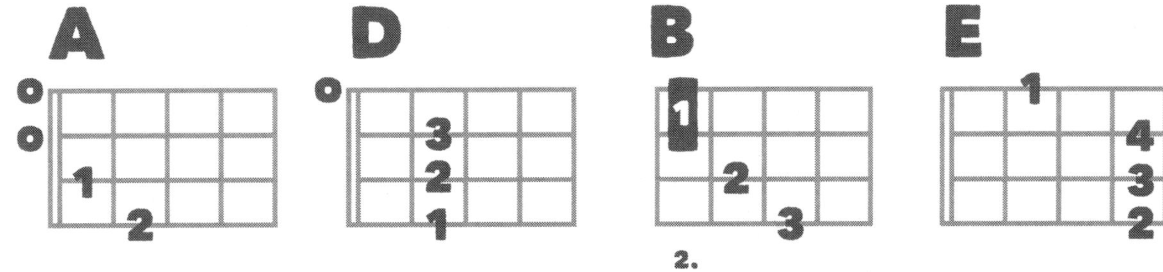

inkum, winkum

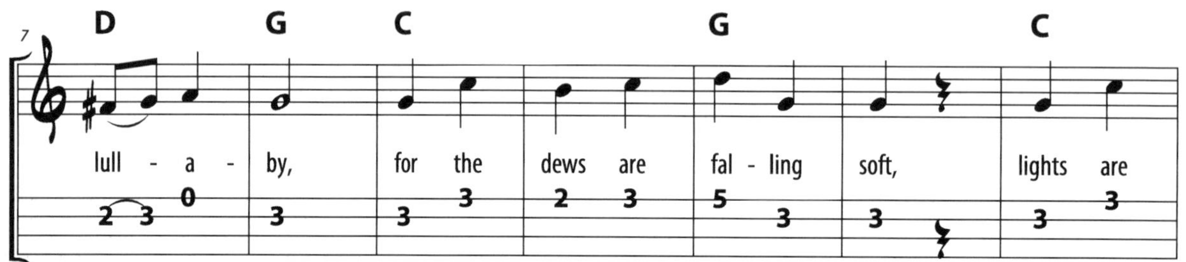

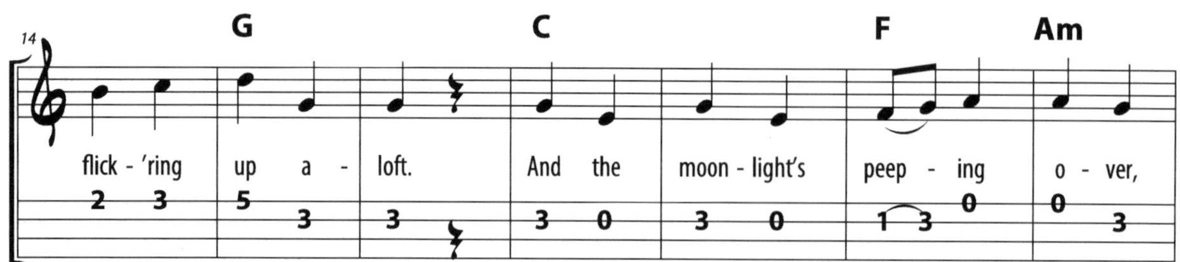

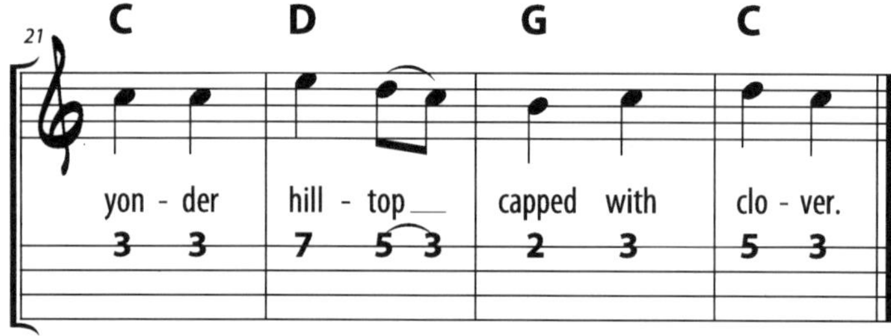

2. *Chickens long have gone to rest,*
birds lie snug within their nest,
and my birdie soon will be
sleeping like a chick-a-dee.
For with only half a try;
Winkum, Winkum shuts her eye.

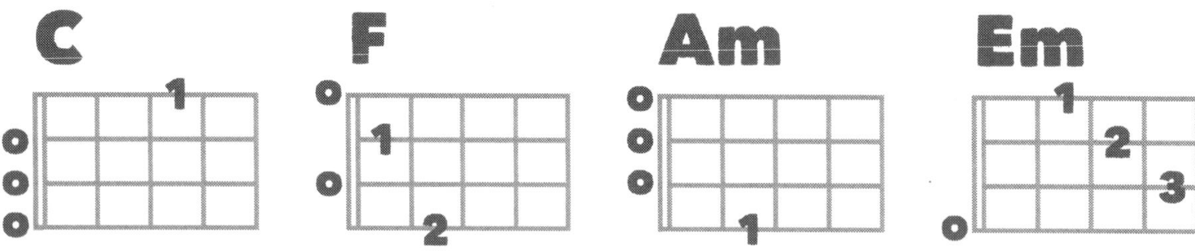

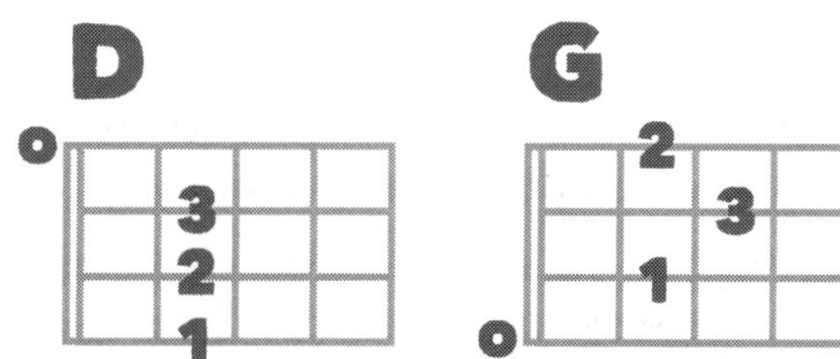

Wee Willi Winkie

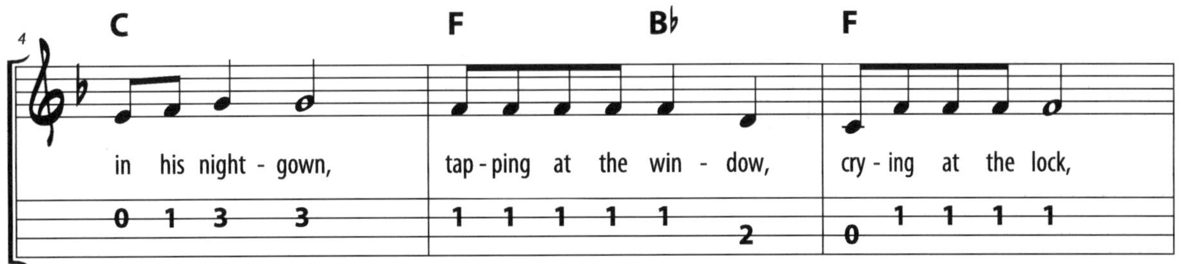

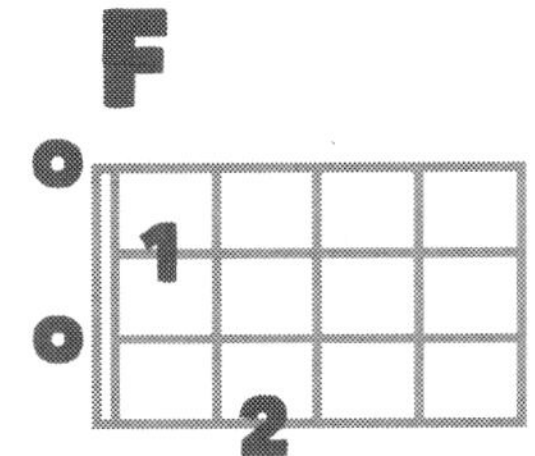

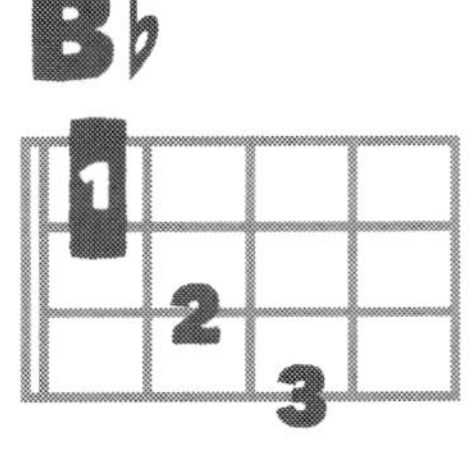

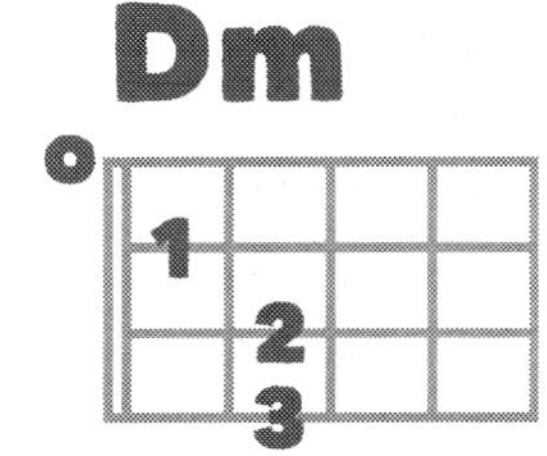

The alphabet song

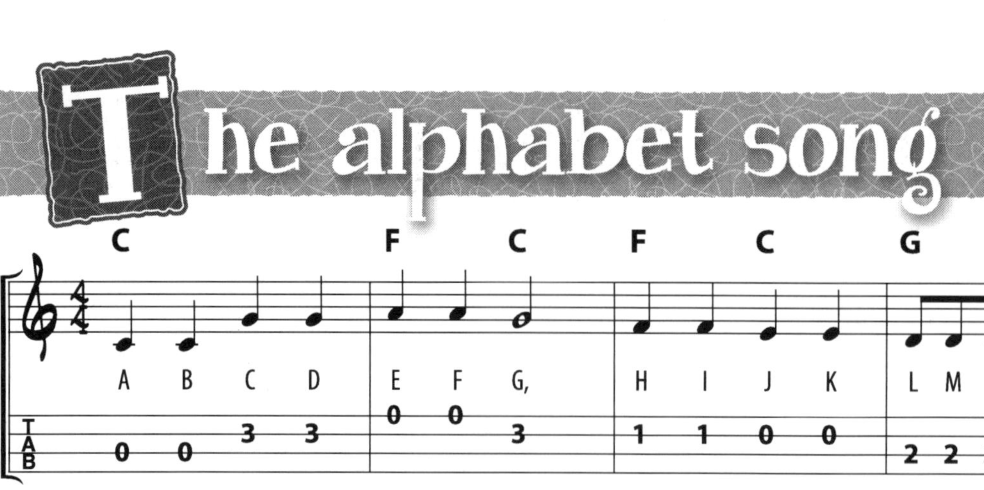

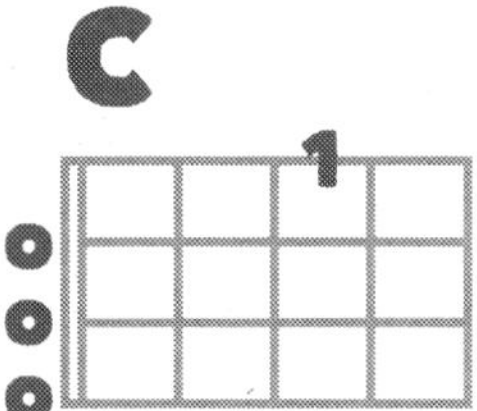

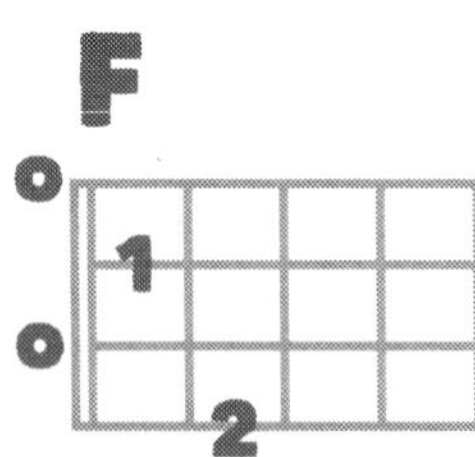

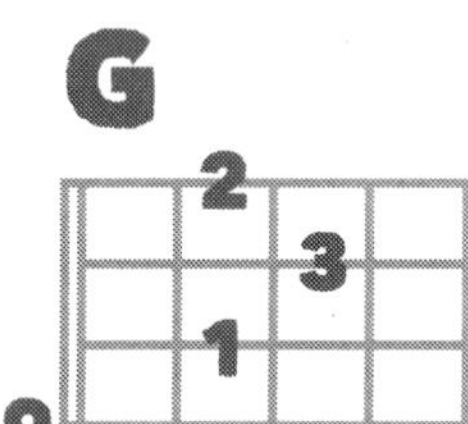

Simple Simon

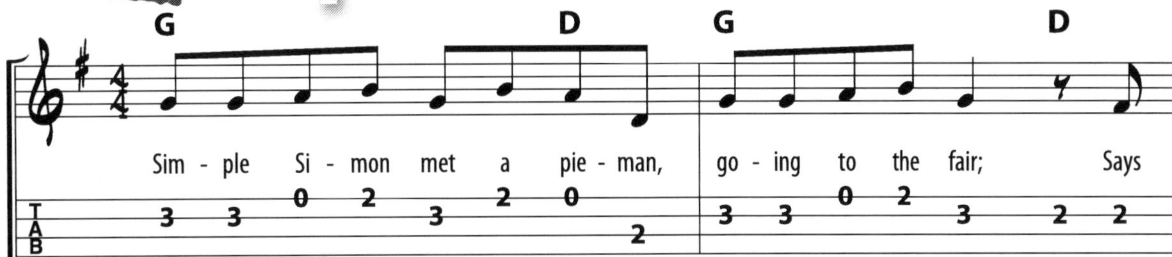

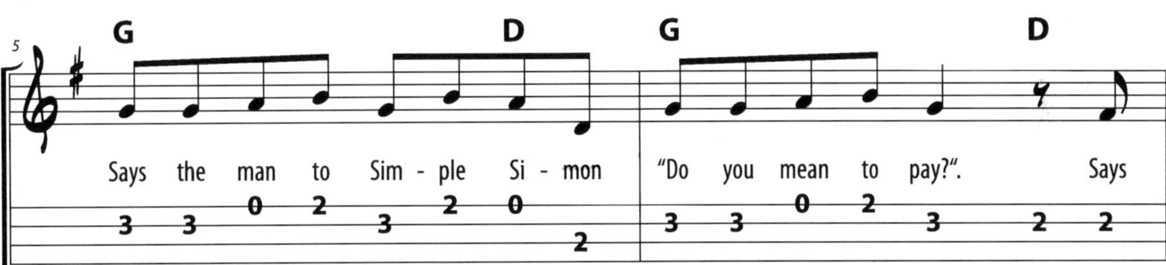

2. *Simple Simon went a-fishing,*
   for to catch a whale;
   All the water he had got,
   was in his mother's pail.

   Simple Simon went to look
   if plums grew on a thistle;
   He pricked his fingers very much,
   which made poor Simon whistle.

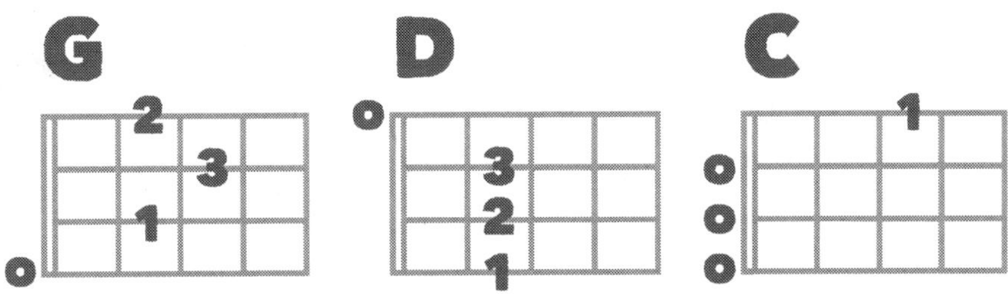

The fox

D
The fox went out on a chil - ly night, prayed to the Moon to

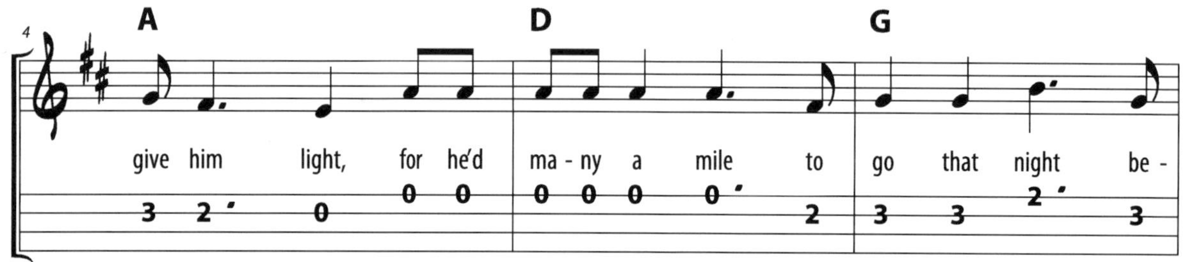
A D G
give him light, for he'd ma - ny a mile to go that night be -

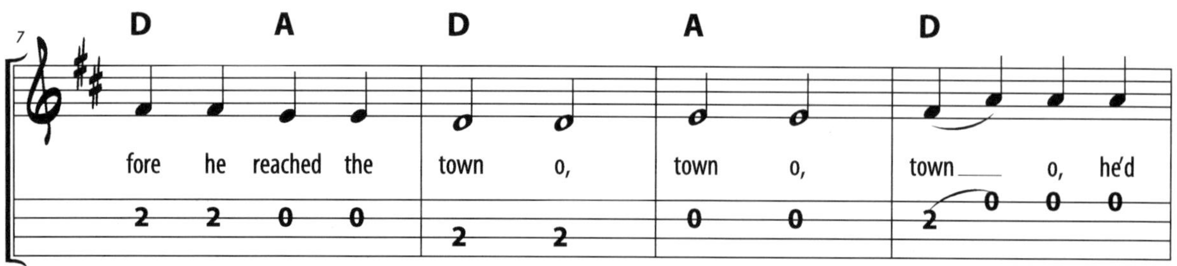
D A D A D
fore he reached the town o, town o, town o, he'd

G D A D
ma - ny a mile to go that night be - fore he reached the town o.

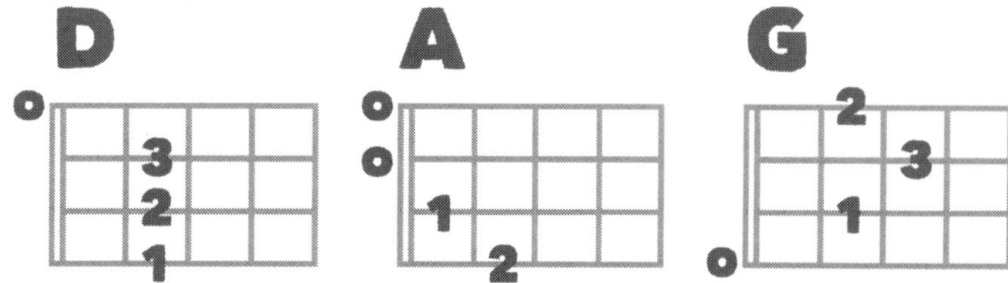
D
A
G

2. *He ran till he came to a great big pen*
where the ducks and the geese were put therein.
"A couple of you will grease my chin
before I leave this town-o, town-o, town-o,
a couple of you will grease my chin
before I leave this town-o."

3. *He grabbed the grey goose by the neck,*
throwed a duck across his back;
he didn't mind their quack, quack, quack,
and their legs all a-dangling down-o, down-o, down-o,
he didn't mind their quack, quack, quack,
and their legs all a-dangling down-o.

4. *Old Mother Flipper-Flopper jumped out of bed;*
out of the window she cocked her head,
Crying, "John, John! The grey goose is gone
and the fox is on the town-o, town-o, town-o!"
Crying, "John, John, the grey goose is gone
and the fox is on the town-o!"

5. *Then John he went to the top of the hill,*
blowed his horn both loud and shrill,
the fox he said, "I'd better flee with my kill
or they'll soon be on my trail-o, trail-o, trail-o."
The fox he said, "I'd better flee with my kill
or they'll soon be on my trail-o."

6. *He ran till he came to his cozy den;*
there were the little ones eight, nine, ten.
They said, "Daddy, better go back again,
'cause it must be a mighty fine town-o, town-o, town-o!"
They said, "Daddy, better go back again,
'cause it must be a mighty fine town-o."

7. *Then the fox and his wife without any strife*
cut up the goose with a fork and knife.
They never had such a supper in their life
and the little ones chewed on the bones-o, bones-o, bones-o,
they never had such a supper in their life
and the little ones chewed on the bones-o.

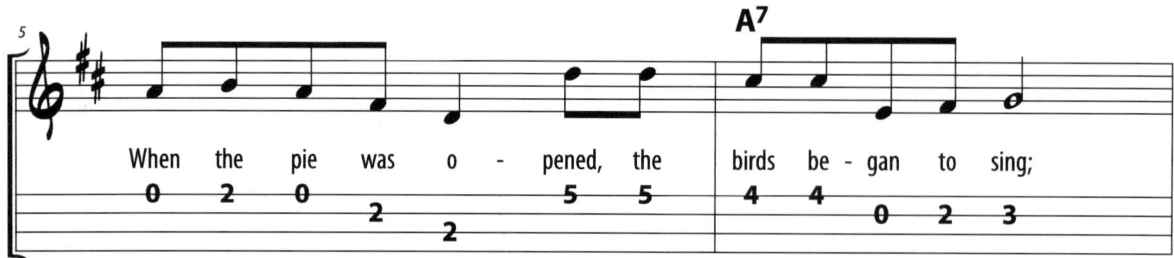

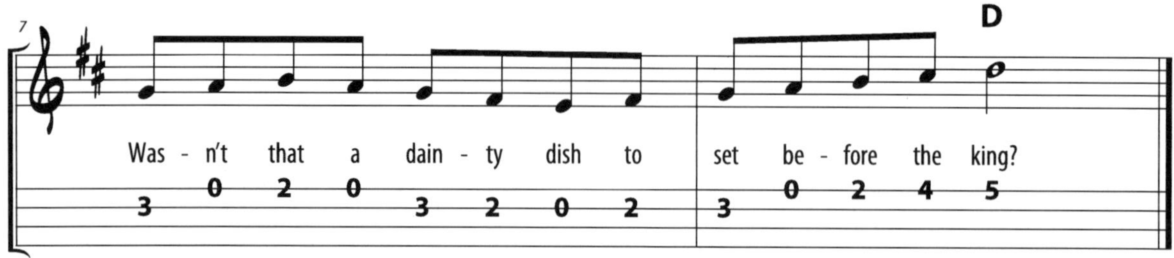

2. *The king was in his counting house, counting out his money;*
The queen was in the parlour, eating bread and honey.
The maid was in the garden, hanging out the clothes,
when down came a blackbird and pecked off her nose.

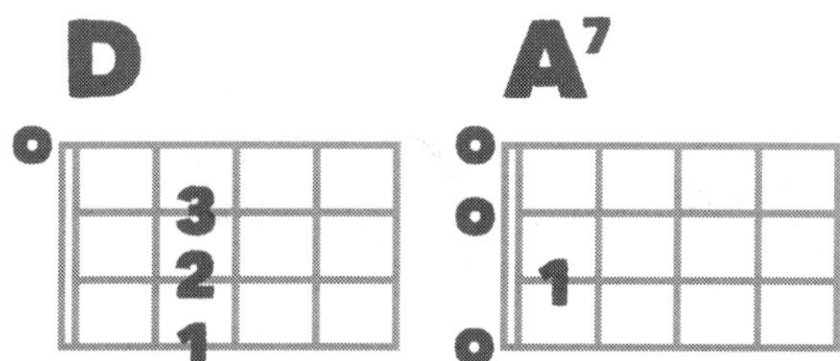

Hark, hark, the dogs do bark

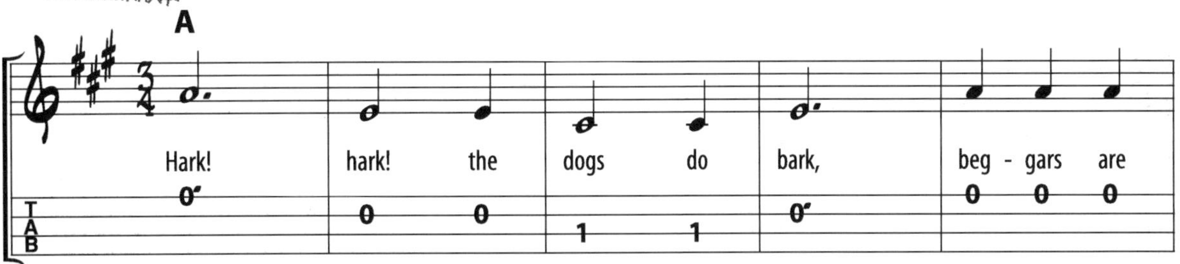

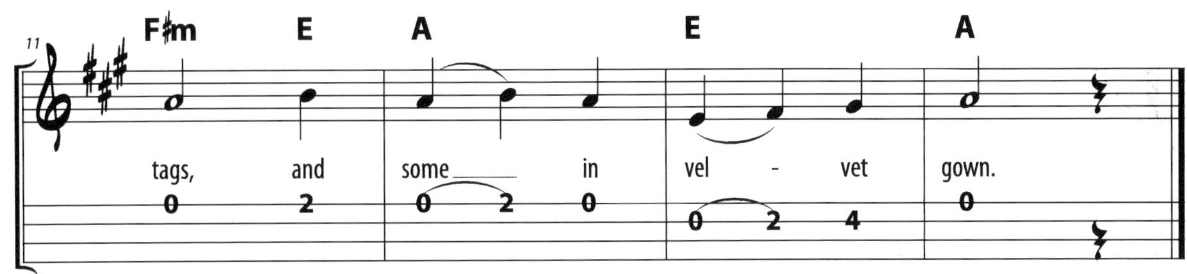

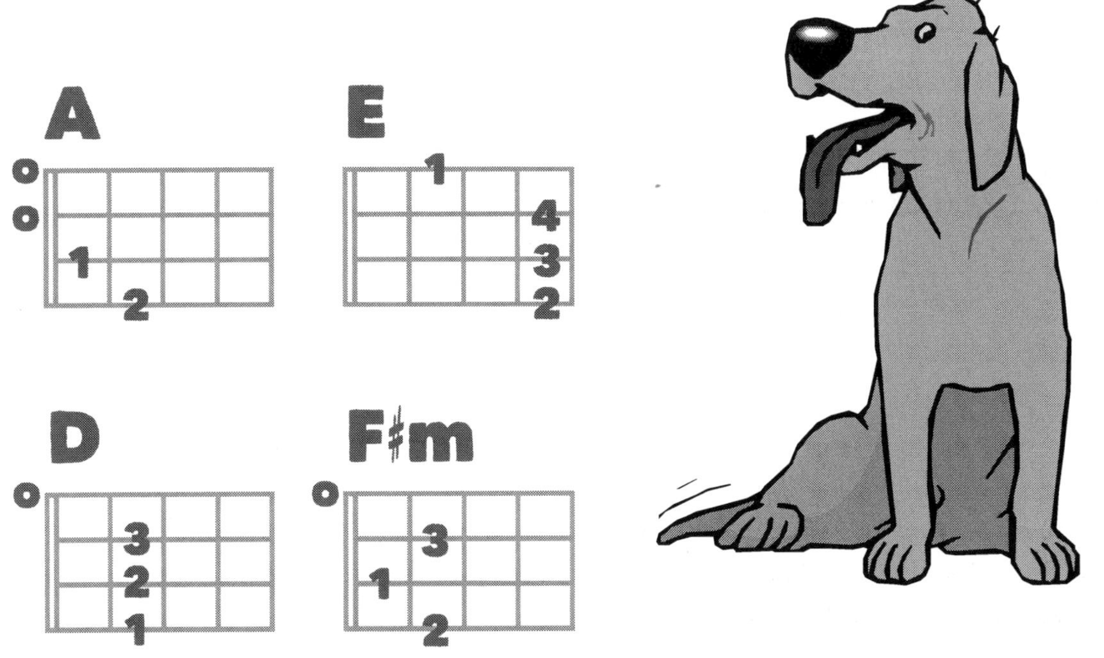

Little Polly Flinders

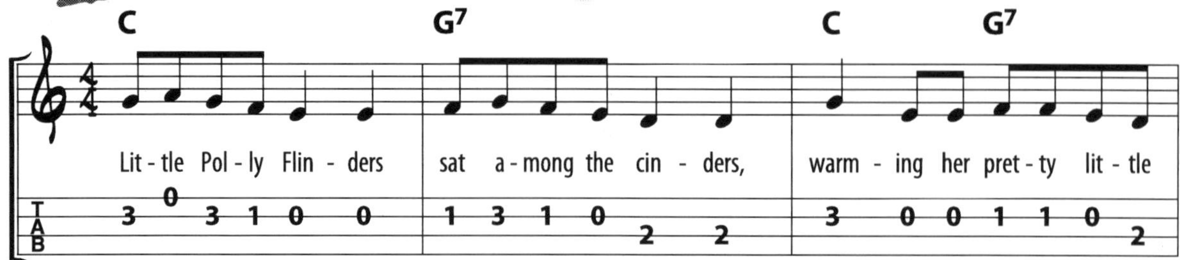

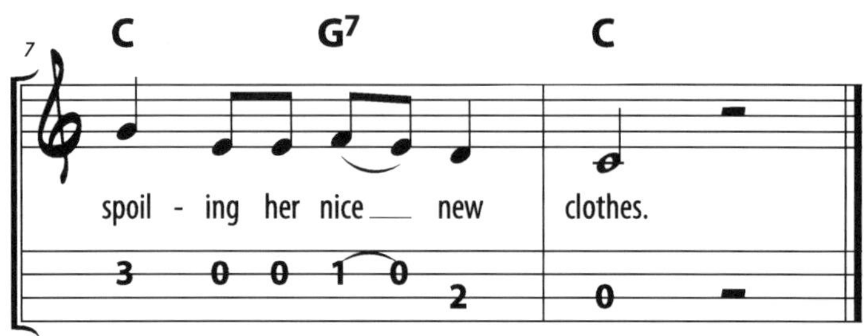

Little Jack Horner

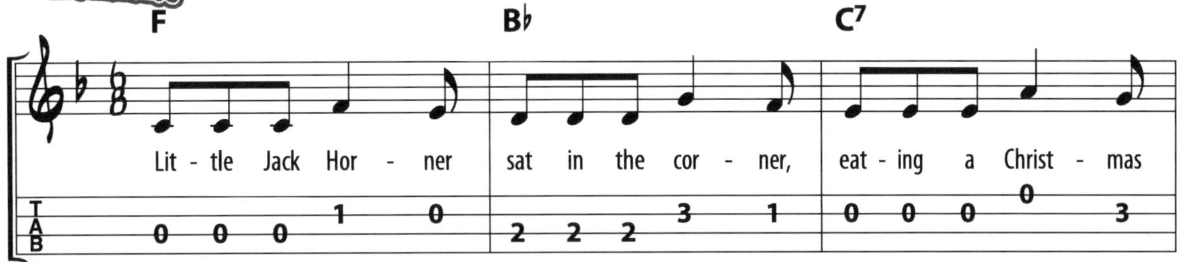

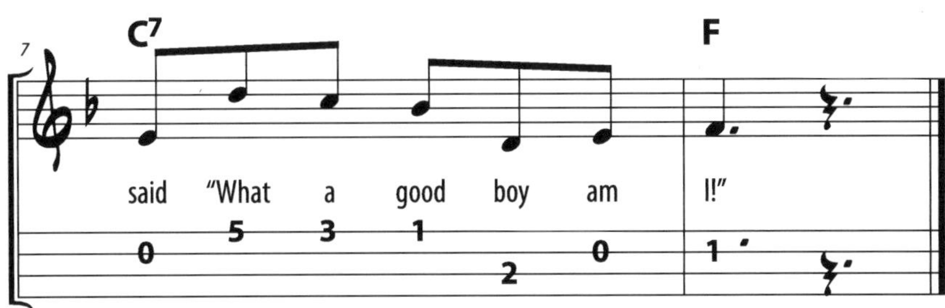

Old mother Hubbard

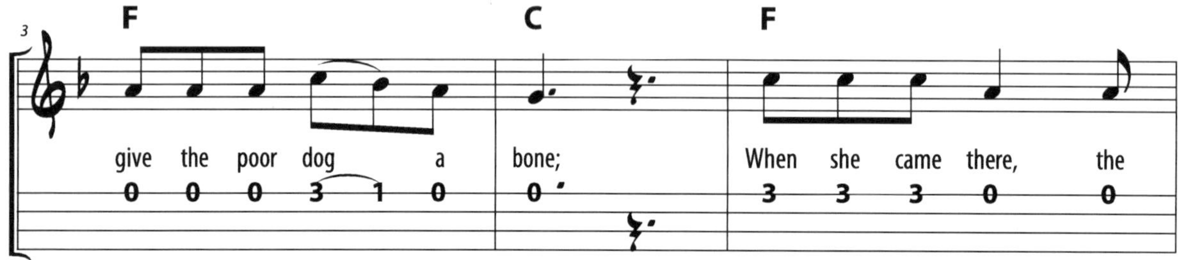

2. *She went to the baker's to buy him some bread;*
   When she came back the dog was dead!

3. *She went to the undertaker's to buy him a coffin;*
   When she came back the dog was laughing.

4. *She took a clean dish to get him some tripe;*
   When she came back he was smoking his pipe.

5. *She went to the alehouse to get him some beer;*
   When she came back the dog sat in a chair.

6. *She went to the tavern for white wine and red;*
   When she came back the dog stood on his head.

7. *She went to the fruiterer's to buy him some fruit;*
   When she came back he was playing the flute.

8. *She went to the tailor's to buy him a coat;*
When she came back he was riding a goat.

9. *She went to the hatter's to buy him a hat;*
When she came back he was feeding her cat.

10. *She went to the barber's to buy him a wig*
When she came back he was dancing a jig.

11. *She went to the cobbler's to buy him some shoes;*
When she came back he was reading the news.

12. *She went to the sempstress to buy him some linen;*
When she came back the dog was spinning.

13. *She went to the hosier's to buy him some hose;*
When she came back he was dressed in his clothes.

14. *The Dame made a curtsy, the dog made a bow;*
The Dame said: "Your servant"; The dog said: "Bow-wow".

15. *This wonderful dog was Dame Hubbard's delight,*
He could read, he could dance, he could sing, he could write.

16. *She gave him rich dainties whenever he fed,*
And erected this monument when he was dead.

All night, all day

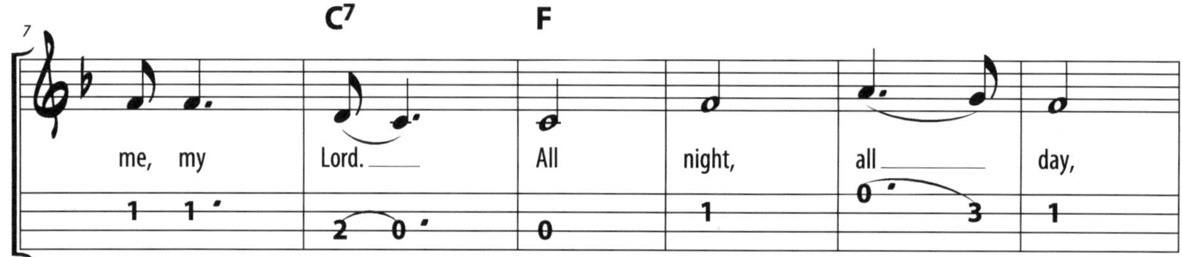

2. *When at night I go to sleep,*
angels watching over me, my Lord.
Pray the Lord my soul to keep,
angels watching over me.

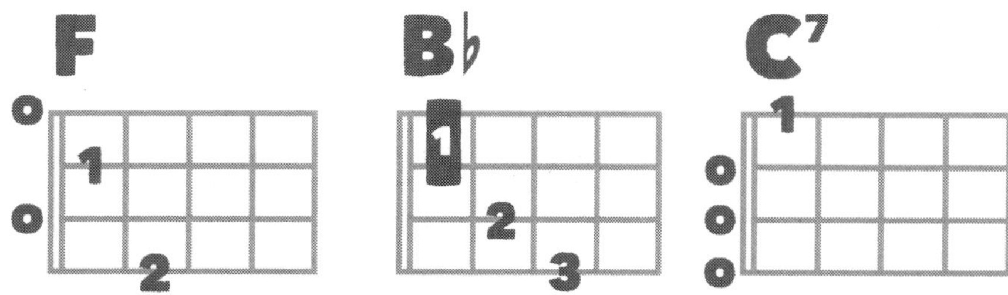

Cock a doodle do

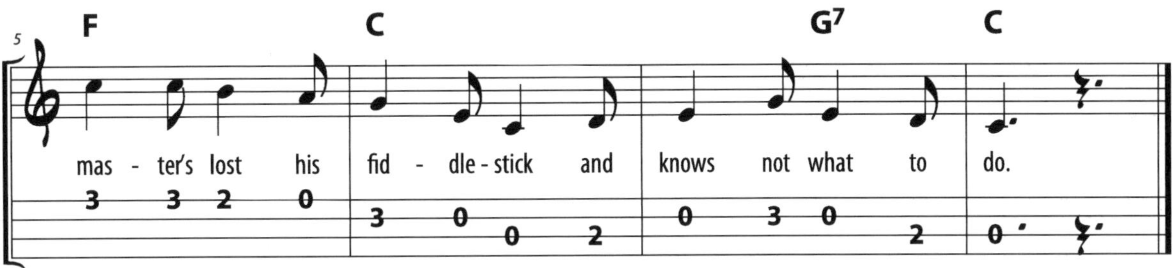

2. *Cock a doodle do!*
   What is my dame to do?
   Till master's found his fiddlingstick,
   She'll dance without her shoe.

3. *Cock a doodle do!*
   My dame has found her shoe,
   And master's found his fiddlingstick,
   Sing cock a doodle do!

4. *Cock a doodle do!*
   My dame will dance with you,
   While master fiddles his fiddlingstick,
   And knows not what to do.

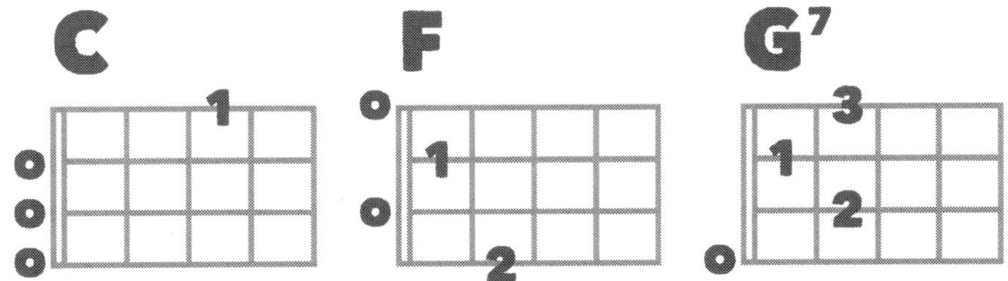

Star light, star bright

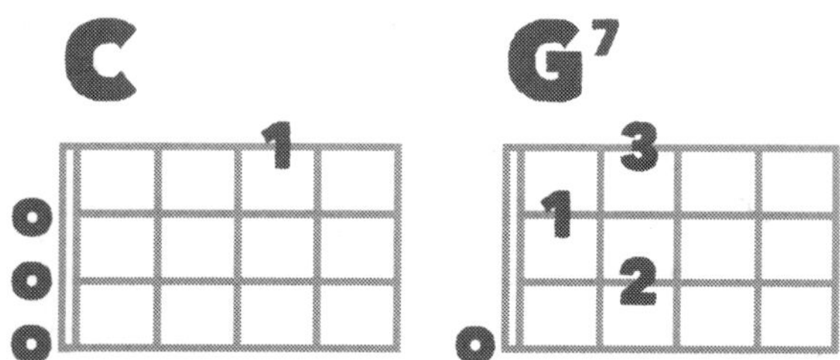

Christmas is coming

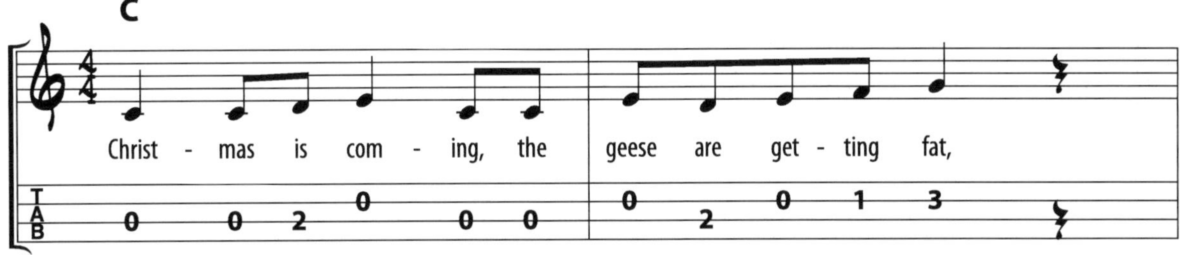

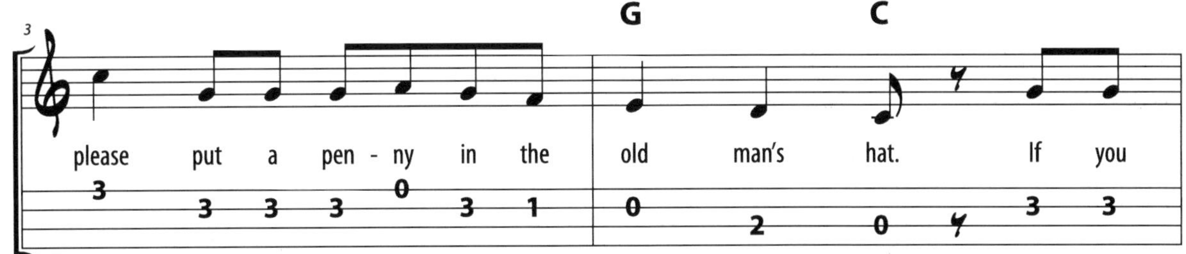

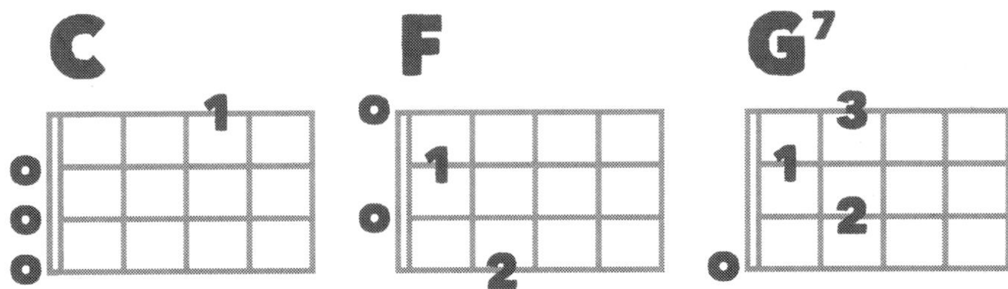

Here we go, looby loo

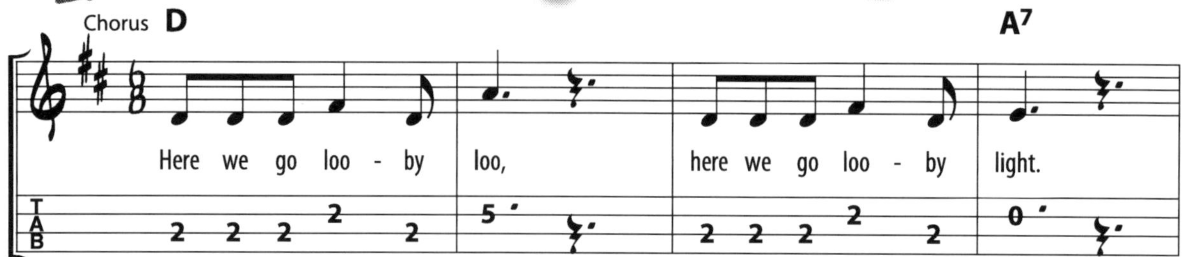

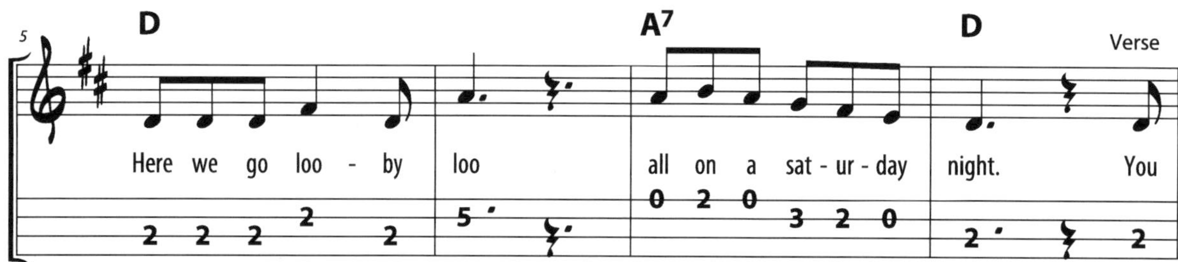

left hand ...
right foot ...
left foot ...
head ...
whole self ...

Join hands and circle around during the chorus. During the verse, stop circling and do as the words indicate. After each verse, join hands and start circling again.

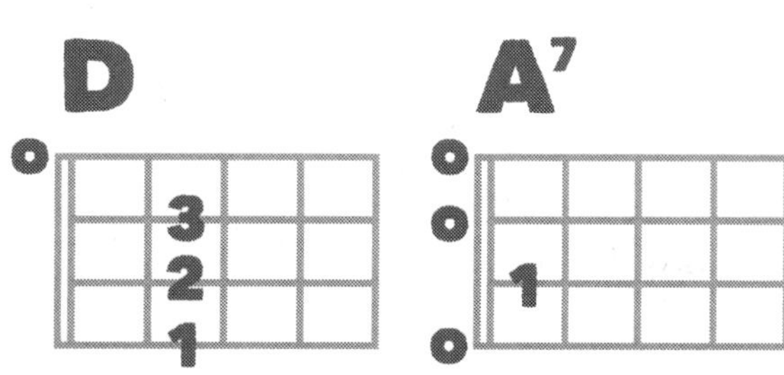

Boys and girls, come out to play

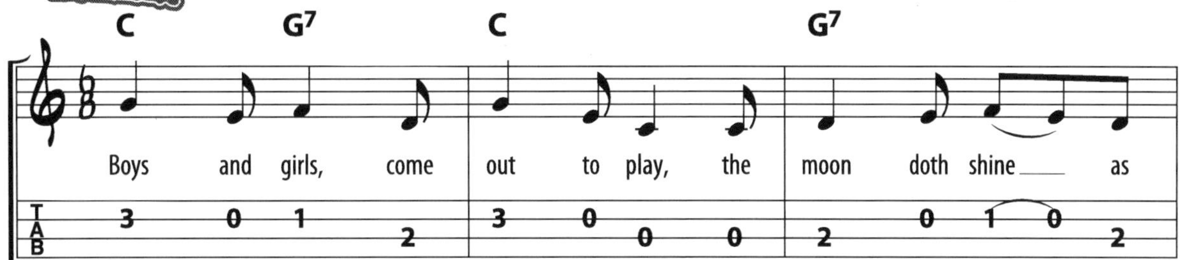

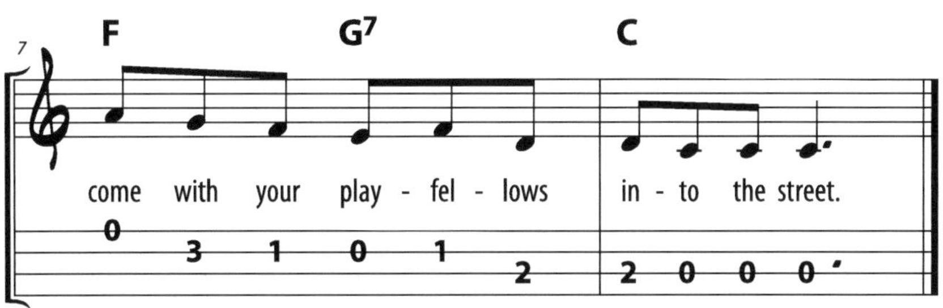

2. *Come with a whoop, come with a call,*
come with a good will or not at all.
Up the ladder and down the wall,
a halfpenny roll will serve us all.

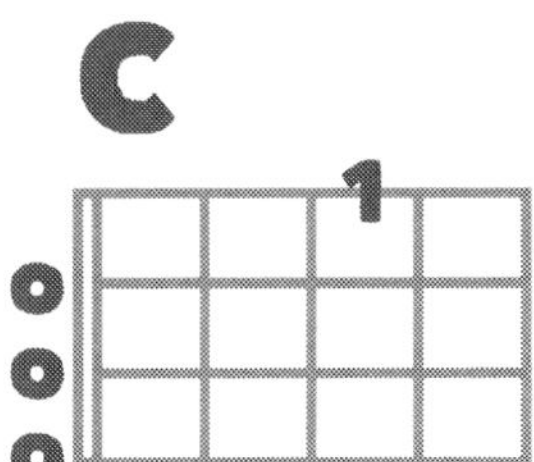

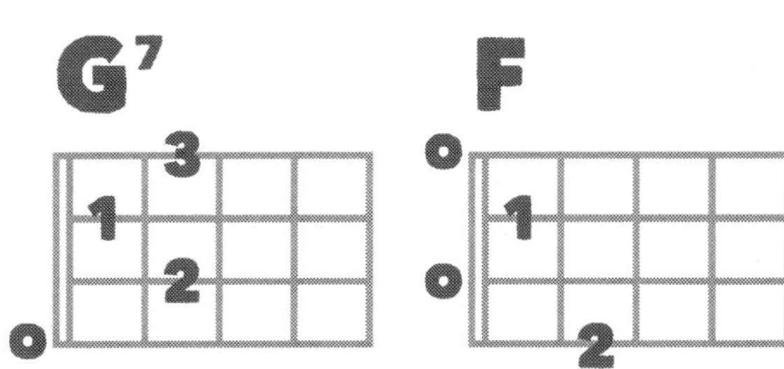

All through the night

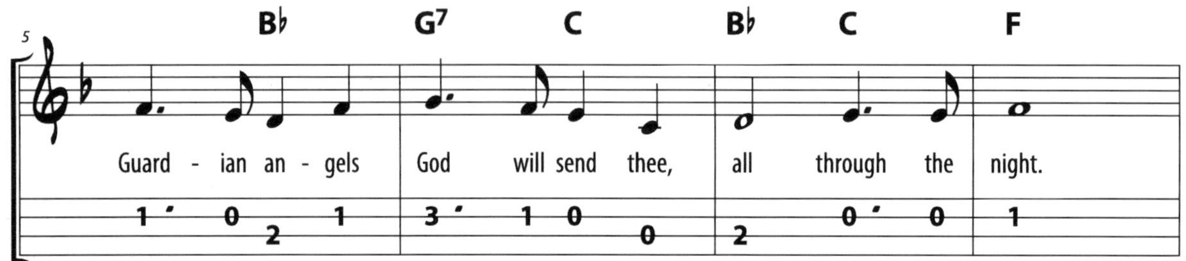

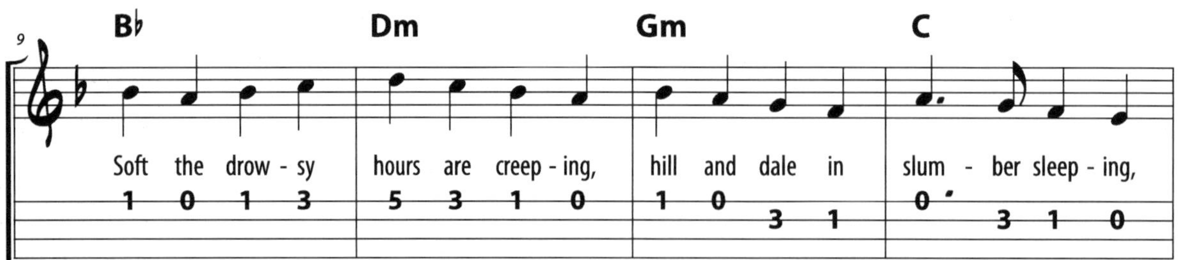

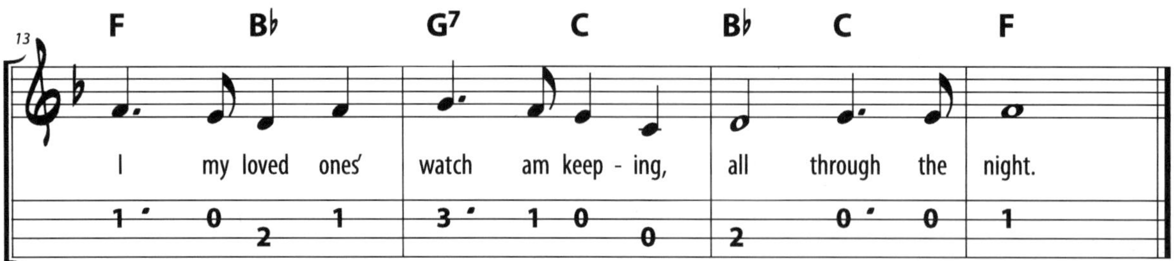

2. *While the moon her watch is keeping,*
all through the night;
While the weary world is sleeping,
all through the night.
O'er thy spirit gently stealing,
visions of delight revealing,
breathes a pure and holy feeling,
all through the night.

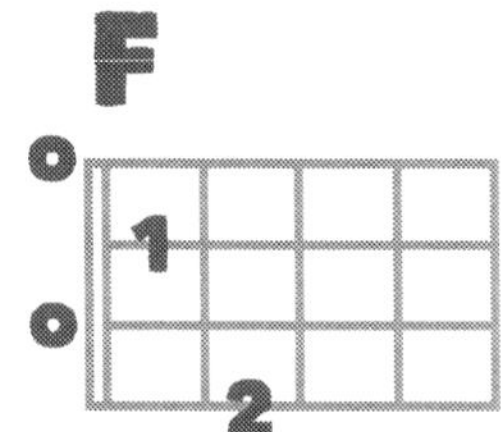

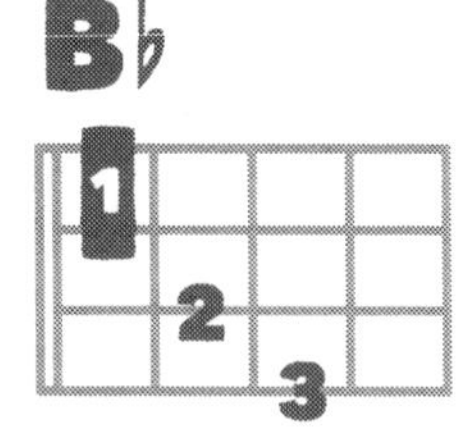

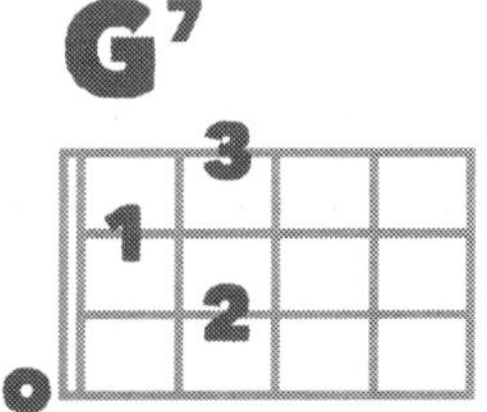

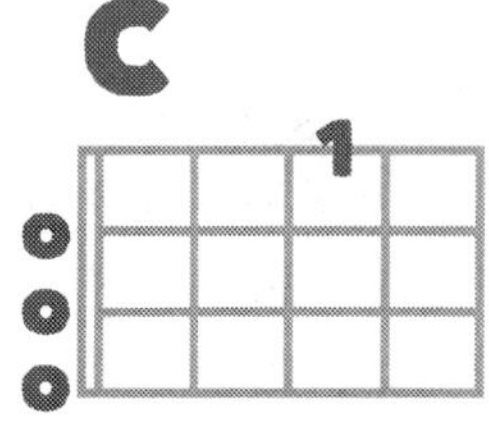

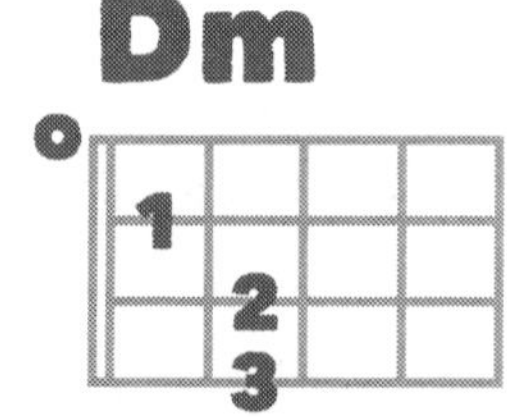

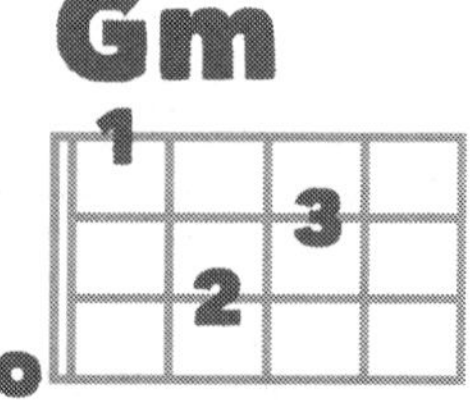

It's raining, it's pouring

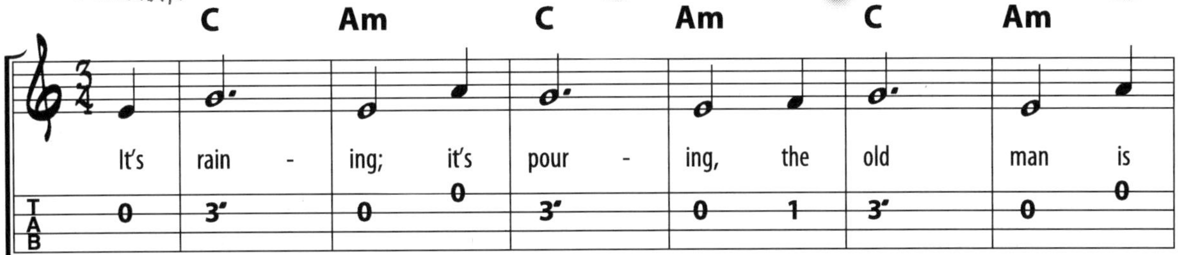

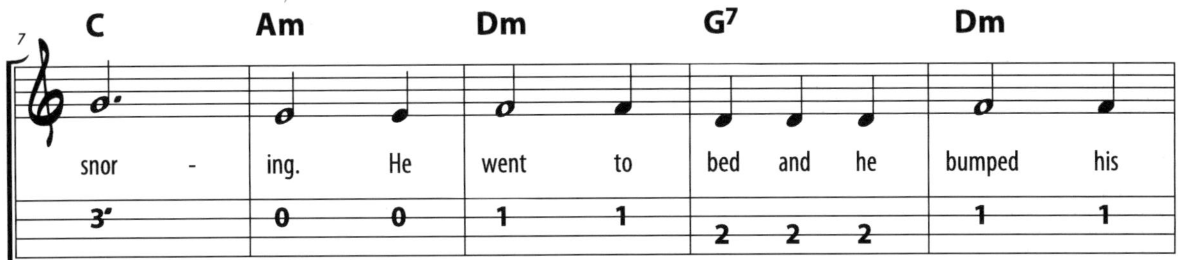

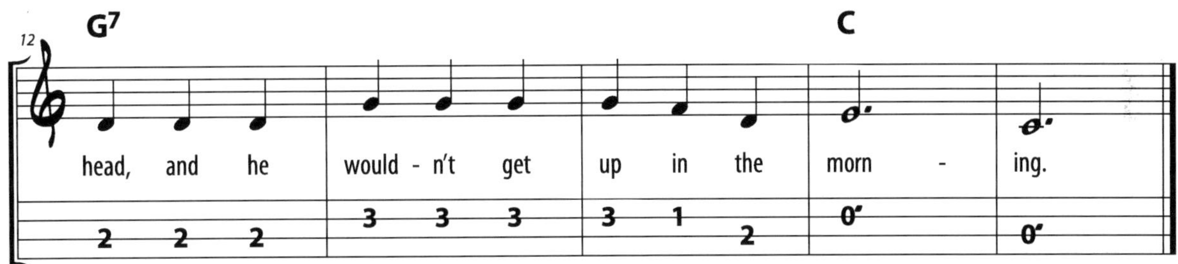

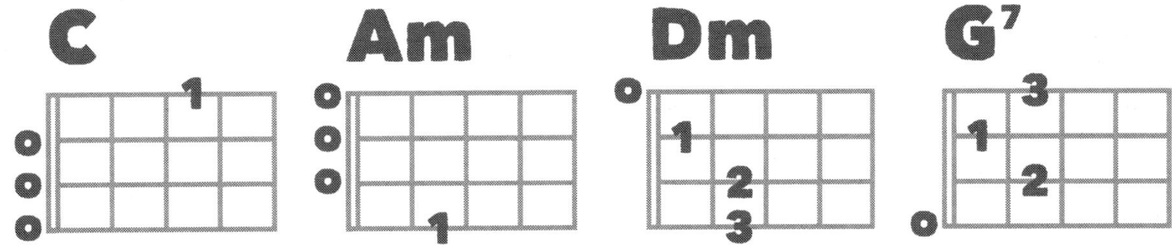

I had a little nut tree

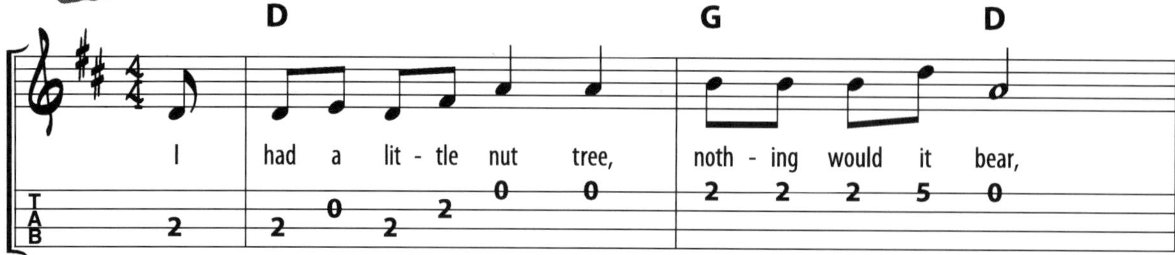

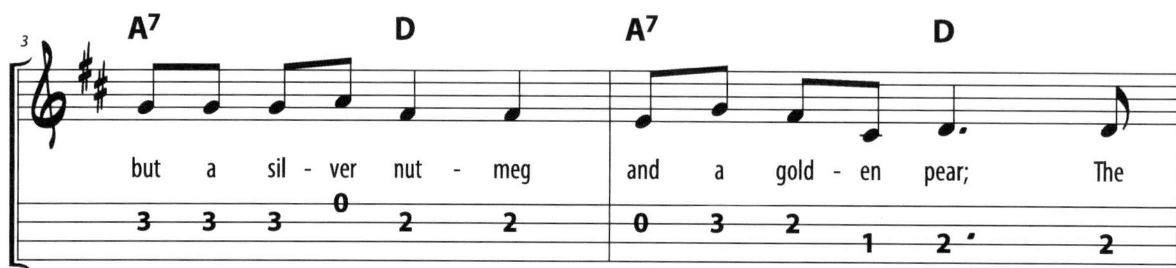

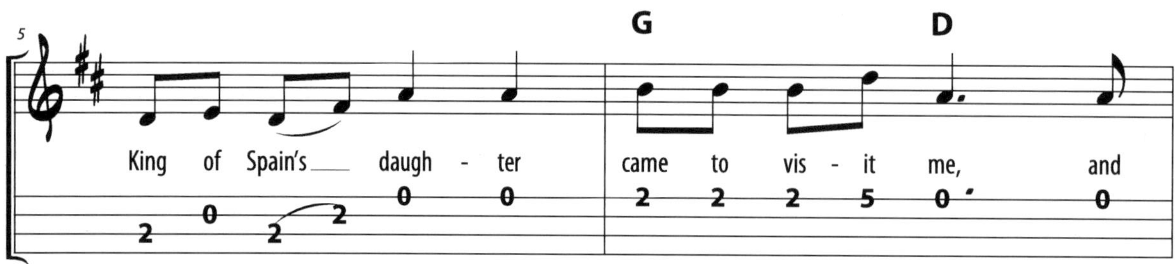

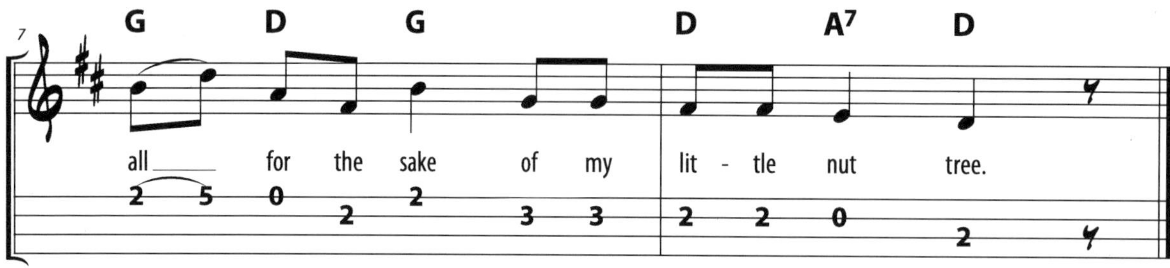

2. *Her dress was made of crimson,*
jet black was her hair,
she asked me for my nutmeg
and my golden pear.

I said, "So fair a princess
never did I see,
I'll give you all the fruit
from my little nut tree."

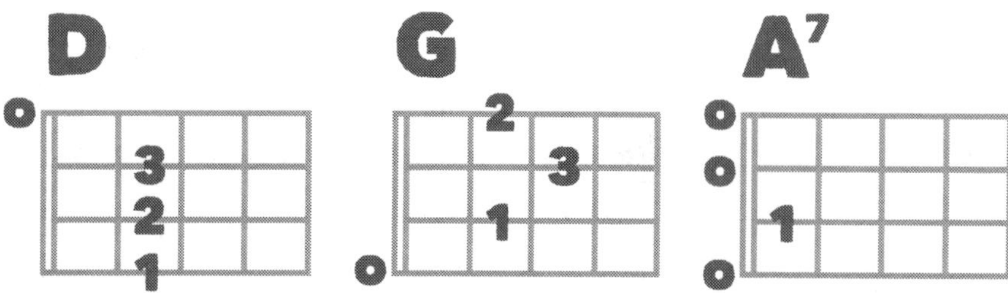

Miss Polly had a dolly

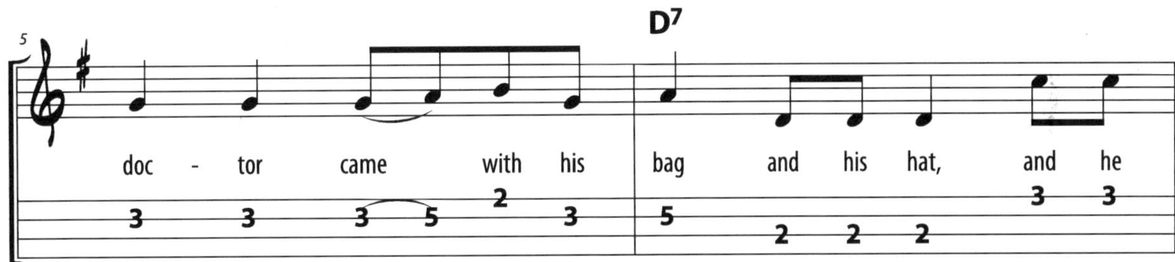

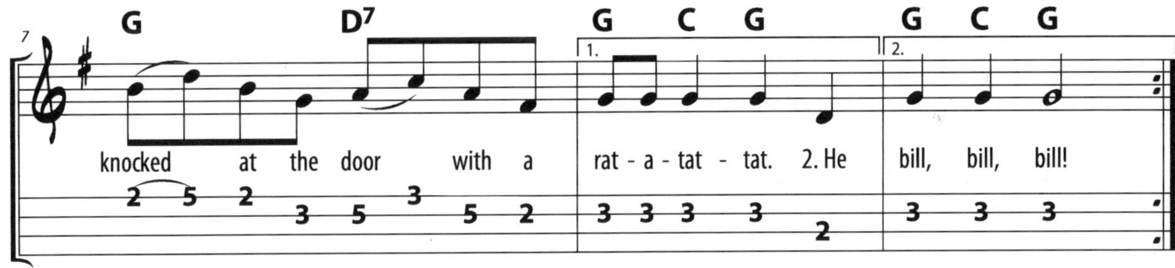

2. *He looked at the dolly and he shook his head,*
   And he said "Miss Polly, put her straight to bed."
   He wrote out a paper for a pill, pill, pill,
   „I'll be back in the morning with the bill, bill, bill!"

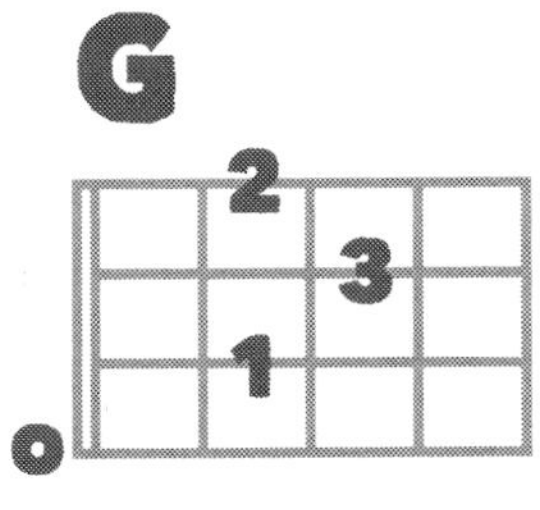

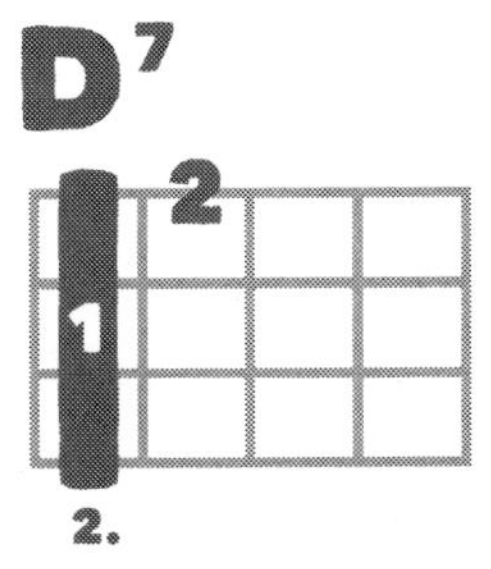

Mother, may I go out to swim

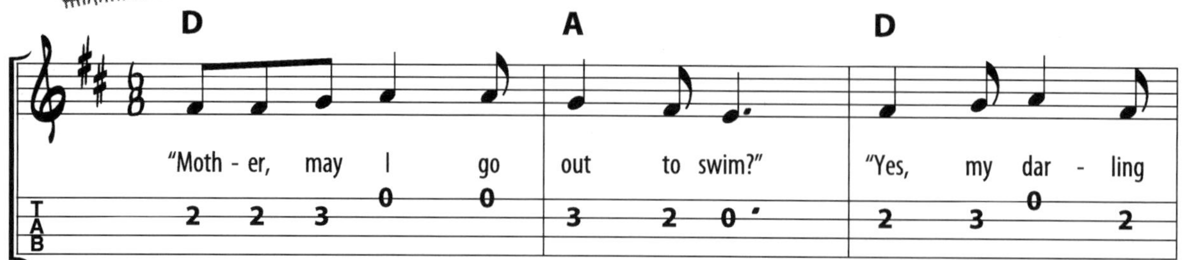

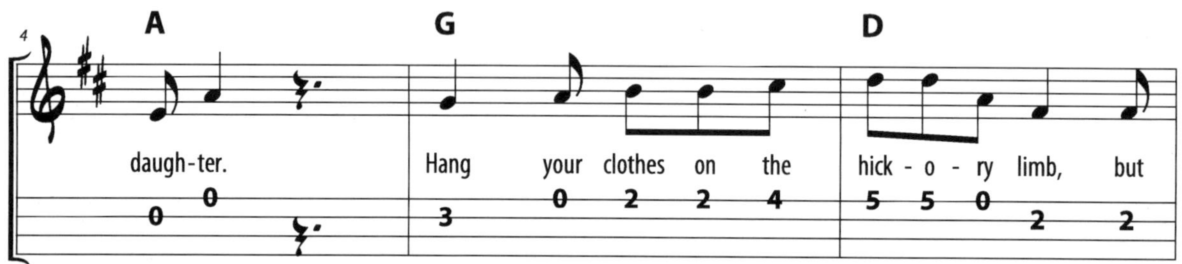

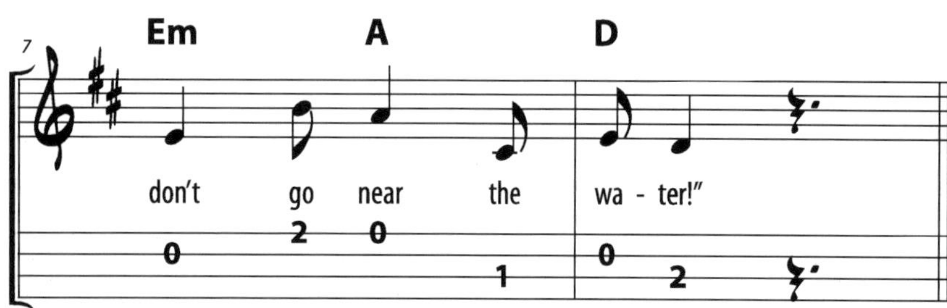

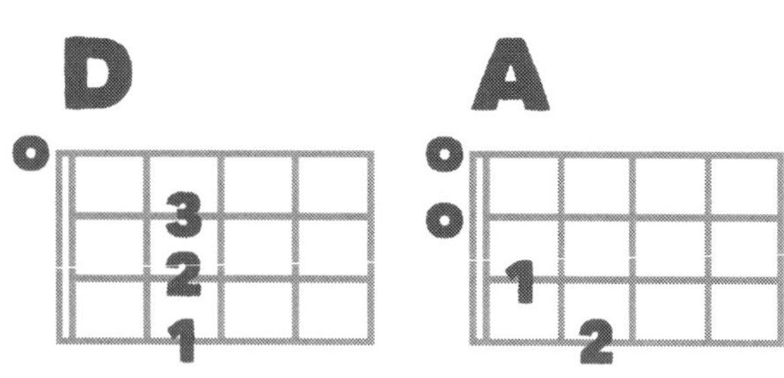

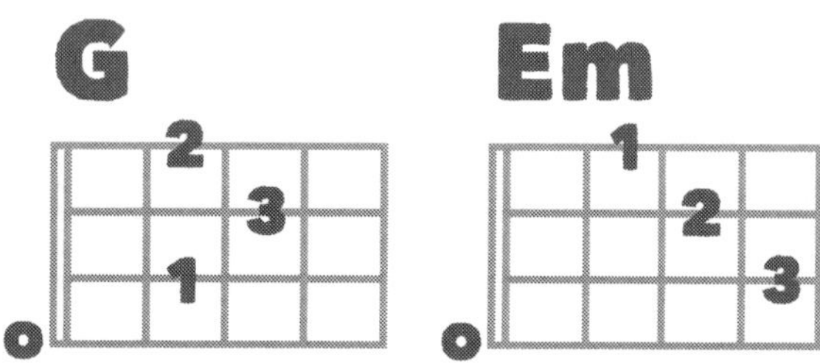

Pussy-cat, Pussy-cat

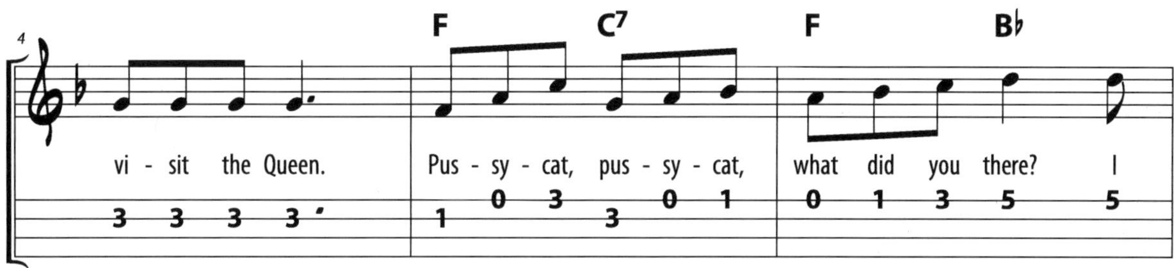

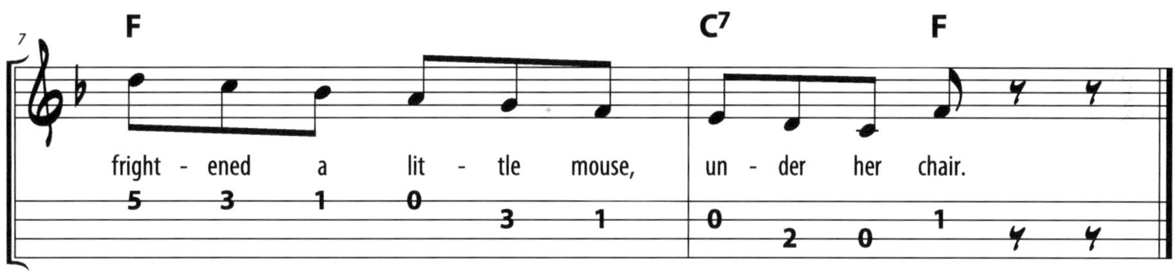

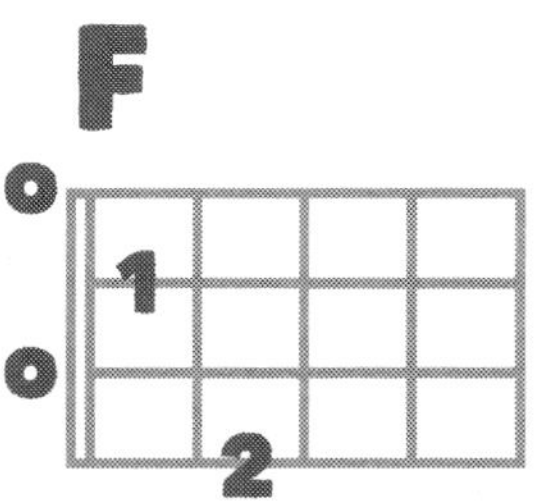

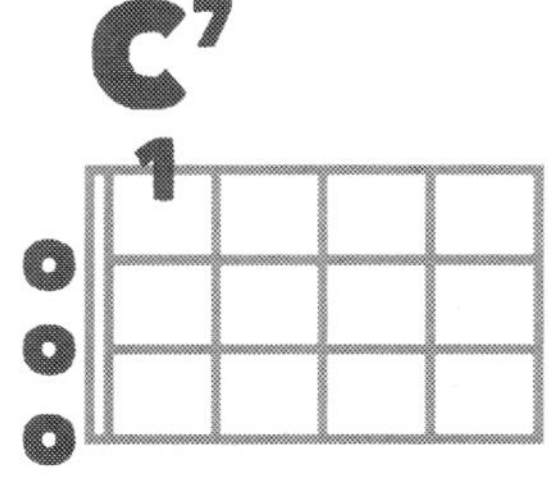

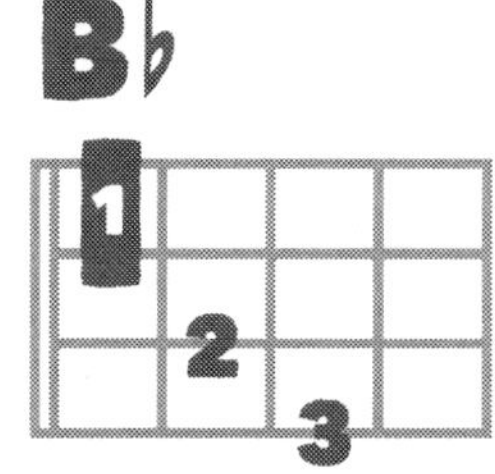

Ride a cock-horse

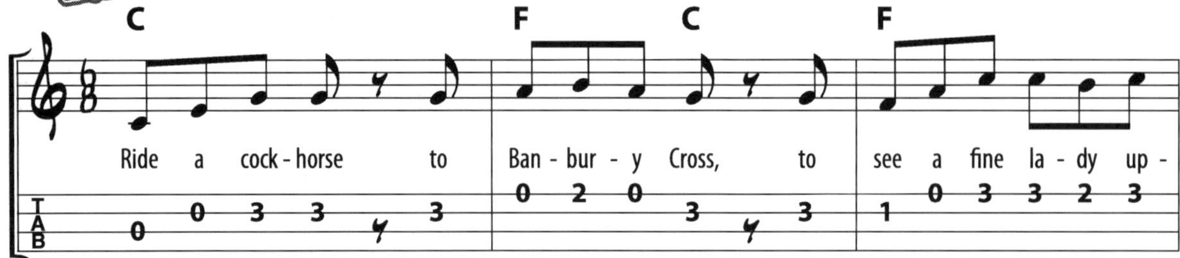

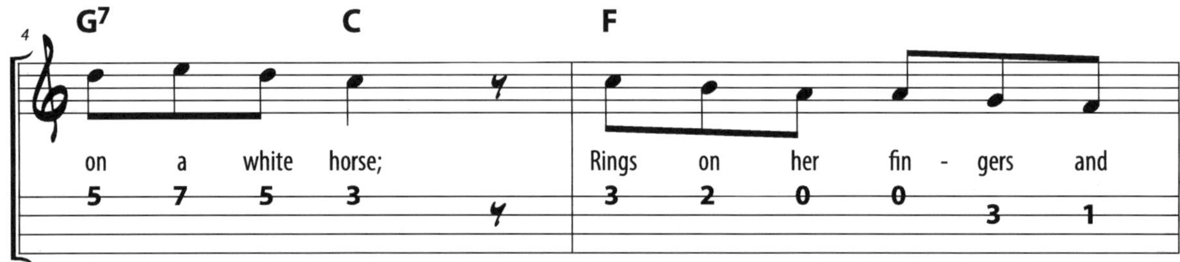

To market, to market

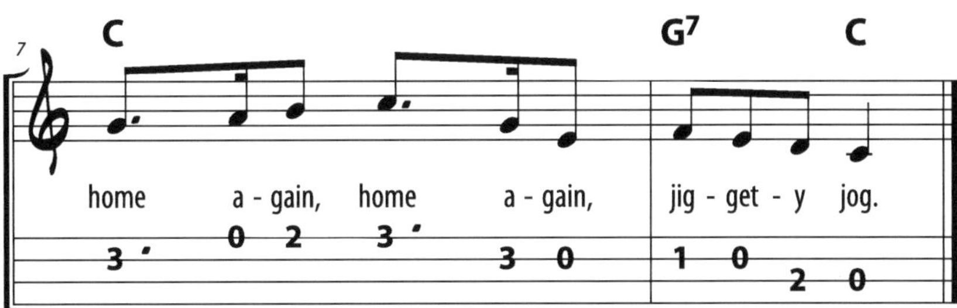

2. *To market, to market, to buy a fat hog,*
   Home again, home again, jiggety-jog.

3. *To market, to market, to buy a plum bun,*
   Home again, home again, market is done.

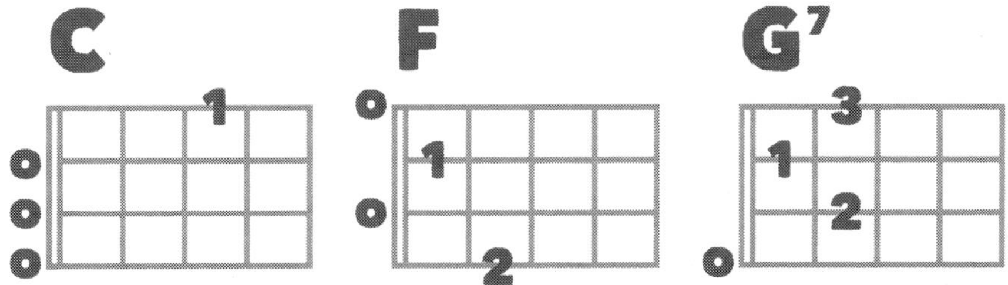

Three blind mice

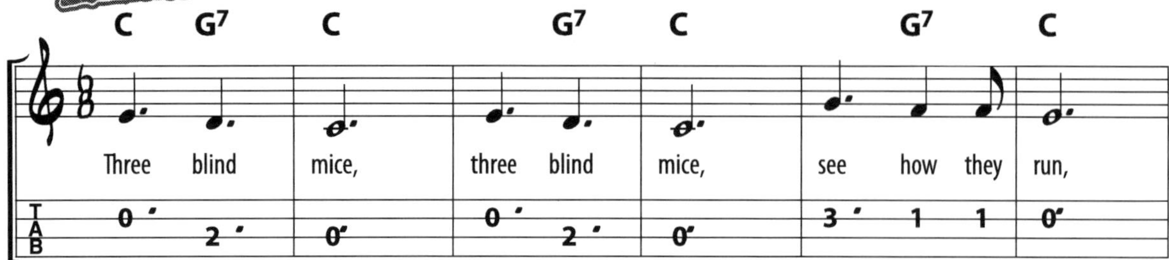

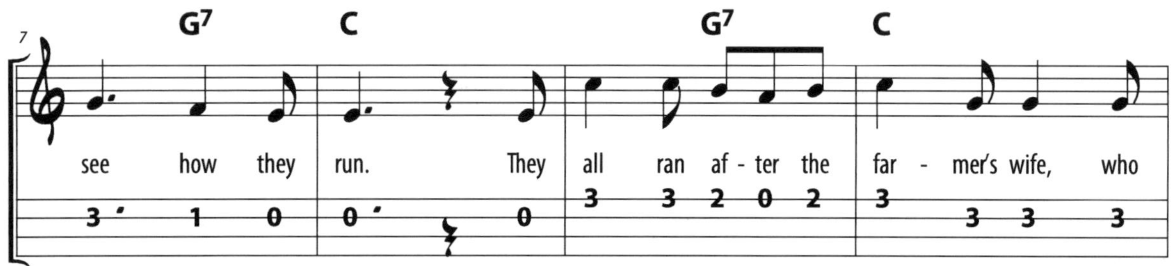

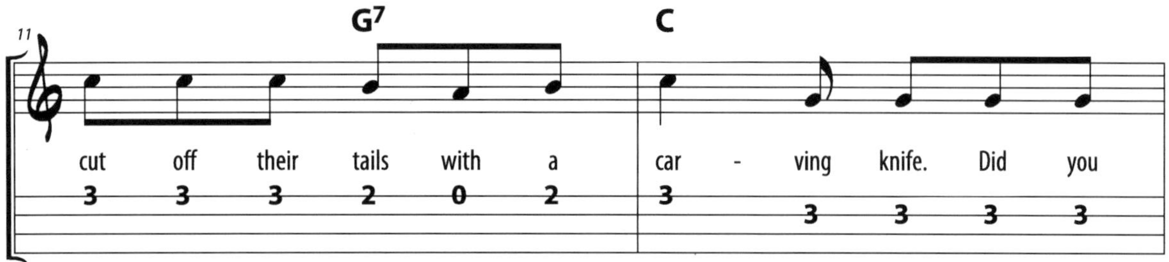

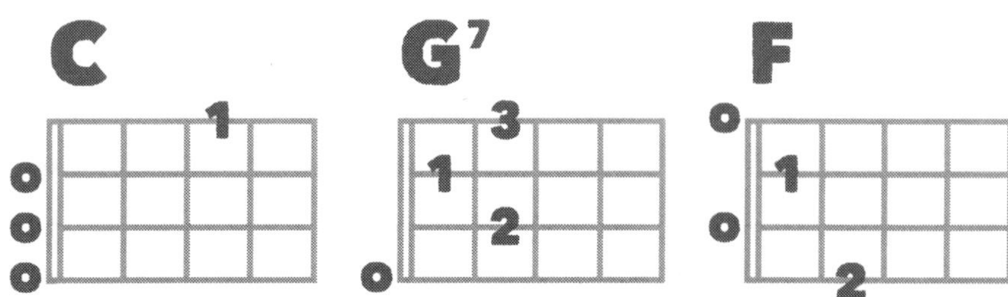

The muffin man

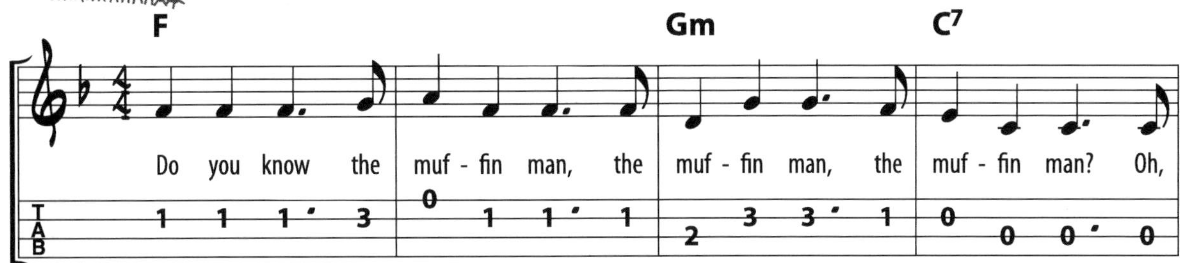
F
Gm
C7
Do you know the muf - fin man, the muf - fin man, the muf - fin man? Oh,
T
A
B
1 1 1 3 0 1 1 1 2 3 3 1 0 0 0 0

5
F
Gm
C7
F
do you know the muf - fin man, who lives in Dru - ry Lane?
1 1 1 3 0 1 1 0 2 3 1 0 1

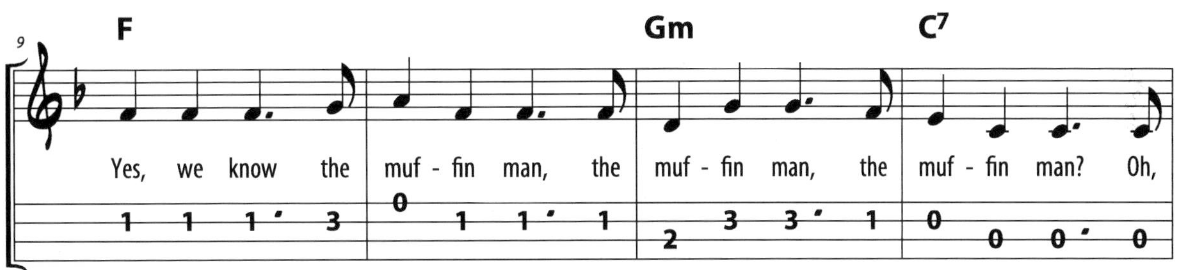
9
F
Gm
C7
Yes, we know the muf - fin man, the muf - fin man, the muf - fin man? Oh,
1 1 1 3 0 1 1 1 2 3 3 1 0 0 0 0

13
F
Gm
C7
F
yes we know the muf - fin man, who lives in Dru - ry Lane.
1 1 1 3 0 1 1 0 2 3 1 0 1

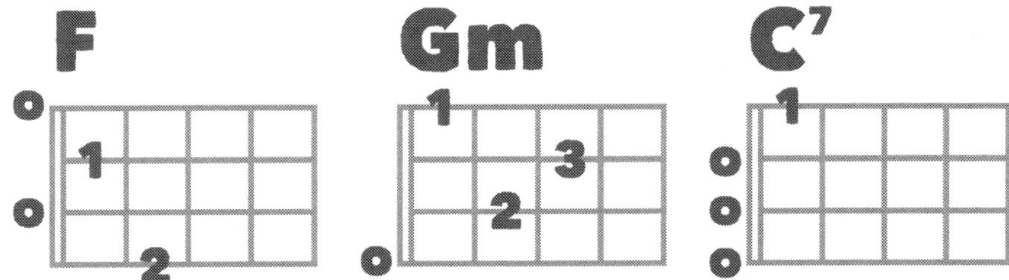
F
Gm
C7
1
2
1
2
3
1

Ten in a bed

2. *There were nine in a bed …*
3. *There were eight in a bed …*
4. *There were seven in a bed …*
5. *There were six in a bed …*
6. *There were five in a bed …*
7. *There were four in a bed …*
8. *There were three in a bed …*
9. *There were two in a bed …*
10. *There was one in a bed*
    and the little one said
    "Good night!"

First line: hold up all ten fingers.

Second line: slowly bring hands together, indicating „small".

Third line: rotate hands over each other.

Last two lines: imitate falling out of bed with your hands.

Second verse
First line: hold up all ten fingers.

... continue down to „one"

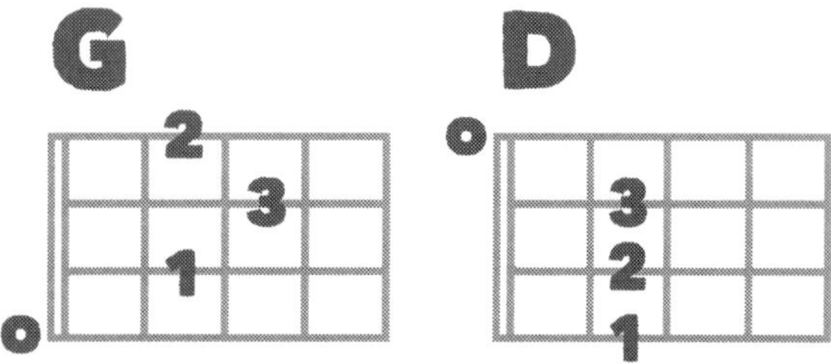

Alice the camel

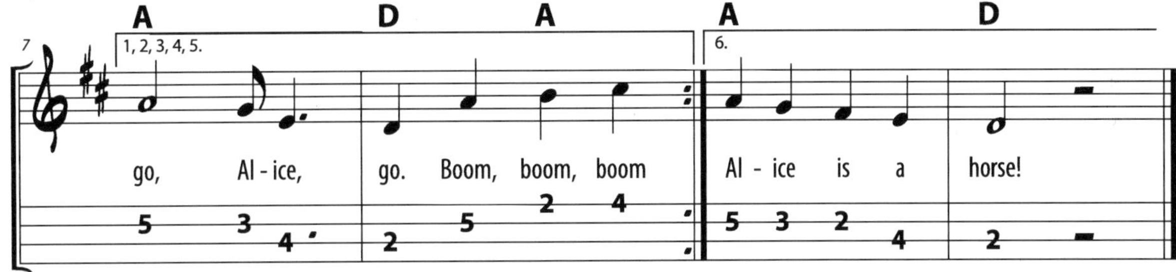

2. *Alice the camel has four humps. (3x)*
   So go, Alice, go.

3. *Alice the camel has three humps. (3x)*
   So go, Alice, go.

4. *Alice the camel has two humps. (3x)*
   So go, Alice, go.

5. *Alice the camel has one hump. (3x)*
   So go, Alice, go.

6. *Alice the camel has no humps. (3x)*
   Boom, Boom; Boom - Alice is a horse!

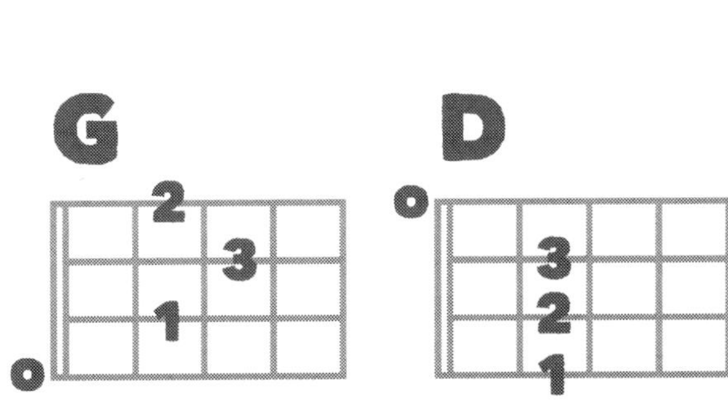

Head and shoulders, knees and toes

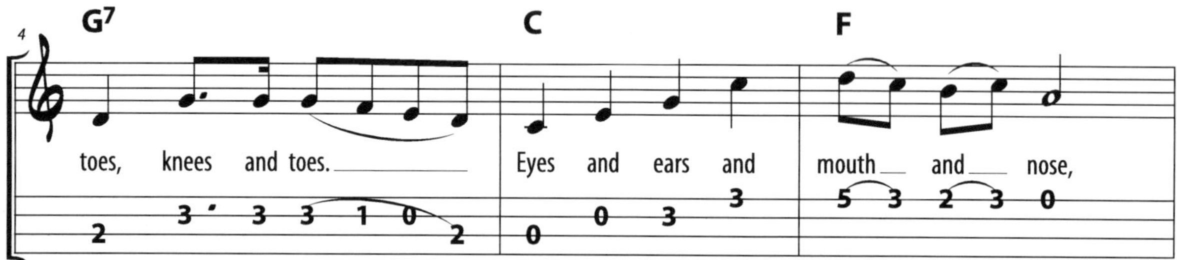

2. *Feet and tummies arms and chins, arms and chins.*
   Feet and tummies arms and chins, arms and chins.
   Eyes and ears and mouth and shins,
   feet and tummies arms and chins, arms and chins.

3. *Hands and fingers legs and lips, legs and lips.*
   Hands and fingers legs and lips, legs and lips.
   Eyes and ears and mouth and hips,
   hands and fingers legs and lips, legs and lips.

The children touch the different parts of the body when singing about them.
Variant: the children repeat the song, omitting the word „head", but still touching their heads. Repeat, leaving out „head and shoulders". Keep on omitting until you do all actions silently.

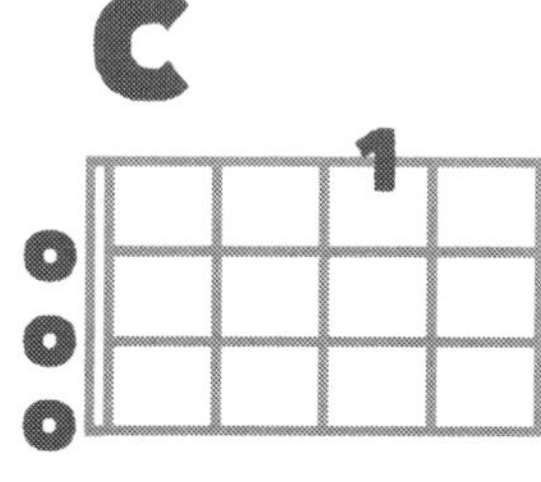

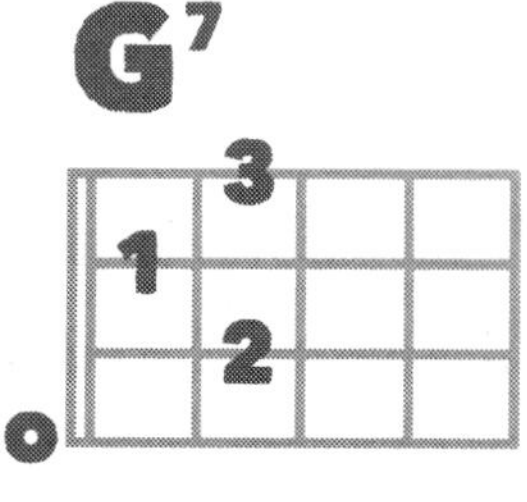

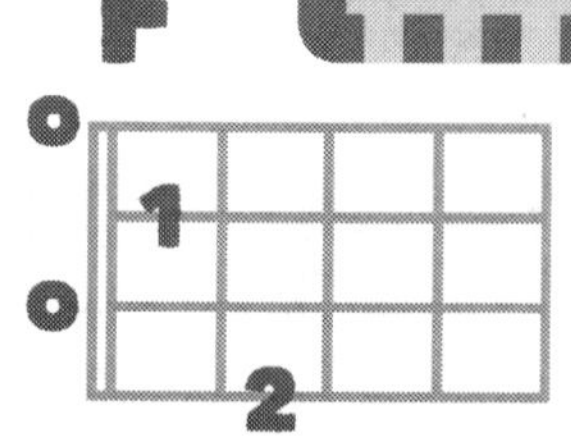

Hickety, pickety, my black hen

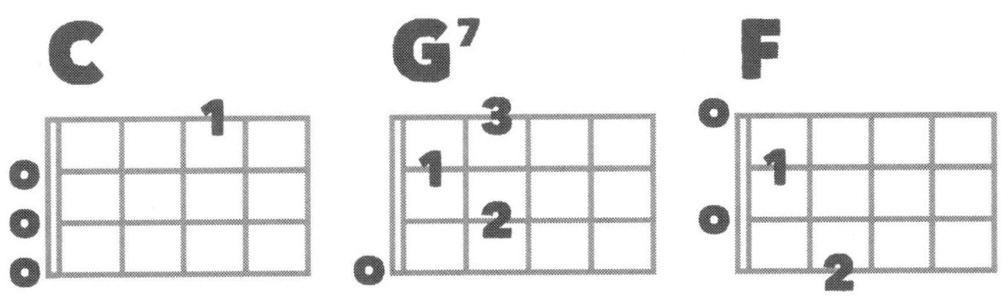

If all the world were paper

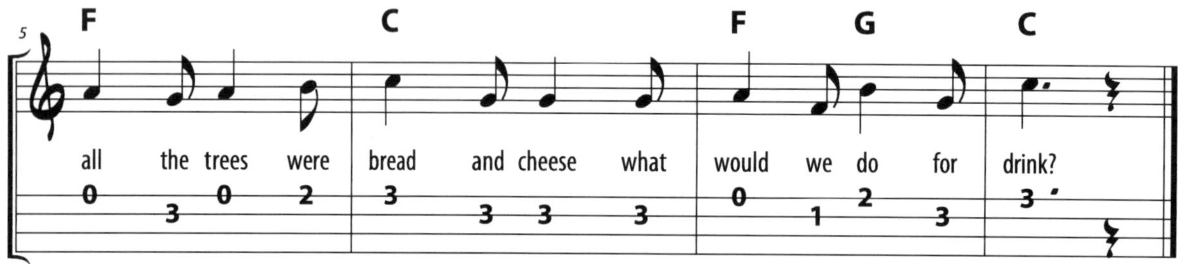

2. *If all the world were sand-o,*
   oh then what should we lack-o,
   if as they say there were no clay
   how should we take Tobacco?

3. *If all our vessels ran-a,*
   if none but had a crack-a,
   if Spanish apes ate all the grapes
   how should we do for sack-a?

4. *If all the world were men*
   and men lived all in trenches,
   and there were none but we alone,
   how should we do for wenches?

5. *If friars had no bald pates,*
   nor nuns had no dark cloisters,
   if all the seas were beans and peas
   how should we do for oysters?

6. *If there had been no projects*
   nor none that did great wrongs,
   if fiddlers shall turn players all
   how should we do for songs?

7. *If all things were eternal*
   and nothing their end bringing,
   if this should be, then how should we
   here make an end of singing?

This comic poem appears in John Mennes and James Smiths "Facetiae", probably published in1658. Today, mostly the first verse is sung as a children's song.

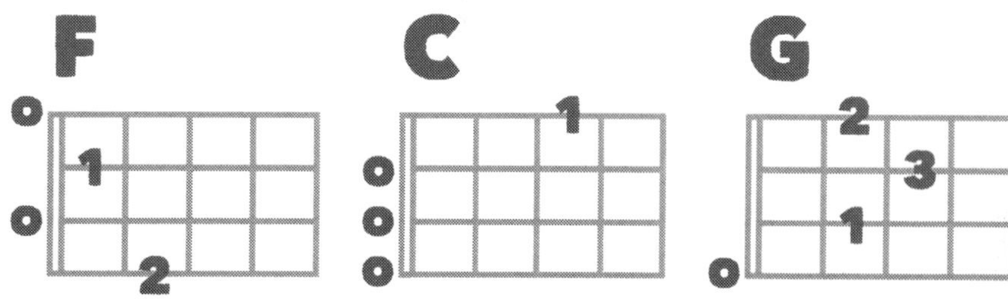

Little Bo-Peep

2. *Little Bo-Peep fell fast asleep,*
   and dreamt she heard them bleating,
   but when she awoke, she found it a joke,
   for they were still a-fleeting.

3. *Then up she took her little crook,*
   determined for to find them,
   she found them indeed, but it made her heart bleed,
   for they'd left their tails behind them.

4. *It happened one day, as Bo-Peep did stray*
   into a meadow hard by,
   there she espied their tails side by side,
   all hung on a tree to dry.

5. *She heaved a sigh and wiped her eye,*
   and over the hillocks went rambling,
   and tried what she could, as a shepherdess should,
   to tack each again to its lambkin.

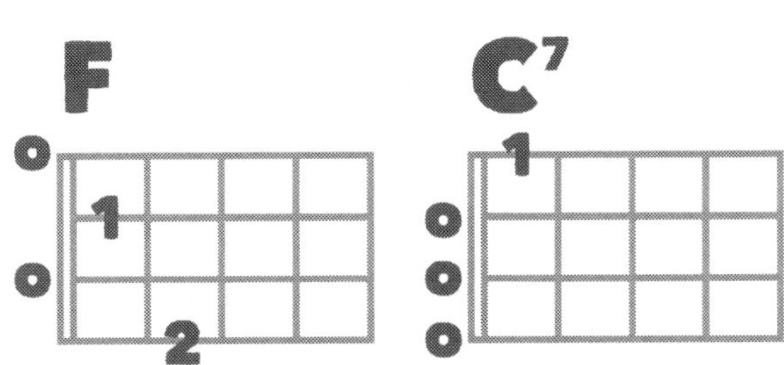

Little boy blue

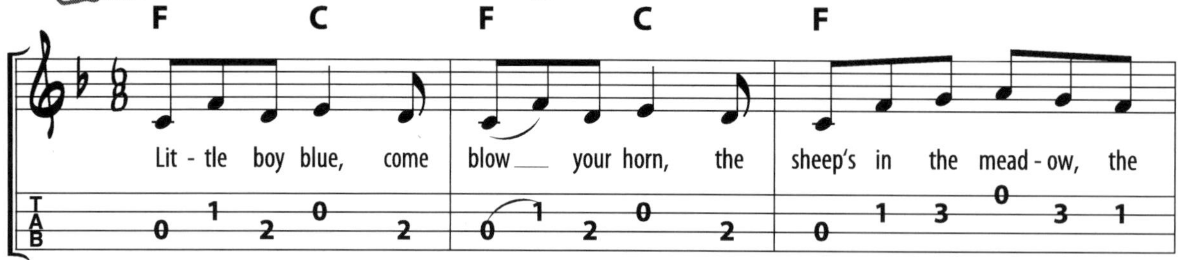
F C F C F
Lit - tle boy blue, come blow your horn, the sheep's in the mead - ow, the

G7 C F B♭ C F
cow's in the corn. Where is the boy who looks af - ter the sheep? He's

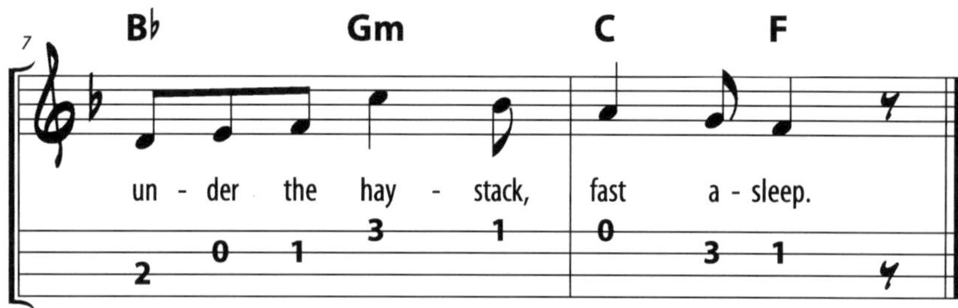
B♭ Gm C F
un - der the hay - stack, fast a - sleep.

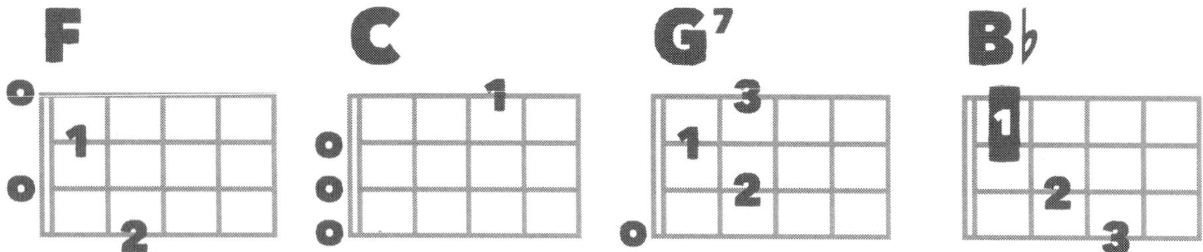
F
C
G7
B♭

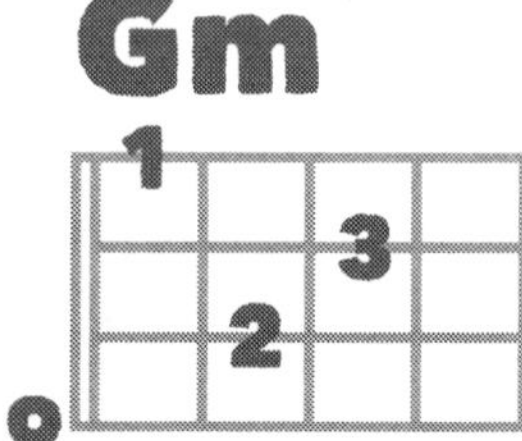
Gm

Little Tommy Tucker

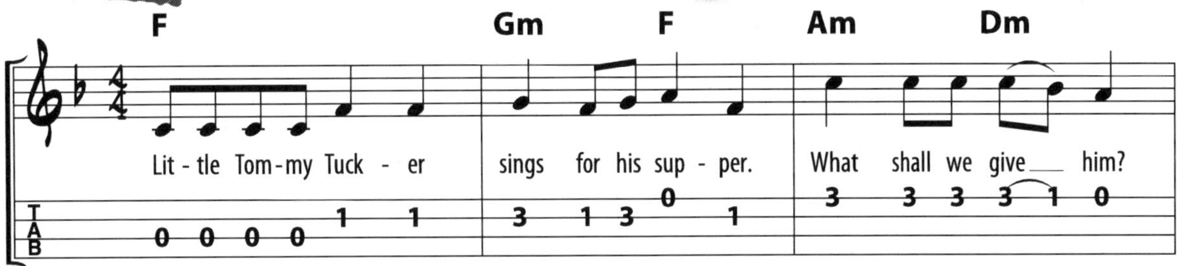

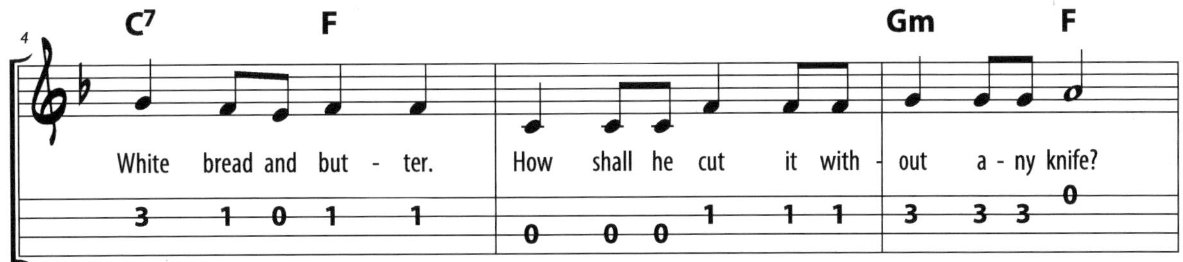

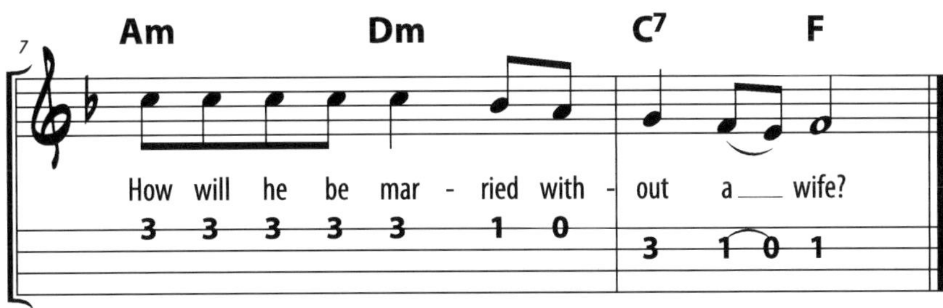

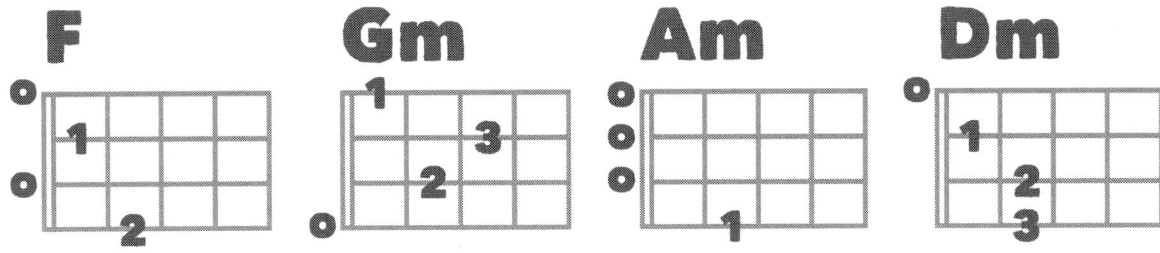

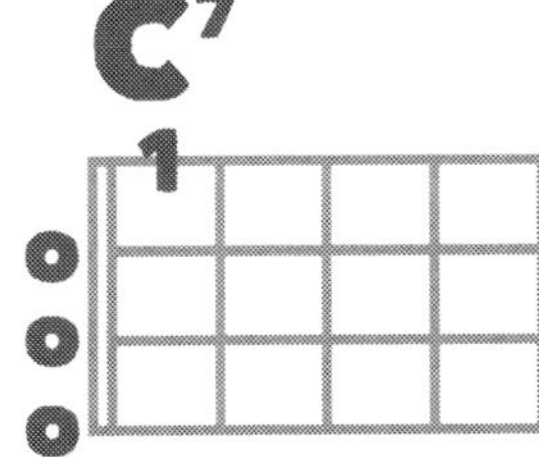

Old King Cole

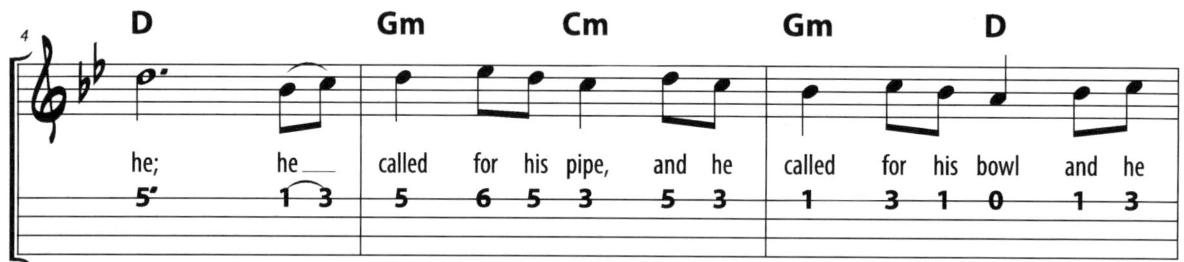

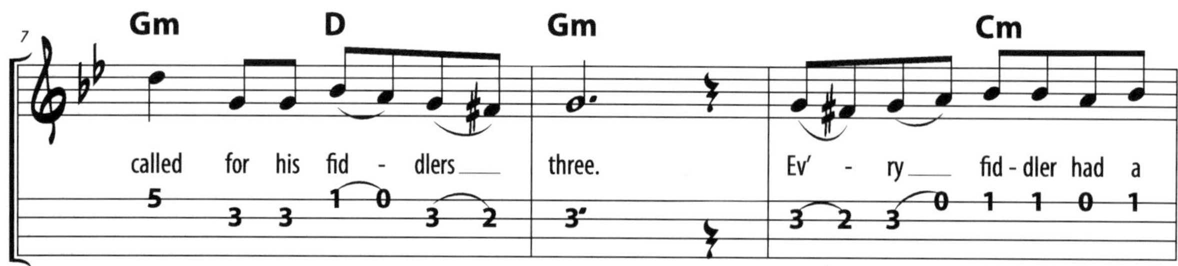

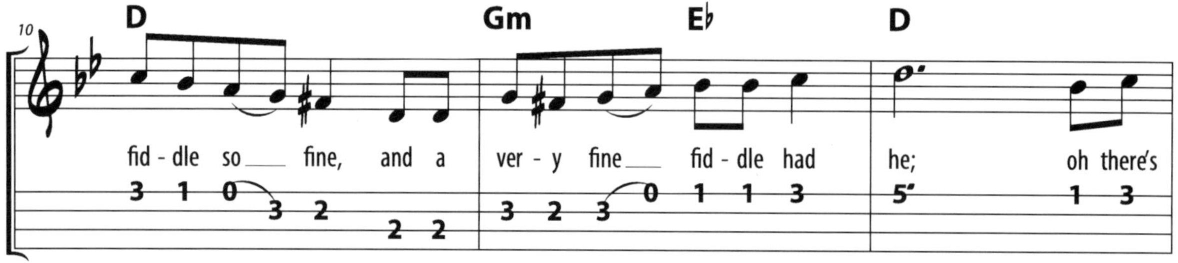

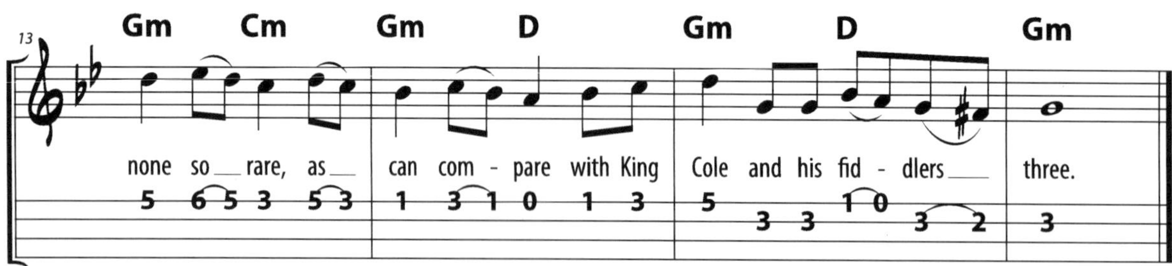

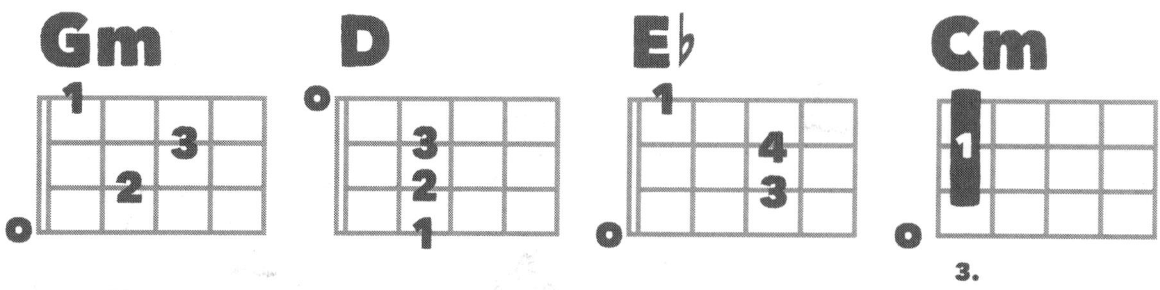

h were, oh where has my little dog gone?

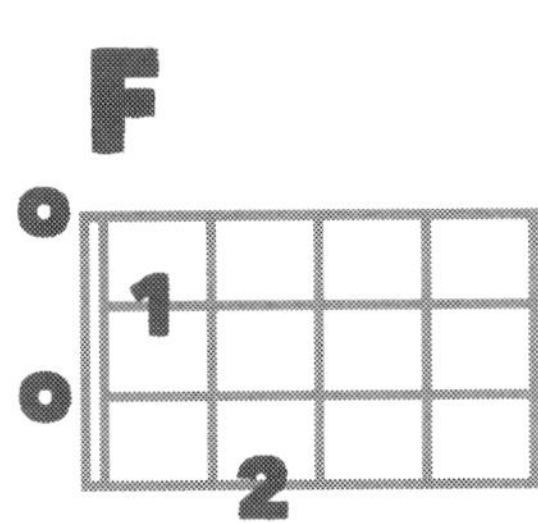

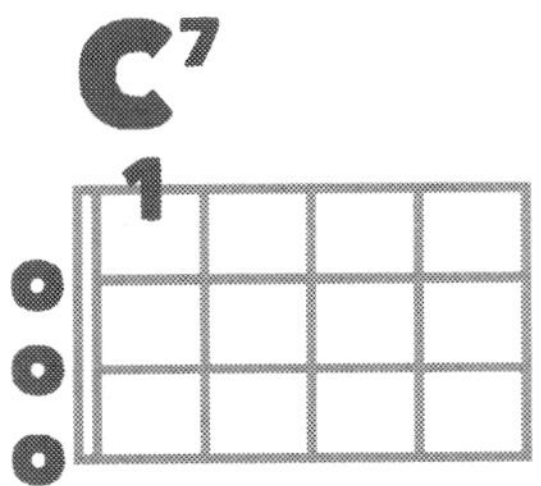

One, two, three, four, five

2. *Why did you let it go?*
   Because it bit my finger so.
   Which finger did it bite?
   This little finger on the right.

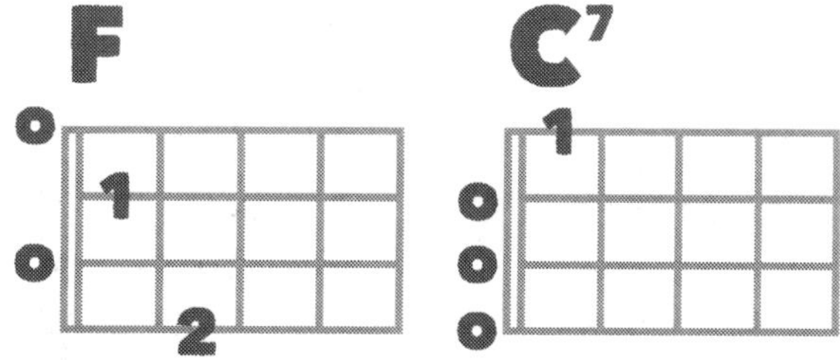

Over the river

2. *Over the river and through the woods,*
   oh, how the wind does blow!
   It stings the toes and bites the nose,
   as over the ground we go.

3. *Over the river and through the woods,*
   and straight through the barnyard gate;
   We seem to go extremely slow,
   it is so hard to wait!

4. *Over the river and through the woods,*
   when Grandmother sees us come,
   She will say, "O, dear, the children are here,
   bring a pie for everyone."

5. *Over the river and through the woods,*
   now Grandmother's cap I spy!
   Hurrah for the fun! Is the pudding done?
   Hurrah for the pumpkin pie!

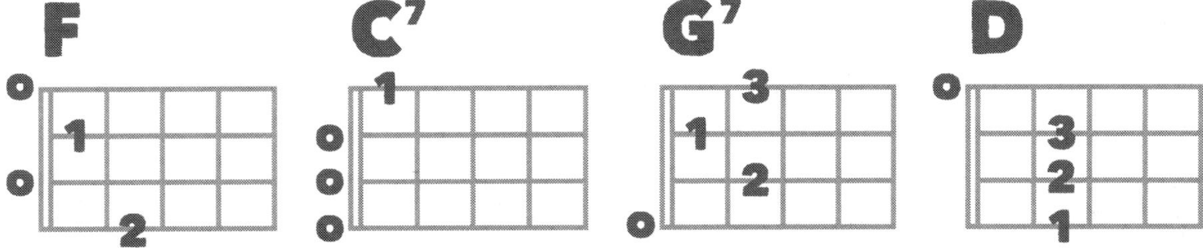

Rub-a-dub-dub

C
Am
G
Rub - a - dub - dub, three
men in a tub, and
who do you think they
T
A
B
0 0 0 0 0
4 4 4 4 4
3 3 3 3 3

4
C
Am
G
C
Am
were? The
but - cher, the ba - ker, the
can - dle - stick - mak - er, and
3 3
3 3 3 3 3 3
4 4 4 0 0 0

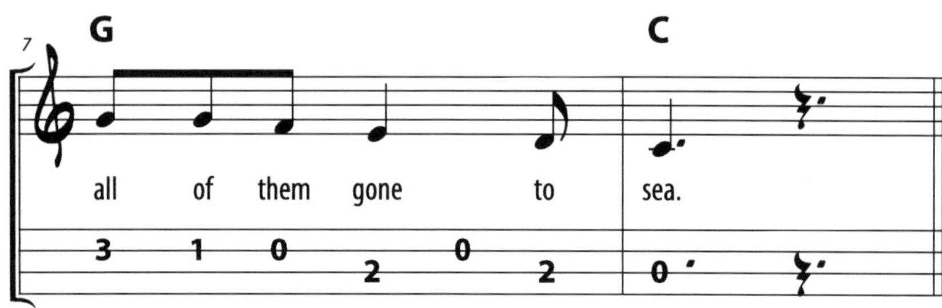
7
G
C
all of them gone to
sea.
3 1 0 2 0 2
0

C
Am
G
1
1
2
3
1

Ten green bottles

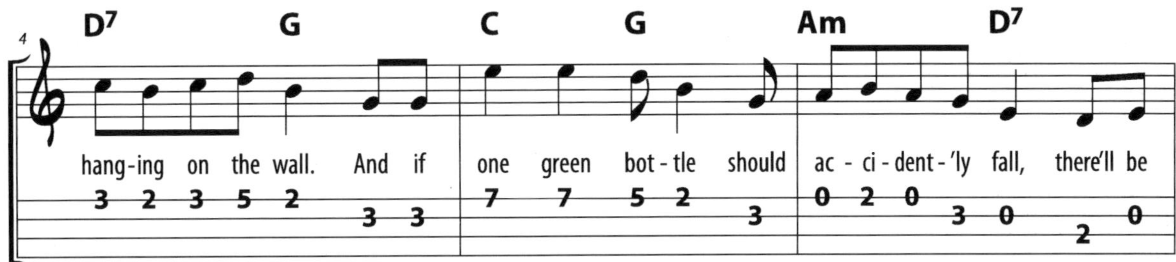

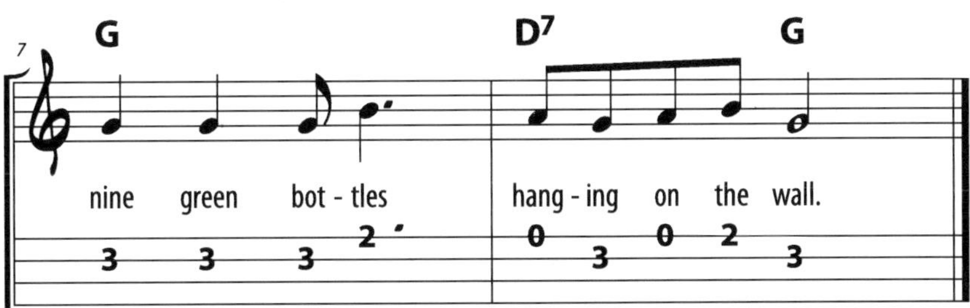

2. *Nine green bottles hanging on the wall ...*
3. *Eight green bottles hanging on the wall ...*
4. *Seven green bottles hanging on the wall ...*
5. *Six green bottles hanging on the wall ...*
6. *Five green bottles hanging on the wall ...*
7. *Four green bottles hanging on the wall ...*
8. *Three green bottles hanging on the wall ...*
9. *Two green bottles hanging on the wall ...*

10. *One green bottle hanging on the wall,*
one green bottle hanging on the wall.
And if that green bottle should accidentally fall,
there'll be no more bottles hanging on the wall.

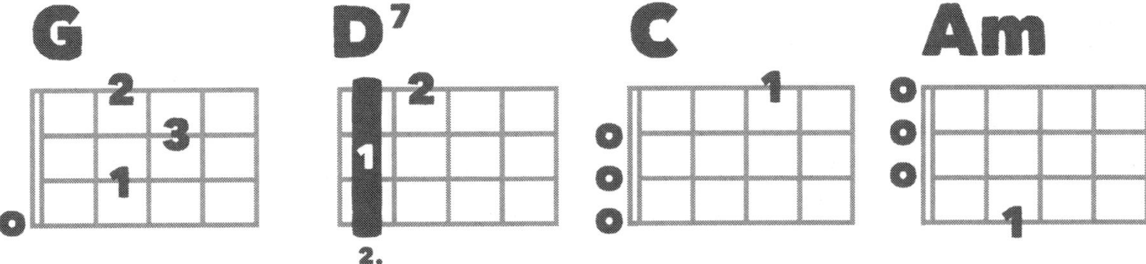

Sweetly sings the donkey

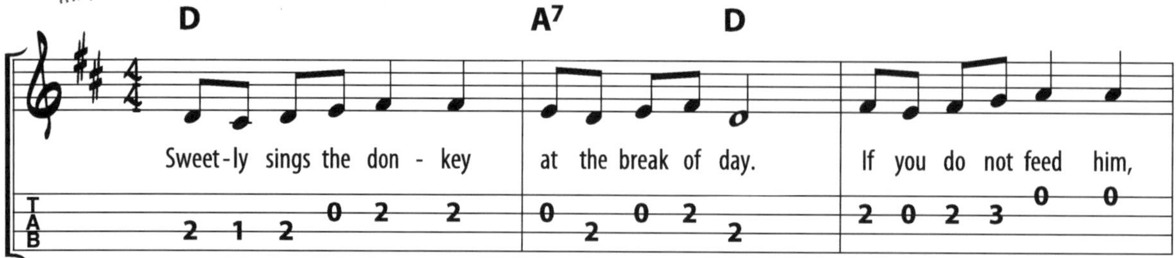

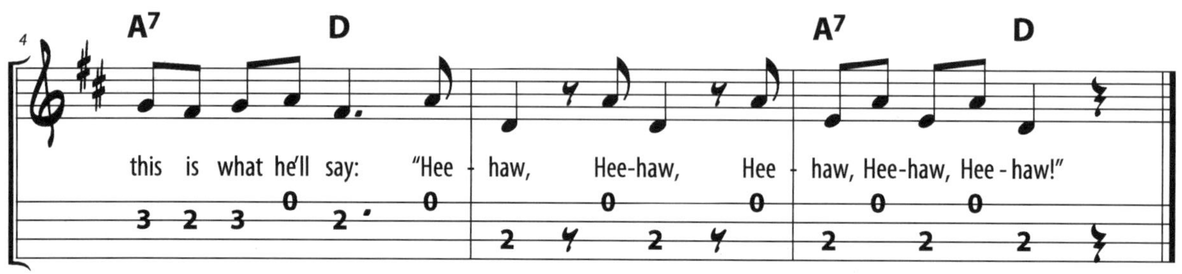

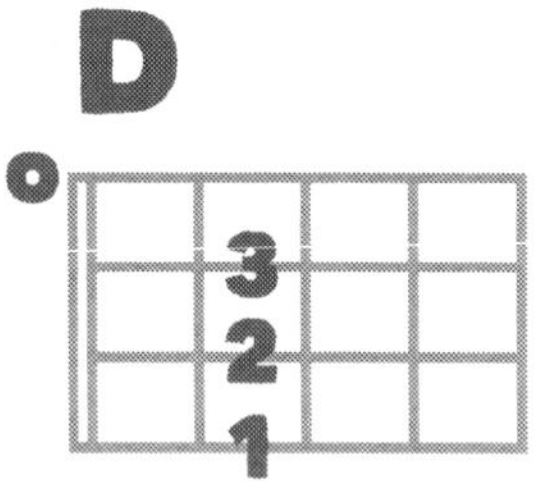

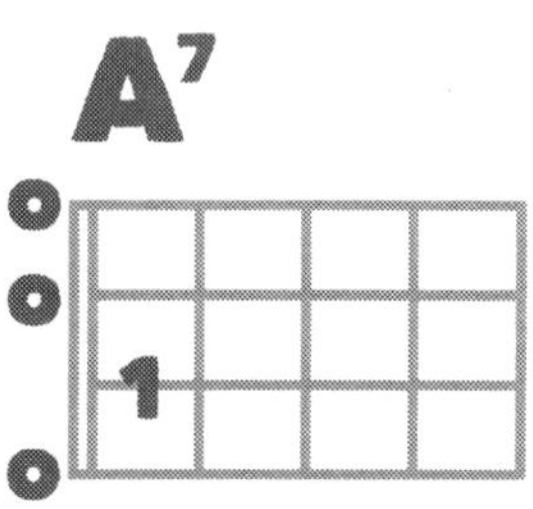

D

A7

Ten little Indians

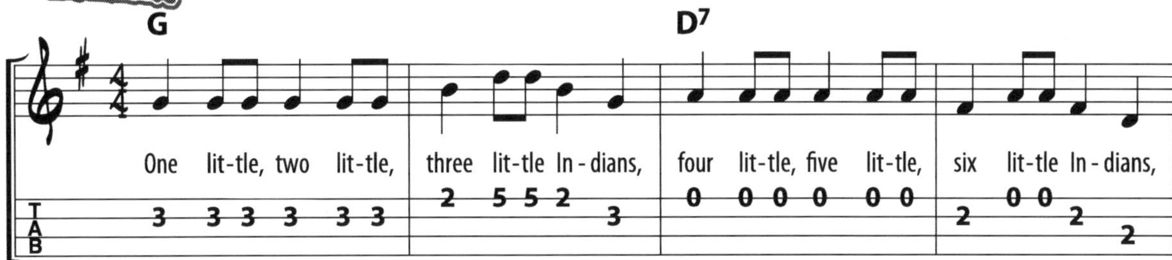
G
D7
One lit-tle, two lit-tle, three lit-tle In-dians, four lit-tle, five lit-tle, six lit-tle In-dians,
T
A
B
3 3 3 3 3 3 2 5 5 2 3 0 0 0 0 0 0 2 0 0 2 2

5
G
D7
G
se-ven lit-tle, eight lit-tle, nine lit-tle In-dians, ten lit-tle In-dian boys.
3 3 3 3 3 3 3 2 5 5 2 3 5 3 3 2 0 3

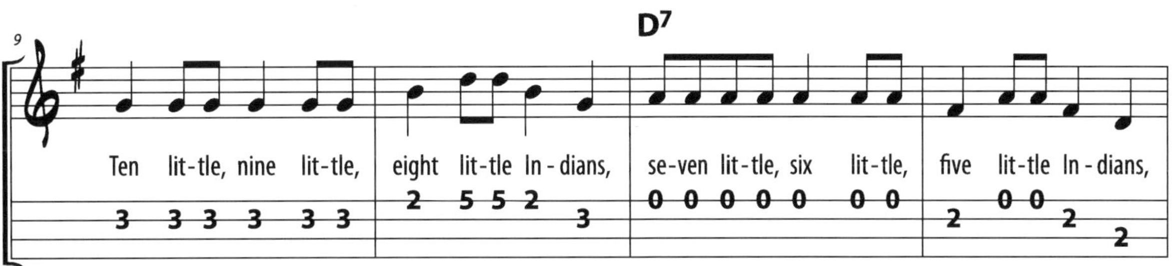
9
D7
Ten lit-tle, nine lit-tle, eight lit-tle In-dians, se-ven lit-tle, six lit-tle, five lit-tle In-dians,
3 3 3 3 3 3 2 5 5 2 3 0 0 0 0 0 0 0 2 0 0 2 2

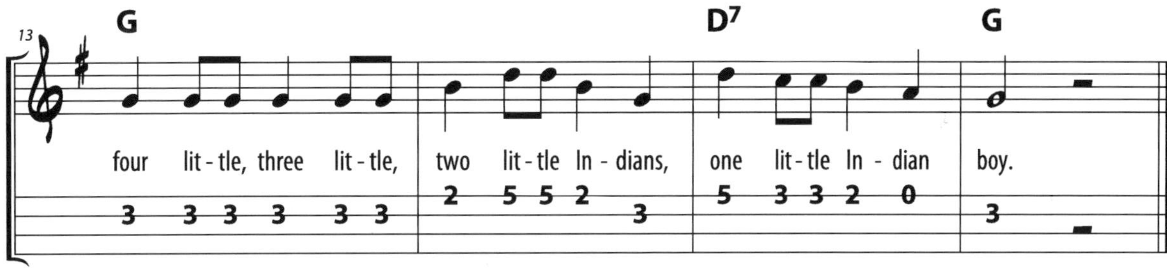
13
G
D7
G
four lit-tle, three lit-tle, two lit-tle In-dians, one lit-tle In-dian boy.
3 3 3 3 3 3 2 5 5 2 3 5 3 3 2 0 3

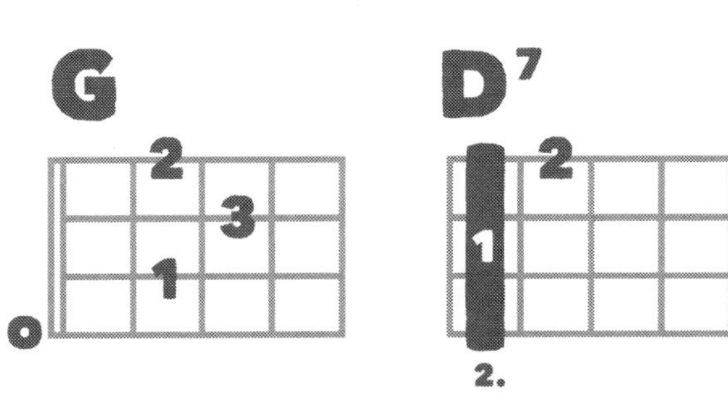
G
2
3
1
o
D7
2
1
2.

The ants go marching

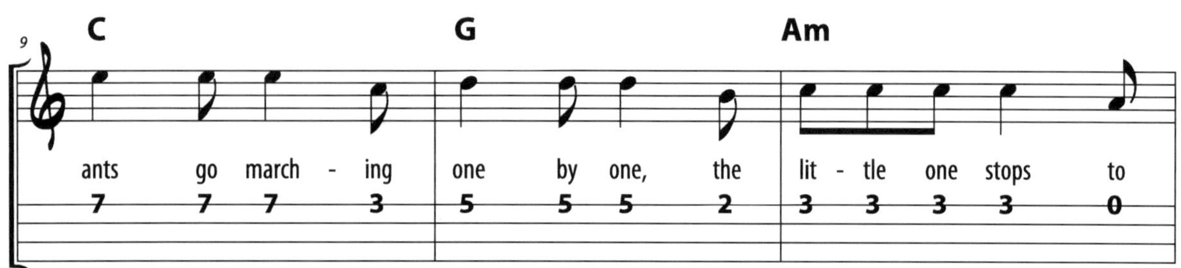

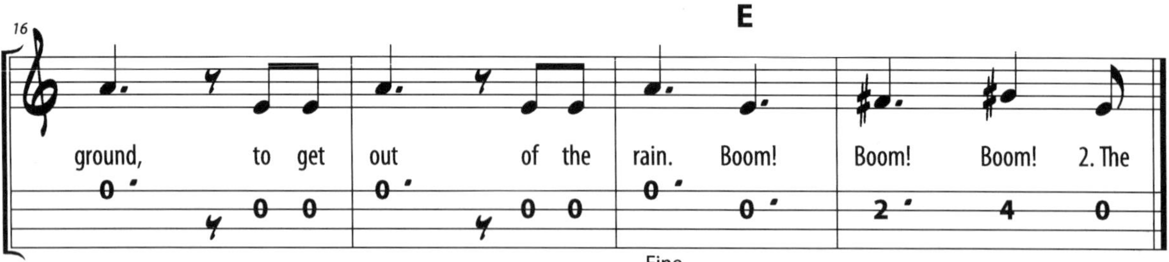

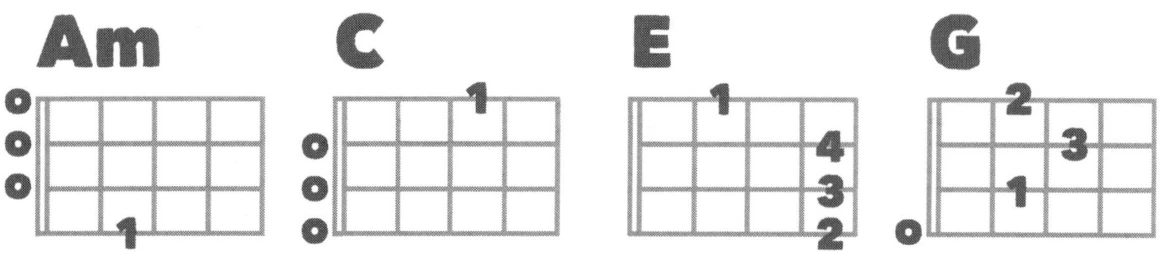

The ants go marching two by two, hoorah, hoorah,
the ants go marching two by two, hoorah, hoorah.
The ants go marching two by two,
the little one stops to tie his shoe,
and they all go marching down to the ground,
to get out of the rain. Boom! Boom! Boom!

The ants go marching three by three, hoorah, hoorah,
the ants go marching three by three, hoorah, hoorah.
The ants go marching three by three,
the little one stops to climb a tree,
and they all go marching down to the ground,
to get out of the rain. Boom! Boom! Boom!

The ants go marching four by four,hoorah, hoorah,
the ants go marching four by four, hoorah, hoorah.
The ants go marching four by four,
the little one stops to shut the door,
and they all go marching down to the ground,
to get out of the rain. Boom! Boom! Boom!

The ants go marching five by five, hurrah, hurrah,
the ants go marching five by five, hurrah, hurrah.
The ants go marching five by five,
the little one stops to take a dive
and they all go marching down to the ground
to get out of the rain. Boom! Boom! Boom!

The ants go marching six by six, hurrah, hurrah,
the ants go marching six by six, hurrah, hurrah.
The ants go marching six by six,
the little one stops to pick up sticks,
and they all go marching down to the ground,
to get out of the rain. Boom! Boom! Boom!

The ants go marching seven by seven, hurrah, hurrah,
the ants go marching seven by seven, hurrah, hurrah.
The ants go marching seven by seven,
the little one stops to pray to heaven,
and they all go marching down to the ground,
to get out of the rain. Boom! Boom! Boom!

The ants go marching eight by eight, hurrah, hurrah,
the ants go marching eight by eight, hurrah, hurrah.
The ants go marching eight by eight,
the little one stops to roller skate,
and they all go marching down to the ground,
to get out of the rain. Boom! Boom! Boom!

The ants go marching nine by nine, hurrah, hurrah,
The ants go marching nine by nine, hurrah, hurrah.
The ants go marching nine by nine,
the little one stops to check the time,
and they all go marching down to the ground,
to get out of the rain. Boom! Boom! Boom!

The ants go marching ten by ten, hurrah, hurrah,
the ants go marching ten by ten, hurrah, hurrah.
The ants go marching ten by ten,
the little one stops to shout "The End",
and they all go marching down to the ground,
to get out of the rain.

The old gray mare

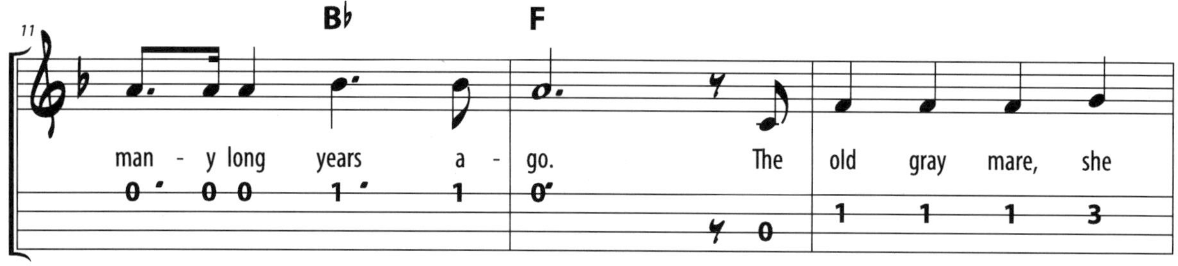

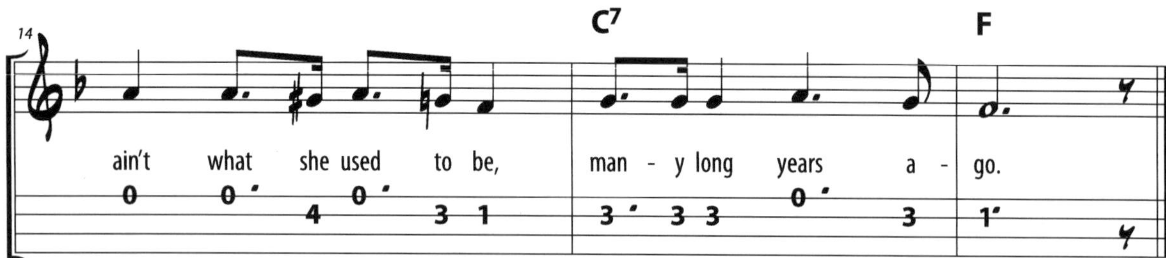

2. *The old gray mare, she kicked on the whiffletree,*
kicked on the whiffletree, kicked on the whiffletree.
The old gray mare, she kicked on the whiffletree,
many long years ago.
Many long years ago, many long years ago.
The old gray mare, she kicked on the whiffletree,
Many long years ago.

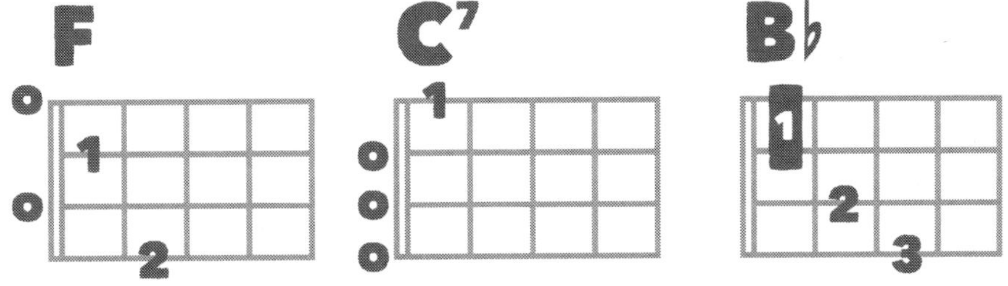

The grand old Duke of York

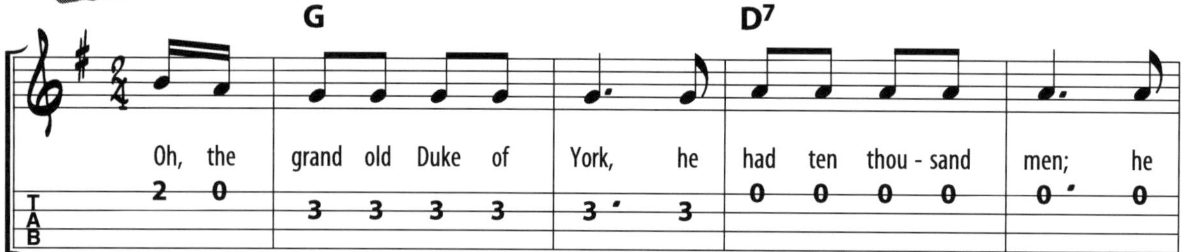

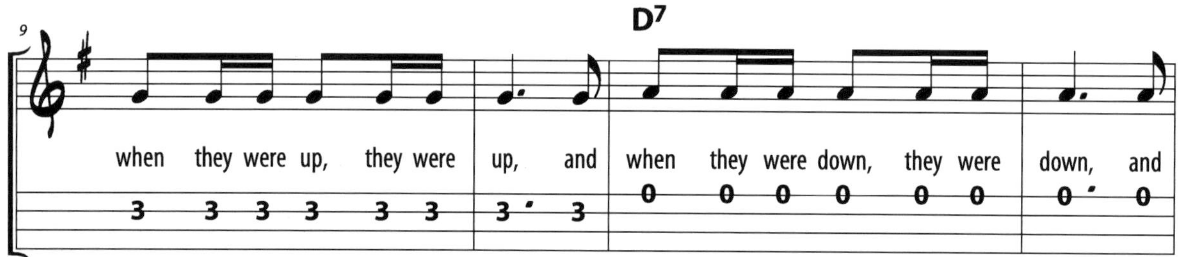

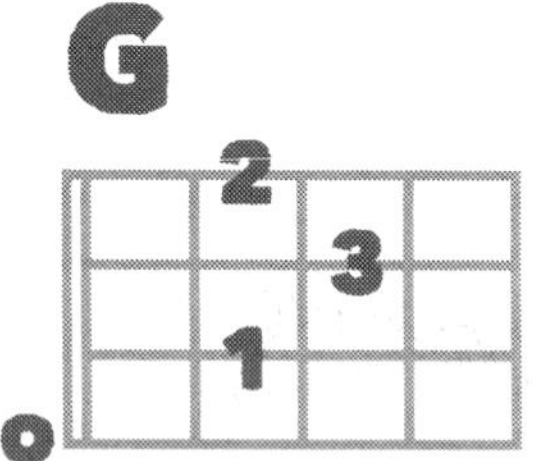

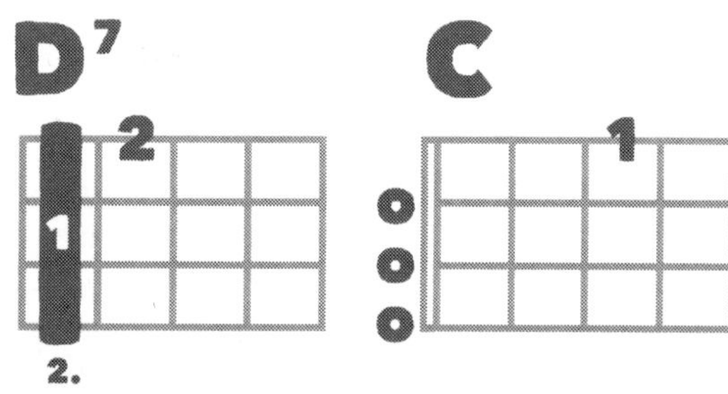

The participants can "act out" this song by standing up, sitting down or standing halfway up at the correspon-ding parts of the verse.
Another popular possibility is to ask the audience not to say various words, for example "up". Here, the idea is to catch out the players.

This little pig went to market

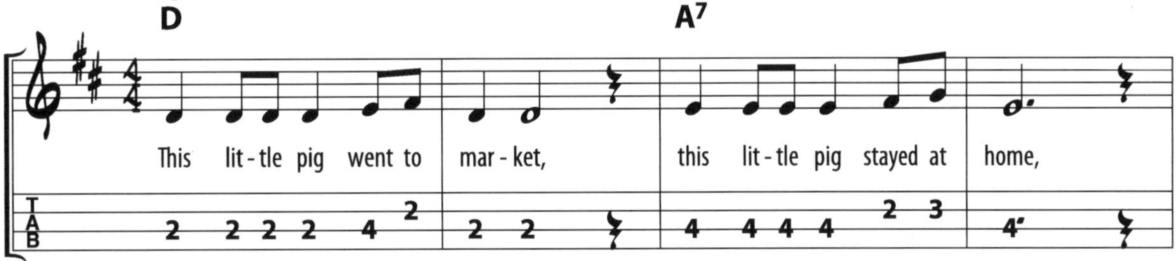

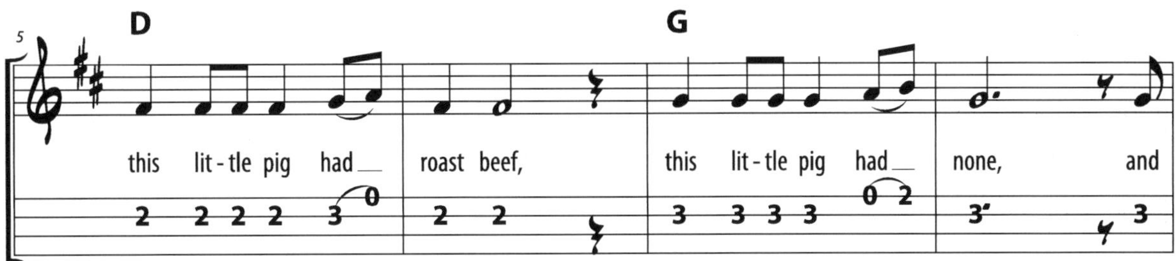

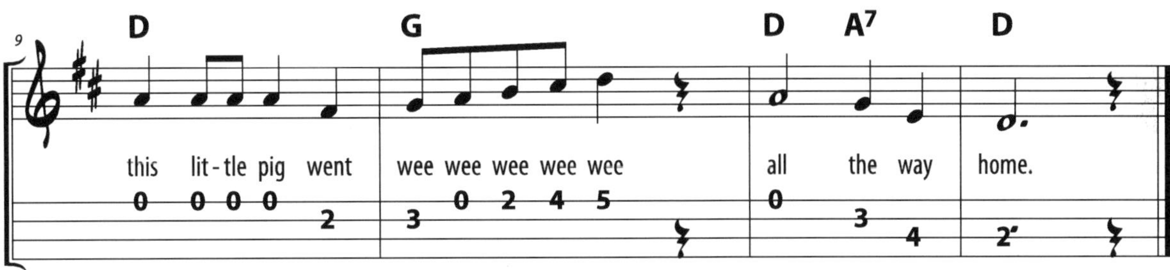

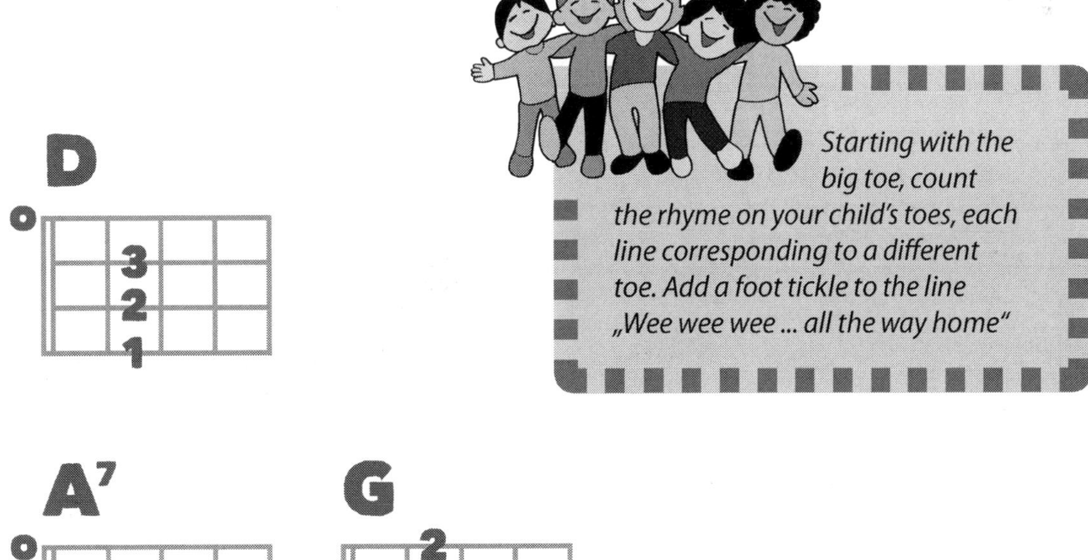

Starting with the big toe, count the rhyme on your child's toes, each line corresponding to a different toe. Add a foot tickle to the line „Wee wee wee ... all the way home"

Ring around the rosy

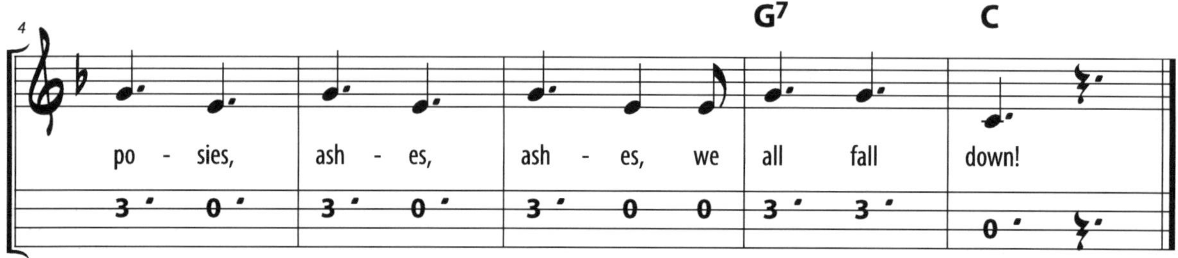

C

1
o
o
o

G^7

3
1
2
o

Punchinello

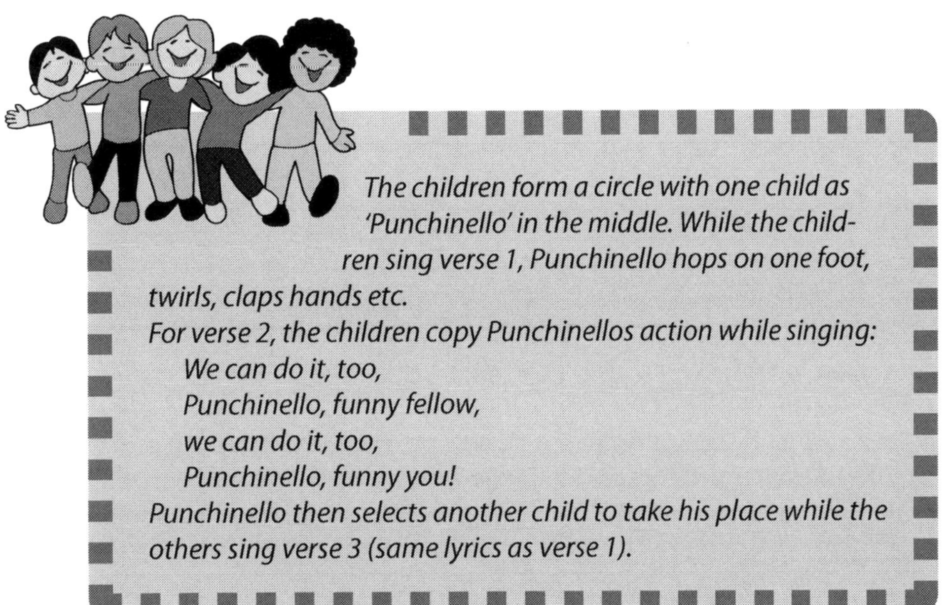

The children form a circle with one child as 'Punchinello' in the middle. While the children sing verse 1, Punchinello hops on one foot, twirls, claps hands etc.

For verse 2, the children copy Punchinellos action while singing:

We can do it, too,
Punchinello, funny fellow,
we can do it, too,
Punchinello, funny you!

Punchinello then selects another child to take his place while the others sing verse 3 (same lyrics as verse 1).

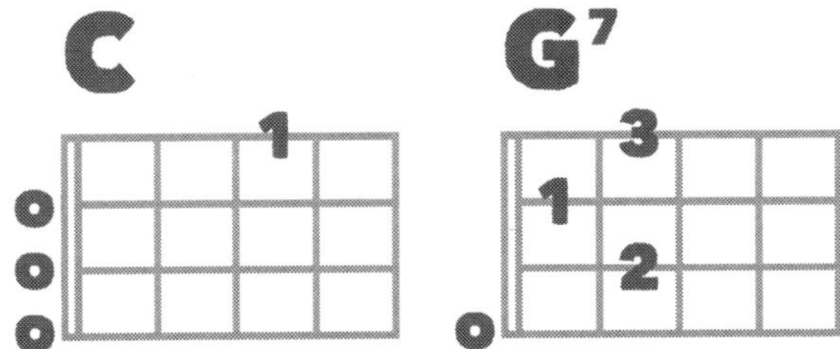

99 Bottles

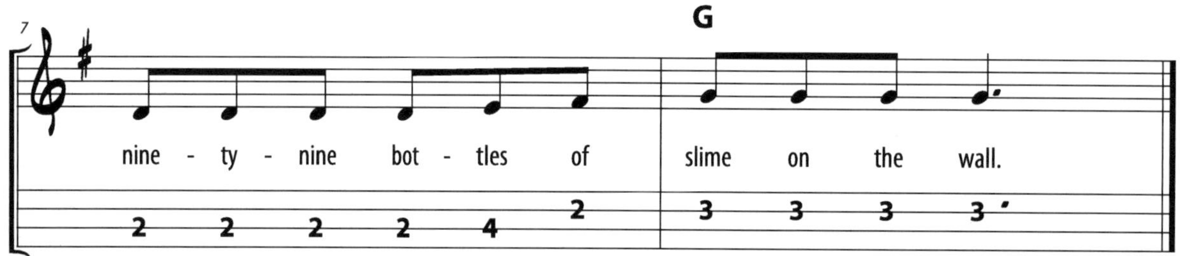

2. 98 bottles of slime on the wall,
98 bottles of slime.
One fell down and broke its crown,
98 bottles of slime on the wall.
etc.

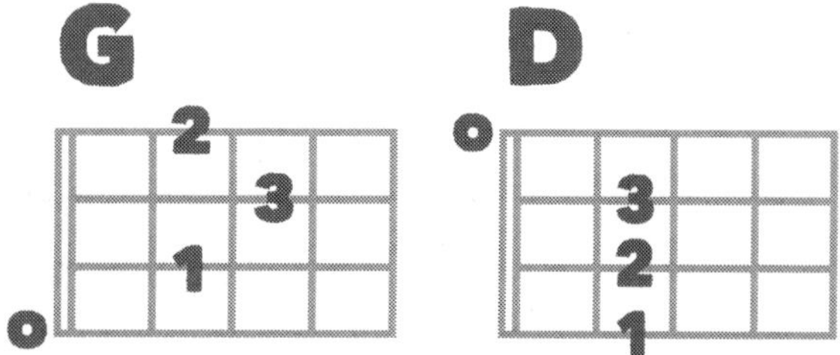

Amazing grace

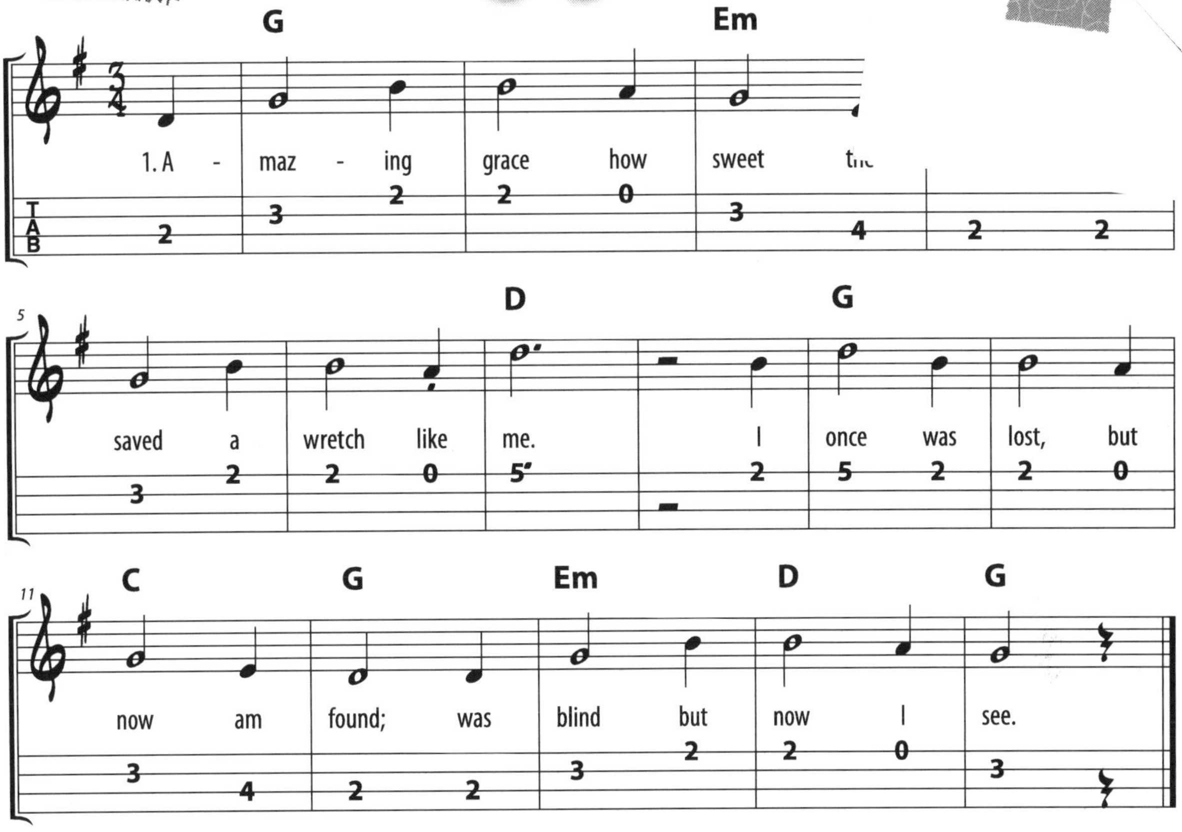

G Em

1. A - maz - ing grace how sweet th...

5 D G

saved a wretch like me. I once was lost, but

11 C G Em D G

now am found; was blind but now I see.

2. 'Twas grace that taught my heart to fear,
And grace my fear relived.
How precious did that grace appear,
The hour I first believed.

3. When we've been there ten thousand years,
Bright shining as the sun.
We've no less days to sing God's praise,
Than when we first begun.

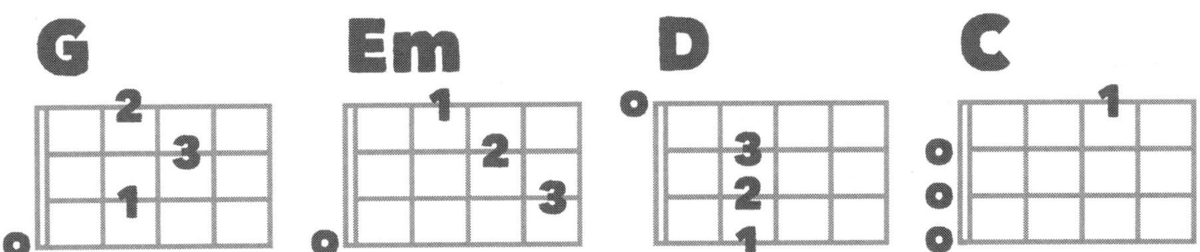

-tisket, a-tasket

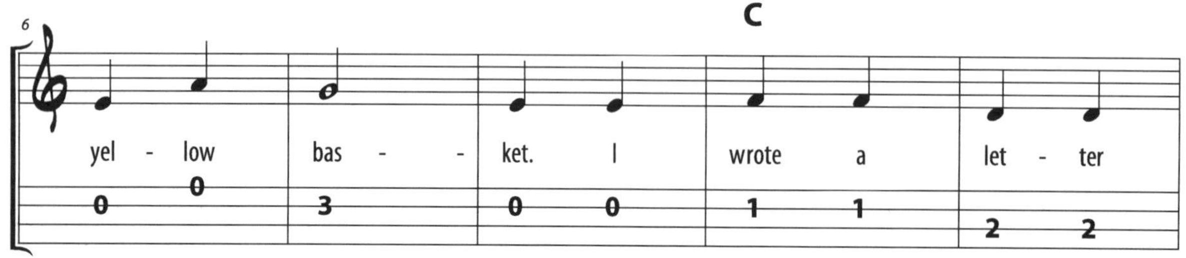

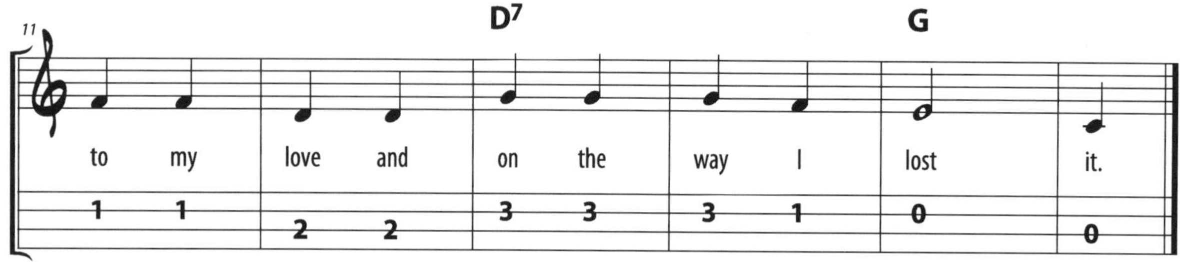

1. *A-tisket a-tasket,*
   a green and yellow basket,
   I wrote a letter to my love
   and on the way I lost it.

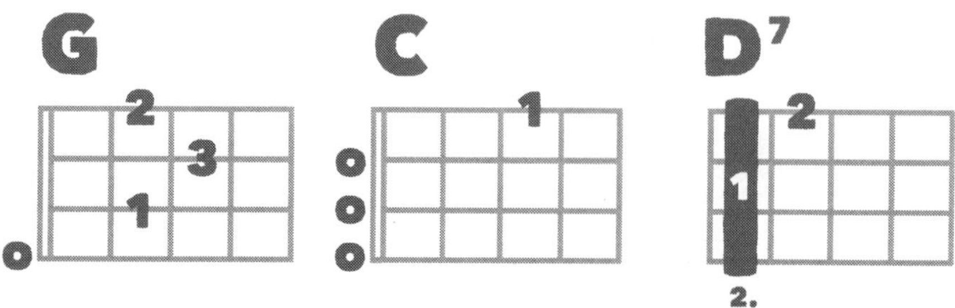

Hush, little baby

2. *If that mockingbird won't sing,*
   mama's gonna buy you a diamond ring.

3. *If that diamond ring turns brass,*
   mama's gonna buy you a looking glass.

4. *If that looking glass gets broke,*
   mama's gonna buy you a billy goat.

5. *If that billy goat don't pull,*
   mama's gonna buy you a cart and bull.

6. *If that cart and bull turn over,*
   mama's gonna buy you a dog named Rover.

7. *If that dog named Rover won't bark,*
   mama's gonna buy you a horse and cart.

8. *If that horse and cart fall down,*
   you'll be the sweetest little baby in town.

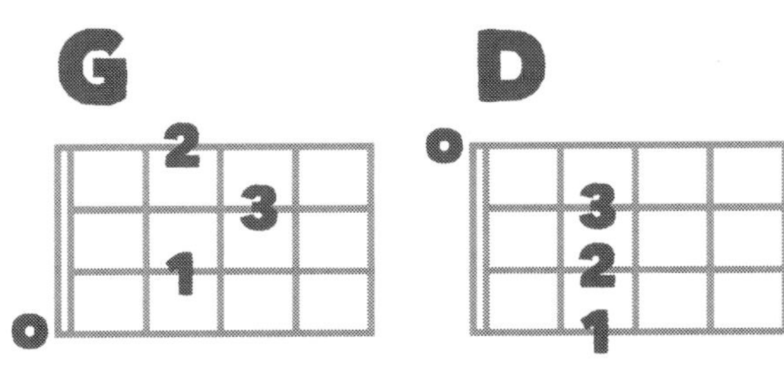

Pop goes the weasel

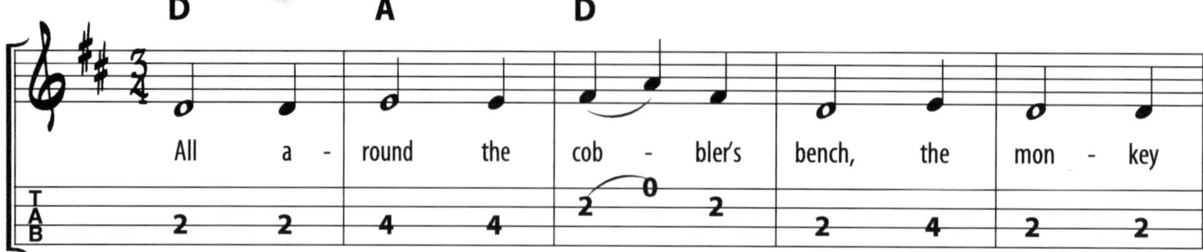

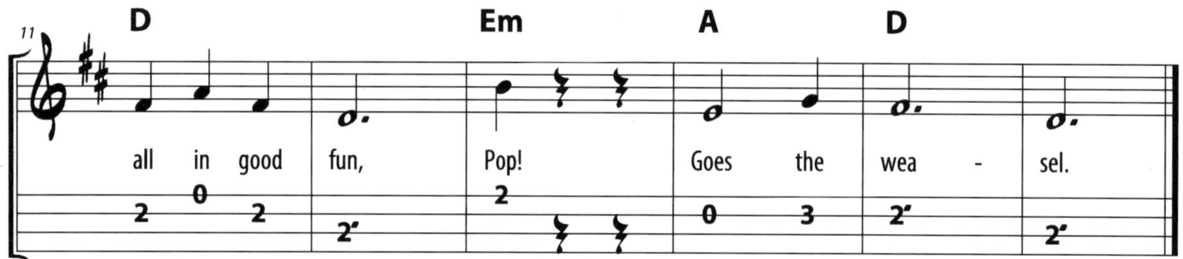

2. *A penny for a spool of thread,*
   a penny for a needle.
   That's the way the money goes,
   Pop! Goes the weasel.

3. *Jimmy's got the whooping cough*
   and Timmy's got the measles.
   That's the way the story goes
   Pop! Goes the weasel.

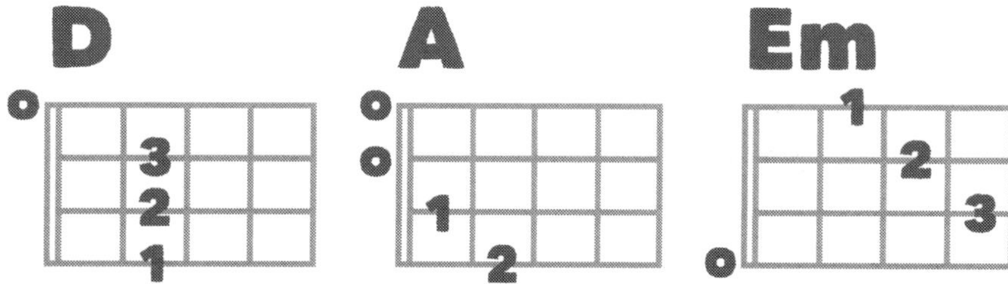

London Bridge is falling down

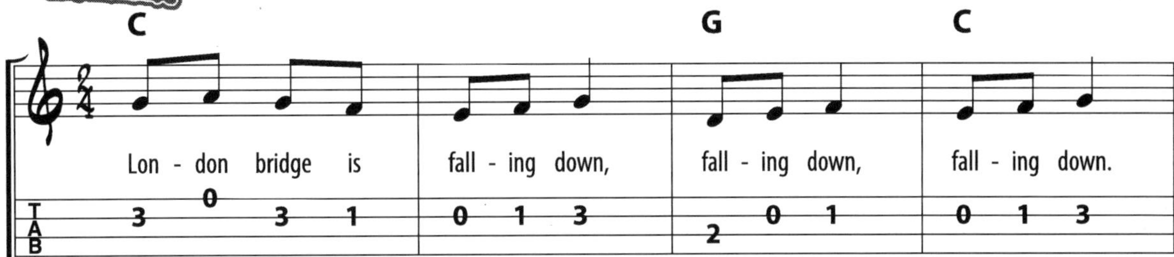

2. *Take a key and lock her up,*
   lock her up, lock her up.
   Take a key and lock her up,
   my fair lady.

3. *How will we build it up,*
   build it up, build it up?
   How will we build it up,
   my fair lady.

4. *Build it up with gold and silver,*
   gold and silver, gold and silver.
   Build it up with gold and silver,
   my fair lady.

5. *Gold and silver I have none,*
   I have none, I have none.
   Gold and silver I have none,
   my fair lady.

6. *Build it up with needles and pins,*
   needles and pins, needles and pins.
   Build it up with needles and pins,
   my fair lady.

7. *Pins and needles bend and break,*
   bend and break, bend and break.
   Pins and needles bend and break,
   my fair lady.

8. *Build it up with wood and clay,*
   wood and clay, wood and clay.
   Build it up with wood and clay,
   my fair lady.

9. *Wood and clay will wash away,*
   wash away, wash away.
   Wood and clay will wash away,
   my fair lady.

10. *Build it up with stone so strong,*
    stone so strong, stone so strong.
    Build it up with stone so strong,
    my fair lady.

11. *Stone so strong will last so long,*
    last so long, last so long.
    Stone so strong will last so long,
    my fair lady.

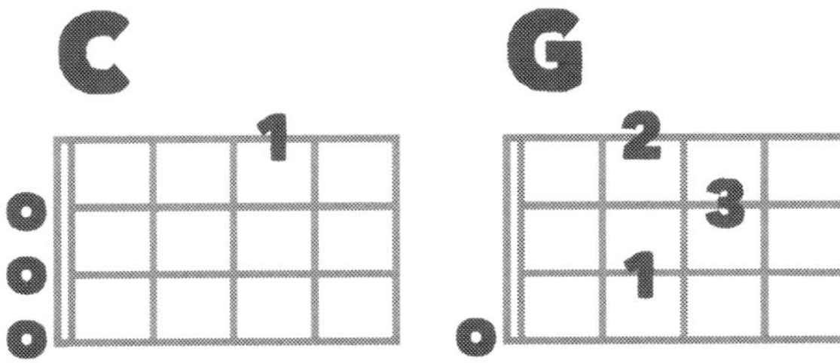

One elephant went out

2. *Two Elephants went out to play upon a spider's web one day.*
   They had such tremendous fun that they called for another Elephant to come!
3. *Three Elephants went out to play upon a spider's web one day.*
   They had such tremendous fun that they called for another Elephant to come!
4. *Four Elephants went out to play upon a spider's web one day.*
   They had such tremendous fun that they called for another Elephant to come!
5. *Five Elephants went out to play upon a spider's web one day.*
   They had such tremendous fun that they all had a picnic in the sun!

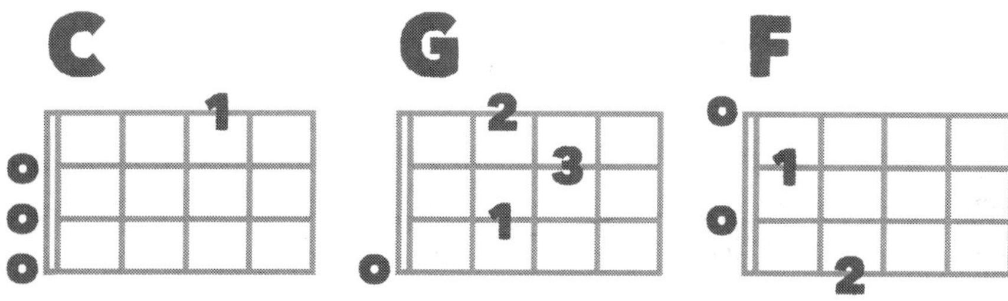

Rain, rain go away

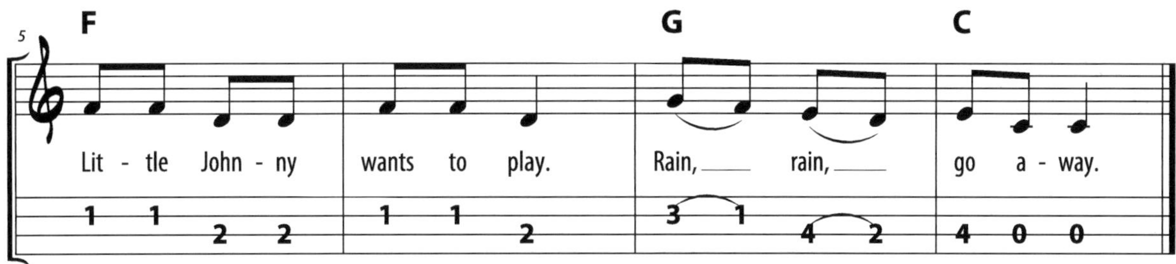

2. *Rain, rain, go away,*
   Come again another day.
   DADDY wants to play.
   Rain, rain, go away

3. *Rain, rain, go away,*
   Come again another day.
   MOMMY wants to play.
   Rain, rain, go away.

5. *Rain, rain, go away,*
   Come again another day.
   BROTHER wants to play.
   Rain, rain, go away.

6. *Rain, rain, go away,*
   Come again another day.
   SISTER wants to play.
   Rain, rain, go away.

7. *Rain, rain, go away,*
   Come again another day.
   BABY wants to play.
   Rain, rain, go away.

8. *Rain, Rain, go away,*
   Come again another day.
   ALL THE FAMILY wants to play.
   Rain, rain, go away.

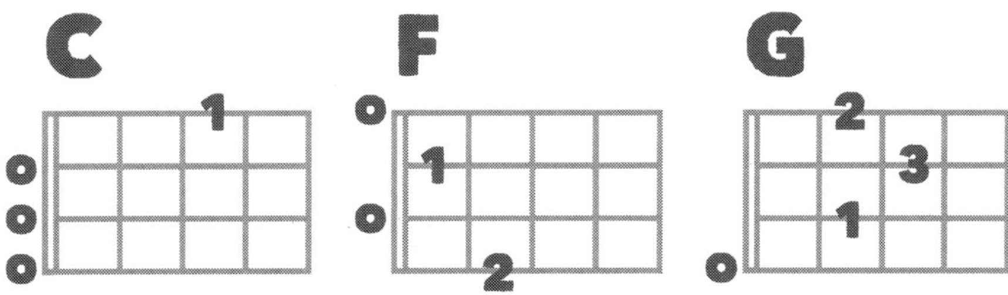

Polly wolly doodle

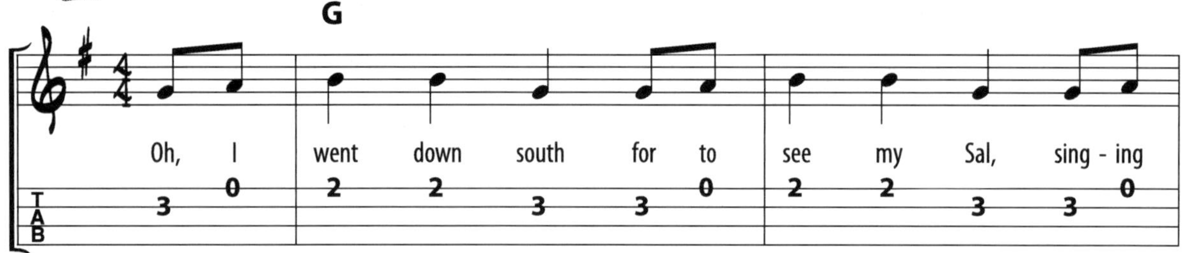

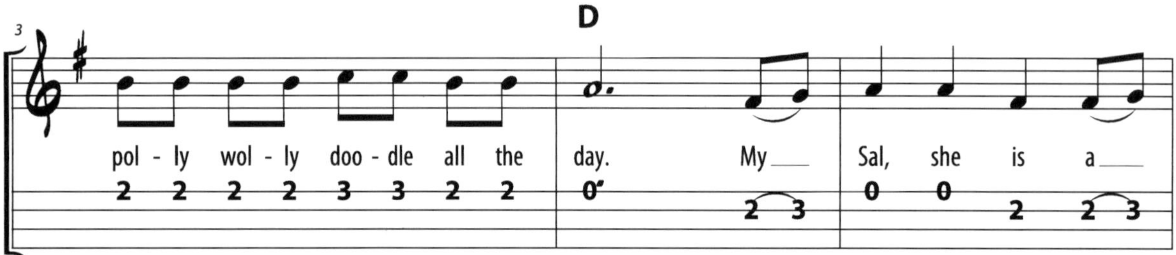

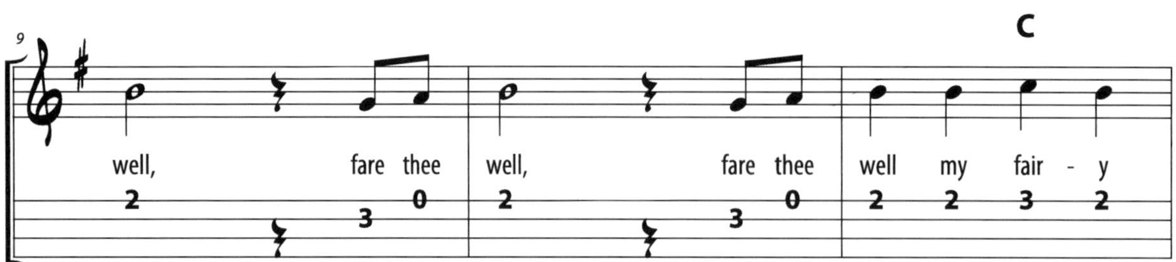

2. *Oh, my Sal, she is a maiden fair,*
   singing Polly wolly doodle all the day.
   With curly eyes and laughing hair,
   singing Polly wolly doodle all the day.
   Fare thee well ...

3. *Behind the barn, down on my knees,*
   singing Polly wolly doodle all the day.
   I thought I heard a chicken sneeze,
   singing Polly wolly doodle all the day.
   Fare thee well ...

4. *He sneezed so hard with the whooping cough,*
   singing Polly wolly doodle all the day.,
   He sneezed his head and the tail right off,
   singing Polly wolly doodle all the day.
   Fare thee well...

5. *Oh, a grasshopper sittin' on a railroad track,*
   singing Polly wolly doodle all the day.
   A-pickin' his teeth with a carpet tack,
   singing Polly wolly doodle all the day
   Fare thee well ...

6. *Oh, I went to bed but it wasn't any use,*
   singing Polly wolly doodle all the day.
   My feet stuck out like a chicken roost,
   singing Polly wolly doodle all the day
   Fare thee well ...

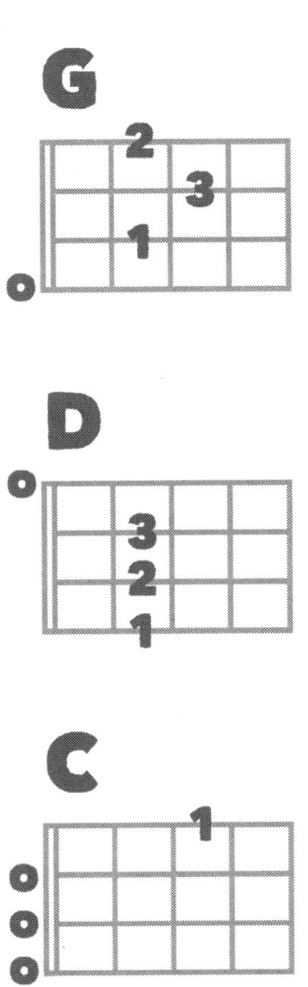

Lavender's blue

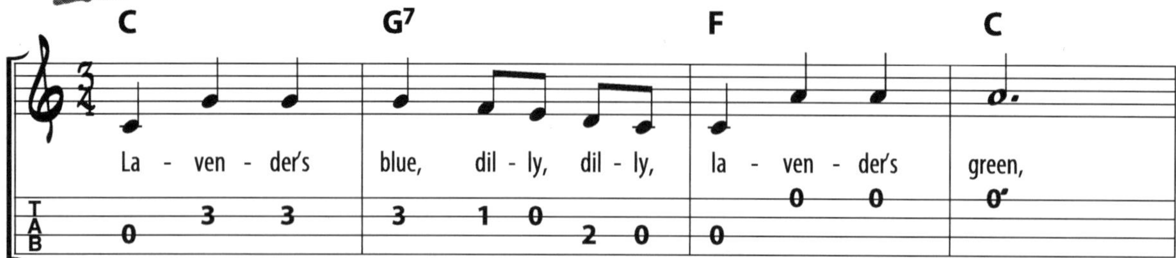

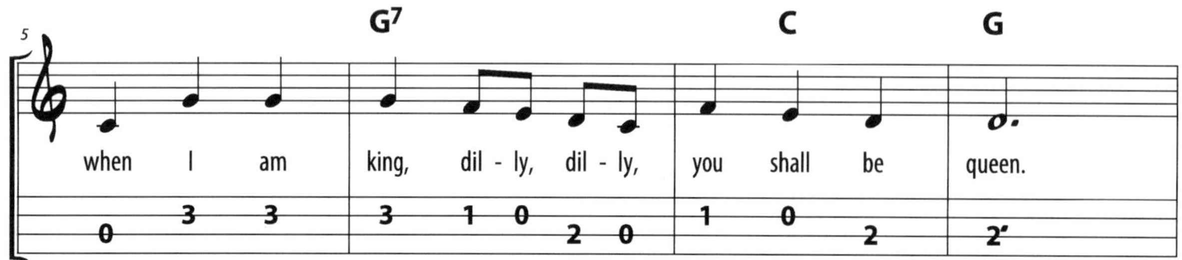

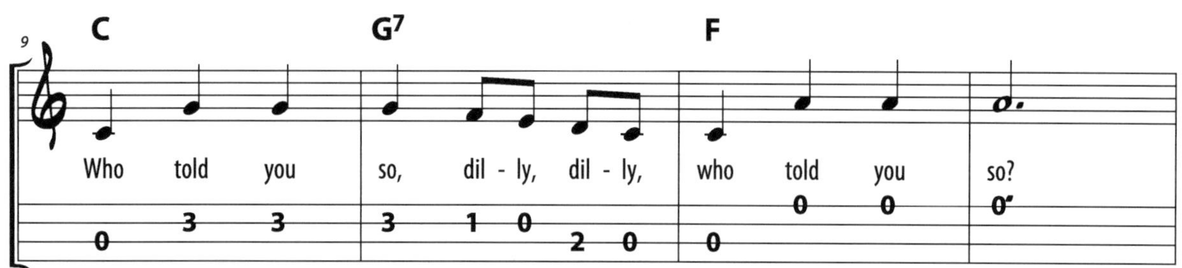

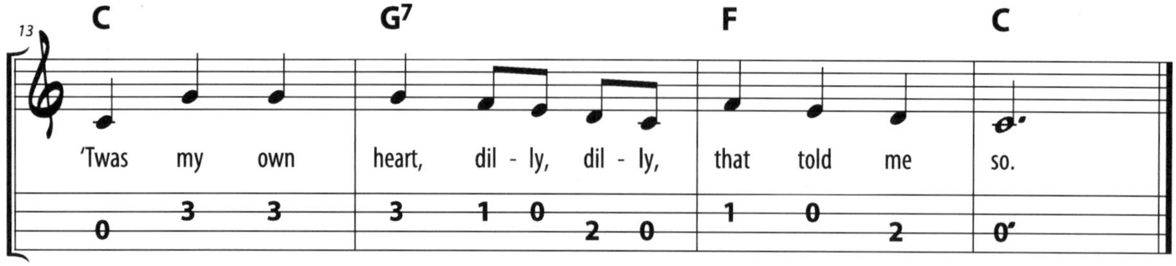

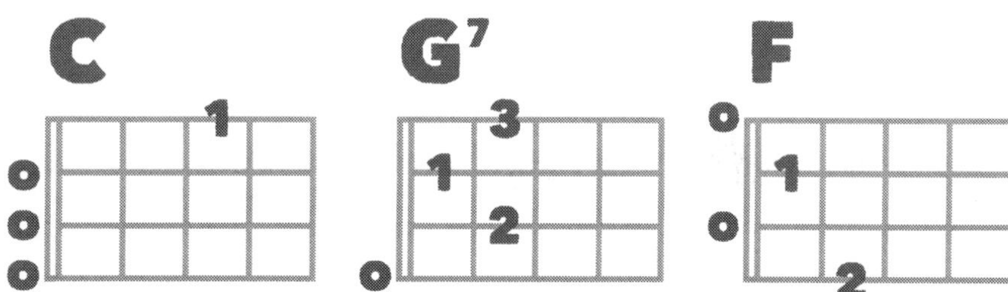

2. *Call up your men, dilly, dilly, set them to work,*
   some to the plough, dilly, dilly, some to the fork,
   some to make hay, dilly, dilly, some to cut corn,
   while you and I, dilly, dilly, keep ourselves warm.

3. *Lavender's green, dilly, dilly, Lavender's blue,*
   if you love me, dilly, dilly, I will love you.
   Let the birds sing, dilly, dilly, and the lambs play;
   we shall be safe, dilly, dilly, out of harm's way.

4. *I love to dance, dilly, dilly, I love to sing;*
   when I am queen, dilly, dilly, you'll be my king.
   Who told me so, dilly, dilly, who told me so?
   I told myself, dilly, dilly, I told me so.

Hickory dickory dock

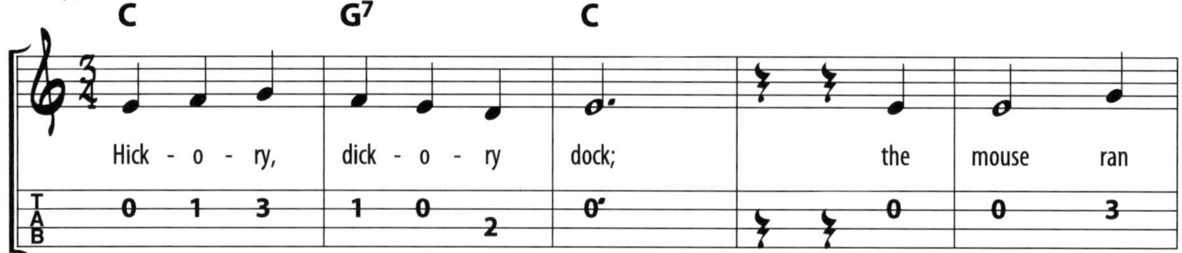

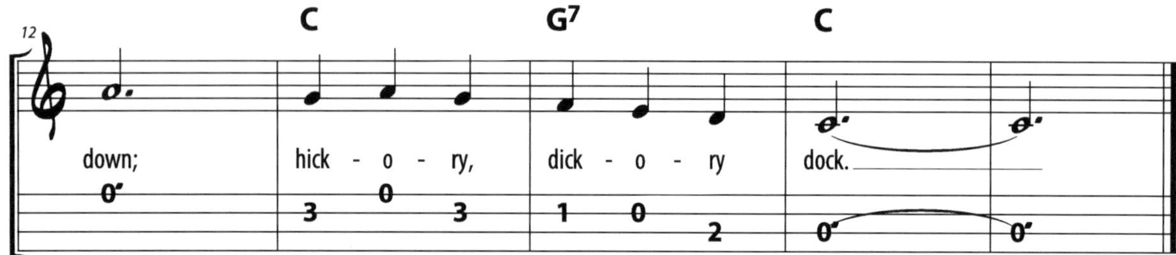

2. *Hickory dickory dock,*
the mouse ran up the clock,
the clock struck two
and down he flew,
hickory dickory dock.

3. *Hickory dickory dock,*
the mouse ran up the clock,
the clock struck three
and he did flee,
hickory dickory dock.

4. *Hickory dickory dock,*
the mouse ran up the clock,
the clock struck four,
he hit the floor,
hickory dickory dock.

5. *Hickory dickory dock,*
the mouse ran up the clock,
the clock struck five,
the mouse took a dive,
hickory dickory dock.

6. *Hickory dickory dock,*
the mouse ran up the clock,
the clock struck six,
the mouse, he split,
hickory dickory dock.

7. *Hickory dickory dock,*
the mouse ran up the clock,
the clock struck seven,
8, 9, 10, 11,
hickory dickory dock.

8. *Hickory dickory dock,*
the mouse ran up the clock,
as twelve bells rang,
the mousie sprang,
hickory dickory dock.

9. *Hickory dickory dock,*
"Why scamper?" asked the clock,
"You scare me so
I have to go!"
hickory dickory dock.

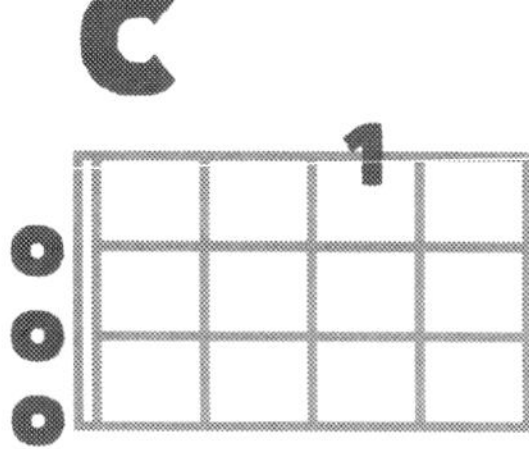

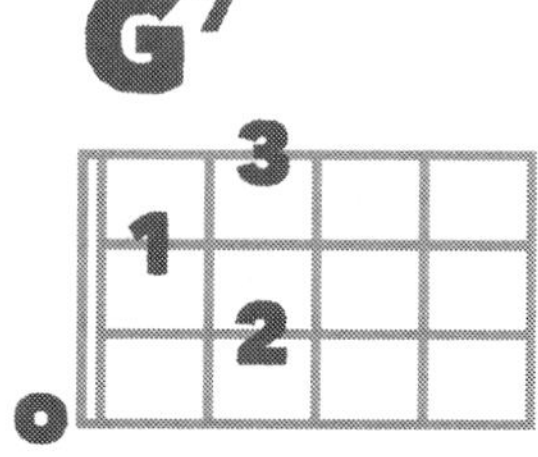

Teddy bear

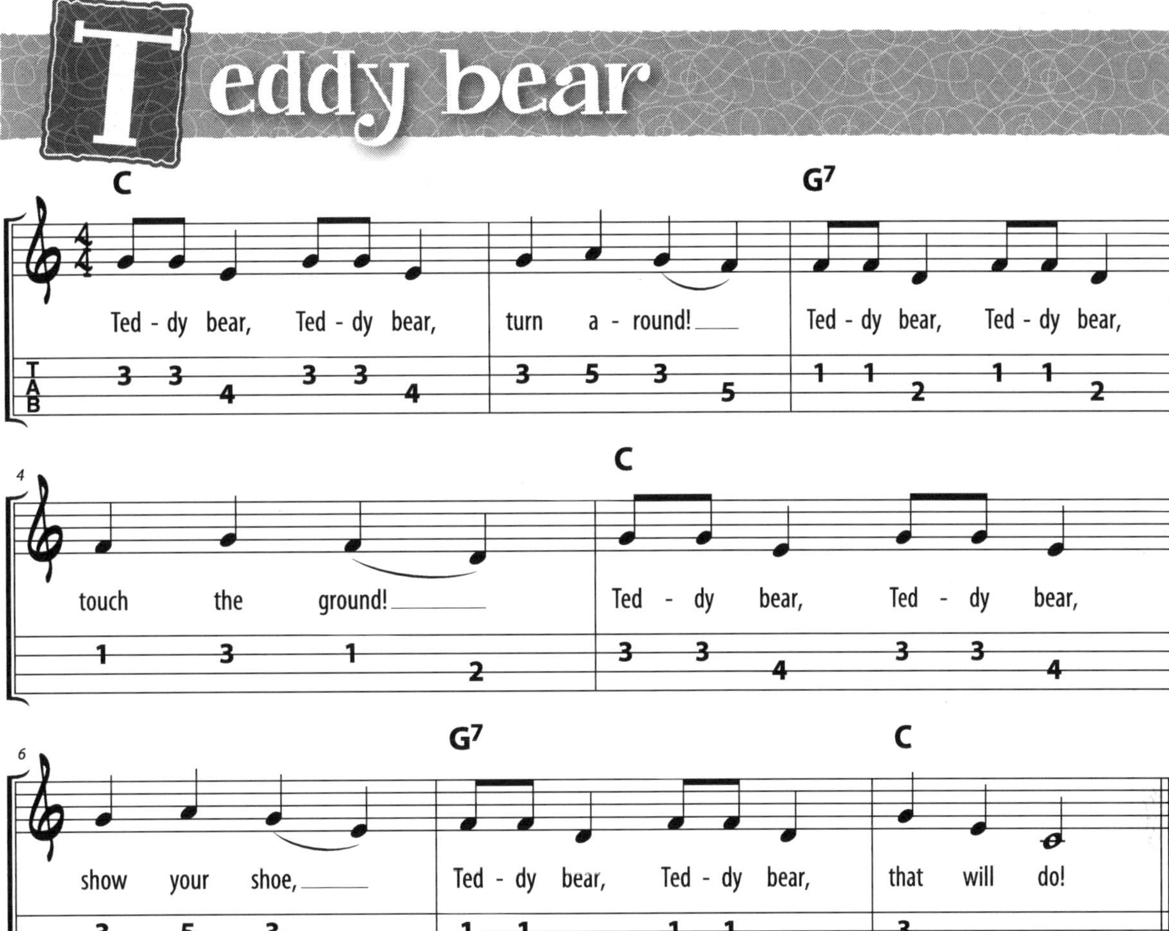

2. *Teddy bear, teddy bear, turn around!*
   Teddy bear, teddy bear, touch the ground!
   Teddy bear, teddy bear, jump up high!
   Teddy bear, teddy bear, touch the sky!

3. *Teddy bear, teddy bear, bend down low!*
   Teddy bear, teddy bear, touch you toes!
   Teddy bear, teddy bear, turn out the light!
   Teddy bear, teddy bear, say good night!

Rock-a-bye, baby

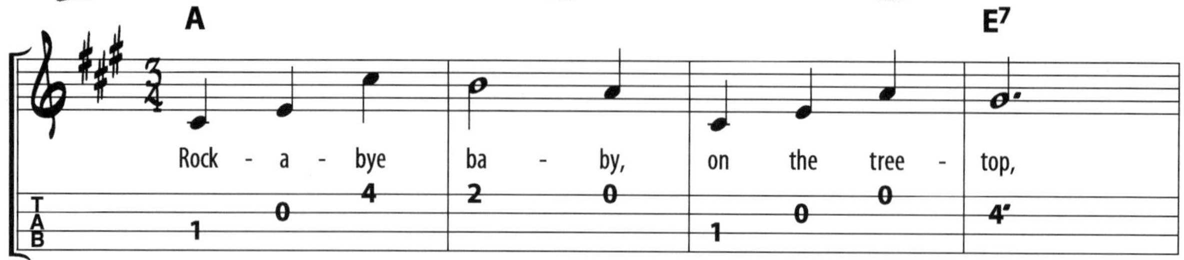

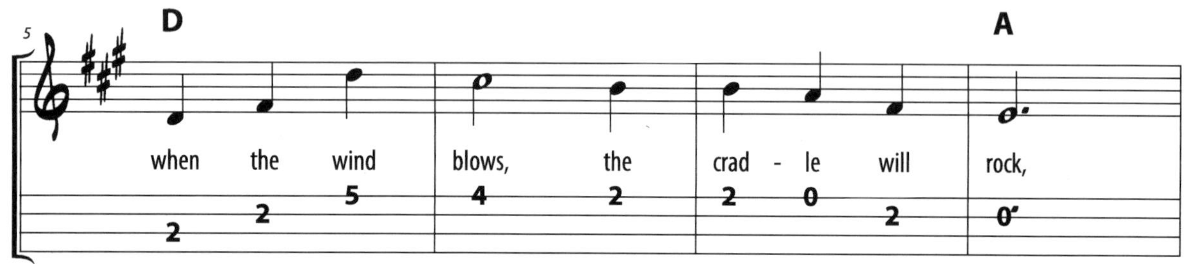

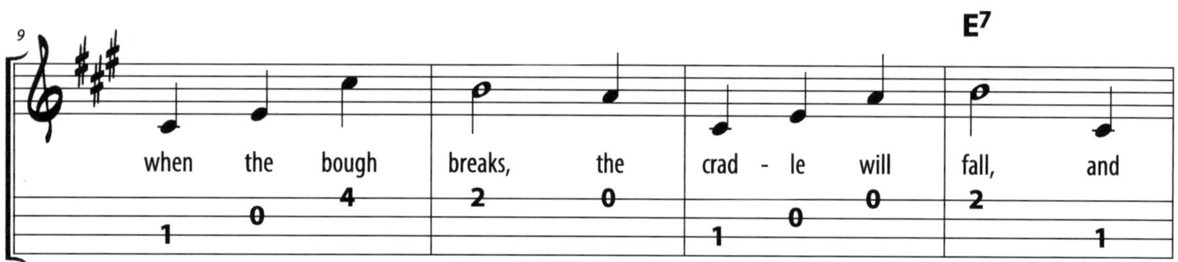

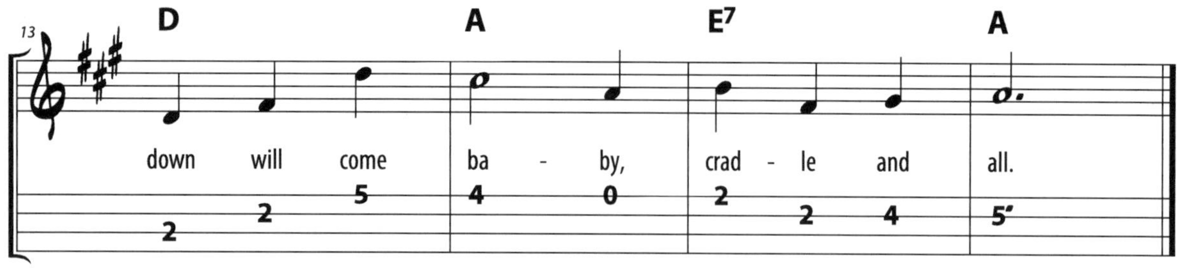

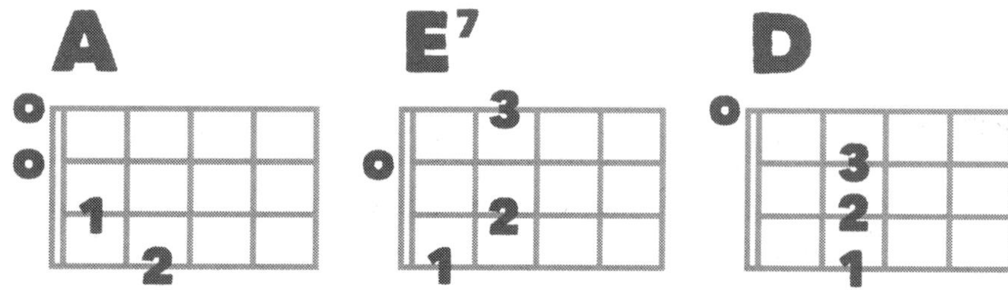

Itsy-bitsy spider

F C

The it - sy - bit - sy spi - der went up the wa - ter

F B♭ F

spout. Down came the rain and washed the spi - der out.

C F

Out came the sun and dried up all the rain, so the

C F

it - sy - bit - sy spi - der went up the spout a - gain.

2. *The great big spider went up the water spout ...*

3. *The teeny tiny spider went up the water spout ...*

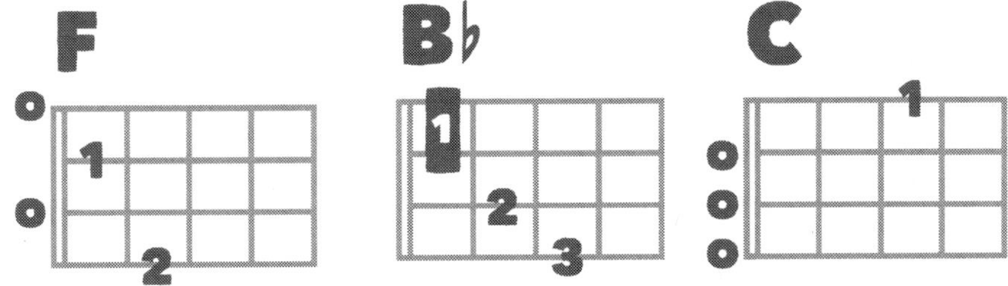

Crawdad song

F
You get a line and I'll get a pole, Hon - ey.
1 1 1 1 1 0 1 1 1 2 1 1

5
C
You get a line and I'll get a pole, Ba - by.
0 3 3 3 3 5 3 3 3 3 3 3

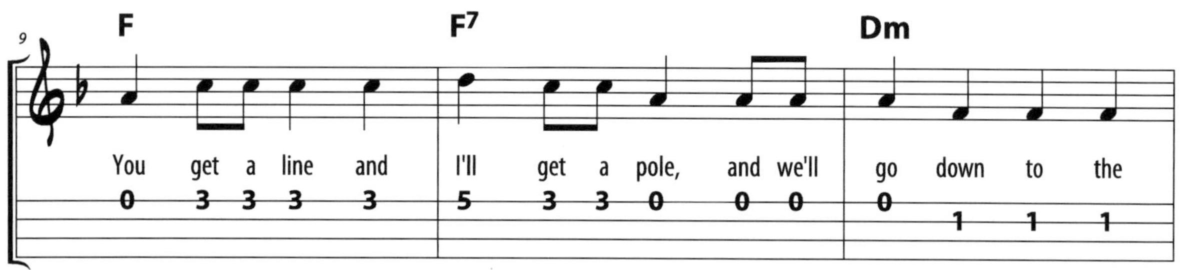
9
F F7 Dm
You get a line and I'll get a pole, and we'll go down to the
0 3 3 3 3 5 3 3 0 0 0 0 1 1 1

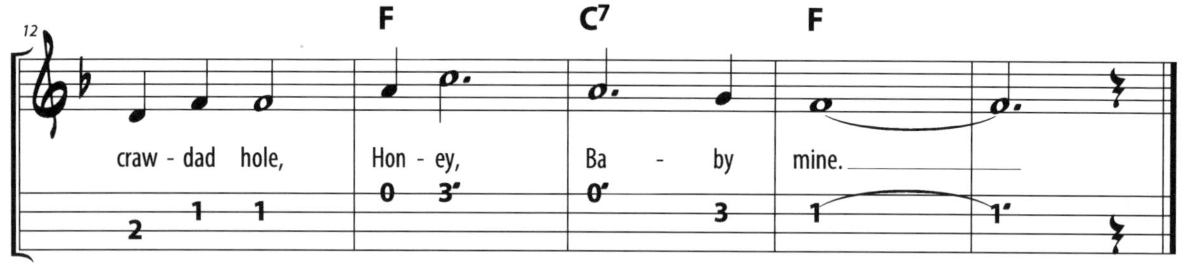
12
F C7 F
craw - dad hole, Hon - ey, Ba - by mine.
2 1 1 0 3 0 3 1 1

2. *Sittin' on the bank 'til my feet get cold, Honey.*
Sittin' on the bank 'til my feet get cold, Baby.
Sittin' on the bank 'til my feet get cold,
lookin' down that crawdad hole, Honey, Baby mine.

3. *Yonder comes a man with a sack on his back, Honey.*
Yonder comes a man with a sack on his Baby.
Yonder comes a man with a sack on his back,
packin' all the crawdads he can pack, Honey, Baby mine.

4. *The man fell down and he broke that sack, Honey.*
The man fell down and he broke that sack, Baby.
The man fell down and he broke that sack,
see those crawdads backing back, Honey, Baby mine.

5. *I heard the duck say to the drake, honey, honey.*
I heard the duck say to the drake, baby, baby.
I heard the duck say to the drake,
there ain't no crawdads in this lake, Honey, Baby mine.

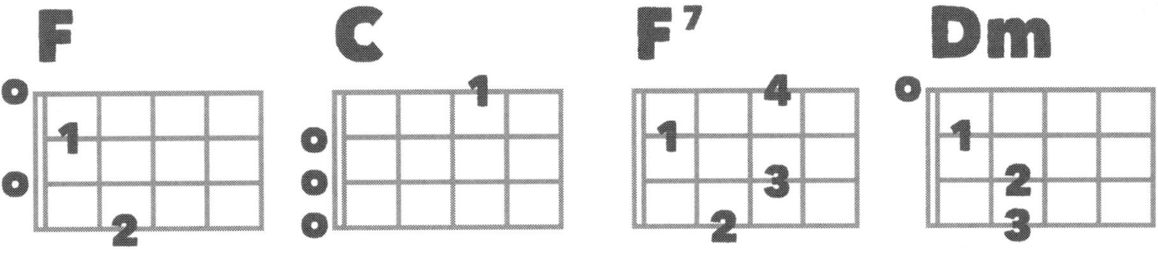

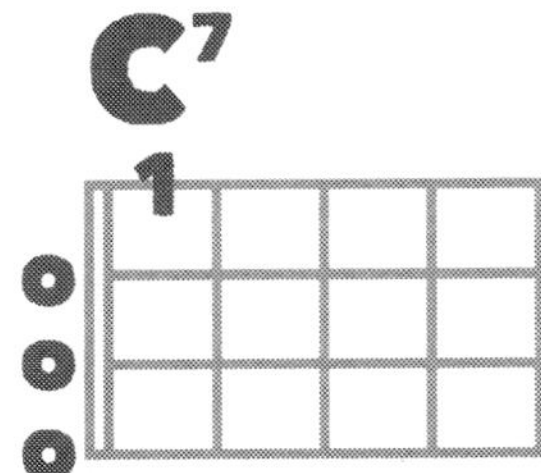

Baa, baa, black sheep

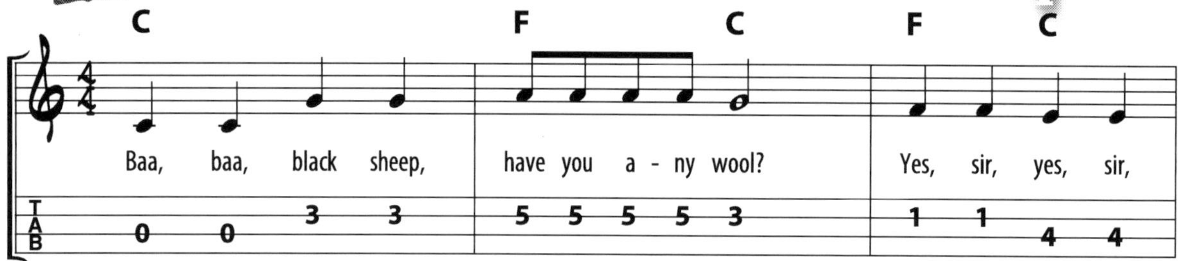

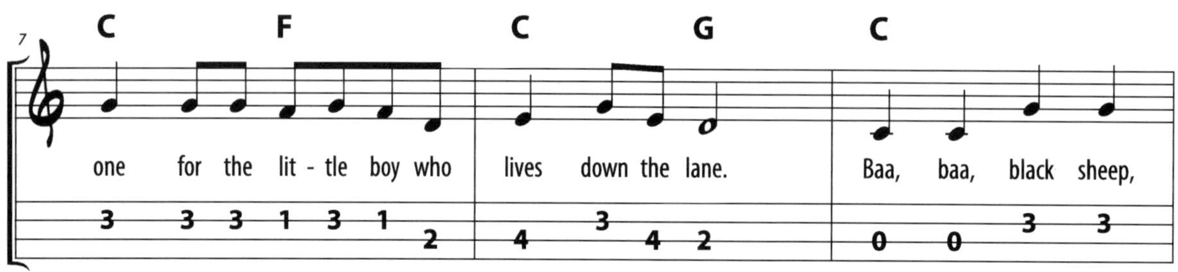

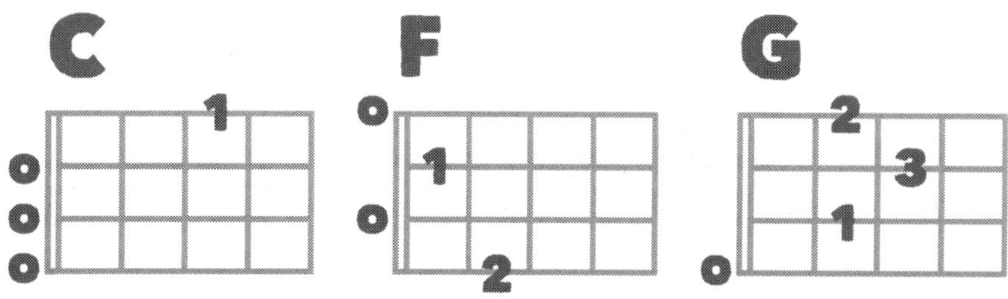

Bingo

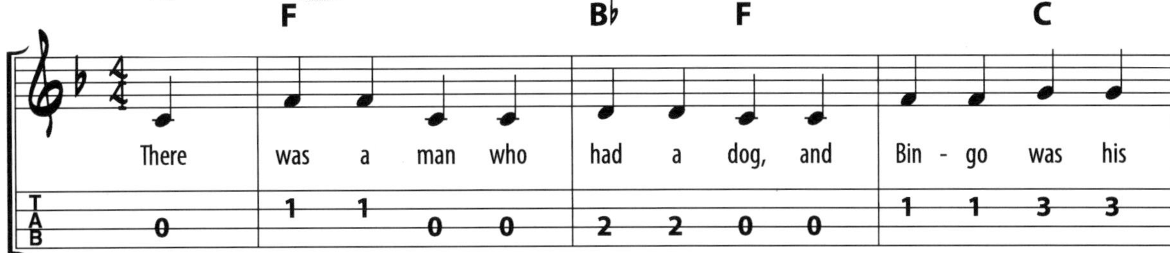

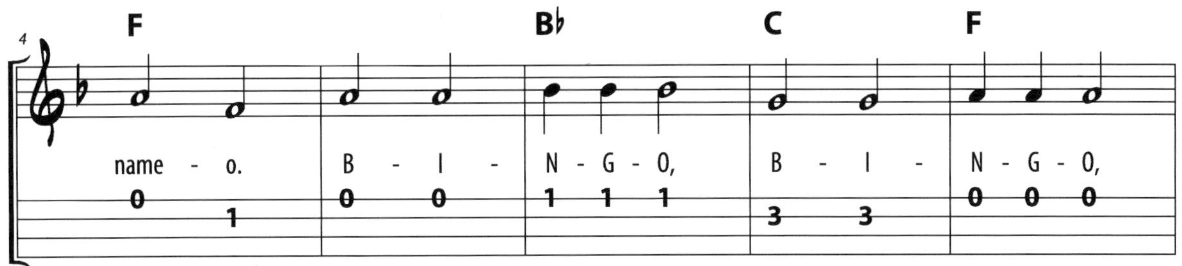

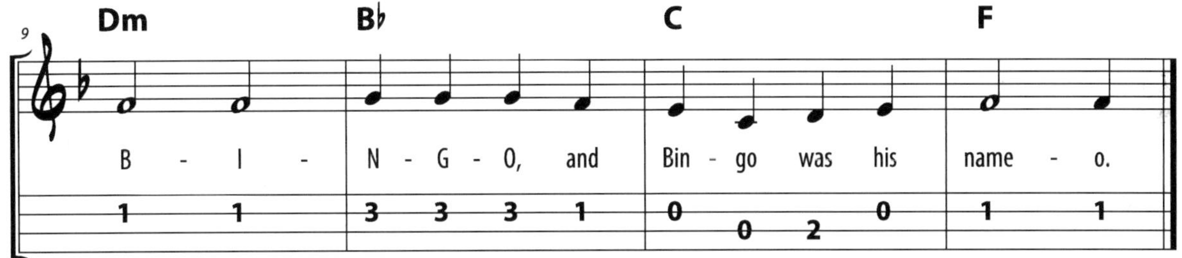

2. *There was a man who had a dog,*
   and Bingo was his name-o.
   (clap)-I-N-G-O (3x)
   and Bingo was his name-o.

3. *There was a man who had a dog,*
   and Bingo was his name-o.
   (clap)-(clap)-N-G-O (3x)
   and Bingo was his name-o.

4. *There was a man who had a dog,*
   and Bingo was his name-o.
   (clap)-(clap)-(clap)-G-O (3x)
   and Bingo was his name-o.

5. *There was a man who had a dog,*
   and Bingo was his name-o.
   (clap)-(clap)-(clap)-(clap)-O (3x)
   and Bingo was his name-o.

6. *There was a man who had a dog,*
   and Bingo was his name-o.
   (clap)-(clap)-(clap)-(clap)-(clap) (3x)
   and Bingo was his name-o.

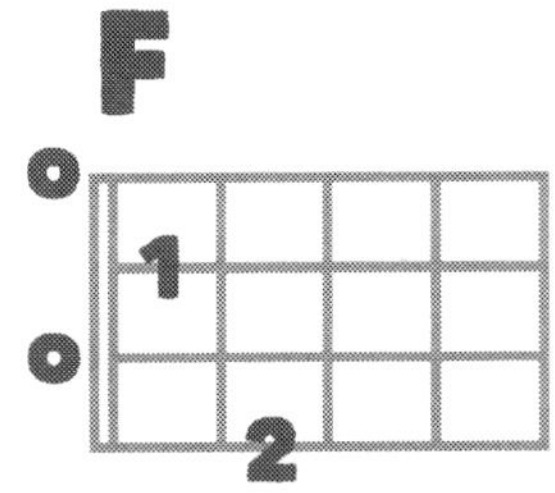

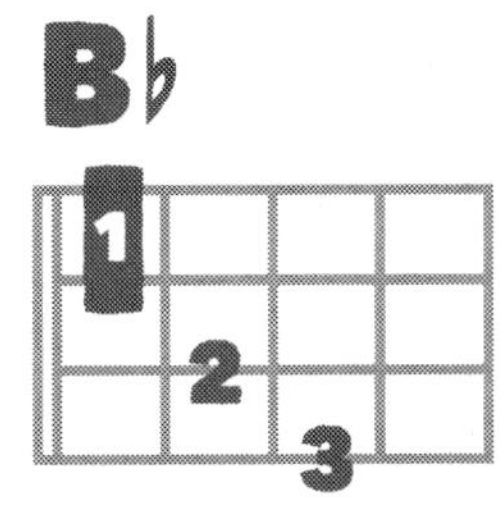

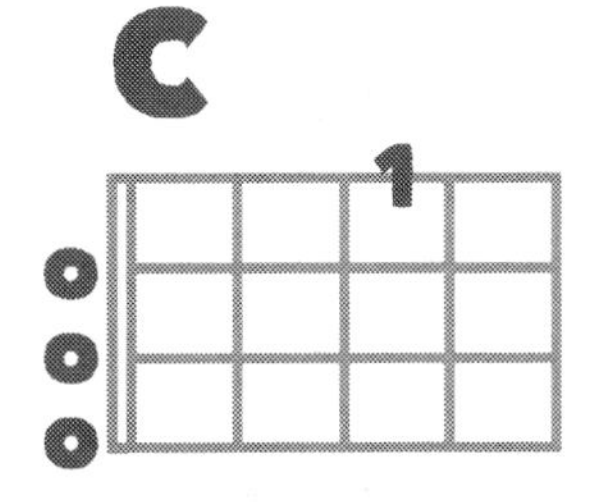

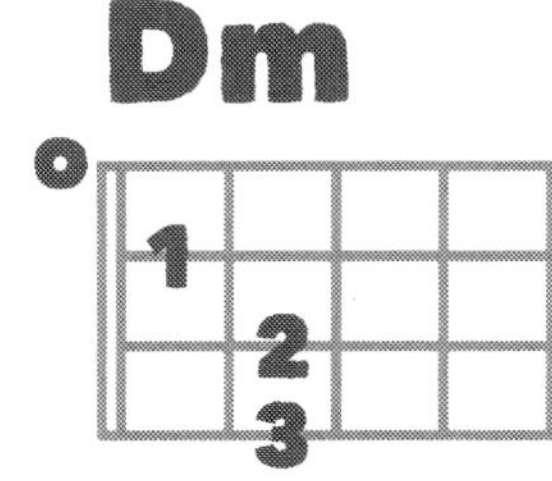

Brahms' Lullaby

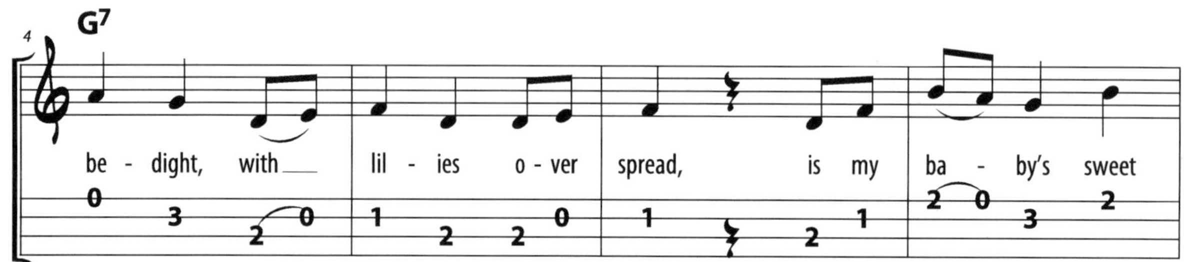

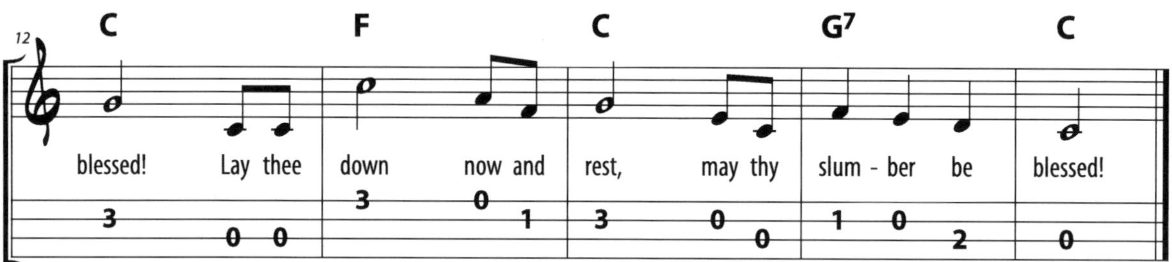

2. *Lullaby, and good night, your mother's delight,*
   shining angels beside my darling abide.
   Soft and warm is your bed,
   close your eyes and rest your head.
   Soft and warm is your bed,
   close your eyes and rest your head.

3. *Sleepyhead, close your eyes,*
   mother's right here beside you.
   I'll protect you from harm,
   you will wake in my arms.
   Guardian angels are near,
   so sleep on, with no fear.
   Guardian angels are near,
   so sleep on, with no fear.

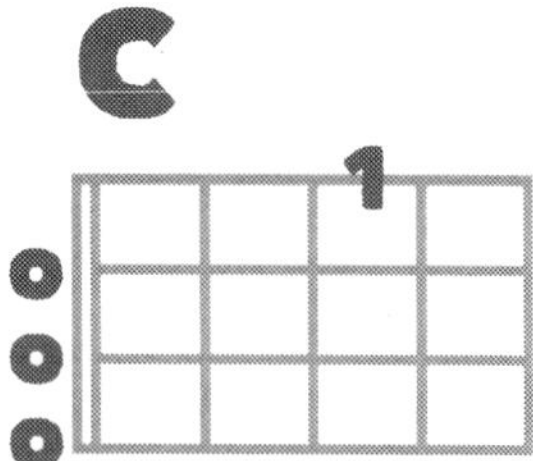

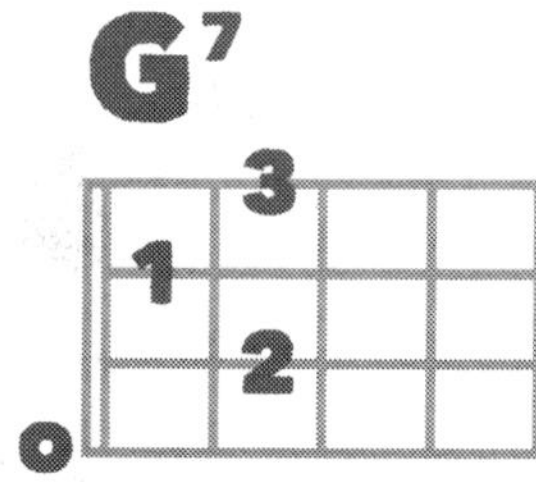

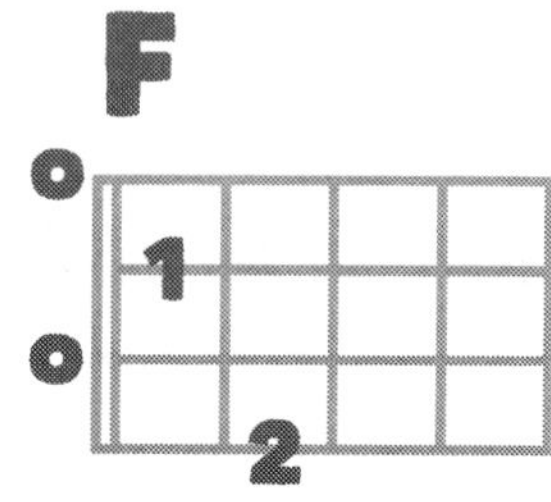

Jack and Jill

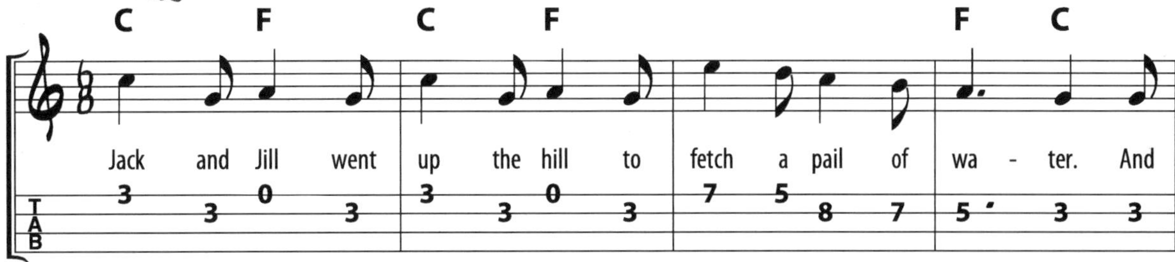

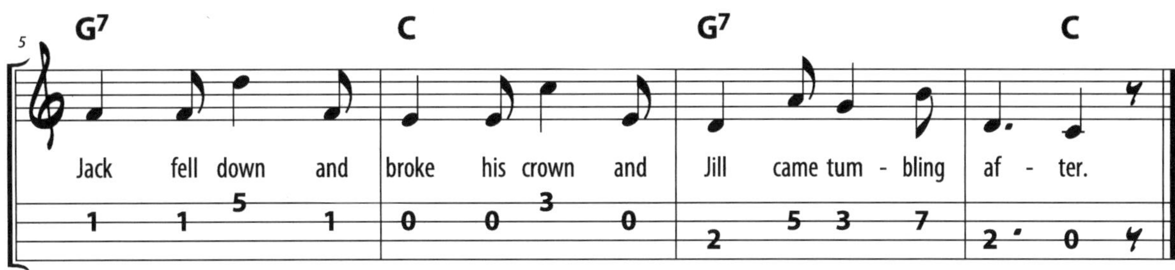

2. *Up Jack got and home did trot,*
   as fast as he could caper;
   and went to bed and bound his head
   with vinegar and brown paper.

3. *When Jill came in how she did grin*
   to see Jack's paper plaster;
   mother vexed did whip her next
   for causing Jack's disaster.

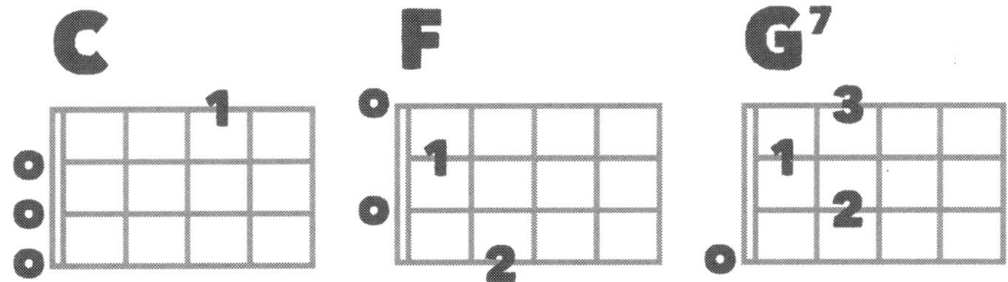

This old man

D
G
This old man, he played one, he played knick - knack
TAB

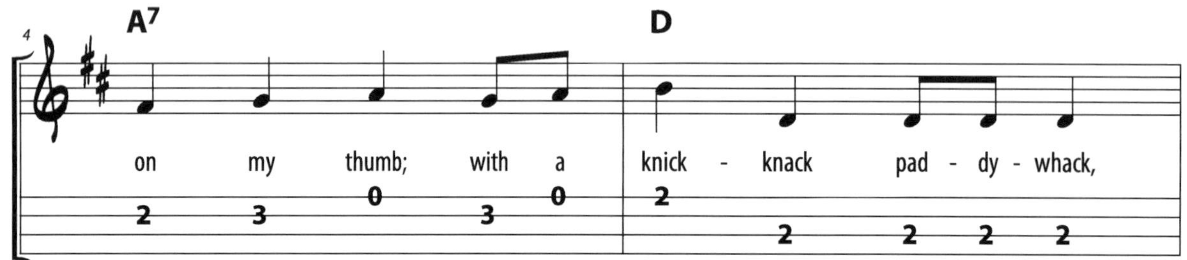
A7
D
on my thumb; with a knick - knack pad - dy - whack,

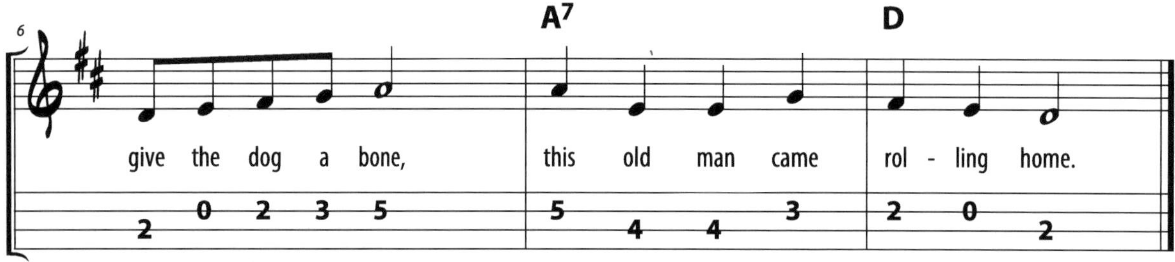
A7
D
give the dog a bone, this old man came rol - ling home.

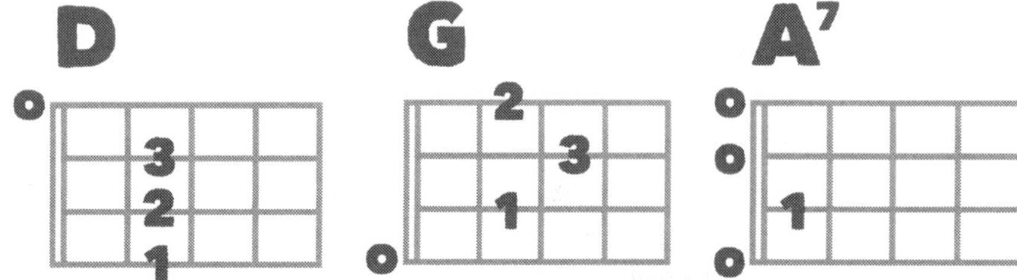
D
G
A7

2. *This old man, he played two,*
   he played knick-knack on my shoe;
   with a knick-knack paddywhack,
   give the dog a bone,
   this old man came rolling home.

3. *This old man, he played three,*
   he played knick-knack on my knee;
   with a knick-knack paddywhack,
   give the dog a bone,
   this old man came rolling home.

4. *This old man, he played four,*
   he played knick-knack on my door;
   with a knick-knack paddywhack,
   give the dog a bone,
   this old man came rolling home.

5. *This old man, he played five,*
   he played knick-knack on my hive;
   with a knick-knack paddywhack,
   give the dog a bone,
   this old man came rolling home.

6. *This old man, he played six,*
   he played knick-knack on my sticks;
   with a knick-knack paddywhack,
   give the dog a bone,
   this old man came rolling home.

7. *This old man, he played seven,*
   he played knick-knack up in heaven;
   with a knick-knack paddywhack,
   give the dog a bone,
   this old man came rolling home.

8. *This old man, he played eight,*
   he played knick-knack on my gate;
   with a knick-knack paddywhack,
   give the dog a bone,
   this old man came rolling home.

9. *This old man, he played nine,*
   he played knick-knack on my spine;
   with a knick-knack paddywhack,
   give the dog a bone,
   this old man came rolling home.

10. *This old man, he played ten,*
    he played knick-knack once again;
    with a knick-knack paddywhack,
    give the dog a bone,
    this old man came rolling home.

J.
J. J. Schmidt

F
C
B♭
C
John Ja - cob Jin - gle - hei - mer Schmidt, his name is my name,
T
A
B
0 3 1 0 1 1 1 1 1 0 1 3 3

4
F
B♭
too. When - ev - er we go out, the peo - ple al - ways shout:
0 0 0 0 0 0 0 1 2 1 1 1 1

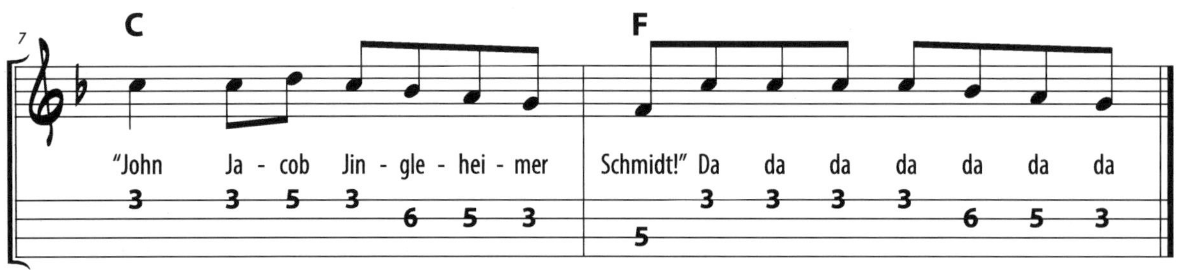
7
C
F
"John Ja - cob Jin - gle - hei - mer Schmidt!" Da da da da da da da
3 3 5 3 6 5 3 5 3 3 3 3 6 5 3

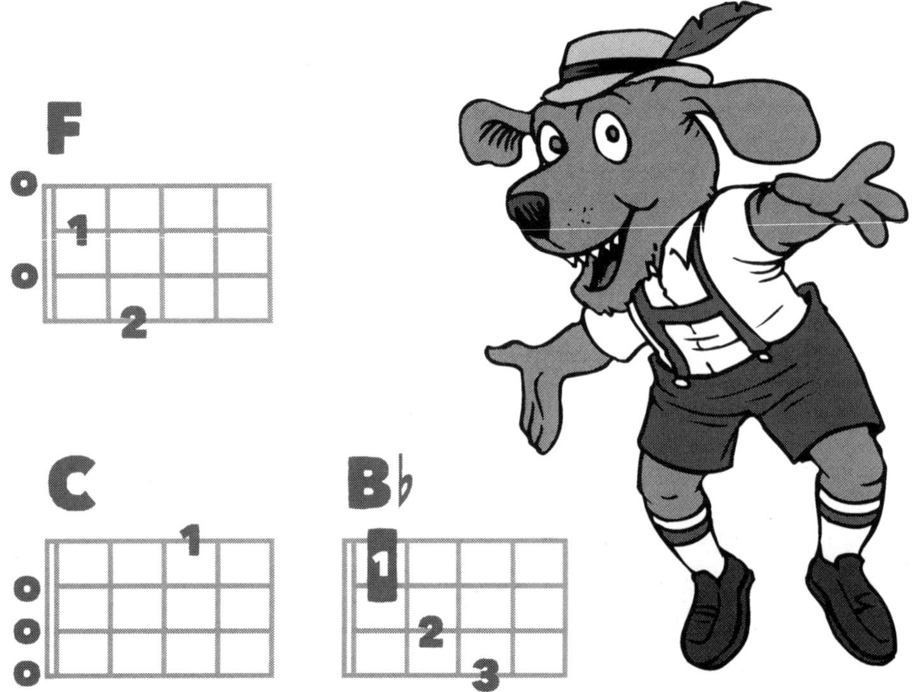
F
1
2
C
1
B♭
1
2
3

Little green frog

F Bb C7 F C7
"Gung, gung", went the lit - tle green frog one day, "gung,
0 1 1 3 0 3 1 3 3 3 0

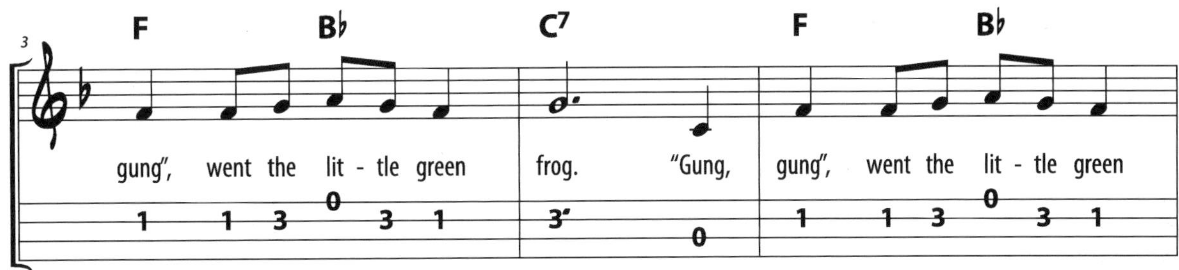
3
F Bb C7 F Bb
gung", went the lit - tle green frog. "Gung, gung", went the lit - tle green
1 1 3 0 3 1 3' 0 1 1 3 0 3 1

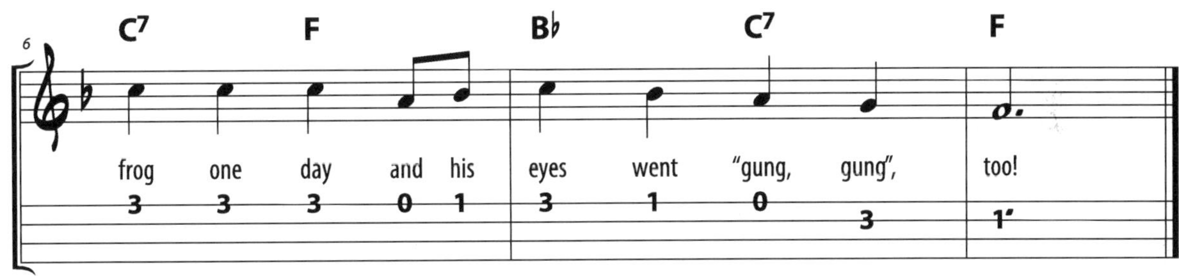
6
C7 F Bb C7 F
frog one day and his eyes went "gung, gung", too!
3 3 3 0 1 3 1 0 3 1'

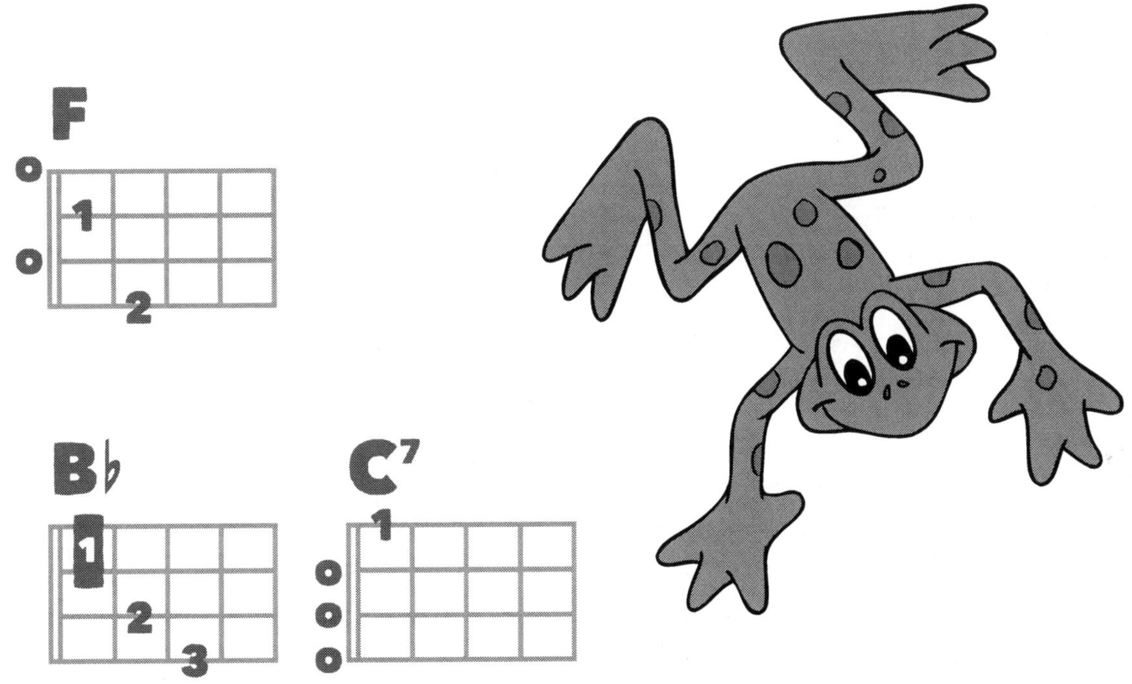
F
1
2
B♭
1
2
3
C7
1

Camptown Races

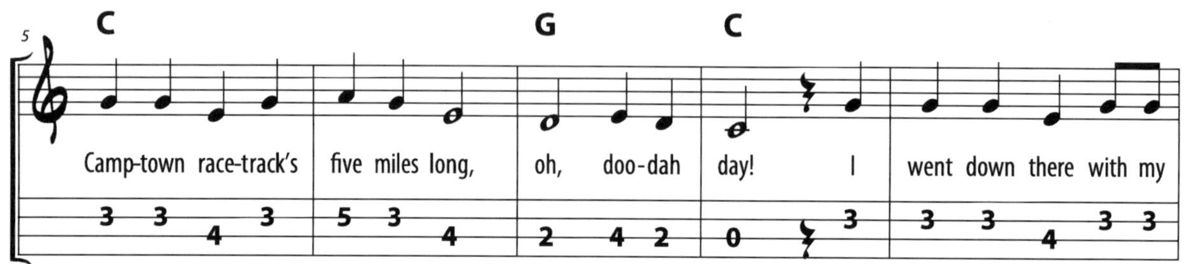

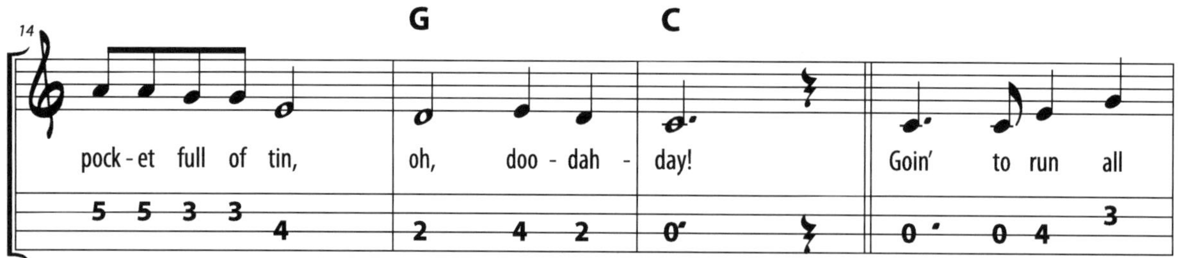

2. *De long tail filly and de big black hoss, Doo-dah! doo-dah!*
Dey fly de track and dey both cut across, Oh, doo-dah-day!
De blind hoss sticken in a big mud hole, Doo-dah! doo-dah!
Can't touch bottom wid a ten foot pole, Oh, doo-dah-day

Refrain

3. *Old muley cow come on to de track, Doo-dah! doo-dah!*
De bob-tail fling her ober his back, Oh, doo-dah-day!
Den fly along like a rail-road car, Doo-dah! doo-dah!
Runnin' a race wid a shootin' star, Oh, doo-dah-day!

Refrain

4. *See dem flyin' on a ten mile heat, Doo-dah doo-dah!*
Round de race track, den repeat, Oh, doo-dah-day!
I win my money on de bob-tail nag, Doo-dah! doo-dah!
I keep my money in an old tow-bag, Oh, doo-dah-day!

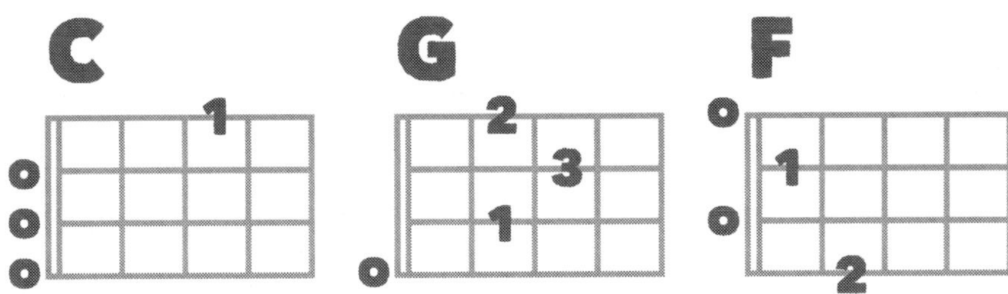

Marianne

D
Em
All day, all night, Ma - ri - anne,
T
A
B
2 0 2 2 2 0 3 3

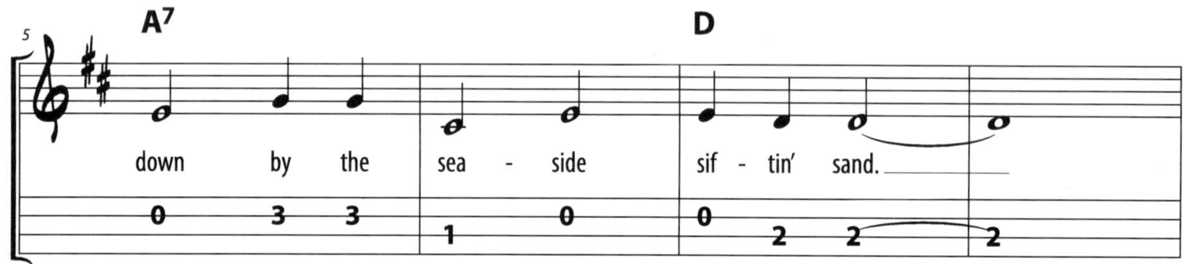
5
A7
D
down by the sea - side sif - tin' sand.
0 3 3 1 0 0 2 2 2

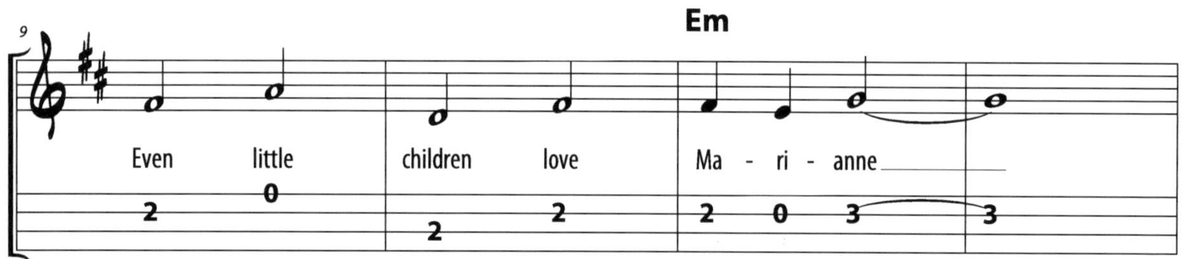
9
Em
Even little children love Ma - ri - anne
2 0 2 2 2 0 3 3

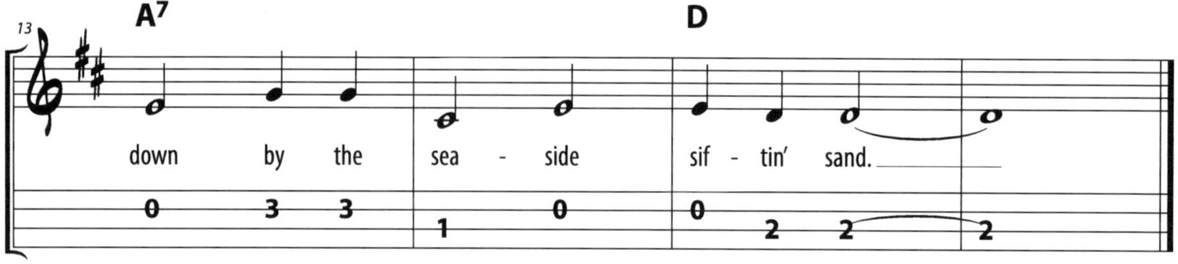
13
A7
D
down by the sea - side sif - tin' sand.
0 3 3 1 0 0 2 2 2

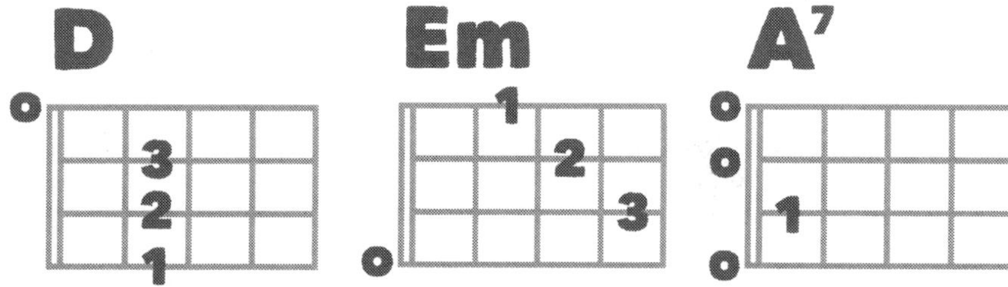
D
Em
A7
3
2
1
1
2
3
1

Good morning

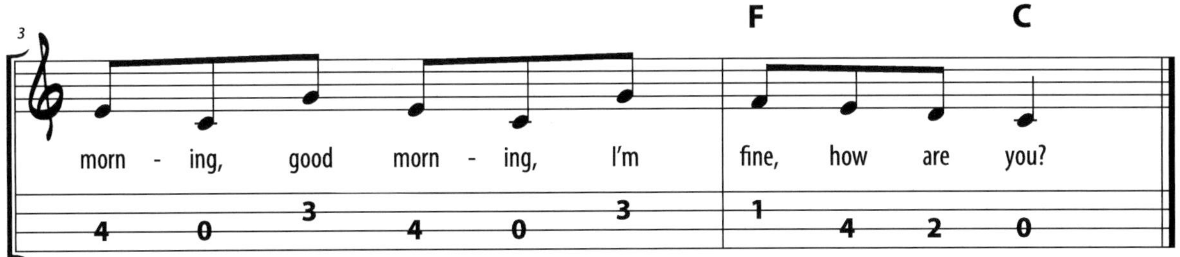

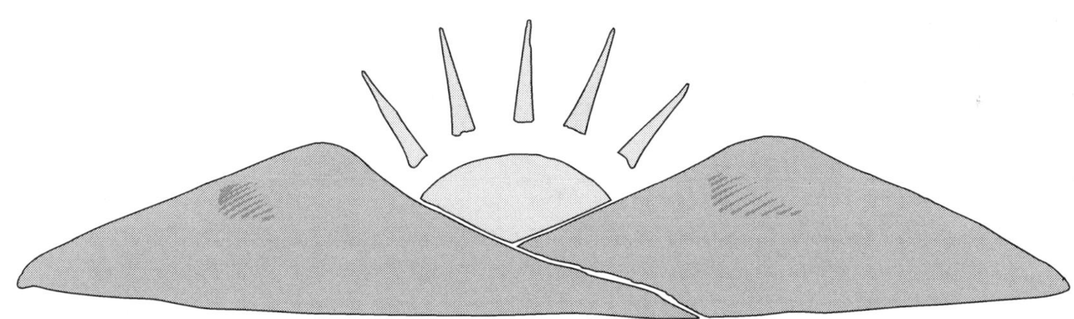

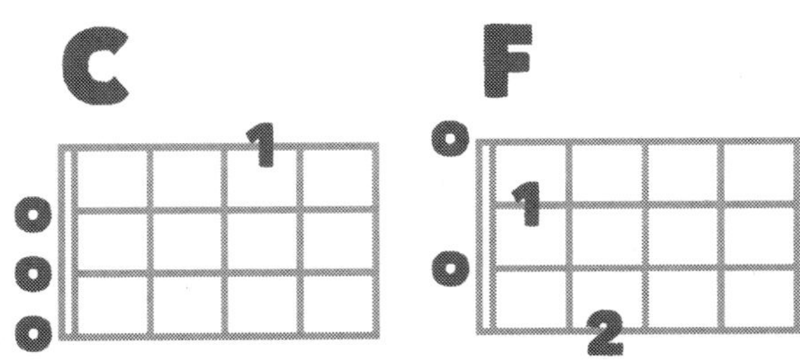

2. ... stomp your feet (stomp, stomp)

3. ... slap your legs (slap slap)

4. ... slap your knees (slap slap)

5. ... nod your head (nod nod)

6. ... tap your toe (tap tap)

7. ... honk your nose (honk honk) etc.

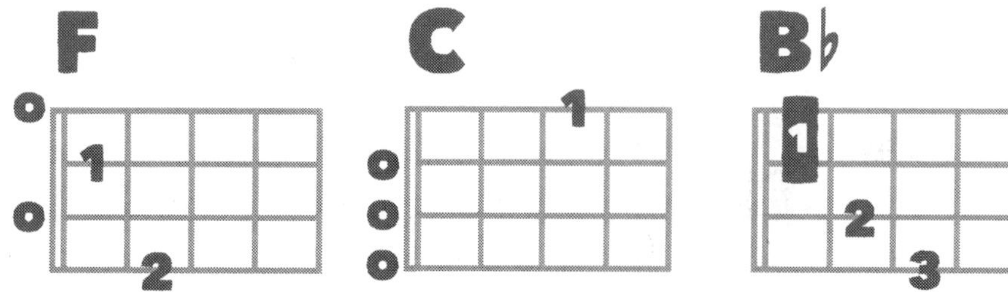

Hey, diddle, diddle

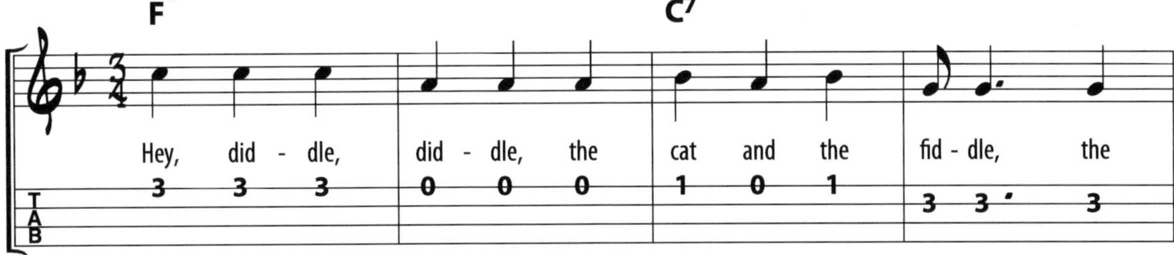
F
C7
Hey, did - dle, did - dle, the cat and the fid - dle, the
3 3 3 0 0 0 1 0 1 3 3 3

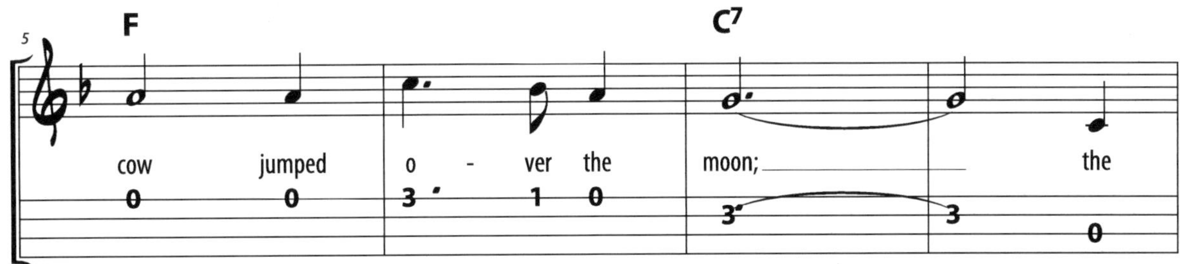
5
F
C7
cow jumped o - ver the moon; the
0 0 3 1 0 3 3 0

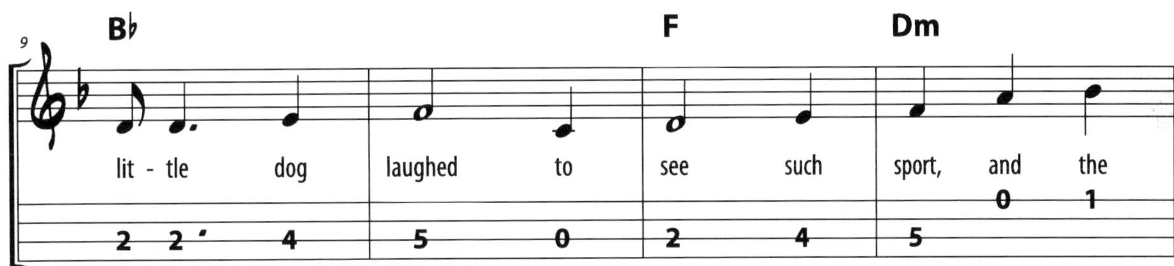
9
B♭
F
Dm
lit - tle dog laughed to see such sport, and the
2 2 4 5 0 2 4 5 0 1

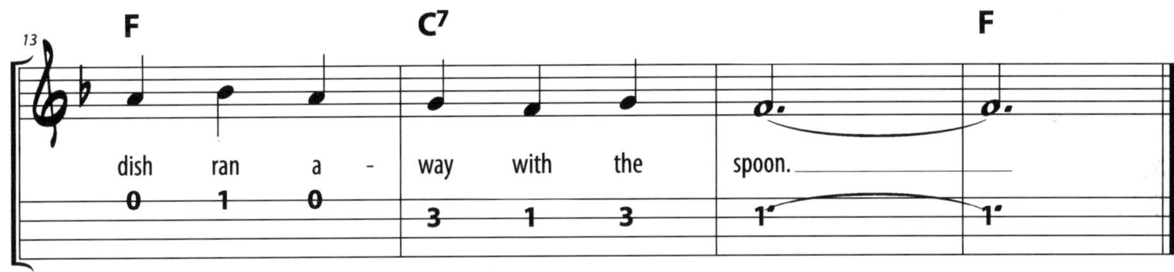
13
F
C7
F
dish ran a - way with the spoon.
0 1 0 3 1 3 1 1

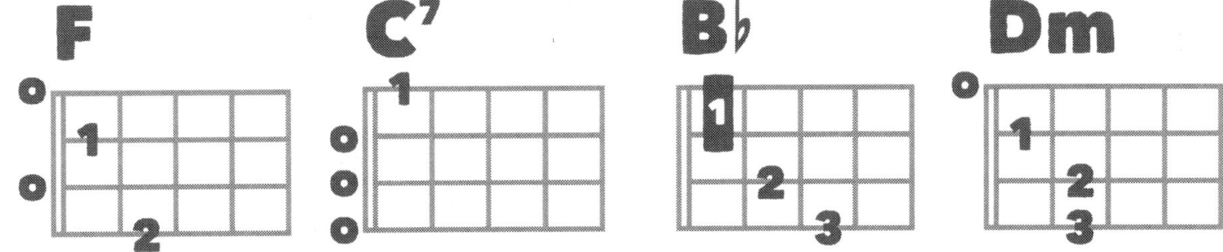
F
C7
B♭
Dm

Old MacDonald had a farm

2. *... he had some geese ...*
   With a gabble-gabble here ...

3. *... he had a pig ...*
   With an oinck-oink here ...

4. *... he had some ducks ...*
   With a quack-quack here ...

5. *... he had a cow ...*
   With a moo-moo here ...

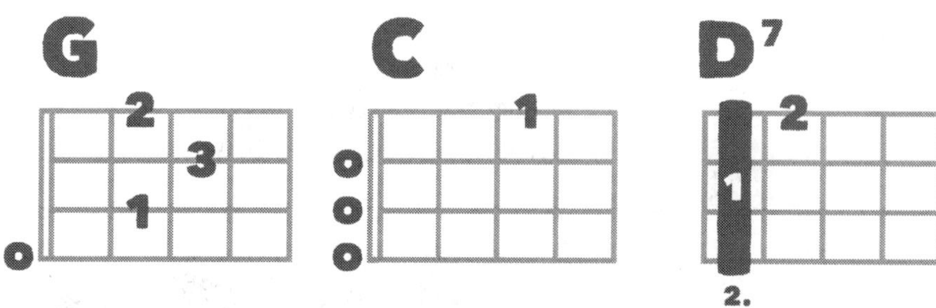

Sleep, baby, sleep

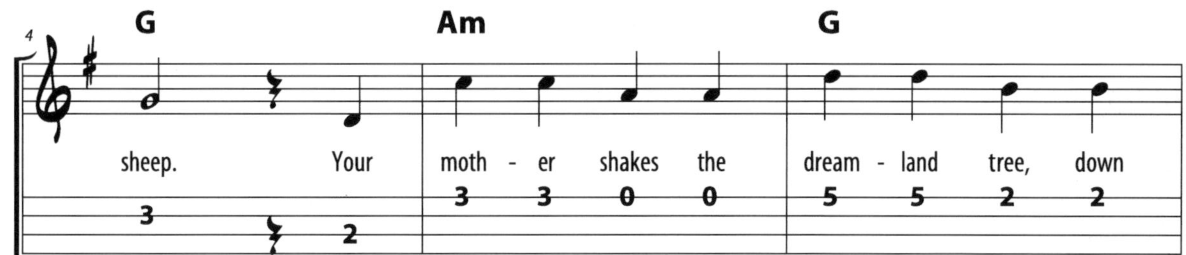

2. *Sleep, baby, sleep.*
   Your father guards the sheep.
   Your mother shakes the dreamland tree,
   down falls a little dream for thee,
   Sleep, baby, sleep.

3. *Sleep, baby, sleep.*
   Your father watches the sheep.
   The wind is blowing fierce and wild,
   it must not wake my little child.
   Sleep, baby, sleep.

4. *Sleep, baby sleep.*
   The large stars are the sheep.
   The little stars are the lambs, I guess,
   the gentle moon's the shepherdess.
   Sleep, baby, sleep.

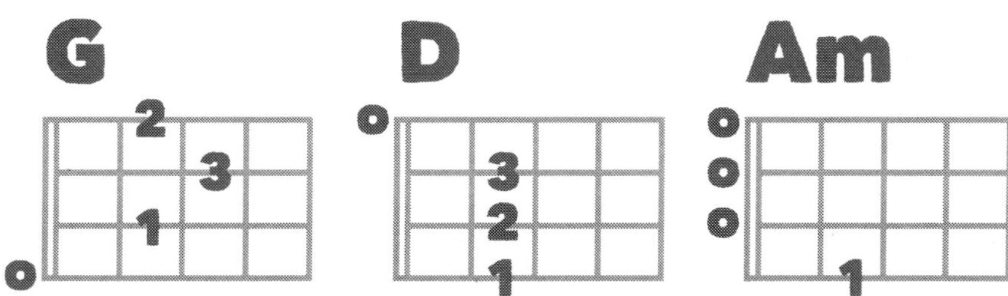

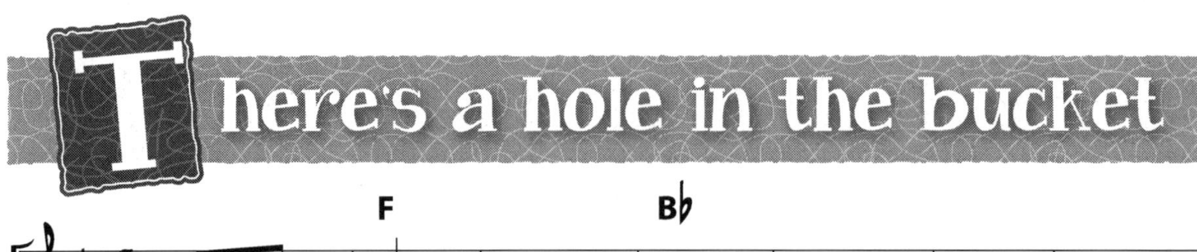

There's a hole in the bucket

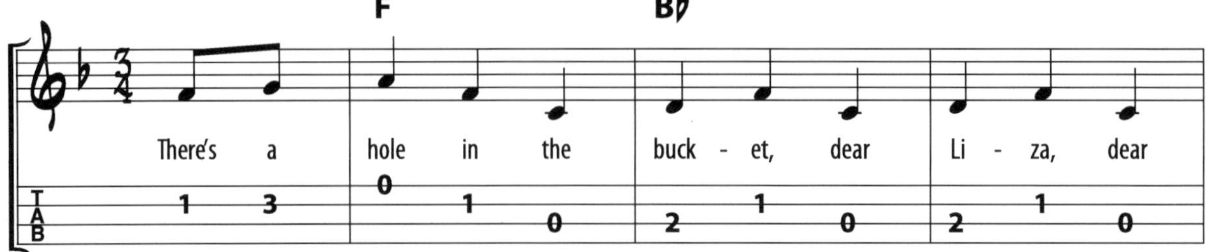

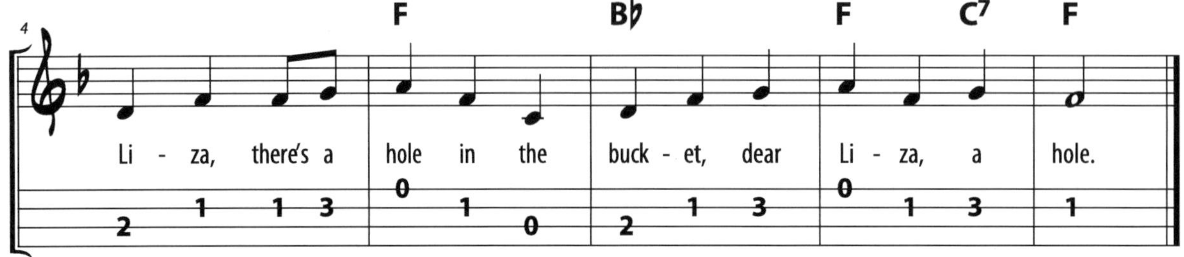

2. *Then fix it, dear Henry, dear Henry, dear Henry,*
   then fix it, dear Henry, dear Henry, fix it.

3. *With what shall I fix it, dear Liza, dear Liza?*
   with what shall I fix it, dear Liza, with what?

4. *With straw, dear Henry, dear Henry, dear Henry,*
   With straw, dear Henry, dear Henry, with straw.

5. *The straw is too long, dear Liza, dear Liza,*
   the straw is too long, dear Liza, too long.

6. *Then cut it, dear Henry, dear Henry, dear Henry,*
   then cut it, dear Henry, dear Henry, cut it.

7. *With what shall I cut it, dear Liza, dear Liza?*
   With what shall I cut it, dear Liza, with what?

8. *With a knife, dear Henry, dear Henry, dear Henry,*
   with a knife, dear Henry, dear Henry, with a knife.

9. *The knife is too dull, dear Liza, dear Liza,*
   the knife is too dull, dear Liza, too dull.

10. *Then sharpen it, dear Henry, dear Henry, dear Henry,*
    then sharpen it, dear Henry, dear Henry, sharpen it.

11. *On what shall I sharpen it, dear Liza, dear Liza?*
On what shall I sharpen it, dear Liza, on what?

12. *On a stone, dear Henry, dear Henry, dear Henry,*
on a stone, dear Henry, dear Henry, a stone.

13. *The stone is too dry, dear Liza, dear Liza,*
the stone is too dry, dear Liza, too dry.

14. *Then wet it, dear Henry, dear Henry, dear Henry,*
then wet it, dear Henry, dear Henry, wet it.

15. *With what shall I wet it, dear Liza, dear Liza?*
With what shall I wet it, dear Liza, with what?

16. *Try water, dear Henry, dear Henry, dear Henry,*
try water, dear Henry, dear Henry, water.

17. *In what shall I fetch it, dear Liza, dear Liza?*
In what shall I fetch it, dear Liza, in what?

18. *In the bucket, dear Henry, dear Henry, dear Henry,*
In the bucket, dear Henry, dear Henry, a bucket.

19. *But there's a hole in my bucket, dear Liza, dear Liza,*
there's a hole in my bucket, dear Liza, a hole.

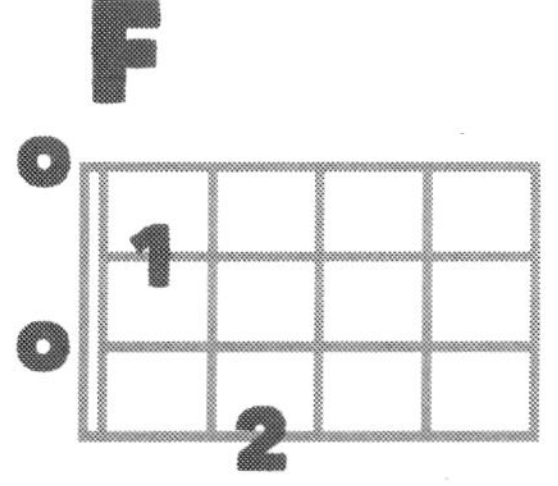

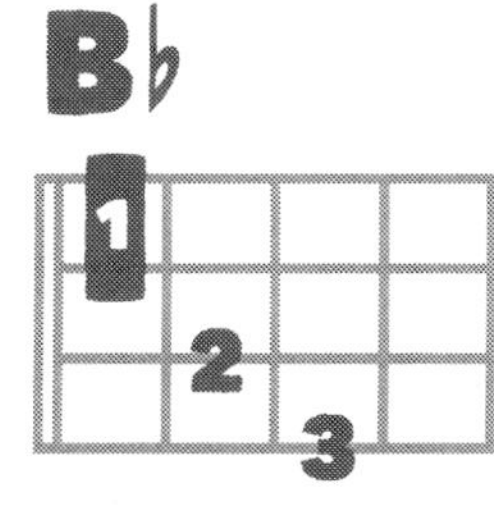

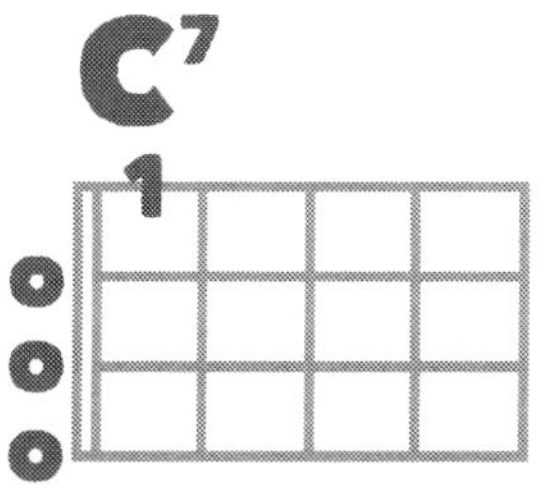

Silent night

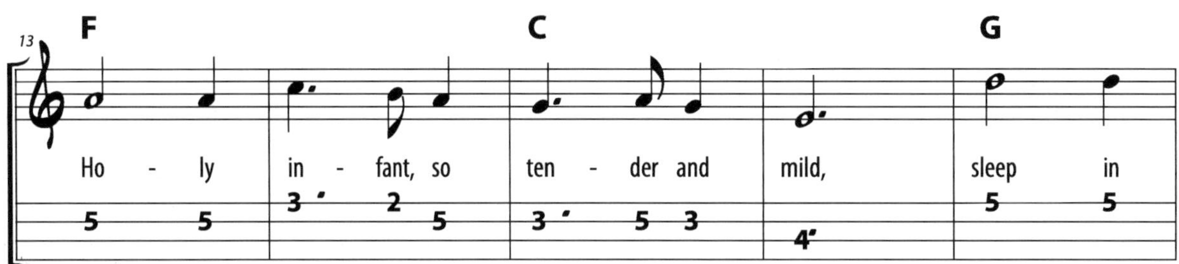

2. *Silent night, Holy night!*
   Son of God, love's pure light.
   Radiant beams from thy holy face.
   With the dawn of redeeming grace,
   Jesus, Lord at thy birth,
   Jesus, Lord at thy birth.

3. *Silent night, Holy night!*
   Shepherds quake, at the sight.
   Glories stream from heaven above.
   Heavenly, hosts sing Hallelujah,
   Christ the Savior is born,
   Christ the Savior is born.

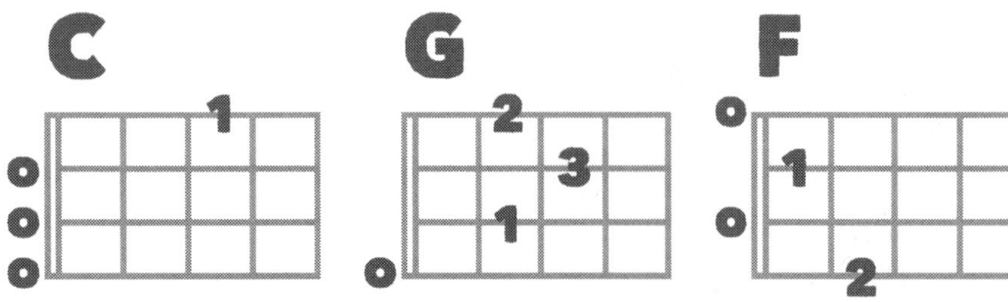

Skip to my Lou

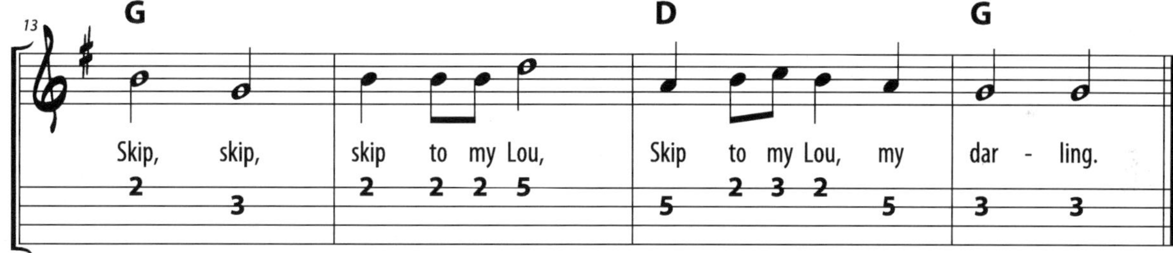

2. *There's a little red wagon, Paint it blue.*
3. *Lost my partner, What'll I do?*
4. *I'll get another one, Prettier than you.*
5. *Can't get a red bird, Jaybird'll do.*
6. *Cat's in the cream jar, Ooh, ooh, ooh.*

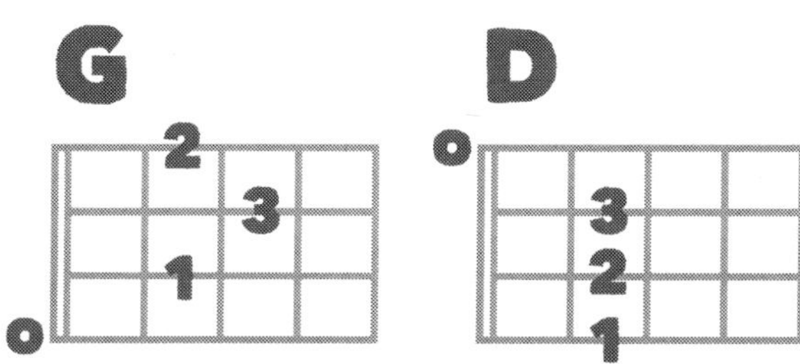

Twinkle, twinkle little Star

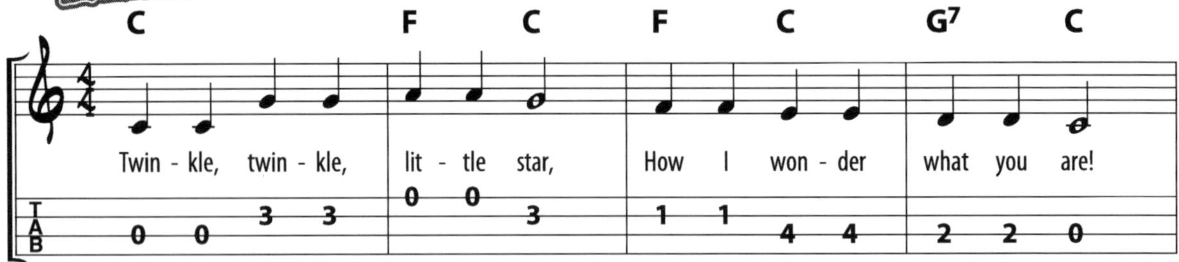

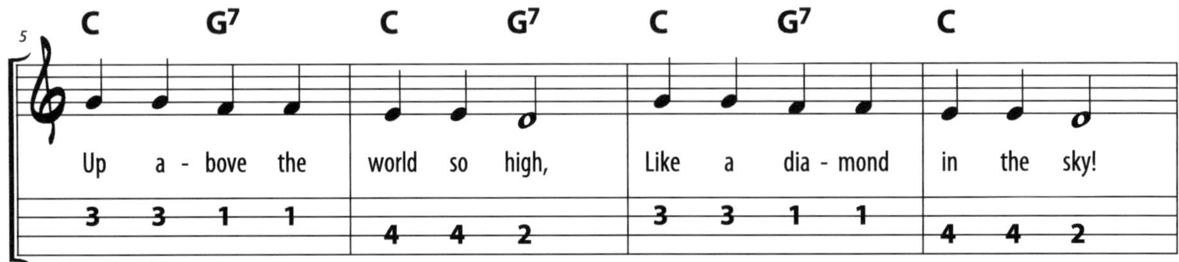

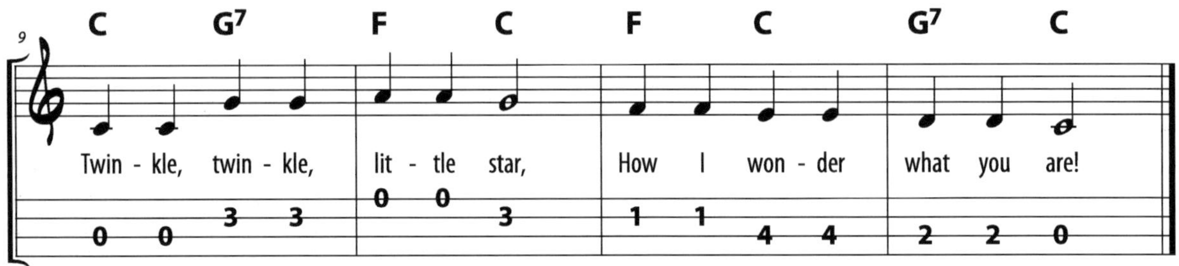

2. *When the blazing sun is gone,*
   when he nothing shines upon,
   then you show your little light,
   twinkle, twinkle, all the night.

3. *Then the traveller in the dark,*
thanks you for your tiny spark,
he could not see which way to go,
if you did not twinkle so.

4. *In the dark blue sky you keep,*
   and often through my curtains peep,
   for you never shut your eye,
   till the sun is in the sky.

5. *As your bright and tiny spark,*
   lights the traveller in the dark,
   though I know not what you are,
   twinkle, twinkle, little star.

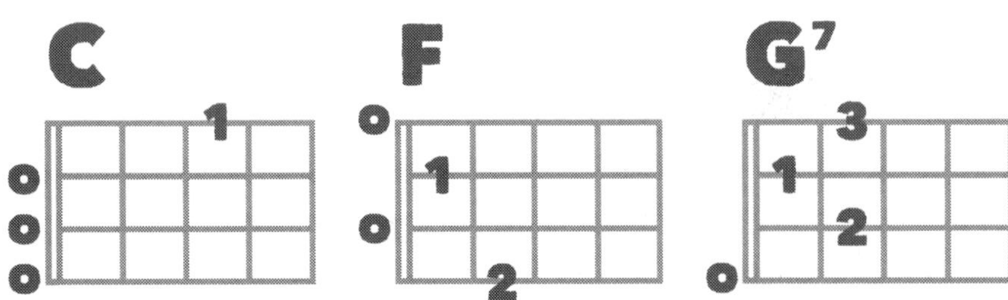

What shall we do with the drunken sailor

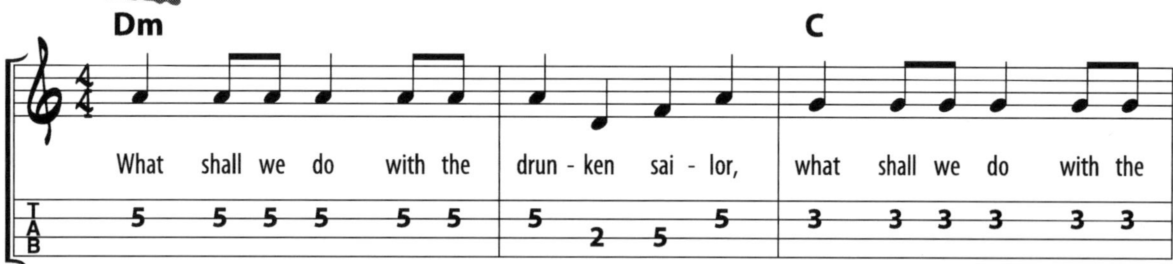

2. Give him a dose of salent water, early ...
3. Give him a dash with a besoms rubber, early ...
4. Pull out the plug and wet him all over, early ...
5. Heave him by the leg in a running bowlin', early ...
6. That's what to do with a drunken sailor, early ...

Jingle bells

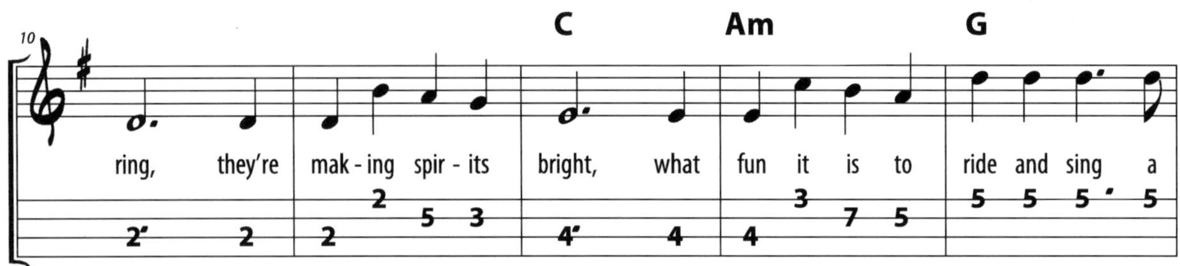

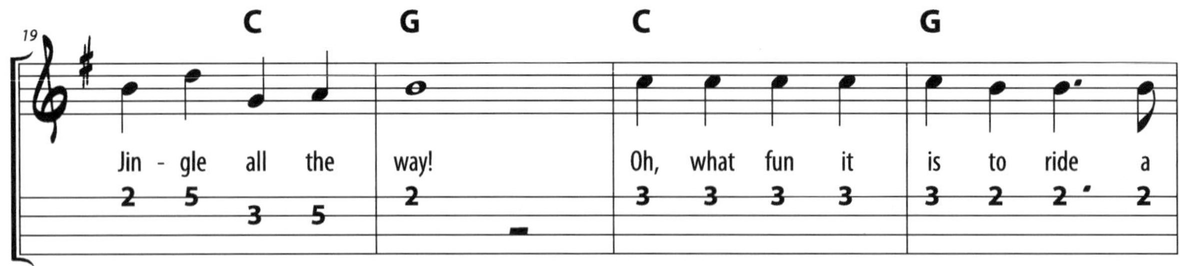

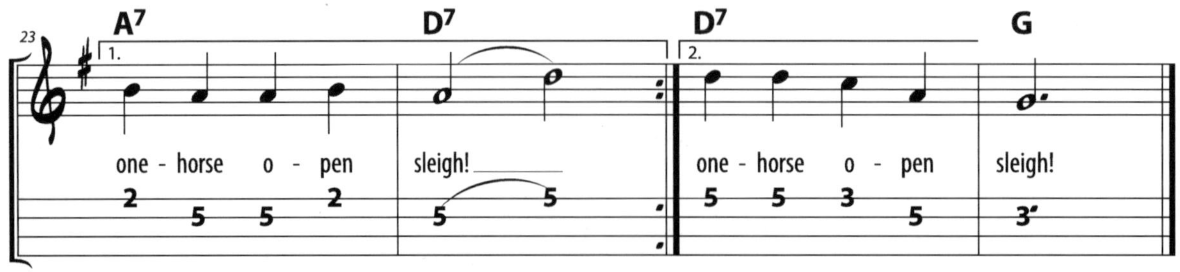

2. *A day or two ago I thought I'd take a ride,*
and soon Miss Fannie Bright was seated by my side.
The horse was lean and lank, misfortune seemed his lot,
he got into a drifted bank and we got upsot.

3. *A day or two ago, The story I must tell*
I went out on the snow, And on my back I fell;
A gent was riding by In a one-horse open sleigh,
he laughed as there I sprawling lie, But quickly drove away.

4. *Now the ground is white, go it while you're young,*
take the girls tonight and sing this sleighing song.
Just get a bobtailed bay, two-forty for his speed,
then hitch him to an open sleigh, and crack! You'll take the lead.

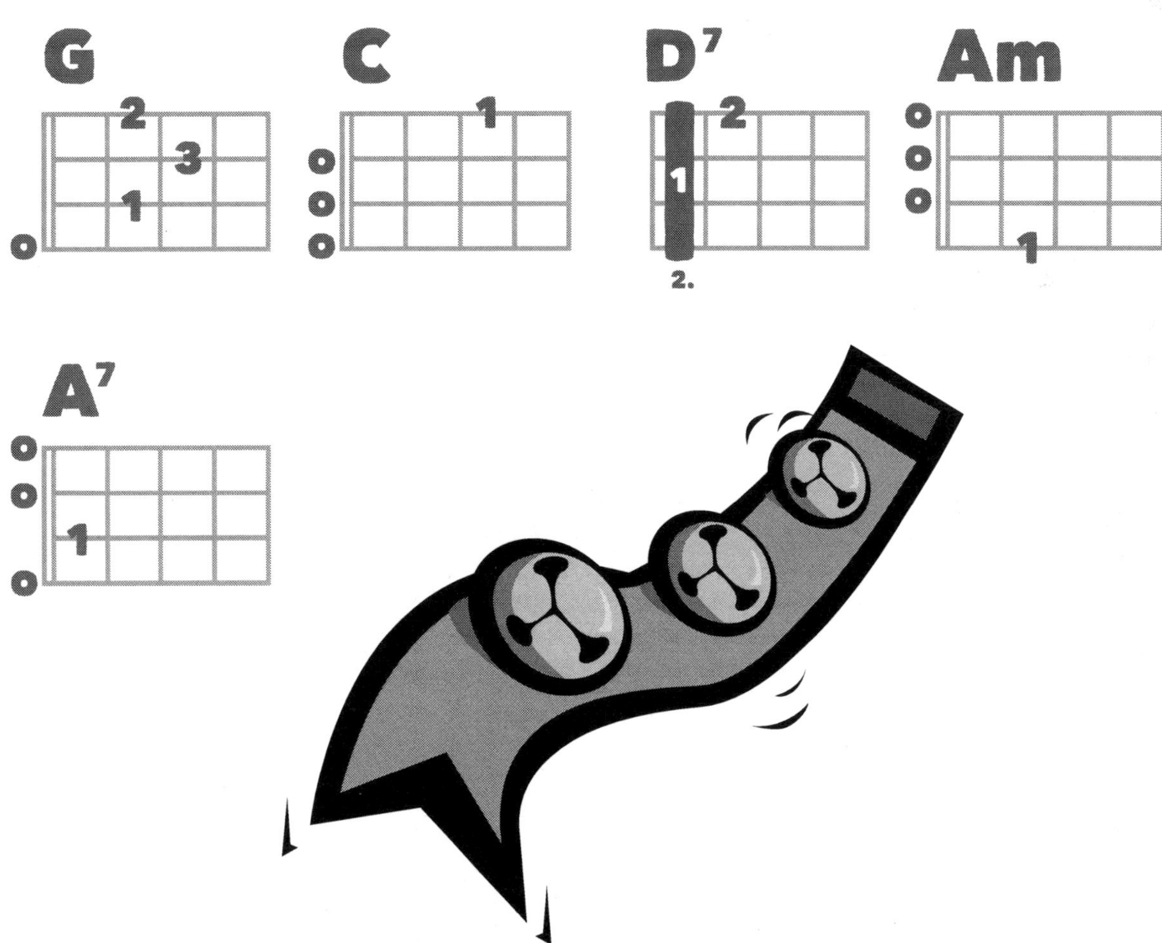

Brother John

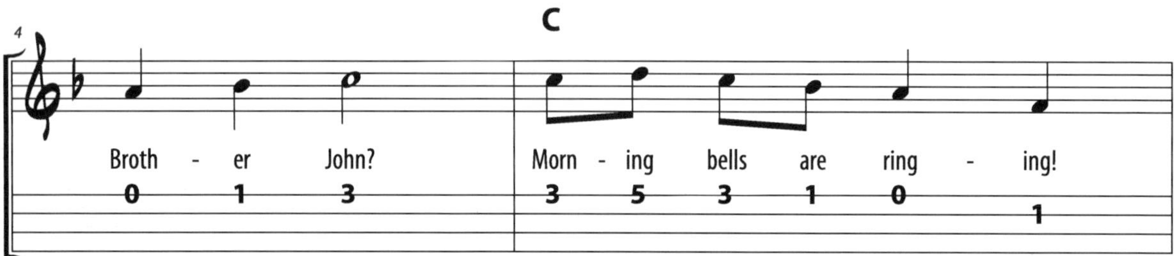

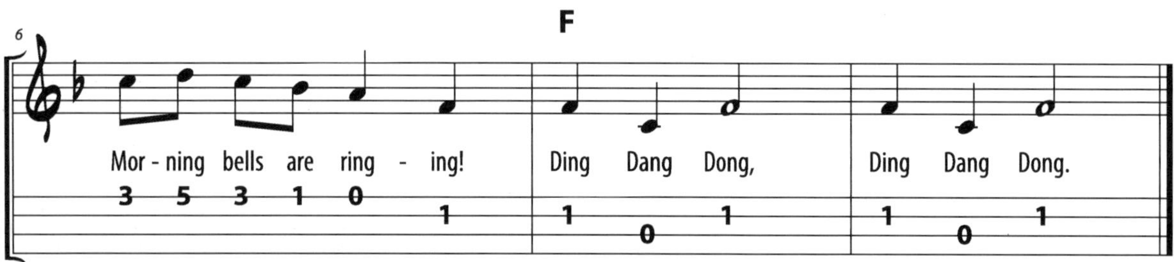

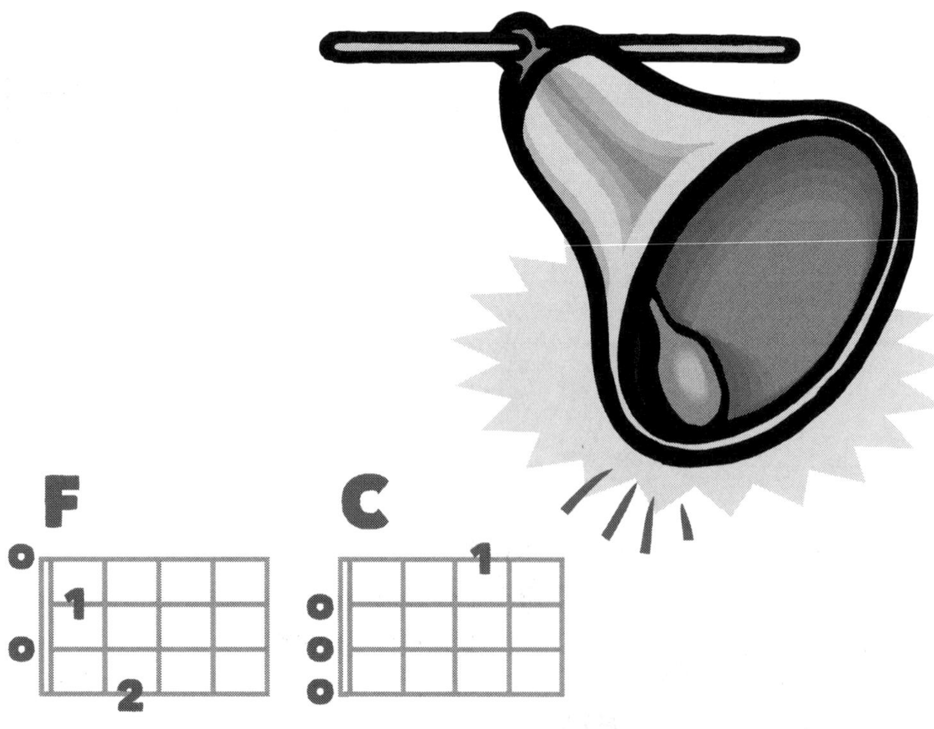

She'll be coming round the mountain

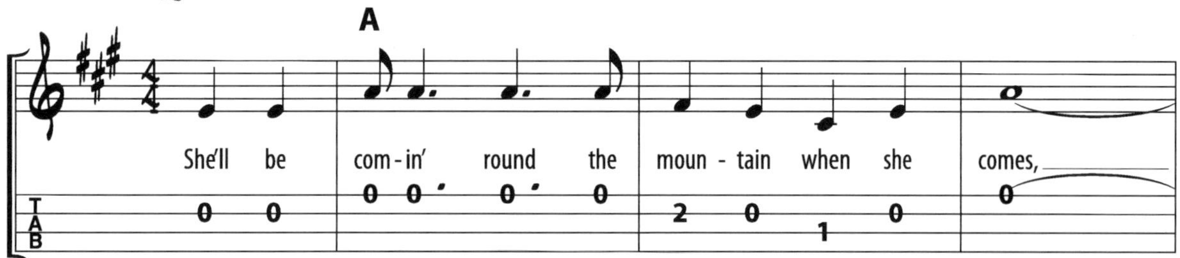

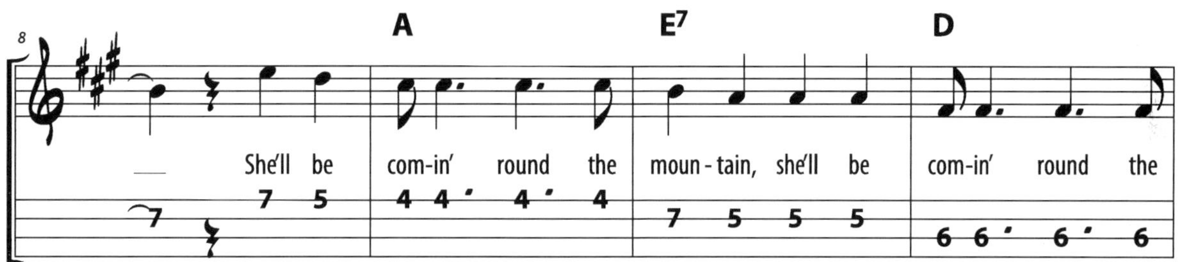

2. *She'll be driving' six white horses when she comes ...*
3. *We will all go out to meet her when she comes ...*
4. *We will have chickden an' dumplin's when she comes ...*
5. *She'll be reelin' an' a-rockin' when she comes ...*
6. *We'll shout glory hallelujah when she comes ...*

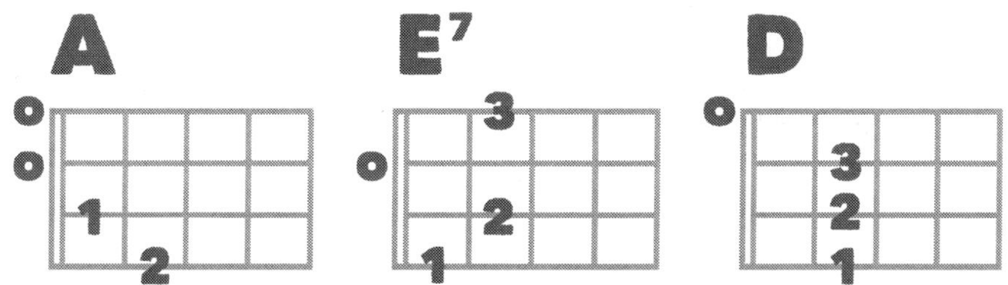

Yankee Doodle

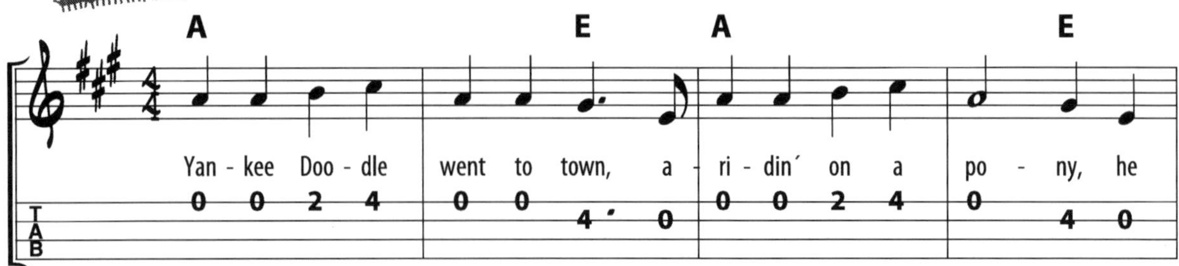

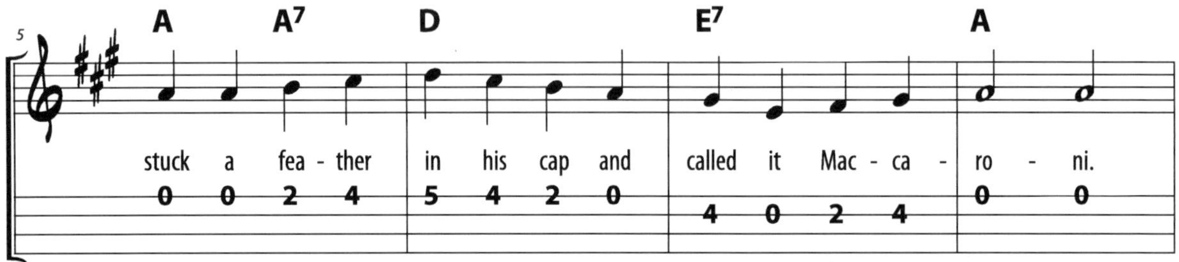

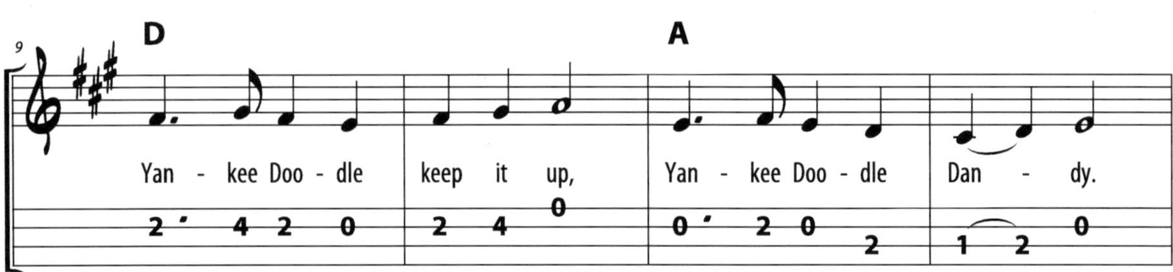

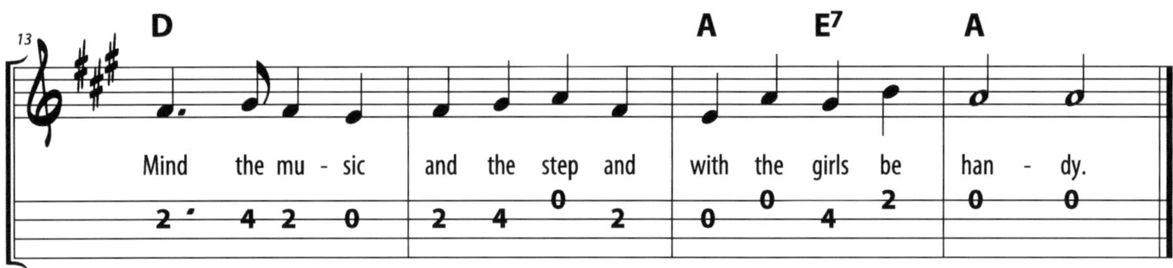

2. *Father and I went down to camp,*
   along with Captain Gooding.
   And there we saw the men and boys,
   as thick as hasty pudding.
   Yankee Doodle, keep it up,
   Yankee Doodle dandy.
   Mind the music and the step,
   and with the girls be handy.

3. *There was Captain Washington,*
   upon a slapping stallion.
   A-giving orders to his men,
   I guess there was a million.
   Yankee Doodle, keep it up,
   Yankee Doodle dandy.
   Mind the music and the step,
   and with the girls be handy.

4. *Yankee Doodle is a tune,*
   that comes in mighty handy,
   The enemies all run away,
   at Yankee Doodle Dandy!
   Yankee Doodle, keep it up,
   Yankee Doodle dandy.
   Mind the music and the step,
   and with the girls be handy.

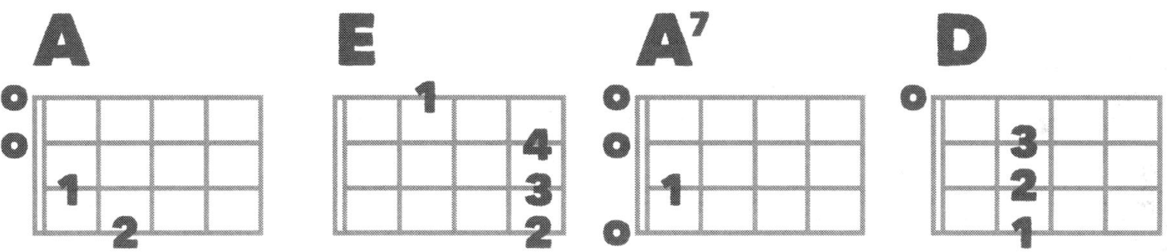

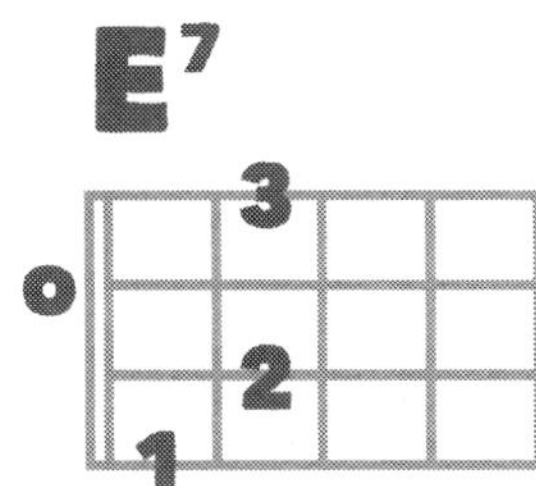

Clementine

G
E7
In a ca - vern, by a can - yon, ex - ca - vat - ing for a

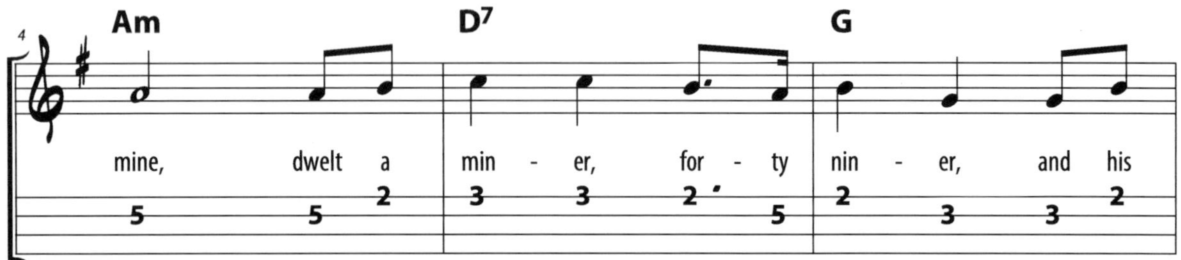

4
Am
D7
G
mine, dwelt a min - er, for - ty nin - er, and his

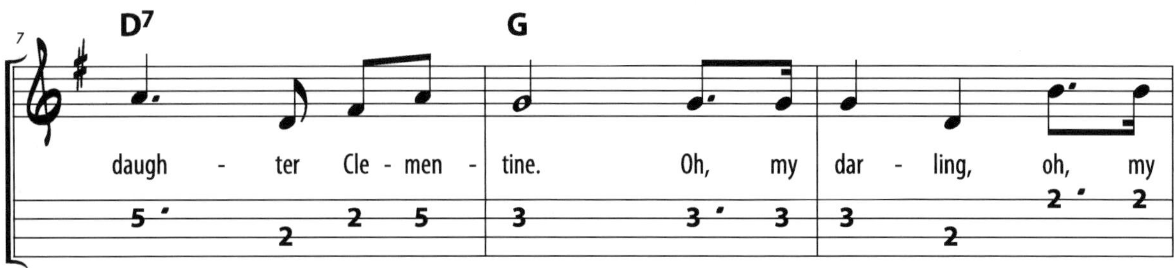

7
D7
G
daugh - ter Cle - men - tine. Oh, my dar - ling, oh, my

10
E7
Am
dar - ling, oh, my dar - ling, Cle - men - tine, thou art

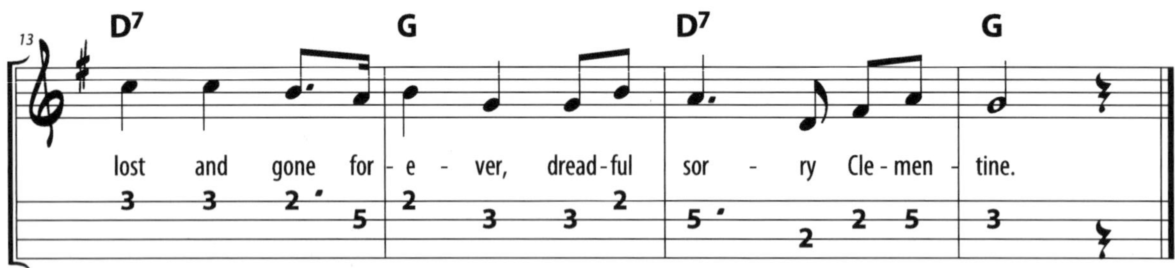

13
D7
G
D7
G
lost and gone for - e - ver, dread - ful sor - ry Cle - men - tine.

2. *Light she was, and like a fairy,*
   and her shoes were number nine,
   herring boxes without topses,
   sandals were for Clementine.

3. *Drove she ducklings to the water*
   every morning just at nine,
   struck her foot agains a splinter,
   fell into the foaming brine.

4. *Rosy lips above the water,*
   blowing bubbles mighty fine,
   but, alas, I was no swimmer,
   so I lost my Clementine.

5. *How I missed her! How I missed her!*
   How I missed my Clementine!
   But I kissed her little sister,
   and forgot my Clementine.

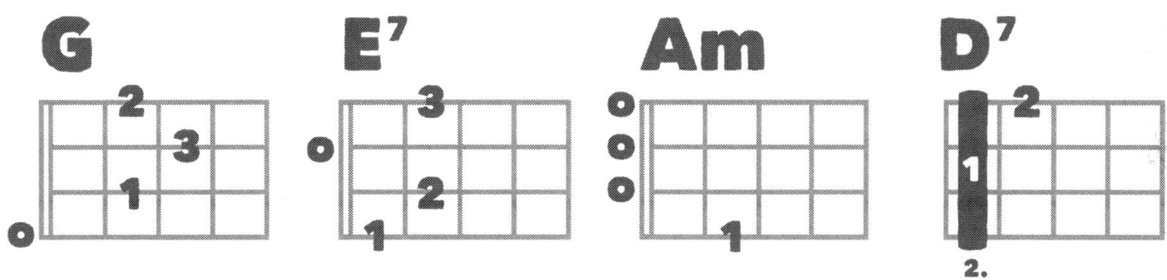

Go, tell it on the mountain

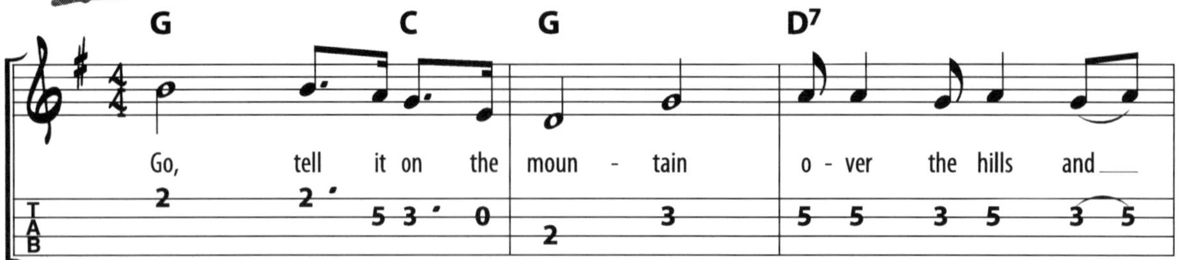

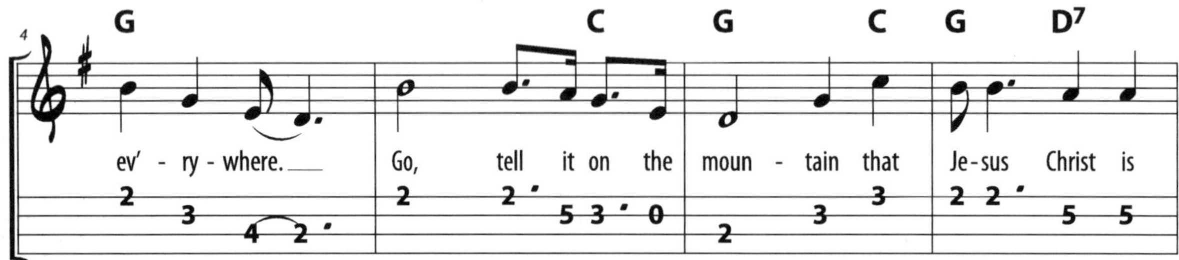

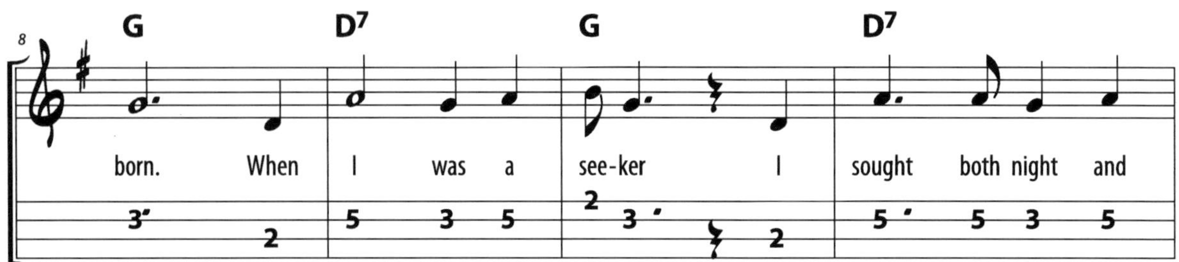

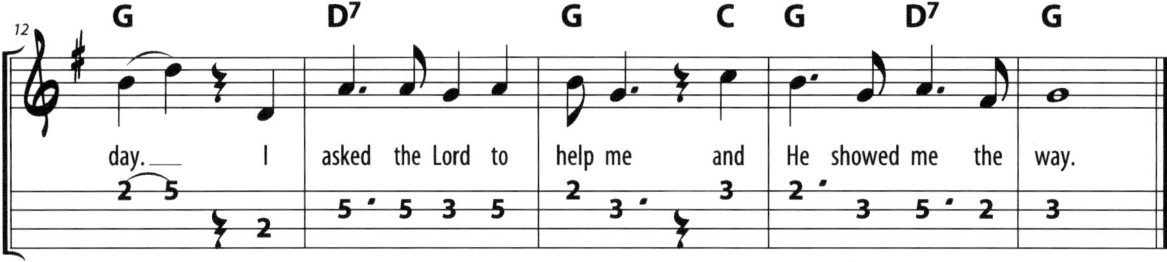

2. *He made me a watchman upon the city-wall, and if I am a christian I am the least of all.*

3. *'T was a lowly manger that Jesus Christ was born. The Lord sent down an angel that bright and glorious morn'.*

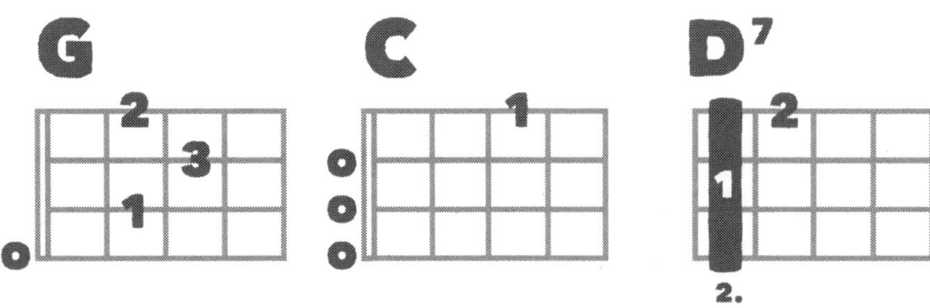

The bear went over the mountain

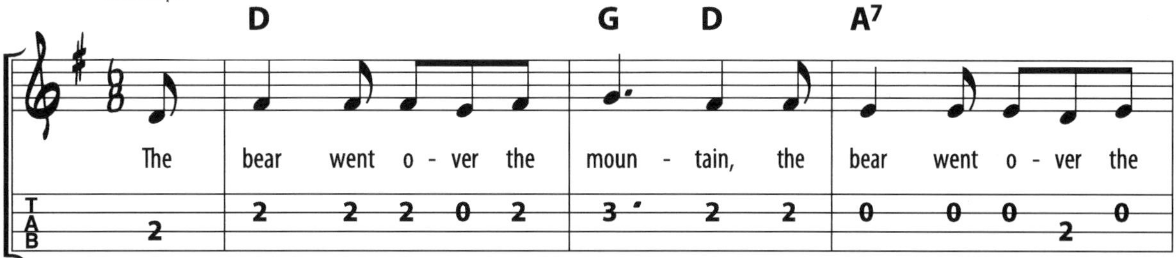

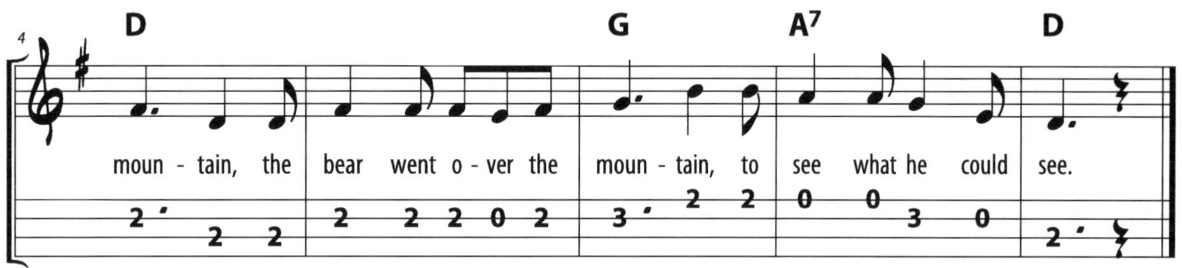

2. *The other side of the mountain,*
   the other side of the mountain,
   the other side of the mountain,
   was all that he could see.

3. *The bear went over the river,*
   the bear went over the river,
   the bear went over the river,
   to see what he could see.

4. *The other side of the river,*
   the other side of the river,
   the other side of the river,
   was all that he could see.

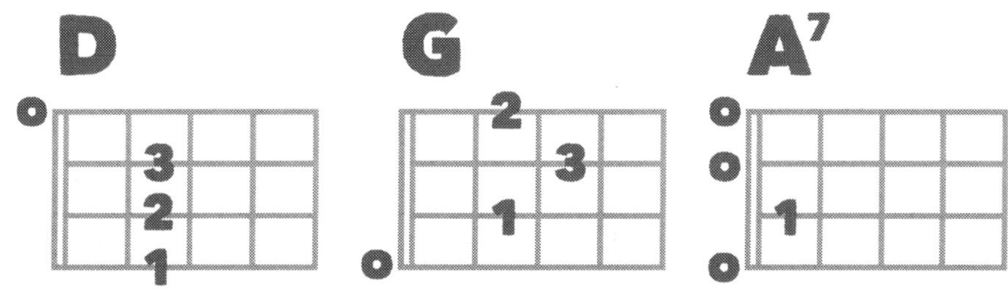

Oh, Susanna

C
I came from A - la - ba - ma with my ban - jo on my
T
A
B
0 2 4 3 3 5 3 4 0 0 2 4 4 2 0

4
G C G7
knee, I'm goin' to Lou' - si - a - na, my Su - san - na for to
2 0 2 4 3 3 5 3 4 0 0 2 4 4 2 2

8
C F C G
see. Oh, Su - san - na, oh don't you cry for me, for I
0 5 5 5 5 5 3 3 4 0 2 0 2

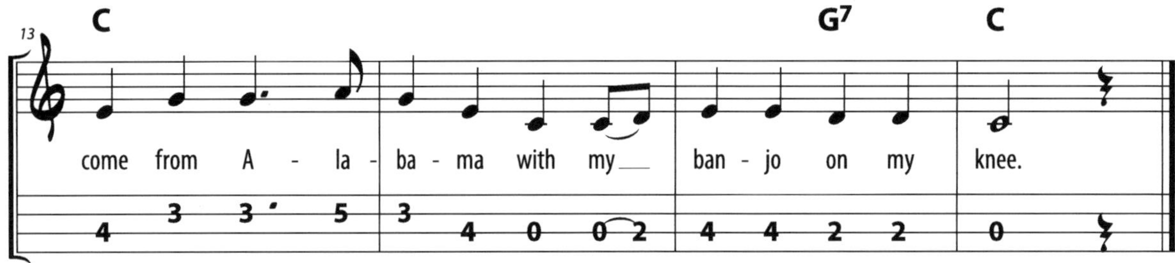
13
C G7 C
come from A - la - ba - ma with my ban - jo on my knee.
4 3 3 5 3 4 0 0 2 4 4 2 2 0

2. *I had a dream the other night*
when ev'rything was still;
I thought I saw Susanna
a-comin' down the hill;
the buckwheat cake was in her mouth,
the tear was in her eye;
says I, I'm comin' from the south,
Susanna, don't you cry.
O, Susanna,
o, don't you cry for me ...

3. *I soon will be in New Orleans,*
and then I'll look around,
and when I find Susanna
I'll fall upon the ground.
And if I do not find her,
then I will surely die,
and when I'm dead and buried,
Susanna, don't you cry.
O, Susanna,
o, don't you cry for me ...

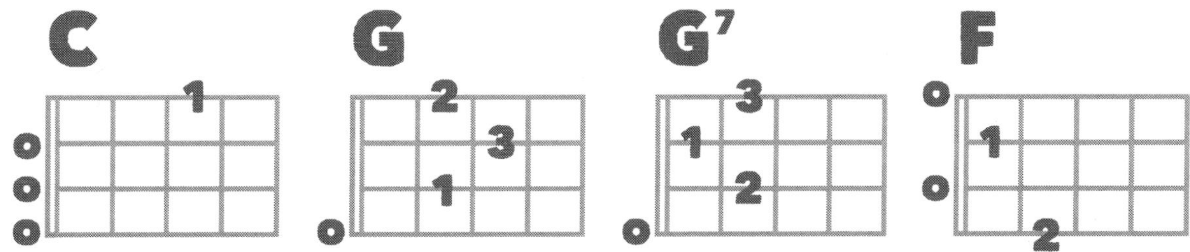

hen the saints go marchin' in

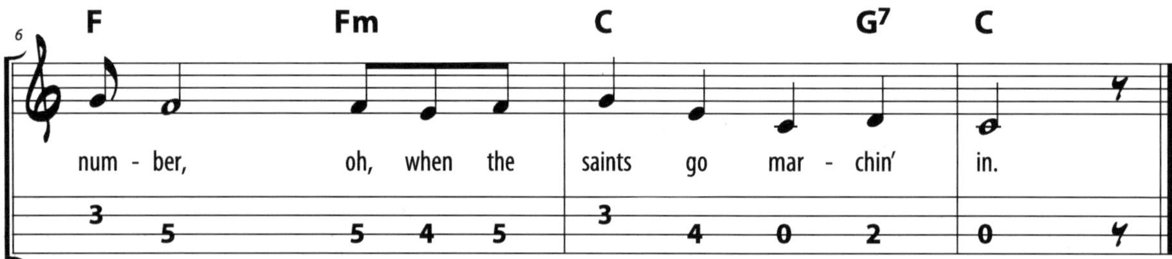

2. *And when the stars begin to shine ...*
3. *And when the band begins to play ...*
4. *When Gabriel blows in his horn ...*
5. *And when the sun refuses to shine ...*
6. *And when they crown Him Lord of Lords ...*
7. *And on that halleluja-day ...*

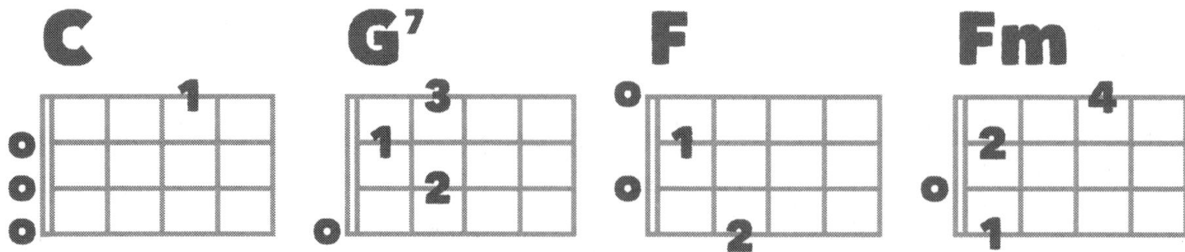

We wish you a merry Christmas

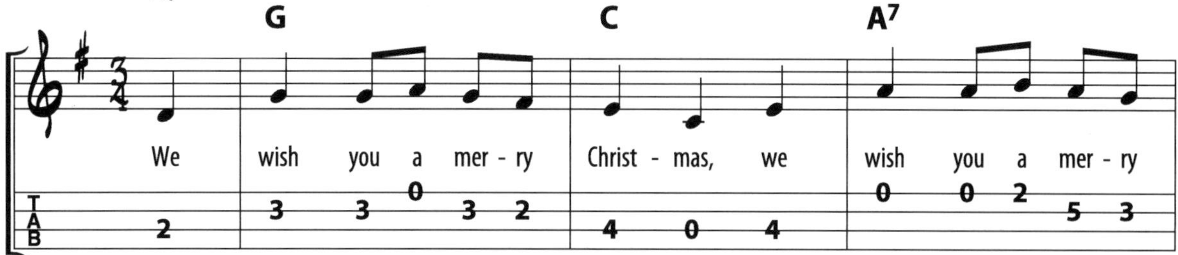

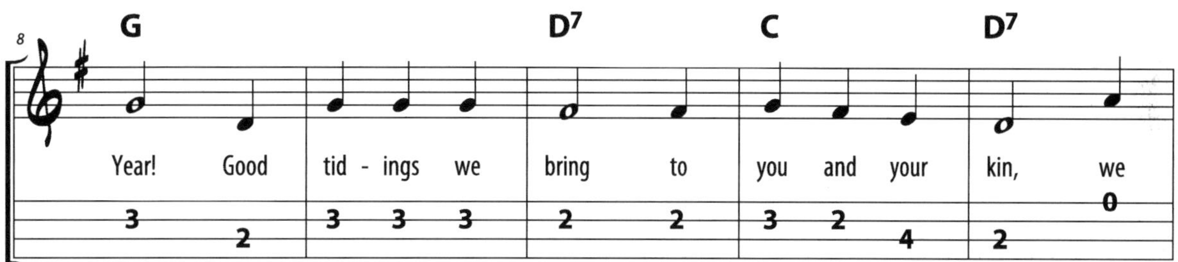

2. Now bring us some figgy pudding (3x)
And bring some out here!

3. For we all like figgy pudding,
We all like figgy pudding (2x)
So bring some out here!

4. And we won't go until we've got some,
We won't go until we've got some (2x)
So bring some out here!

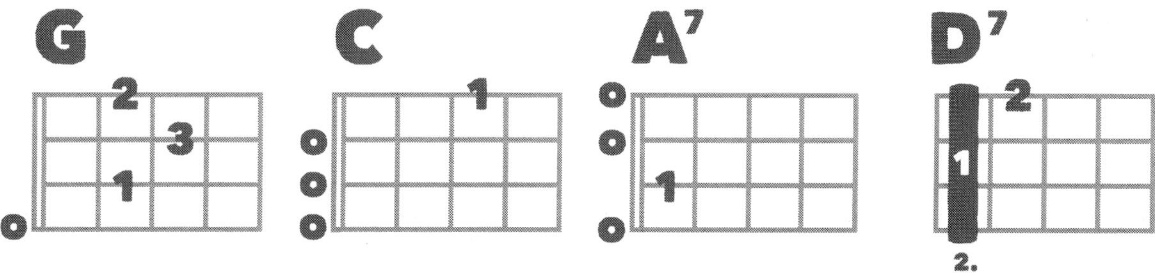

My Bonnie lies over the ocean

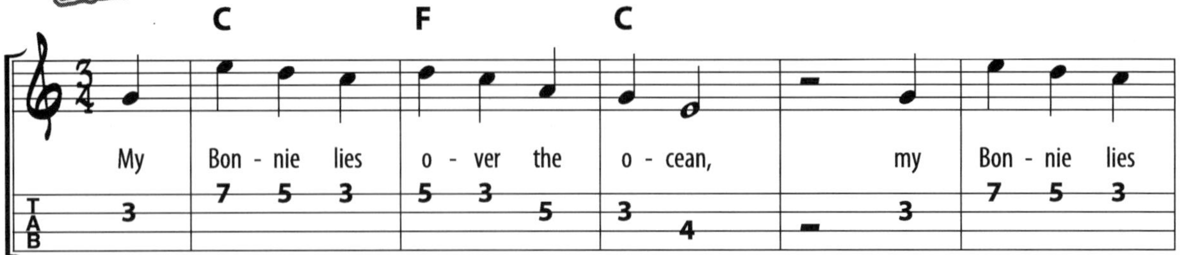

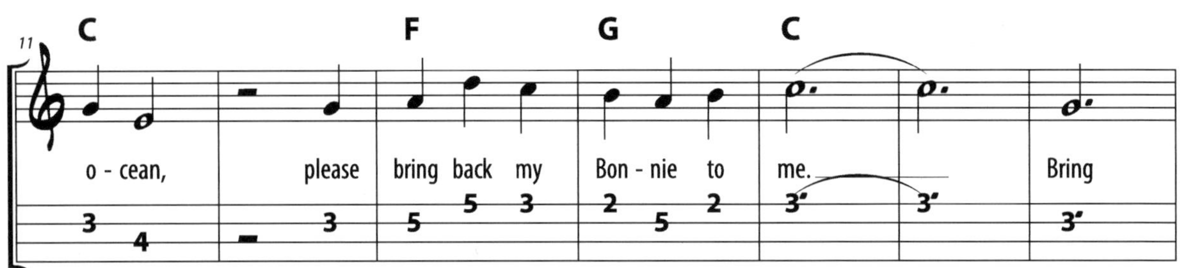

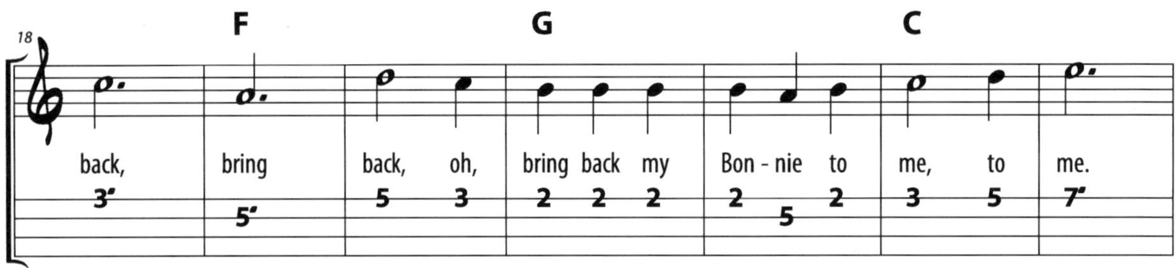

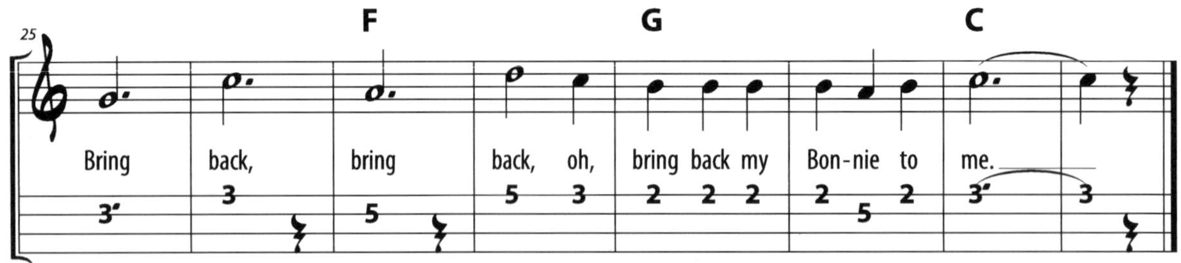

2. *Last night as I lay on my pillow,*
   last night as I lay on my bed.
   Last night as I lay on my pillow,
   I dreamed that my Bonnie was dead,
   Bring back, bring back,
   bring back my Bonnie to me, to me.
   Bring back, bring back,
   bring back my Bonnie to me.

3. *Oh blow ye the winds o'er the ocean,*
   and blow ye the winds o'er the sea.
   Oh blow ye the winds o'er the ocean,
   and bring back my Bonnie to me.
   Bring back, bring back,
   bring back my Bonnie to me, to me.
   Bring back, bring back,
   bring back my Bonnie to me.

4. *The winds have blown over the ocean,*
   the winds have blown over the sea.
   The winds have blown over the ocean,
   and brought back my Bonnie to me.
   Bring back, bring back,
   bring back my Bonnie to me, to me.
   Bring back, bring back,
   bring back my Bonnie to me.

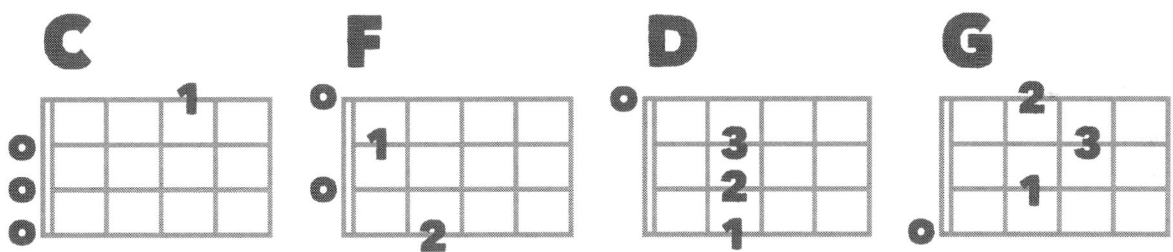

Good night, Ladies

2. *Farewell, ladies! (3x)*
   We're going to leave you now.
   Merrily we roll along,
   roll along, roll along,
   merrily we roll along,
   o'er the deep blue sea.

3. *Sweet dreams, ladies! (3x)*
   We're going to leave you now.
   Merrily we roll along,
   roll along, roll along,
   merrily we roll along,
   o'er the deep blue sea.

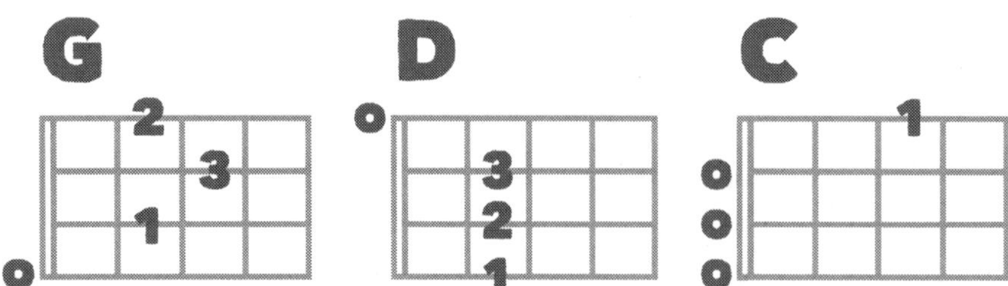

Tom Dooley

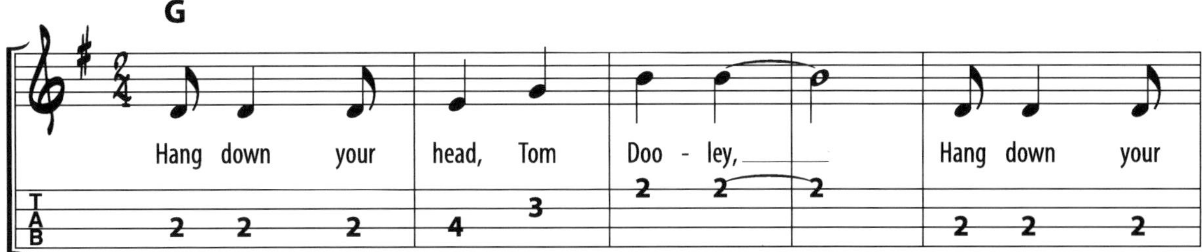

2. *This time tomorrow,*
   Reckon where I'll be?
   If it hadn't been for Grayson,
   I'd a-been in Tennesse.

3. *This time tomorrow,*
   Reckon where I'll be?
   Down in some lonesome valley,
   Hangin' from a white oak tree.

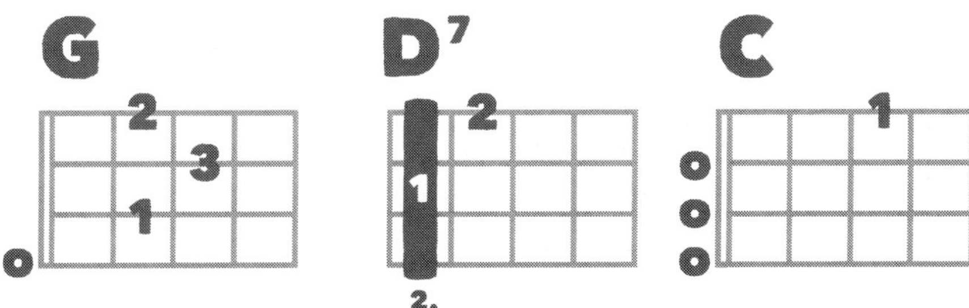

Row, row, row

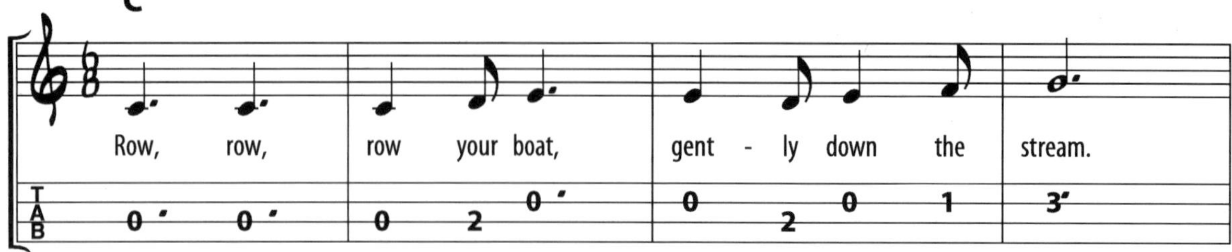
C
Row, row, row your boat, gent - ly down the stream.
T
A
B
0 0 0 2 0 0 2 0 1 3

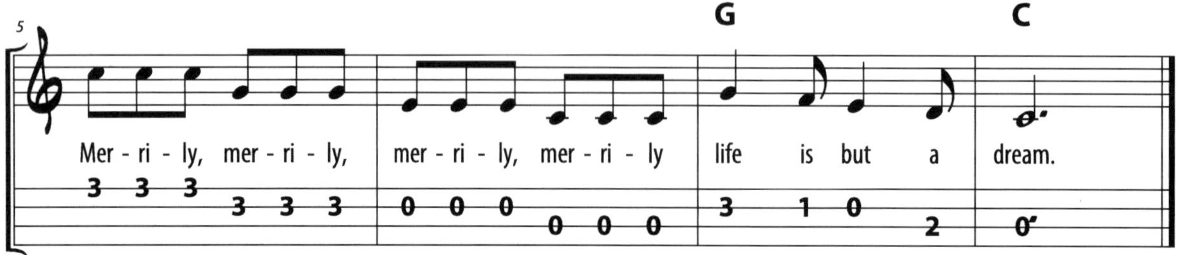
5
G
C
Mer - ri - ly, mer - ri - ly, mer - ri - ly, mer - ri - ly life is but a dream.
3 3 3 3 3 3 0 0 0 0 0 0 3 1 0 2 0

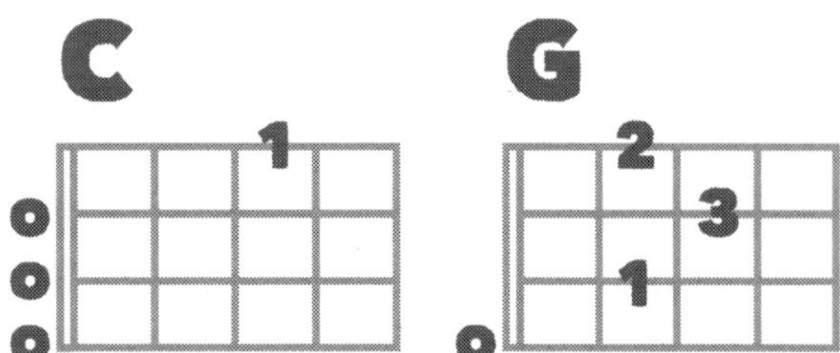
C
1
G
2
3
1

2. *Someone's crying, Lord, kum ba yah!*

3. *Someone's singing, Lord, kum ba yah!*

4. *Someone's praying, Lord, kum ba yah!*

Humpty Dumpty

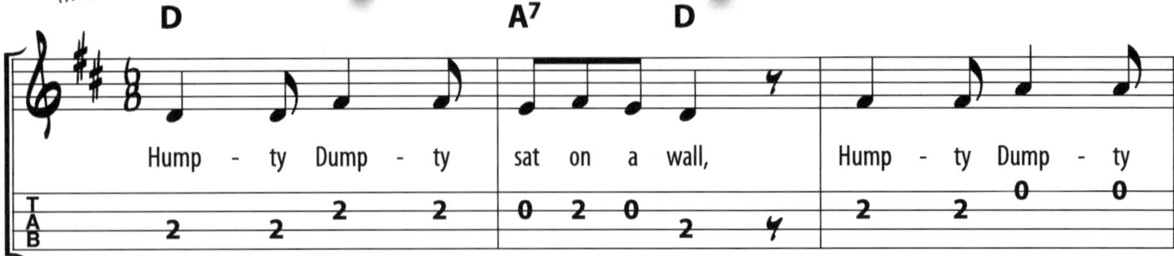

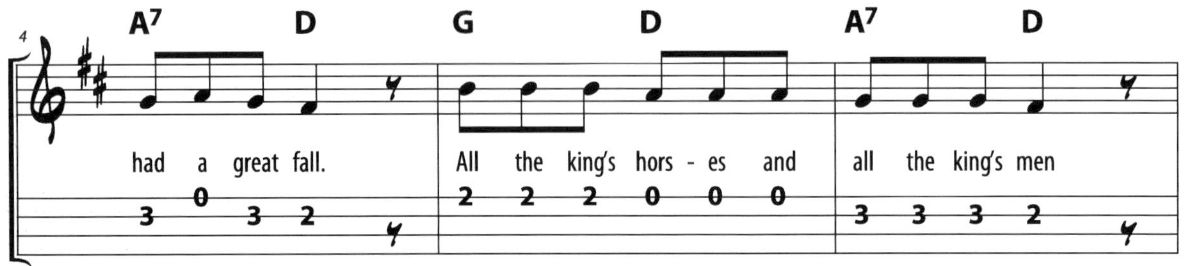

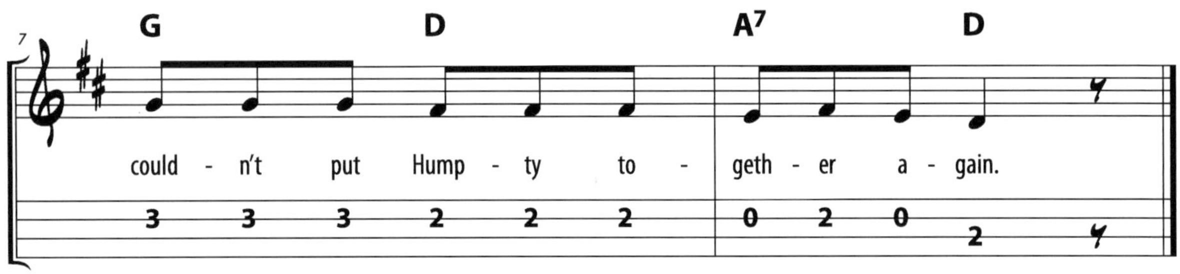

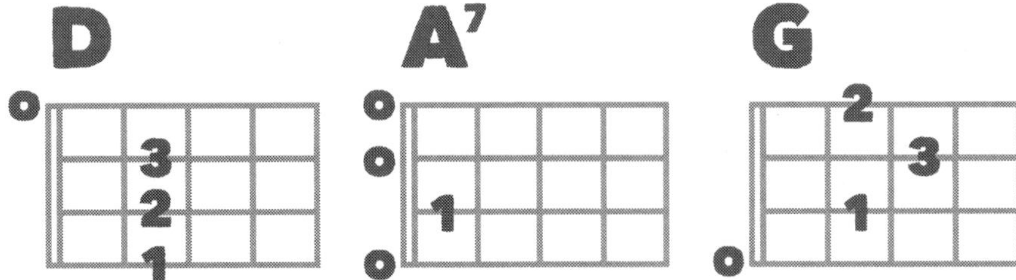

Jack Sprat

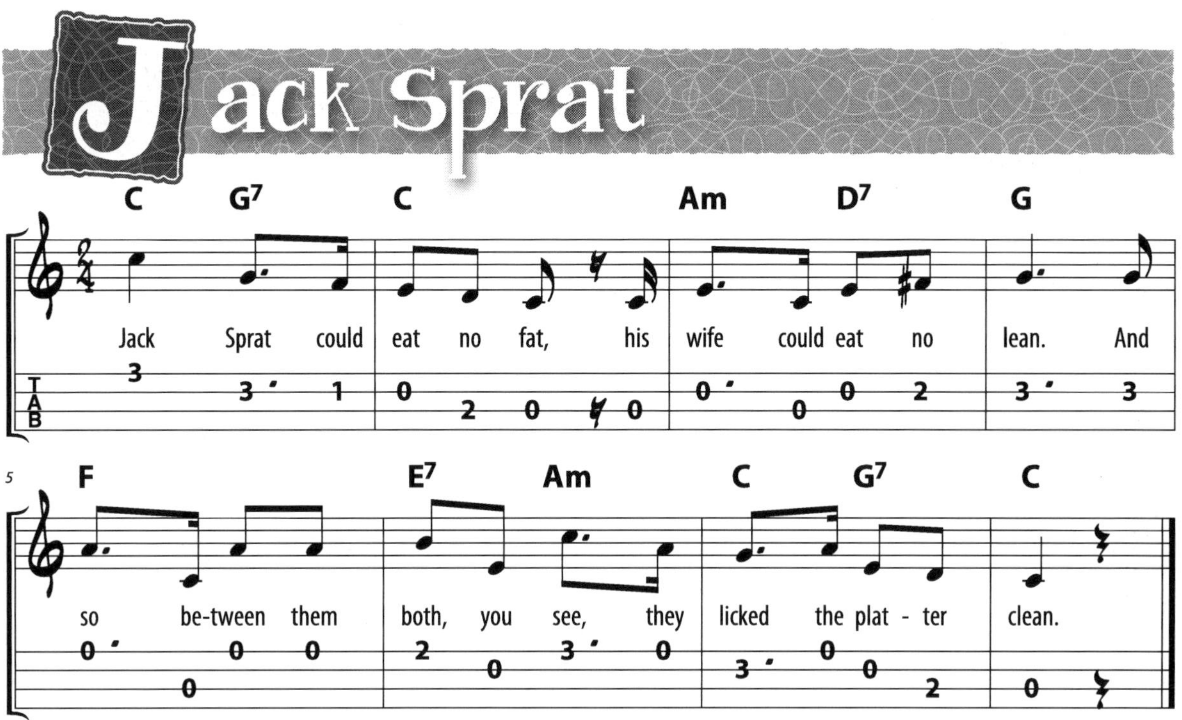
C G7 C Am D7 G
Jack Sprat could eat no fat, his wife could eat no lean. And
F E7 Am C G7 C
so be-tween them both, you see, they licked the plat - ter clean.

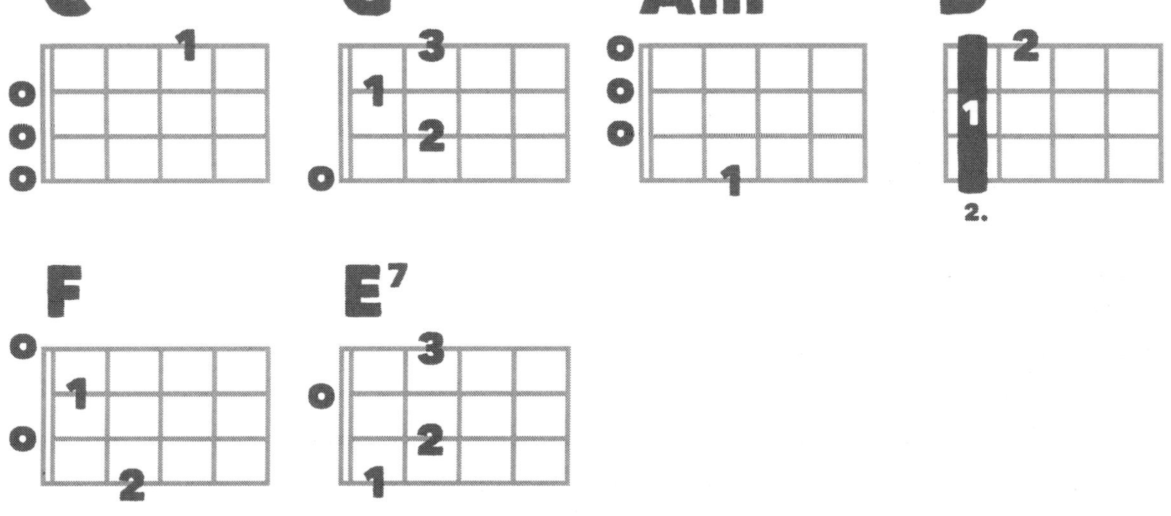
C
G7
Am
D7
F
E7

Mary had a little lamb

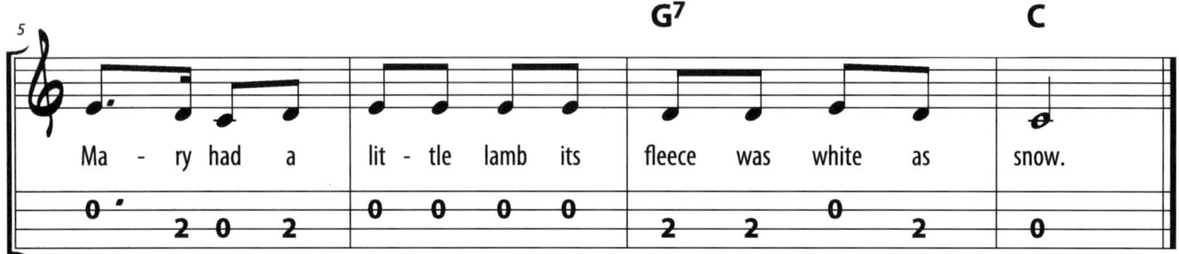

2. *And everywhere that Mary went,*
   Mary went, Mary went,
   everywhere that Mary went
   the lamb was sure to go.

3. *It followed her to school one day,*
   school one day, school one day,
   it followed her to school one day
   which was against the rule.

4. *It made the children laugh and play,*
   laugh and play, laugh and play,
   it made the children laugh and play
   to see a lamb at school.

5. *And so the teacher turned it out,*
   turned it out, turned it out,
   and so the teacher turned it out
   but still it lingered near.

6. *And waited patiently about,*
   Patiently, patiently,
   and waited patiently about
   till Mary did appear.

7. *"Why does the lamb love Mary so,*
   Mary so, Mary so?"
   "Why does the lamb love Mary so?"
   the eager children cry.

8. *"Because the lamb loves Mary so,*
   Mary so, Mary so",
   "Because the lamb loves Mary so",
   the teacher did reply.

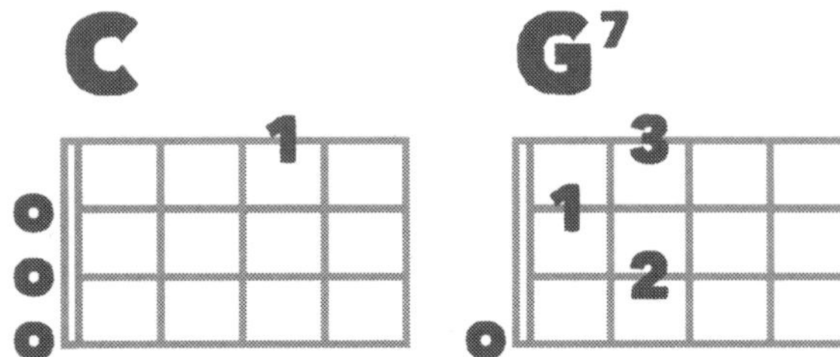

Six little ducks

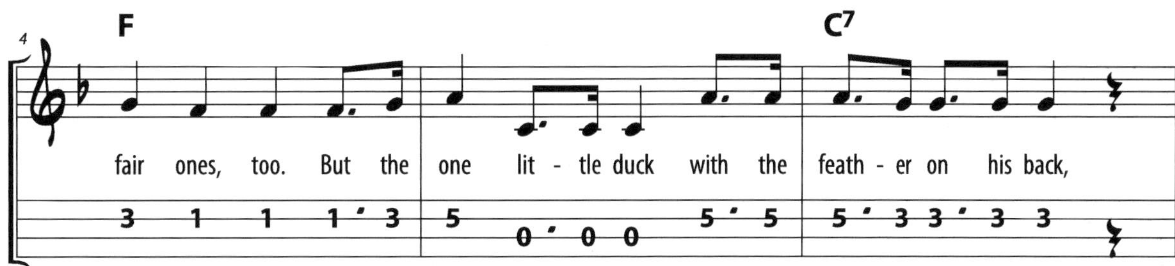

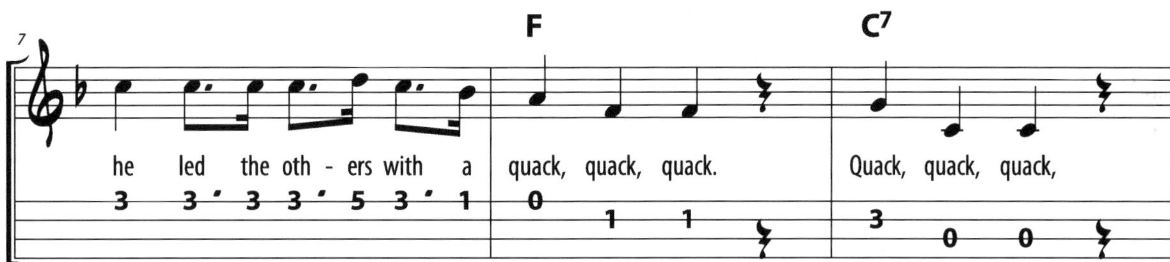

2. *Down to the river they would go,*
   Wibble, wobble, wibble, wobble, to and fro.
   But the one little duck with the feather on his back,
   he led the others with a quack, quack, quack.
   Quack, quack, quack, quack, quack, quack,
   he led the others with a quack, quack, quack.

3. *Back from the river they would come,*
   Wibble, wobble, wibble, wobble, ho, hum, hum.
   But the one little duck with the feather on his back,
   he led the others with a quack, quack, quack.
   Quack, quack, quack, quack, quack, quack,
   he led the others with a quack, quack, quack.

F

C7

One, two, buckle my shoe

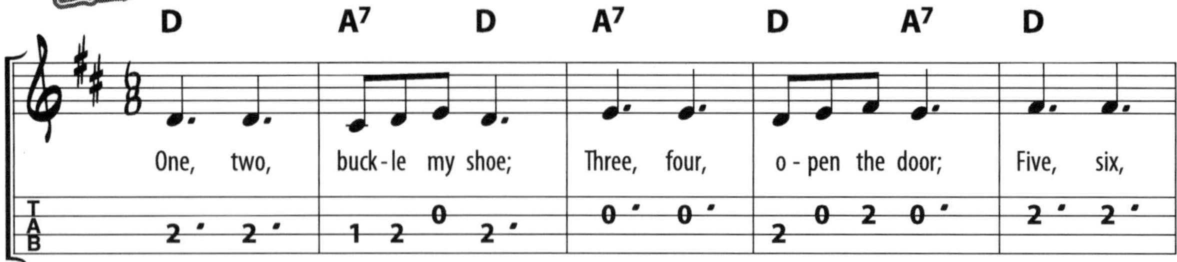

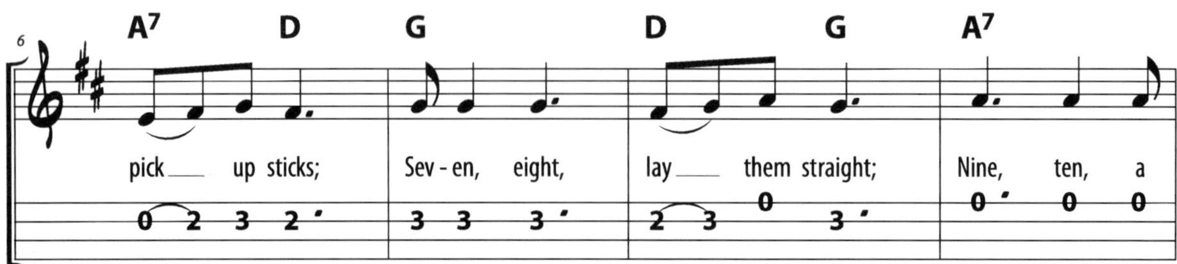

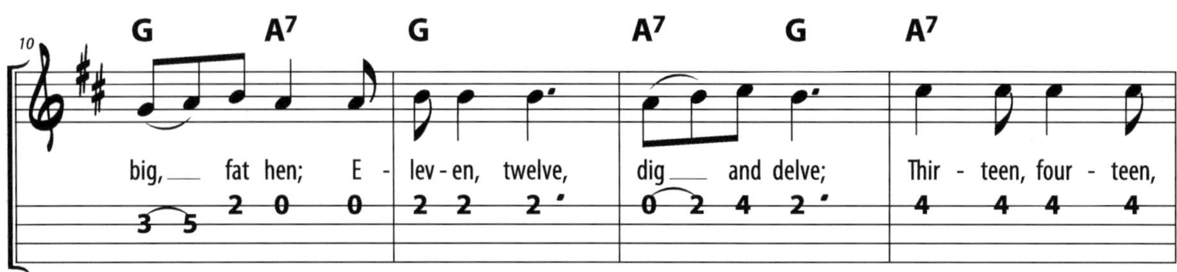

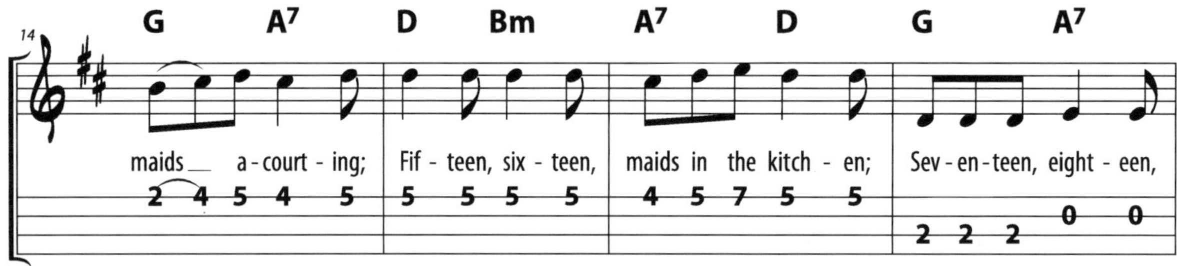

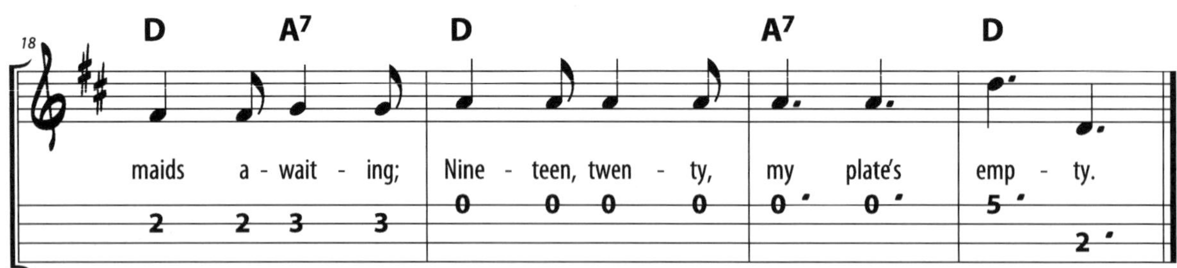

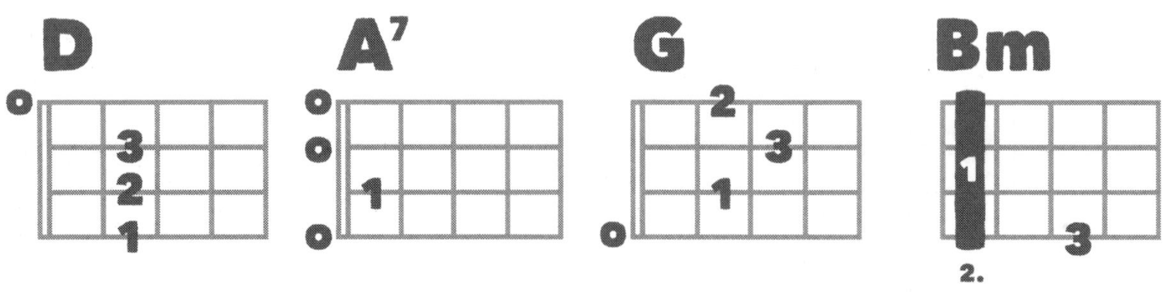

The Hokey Pokey

You put your left hand in ...
You put your right foot in ...
You put your left foot in ...
You put your right shoulder in ...
You put your left shoulder in ...

You put your right hip in ...
You put your left hip in ...
You put your head in ...
You put your whole self in ...

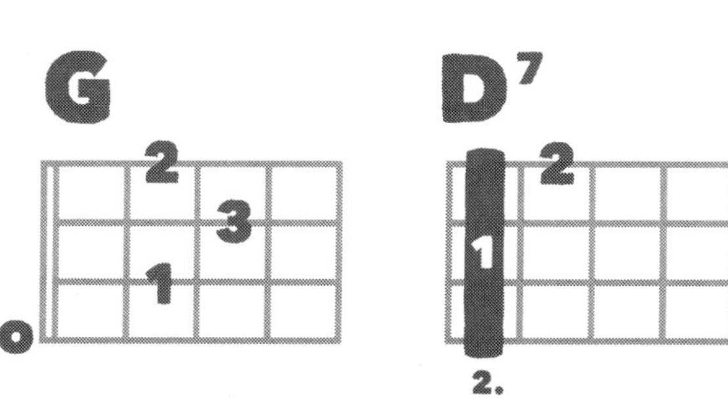

Georgie Porgie

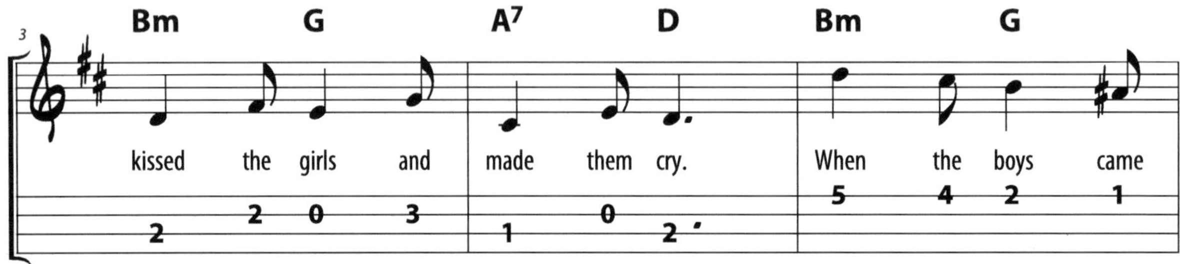

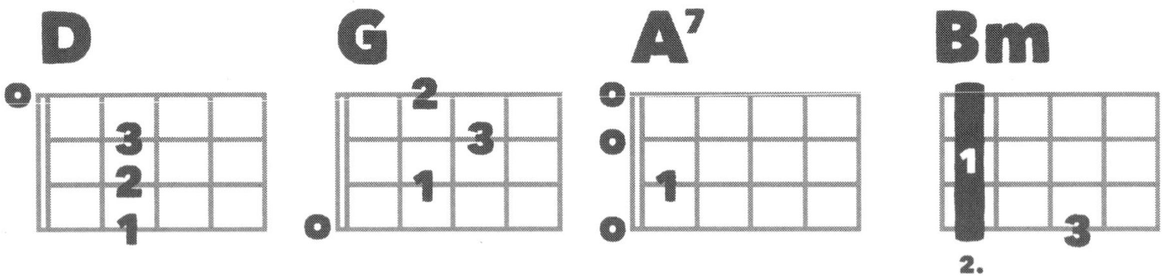

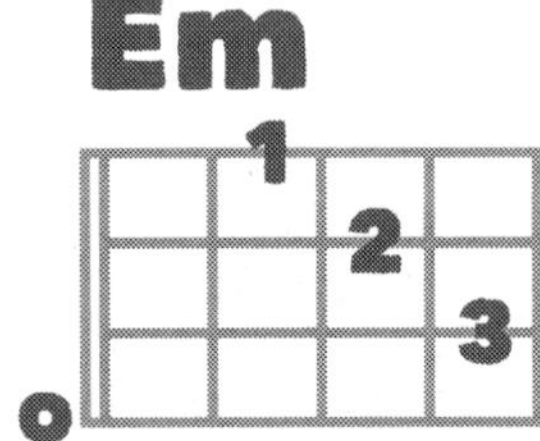

Jack be nimble

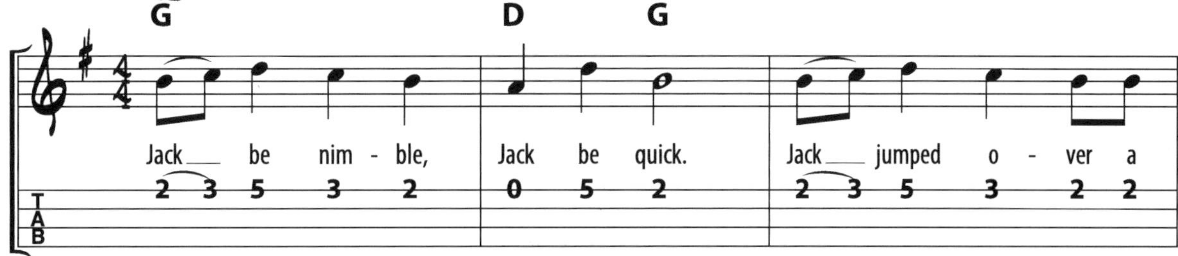

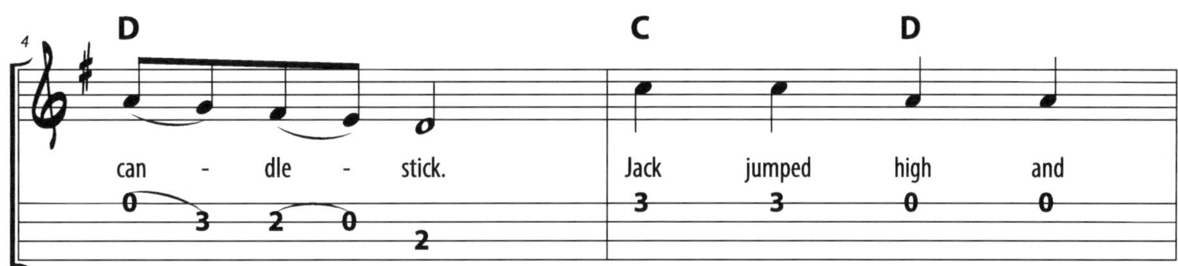

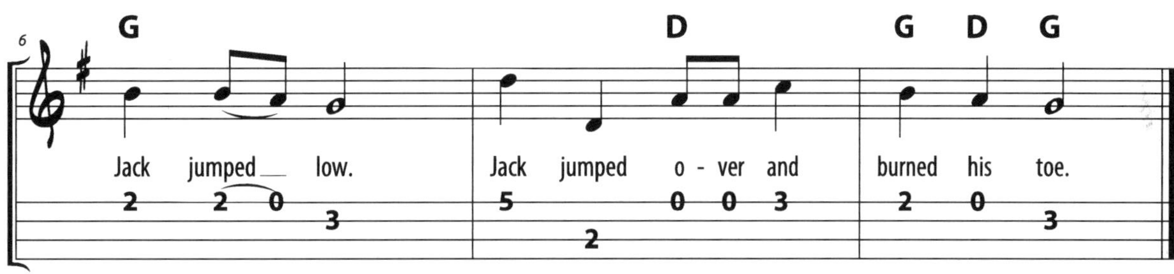

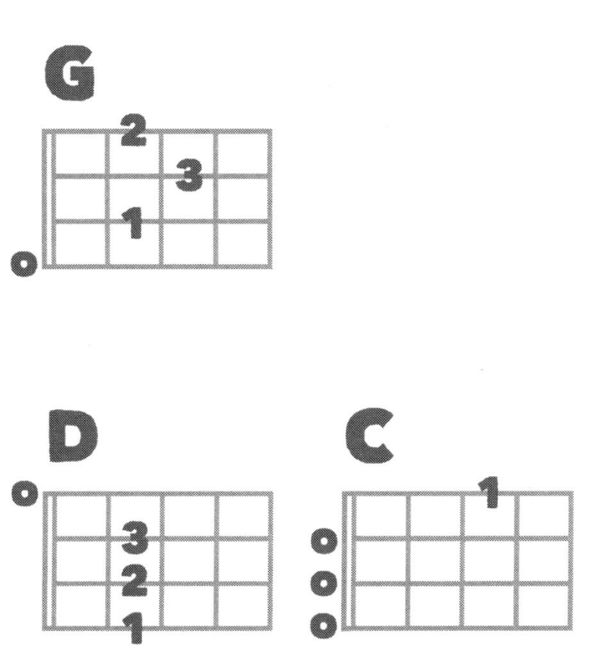

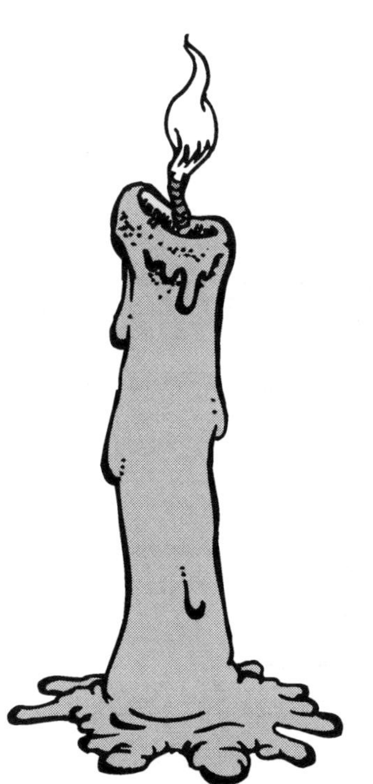

Mulberry bush

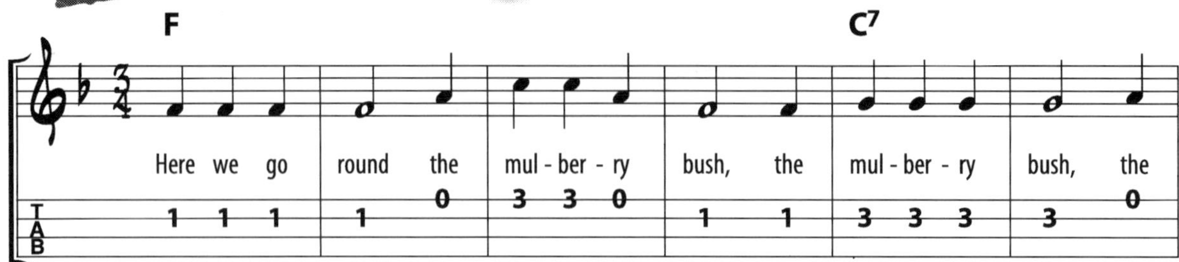

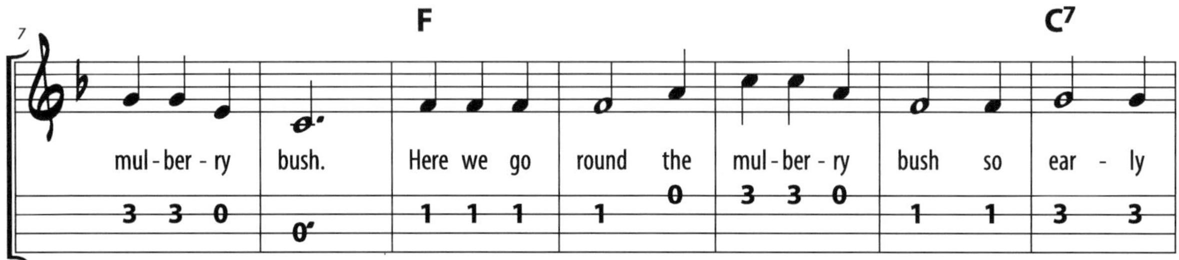

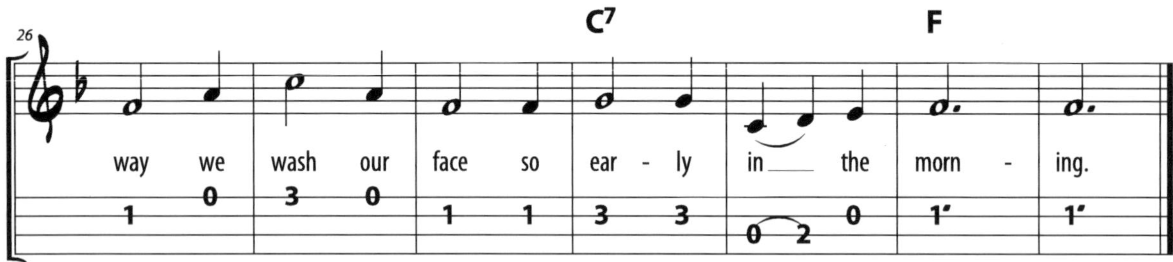

2. *This is the way we comb our hair,*
   we comb our hair, we comb our hair.
   This is the way we comb our hair
   so early in the morning.

3. *This is the way we brush our teeth,*
   we brush our teeth, we brush our teeth.
   This is the way we brush our teeth
   so early in the morning.

4. *This is the way we put on our clothes,*
   we put on our clothes, we put on our clothes.
   This is the way we put on our clothes
   so early in the morning.

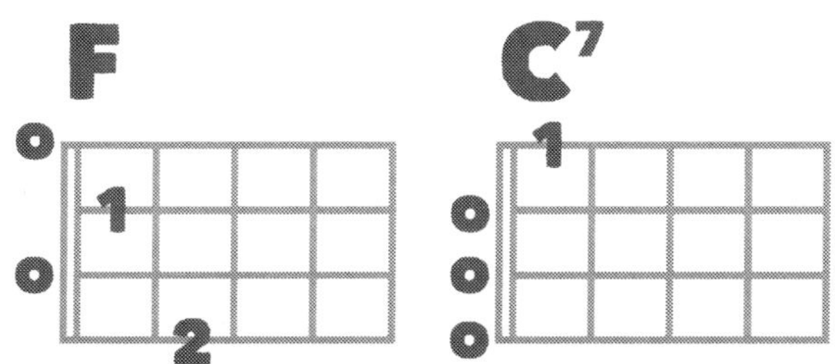

The farmer in the dell

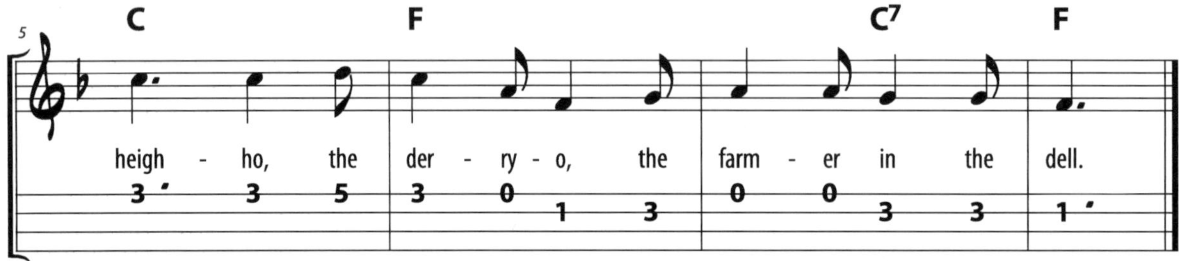

2. *The farmer takes the wife (2×)*
   Heigh-ho, the derry-o …
   The farmer takes the wife

3. *The wife takes the child (2×)*
   Heigh-ho, the derry-o …
   The wife takes the child

4. *The child takes the nurse (2×)*
   Heigh-ho, the derry-o …
   The child takes the nurse

5. *The nurse takes the cow (2×)*
   Heigh-ho, the derry-o …
   The nurse takes the cow

6. *The cow takes the dog (2×)*
   Heigh-ho, the derry-o …
   The cow takes the dog

7. *The dog takes the cat (2×)*
   Heigh-ho, the derry-o …
   The dog takes the cat

8. *The cat takes the mouse (2×)*
   Heigh-ho, the derry-o …
   The cat takes the mouse

9. *The mouse takes the cheese (2×)*
   Heigh-ho, the derry-o …
   The mouse takes the cheese

10. *The cheese stands alone (2×)*
    Heigh-ho, the derry-o …
    The cheese stands alone

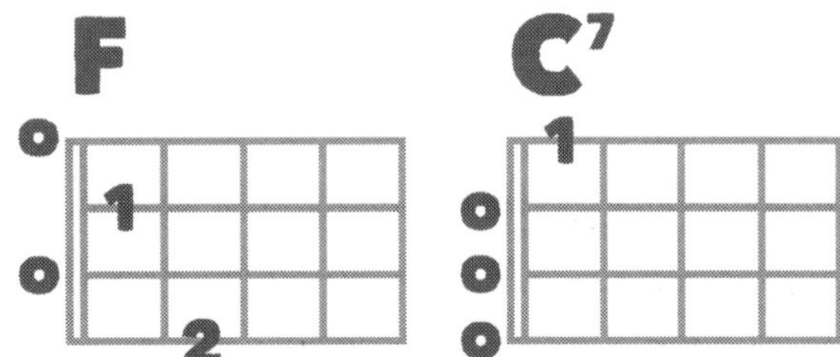

Bye, baby bunting

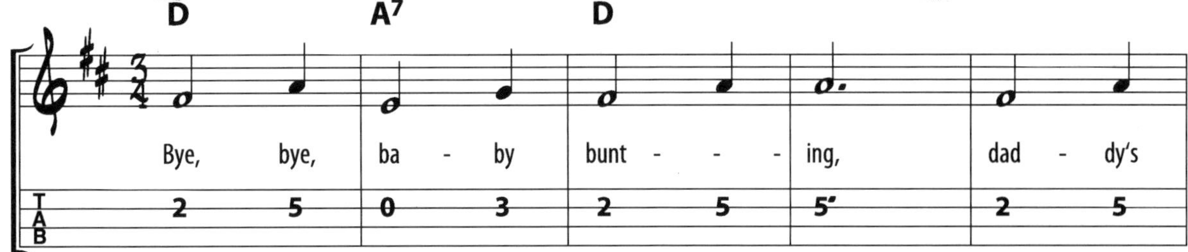

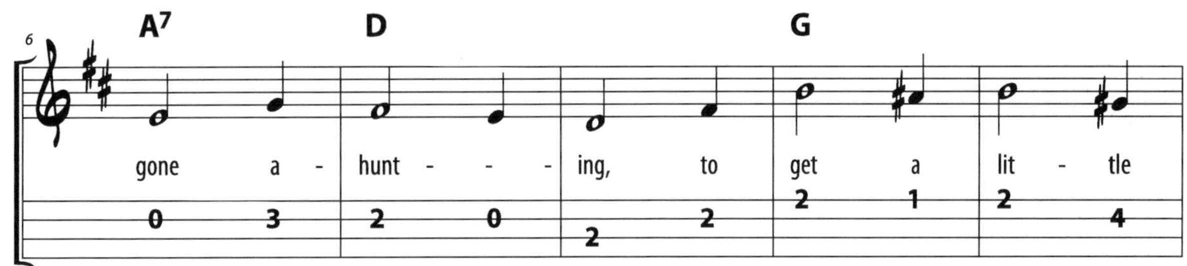

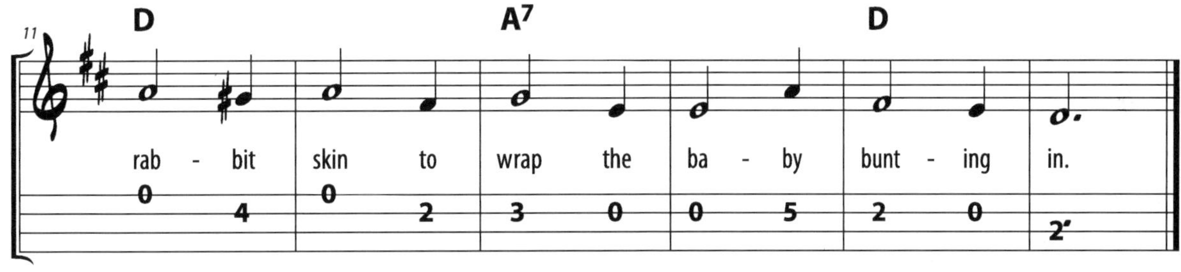

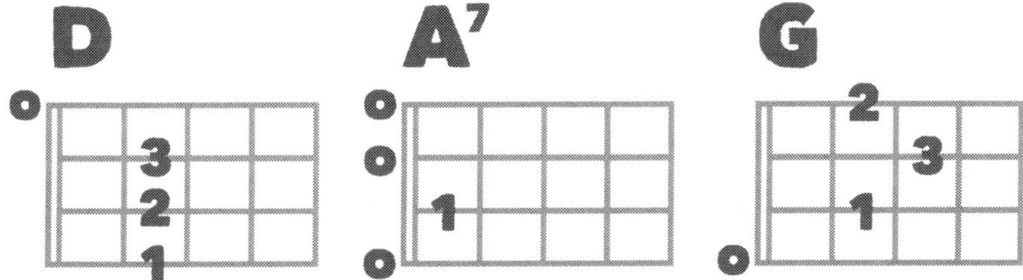

Lucy Locket

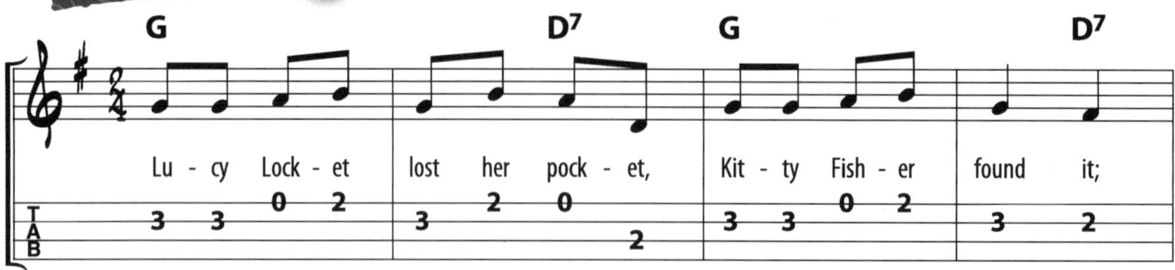
G
D7
G
D7
Lu - cy Lock - et lost her pock - et, Kit - ty Fish - er found it;
T
A
B
3 3 0 2 3 2 0 2 3 3 0 2 3 2

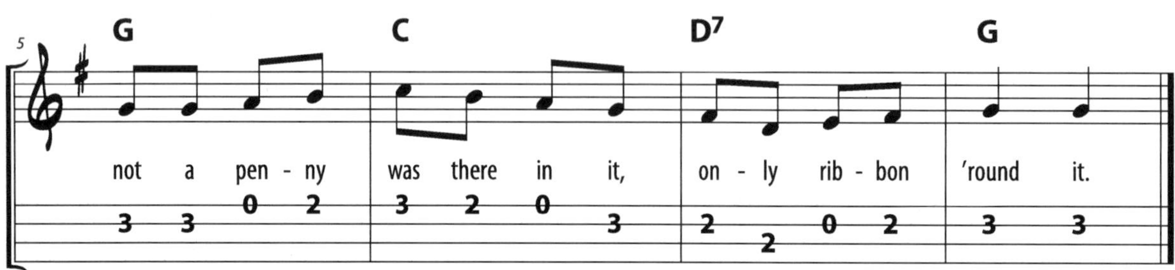
5
G
C
D7
G
not a pen - ny was there in it, on - ly rib - bon 'round it.
3 3 0 2 3 2 0 3 2 2 0 2 3 3

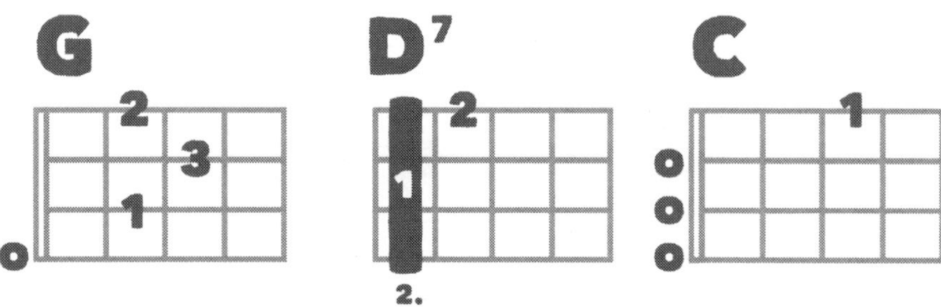
G
D7
C
2
3
1
2
1
1
2.

Pease porridge hot

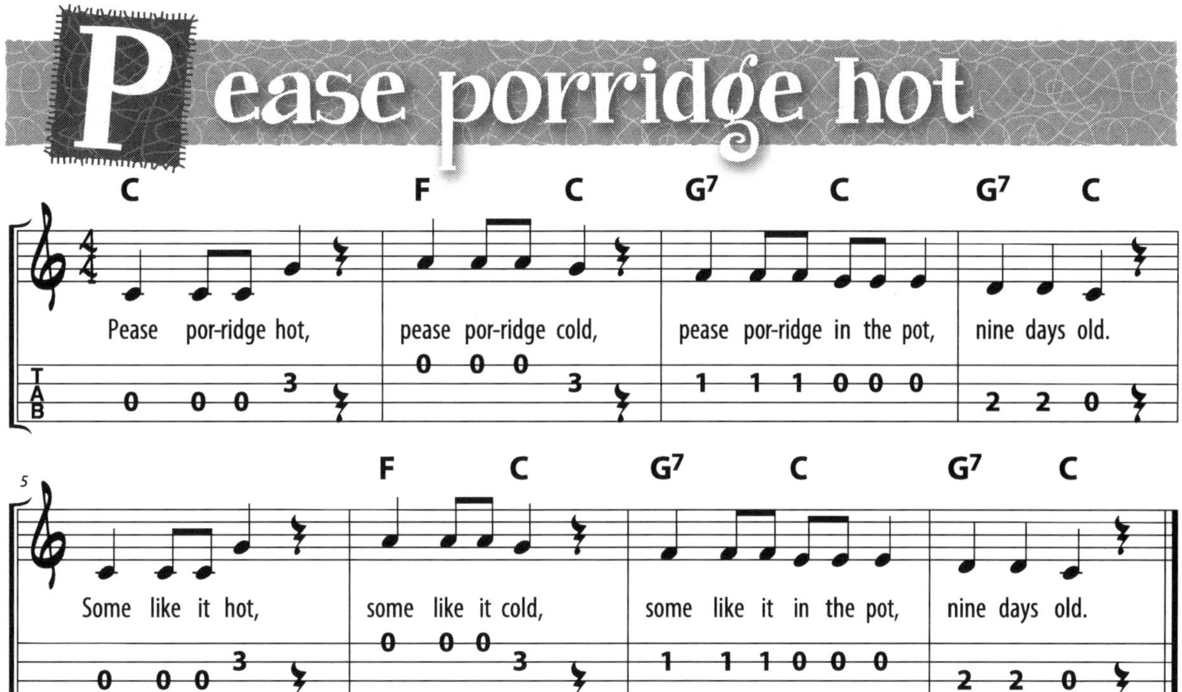

C F G7

2. *Down goes the first one,*
   down goes the second one,
   oh, how they wiggle and squirm.
   Long, thin, slimy ones,
   short, fat, juicy ones
   itsy, bitsy, fuzzy, wuzzy worms.

3. *Up comes the first one,*
   up comes the second one,
   oh, how they wiggle and squirm.
   Long, thin, slimy ones,
   short, fat, juicy ones,
   itsy, bitsy, fuzzy, wuzzy worms.

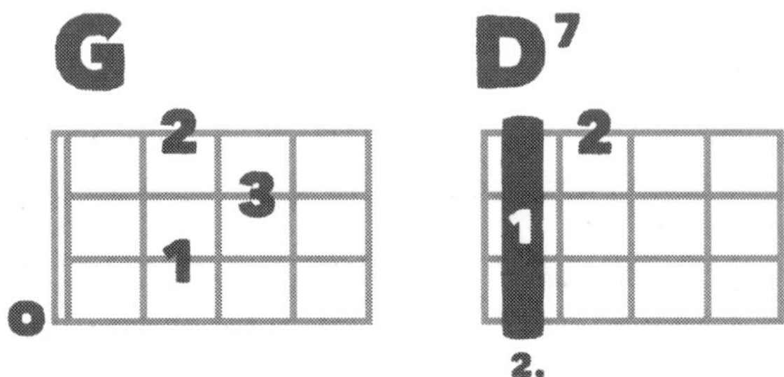

Little Miss Muffet

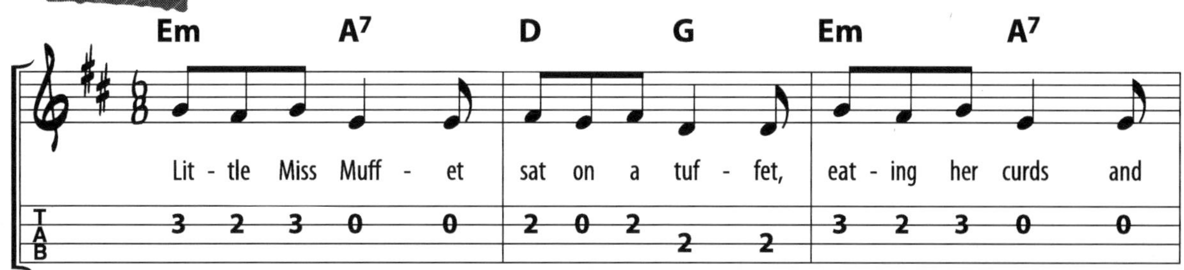

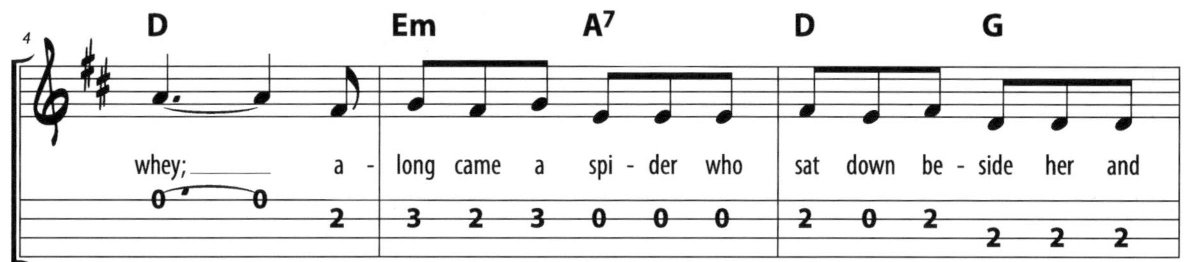

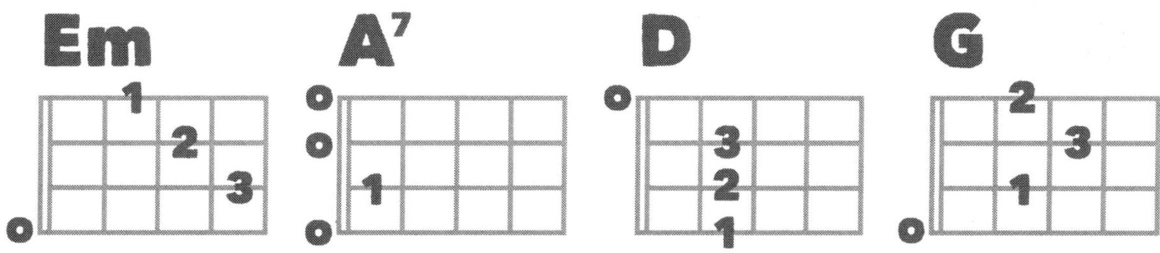

Pat-a-cake

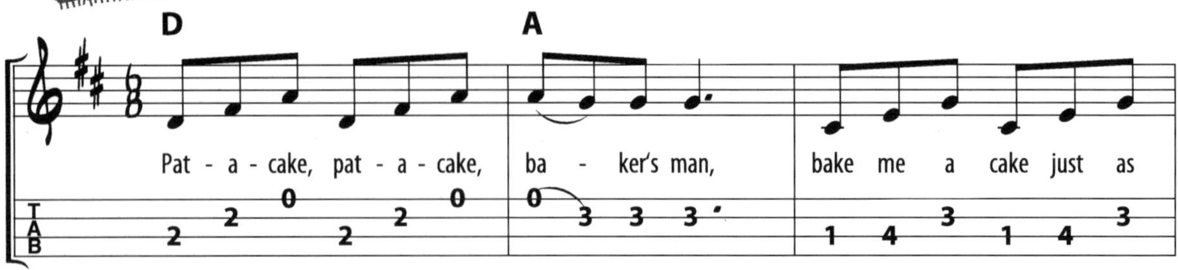
D A
Pat - a - cake, pat - a - cake, ba - ker's man, bake me a cake just as

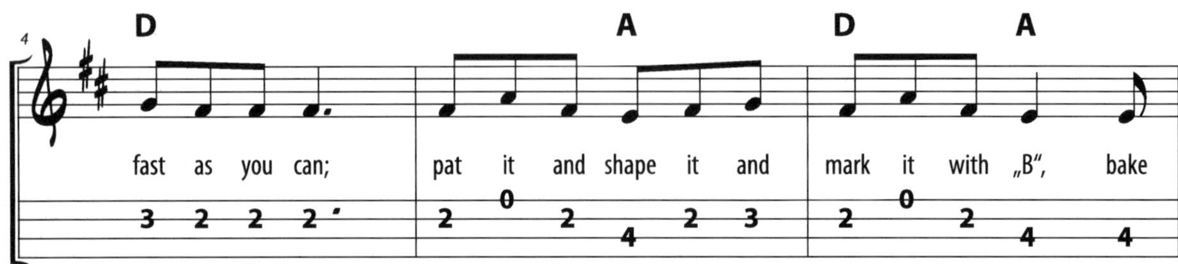
D A D A
fast as you can; pat it and shape it and mark it with „B", bake

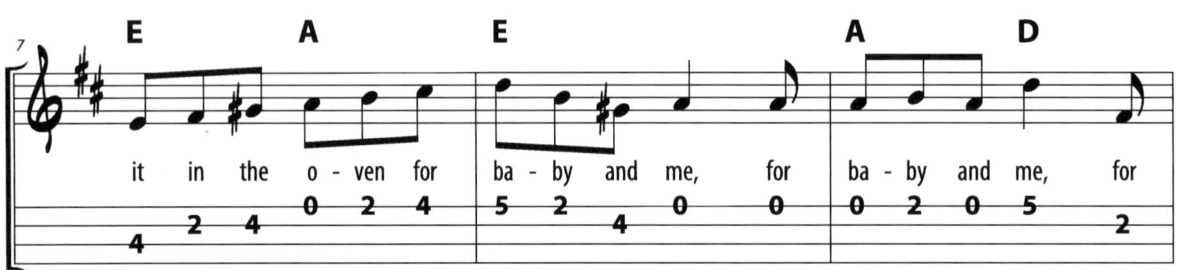
E A E A D
it in the o - ven for ba - by and me, for ba - by and me, for

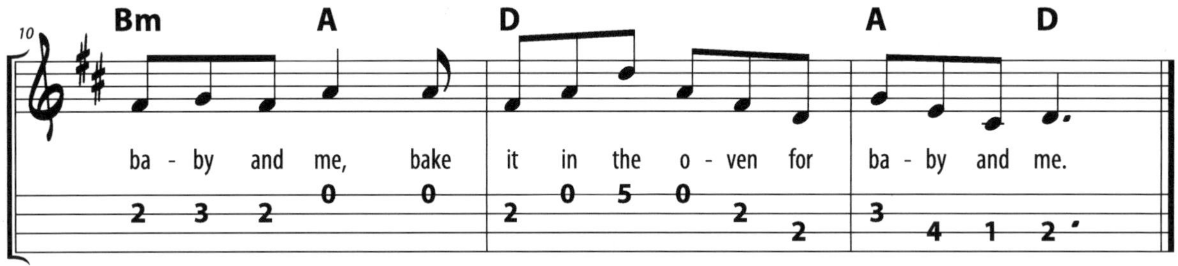
Bm A D A D
ba - by and me, bake it in the o - ven for ba - by and me.

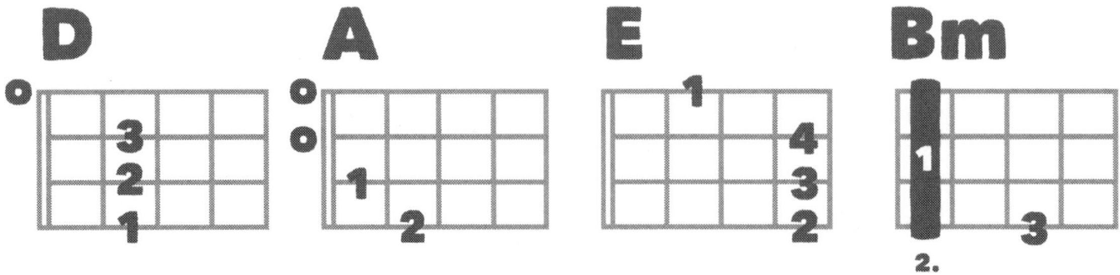
D
A
E
Bm

Peter, Peter, pumpkin eater

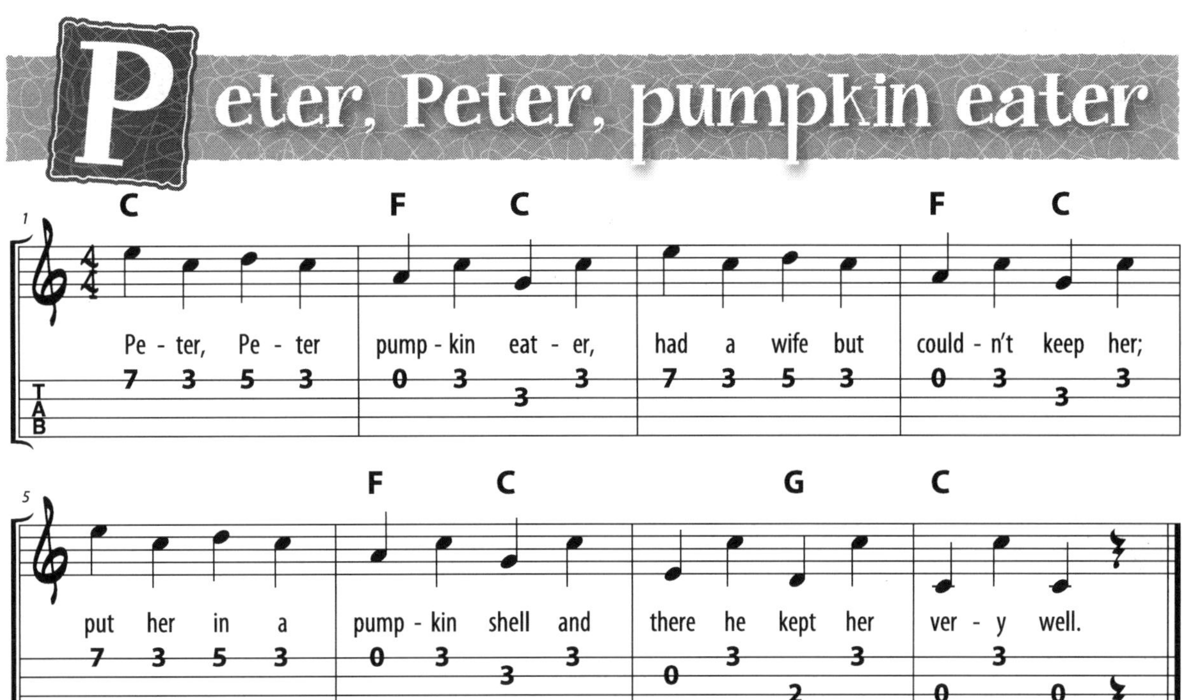

2. *Peter, Peter, pumpkin eater,*
   had another and didn't love her;
   Peter learned to read and spell,
   and then he loved her very well.

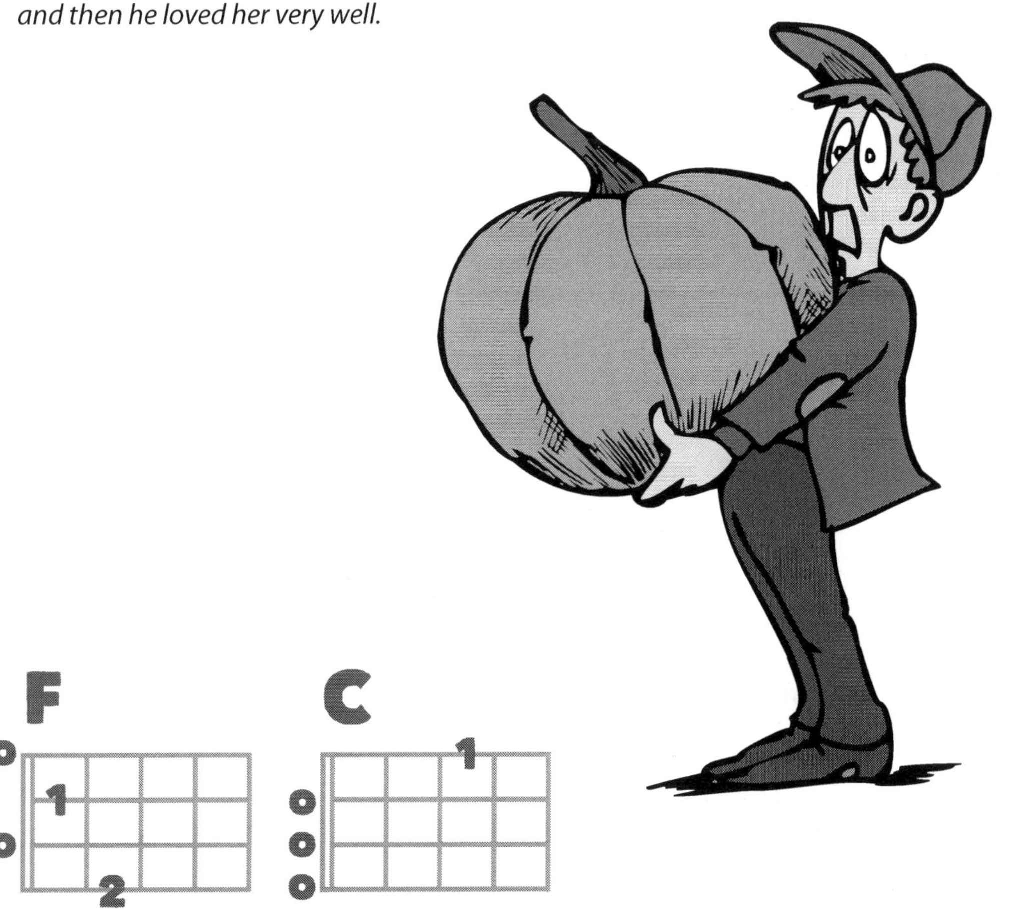

here was a crooked man

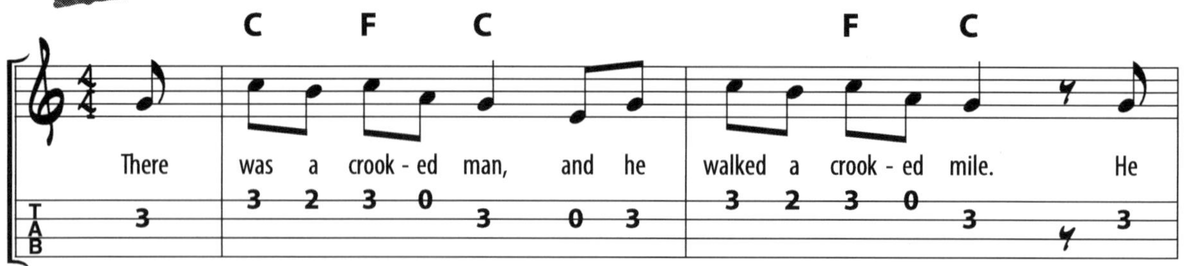

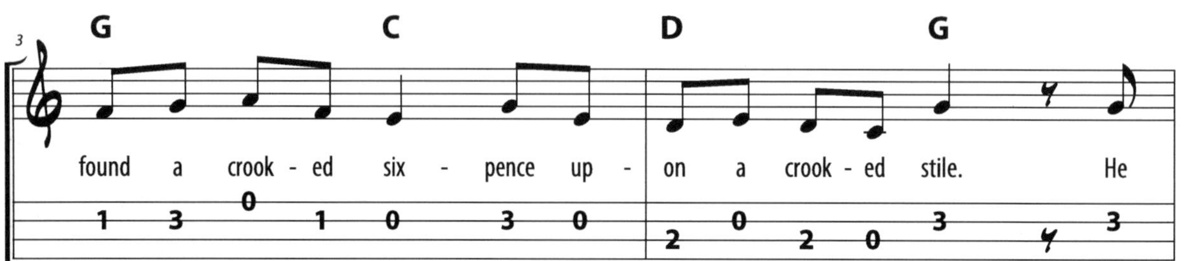

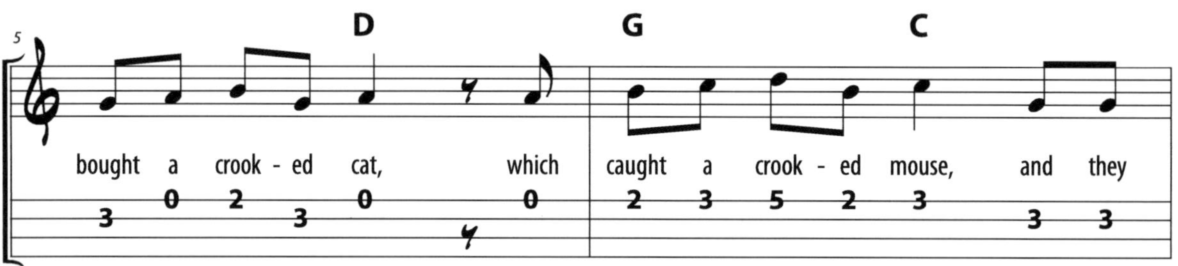

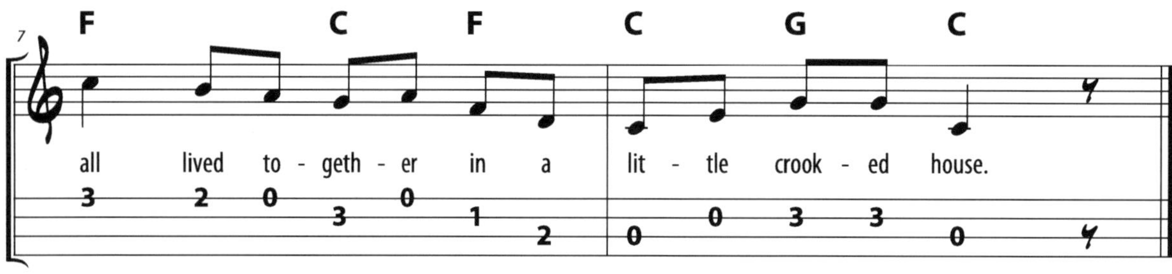

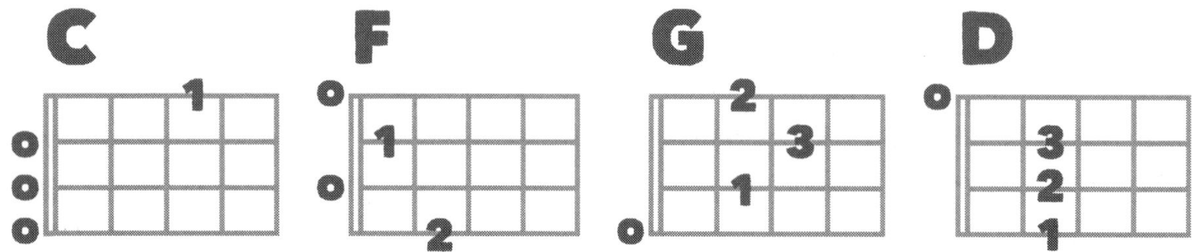

Lazy Mary

2. *No, no, mother I won't get up,*
   I won't get up, I won't get up.
   No, no, mother I won't get up,
   I won't get up today.

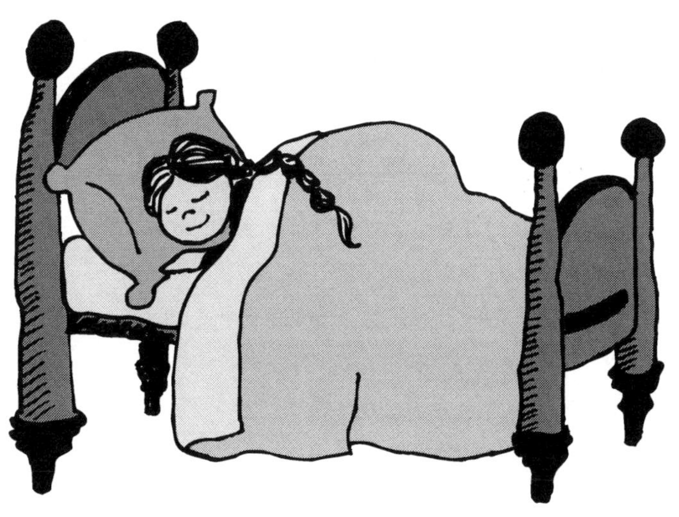

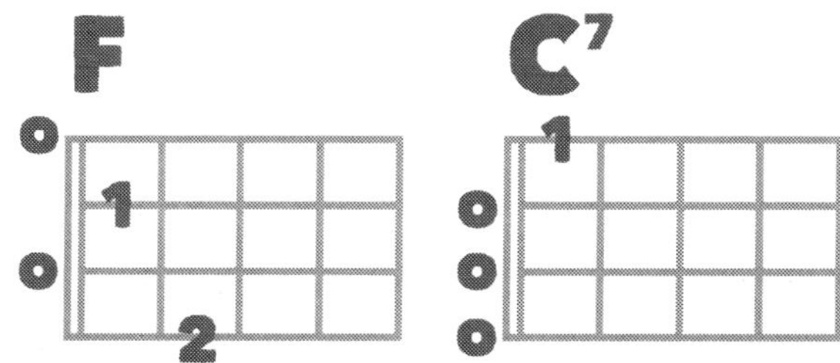

Over in the meadow

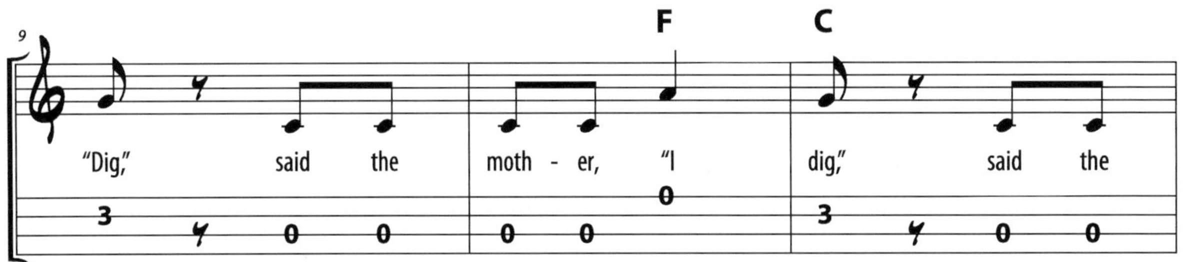

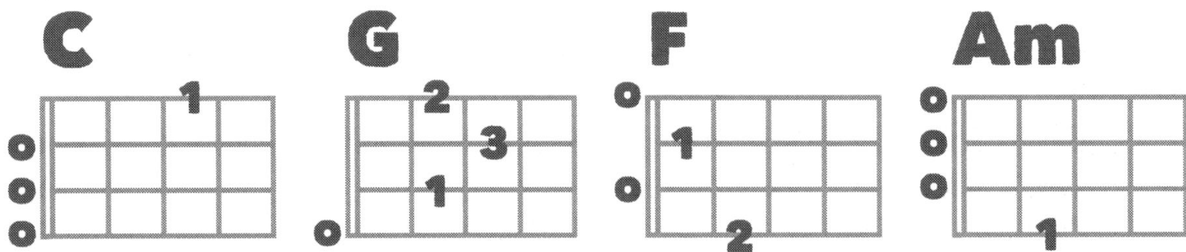

2. *Over in the meadow where the stream runs blue,*
lived an old mother fish and her little fishies two.
"Swim," said the mother, "We swim," said the two,
so they swam and they swam where the stream runs blue.

3. *Over in the meadow in a hole in the tree,*
Lived an old mother owl and her little owls three.
"Whoo," said the mother, "We whoo," said the three,
so they whooed and they whoeed in the hole in the tree.

4. *Over in the meadow by the old barn door,*
Lived an old mother rat and her little ratties four.
"Gnaw," said the mother, "We gnaw," said the four,
so they gnawed and the gnawed by the old barn door.

5. *Over in the meadow in a snug beehive,*
Lived an old mother bee and her little bees five.
"Buzz," said the mother, "We buzz," said the five,
so they buzzed and they buzzed in the snug beehive.

6. *Over in the meadow in a nest built of sticks,*
Lived an old mother crow and her little crows six.
"Caw," said the mother, "We caw," said the six,
so they cawed and the cawed in the nest built of sticks.

7. *Over in the meadow where the grass grows so even,*
Lived an old mother frog and her little froggies seven.
"Jump," said the mother, "We jump," said the seven,
so they jumped and they jumped where the grass grows so even.

8. *Over in the meadow by the old mossy gate,*
Lived an old mother lizard and her little lizards eight.
"Bask," said the mother, "We bask," said the eight,
so they basked and they basked by the old mossy gate.

9. *Over in the meadow by the old scotch pine,*
Lived an old mother duck and her little duckies nine.
"Quack," said the mother, "We quack," said the nine,
so they quacked and they quacked by the old scotch pine.

10. *Over in the meadow in a cozy, wee den,*
Lived an old mother beaver and her little beavers ten.
"Beave," said the mother, "We beave," said the ten,
so they beaved and they beaved in their cozy, wee den.

Three little Kittens

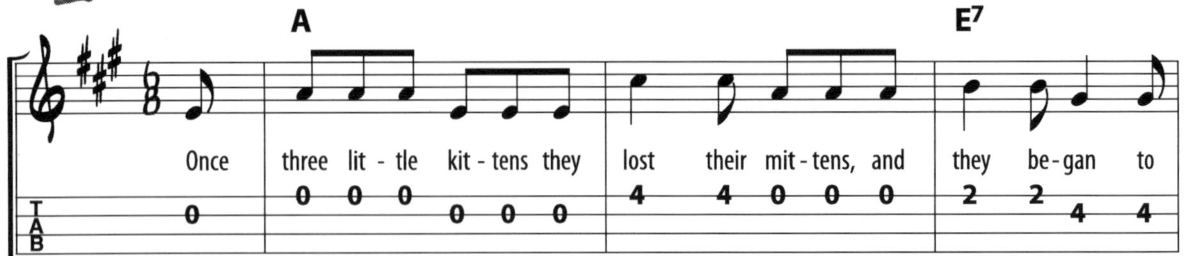

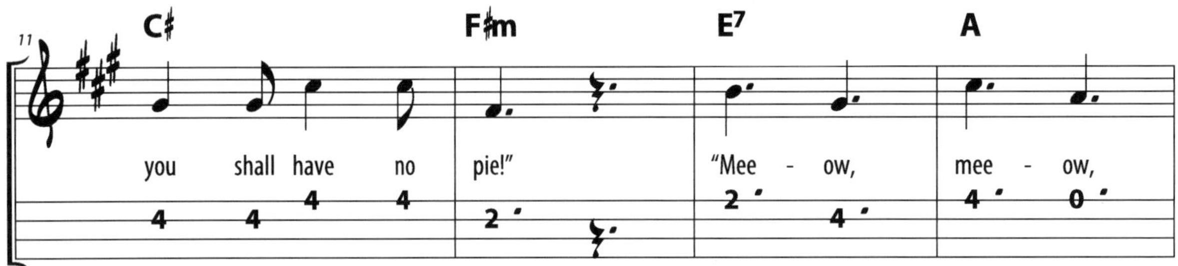

2. *The three little kittens they found their mittens,*
   and they began to cry,
   "Oh, mother dear, see here, see here,
   we have found our mittens."
   "Put on your mittens, you silly kittens,
   and you shall have some pie."
   "Mee-ow, mee-ow, mee-ow."

3. *The three little kittens put on their mittens,*
   and soon ate up the pie;
   "Oh, mother dear, we greatly fear
   we have soiled our mittens."
   "What! soiled your mittens, you naughty kittens!"
   Then they began to sigh,
   "Mee-ow, mee-ow, mee-ow."

4. *The three little kittens they washed their mittens,*
   and hung them out to dry;
   "Oh! mother dear, do you not hear,
   we have washed our mittens."
   "What! washed your mittens, then you're good kittens,
   But I smell a rat close by."
   "Mee-ow, mee-ow, mee-ow."

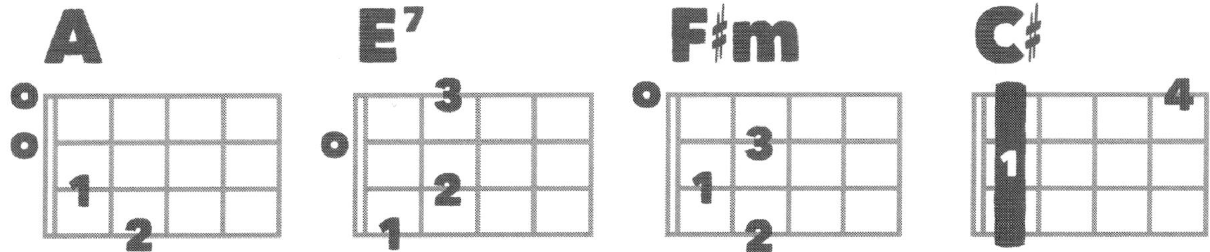

Animal fair

C
G7
I went to the an - i - mal fair, the birds and beasts were there,
0 3 3 3 0 0 0 3′ 0 3 3 0 0 1′

8
C
the big ba - boon, by the light of the moon was comb-ing his au - burn hair.
3 2 2 2 2 2 2 2 2 2 0 3 3 3 0 0 3′

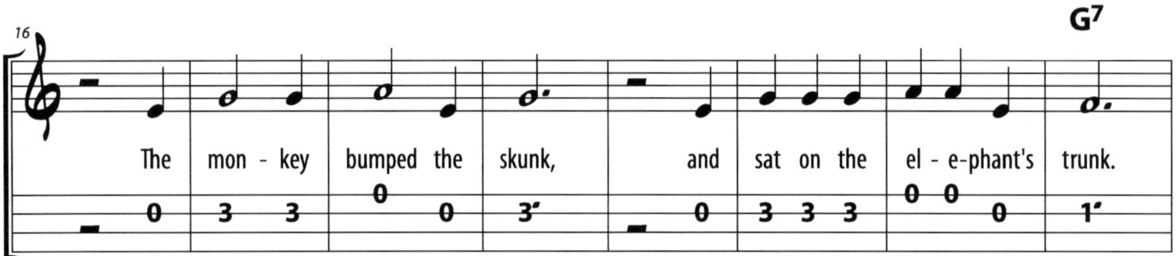
16
G7
The mon - key bumped the skunk, and sat on the el - e-phant's trunk.
0 3 3 0 0 3′ 0 3 3 3 0 0 0 1′

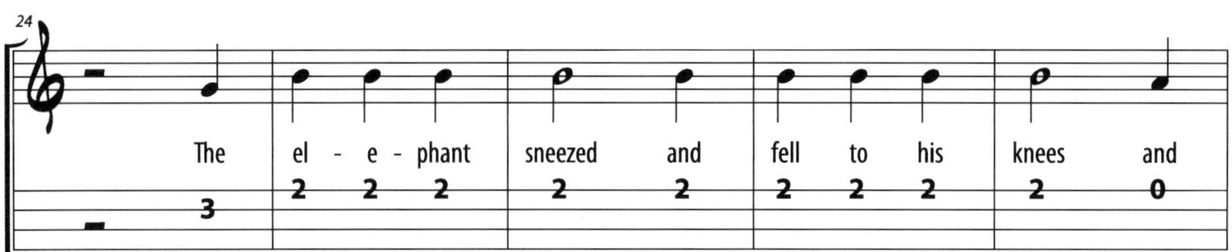
24
The el - e - phant sneezed and fell to his knees and
3 2 2 2 2 2 2 2 2 2 0

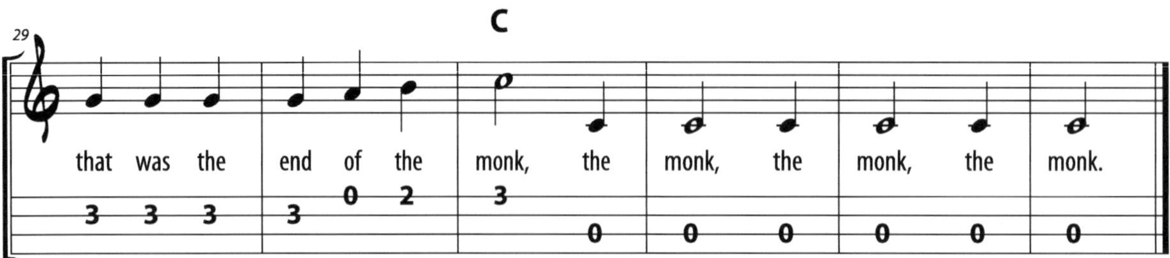
29
C
that was the end of the monk, the monk, the monk, the monk.
3 3 3 3 0 2 3 0 0 0 0 0 0

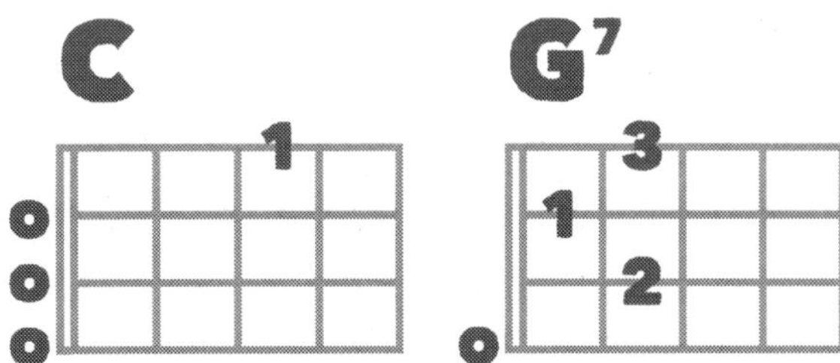
C
G7
1
3
1
2

See-saw, Margery Daw

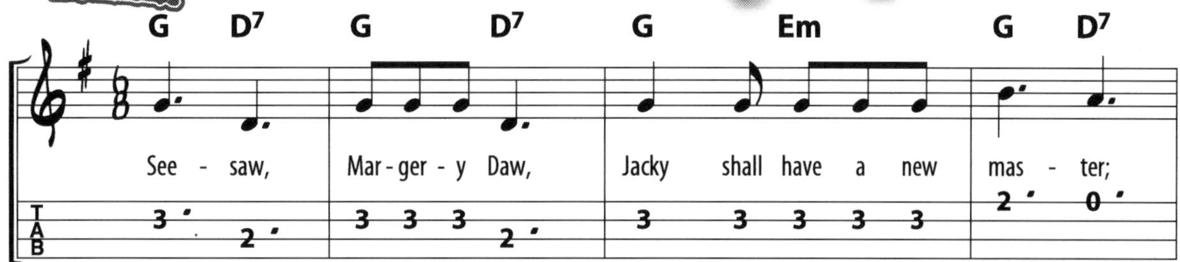

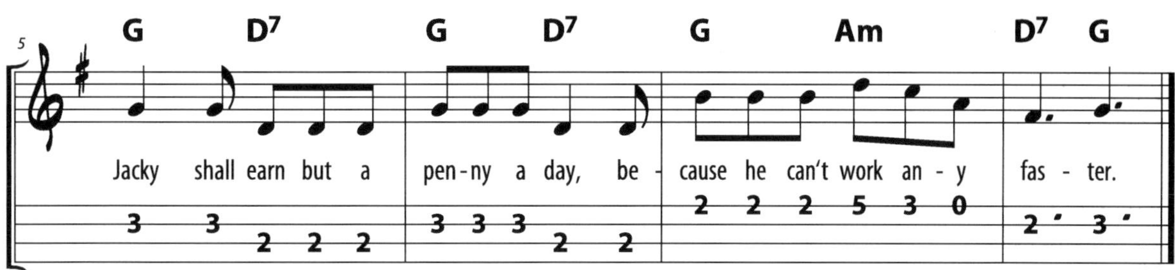

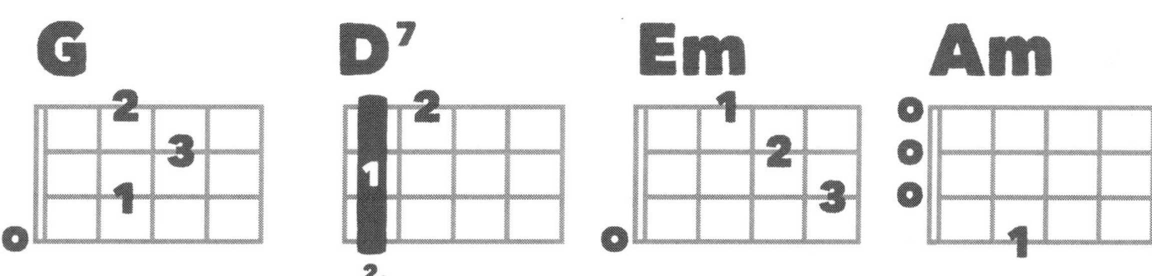

Hot cross buns

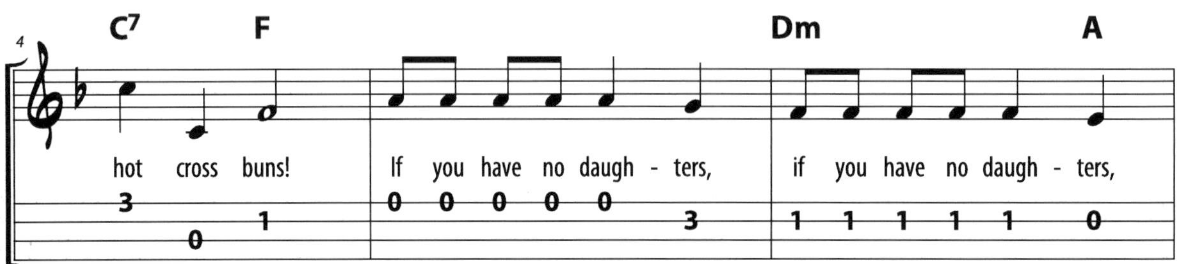

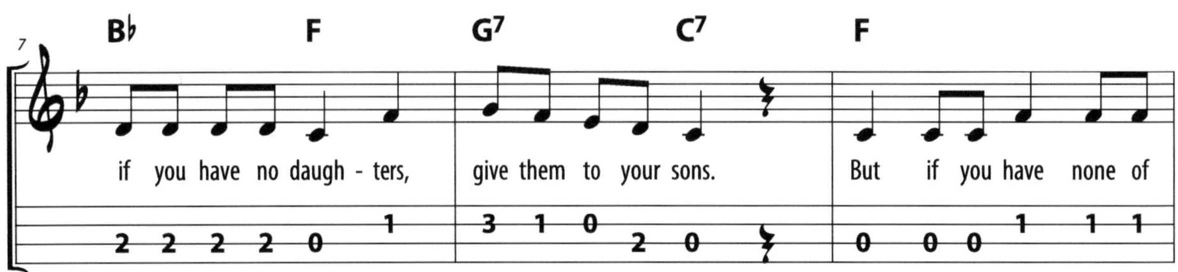

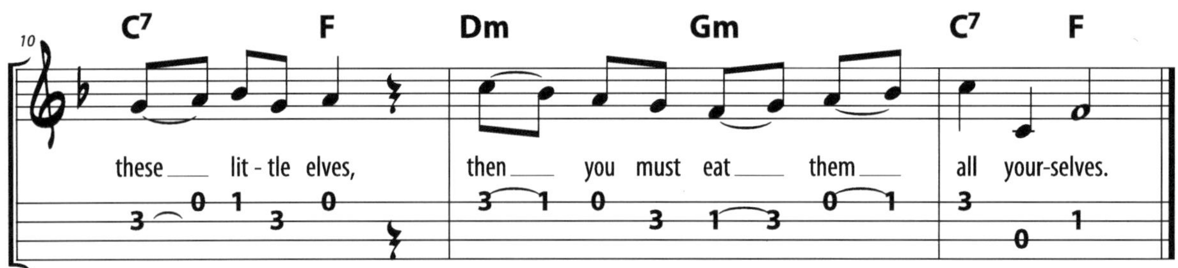

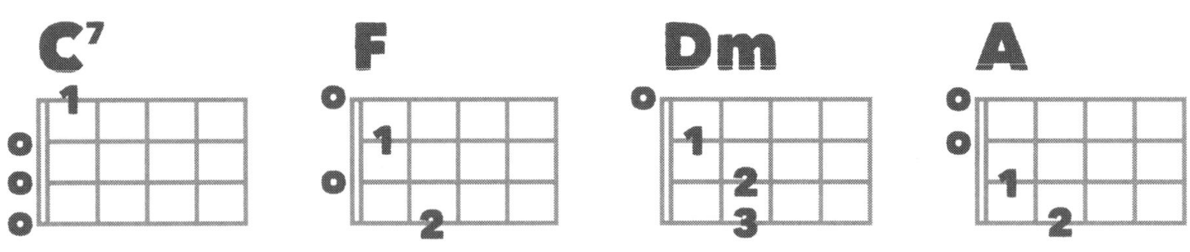

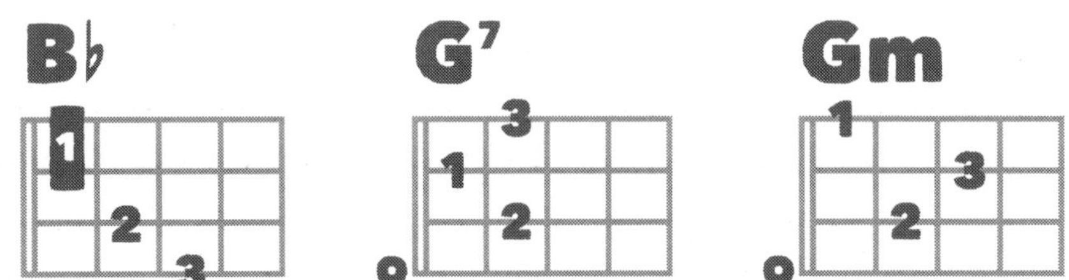

Five little ducks

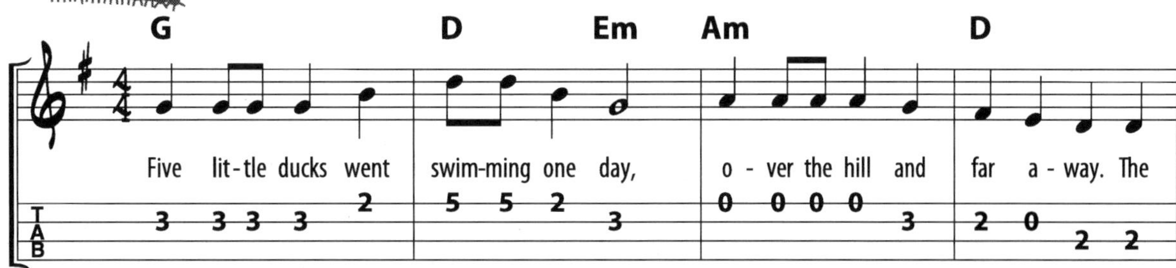

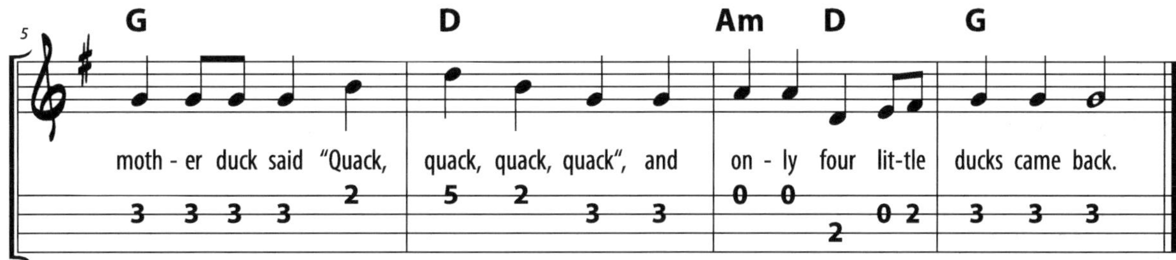

2. *Four little ducks went swimming one day,*
   over the hill and far away.
   The mother duck said "Quack, quack, quack, quack",
   and only three little ducks came back.

3. *Three little ducks went swimming one day,*
   over the hill and far away.
   The mother duck said "Quack, quack, quack, quack",
   and only two little ducks came back.

4. *Two little ducks went swimming one day,*
   over the hill and far away.
   The mother duck said "Quack, quack, quack, quack",
   and only one little duck came back.

5. *One little ducks went swimming one day,*
   over the hill and far away.
   The mother duck said "Quack, quack, quack, quack",
   and all the five little ducks came back.

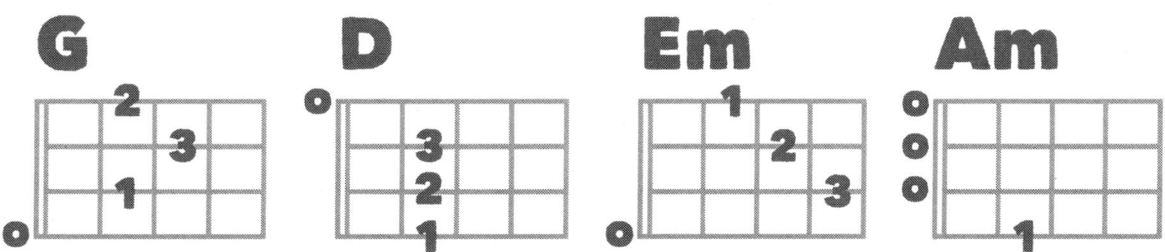

All the pretty little horses

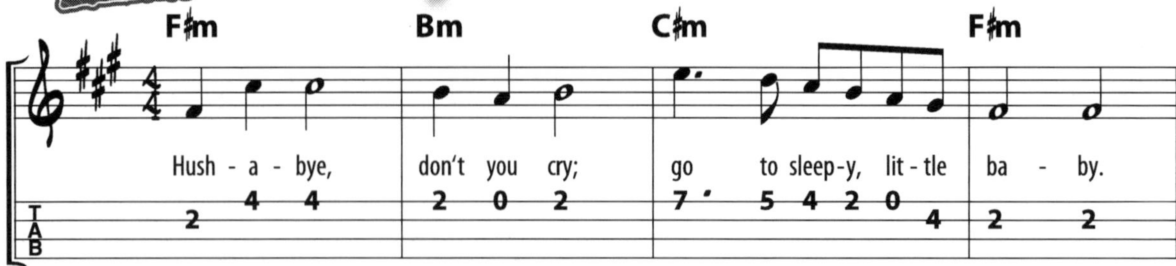

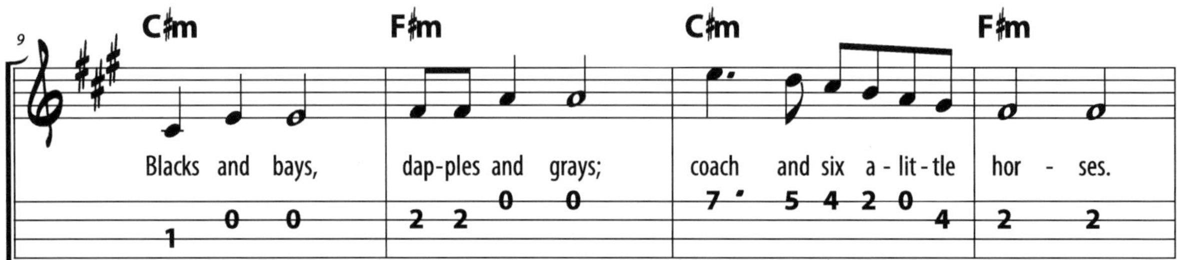

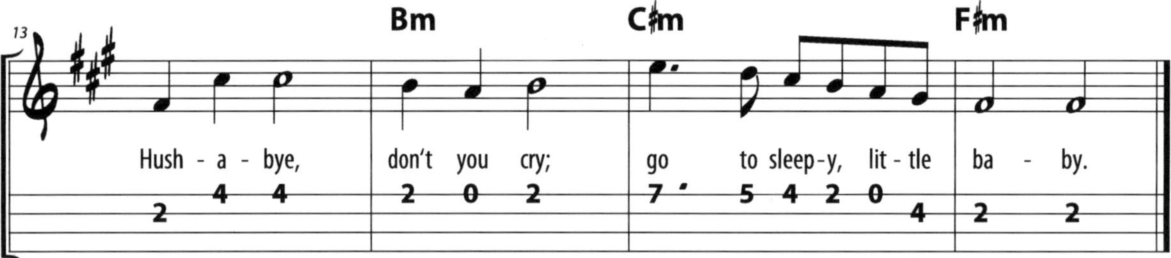

2. *Hush-a-bye, don't you cry; go to sleepy, little baby.*
   When you wake you shall have all the pretty little horses.
   Paint and Bay, sorrel and gray, all the pretty little ponies.
   Hush-a-bye, don't you cry; go to sleepy, little baby.

3. *Hush-a-bye, don't you cry; go to sleepy, little baby.*
   When you wake you shall have all the pretty little horses.
   Way down under the meadow lies a poor little lambie.
   Hush-a-bye, don't you cry; go to sleepy, little baby.

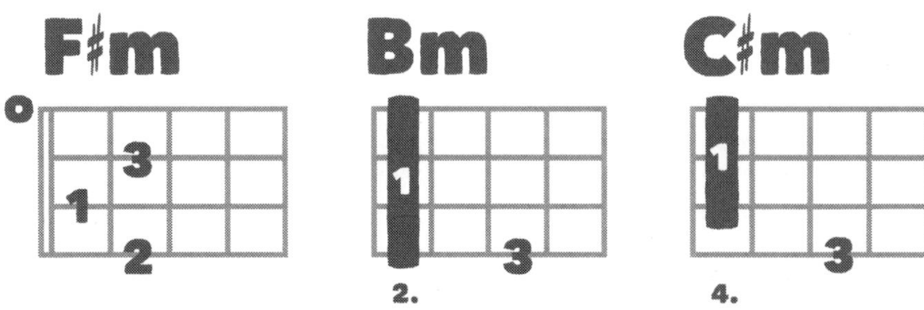

Mary, Mary

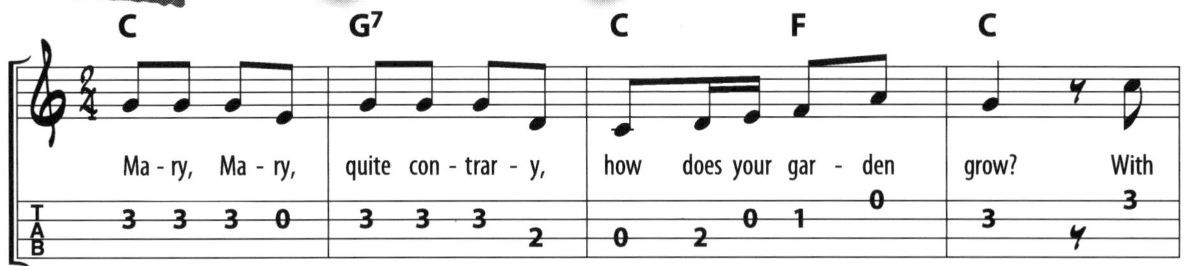
C
G7
C
F
C
Ma - ry, Ma - ry, quite con - trar - y, how does your gar - den grow? With
3 3 3 0 3 3 3 2 0 2 0 1 0 3 3

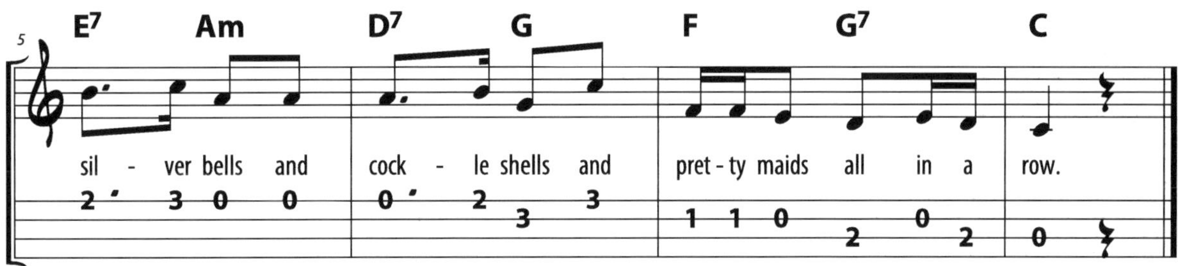
E7
Am
D7
G
F
G7
C
sil - ver bells and cock - le shells and pret - ty maids all in a row.
2 3 0 0 0 2 3 3 1 1 0 2 0 2 0

C
G7
F
E7

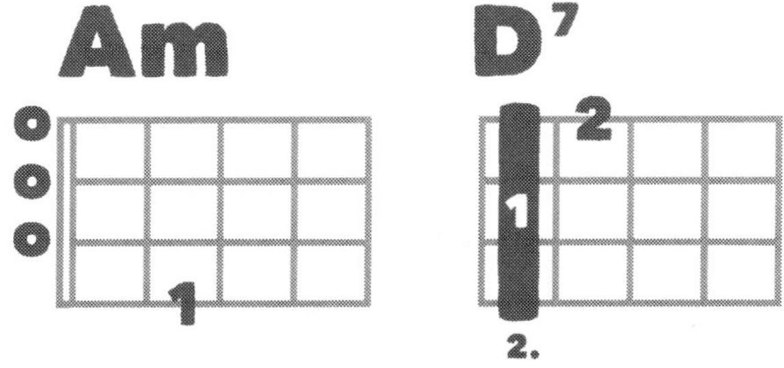
Am
D7
2.

Polly put the kettle on

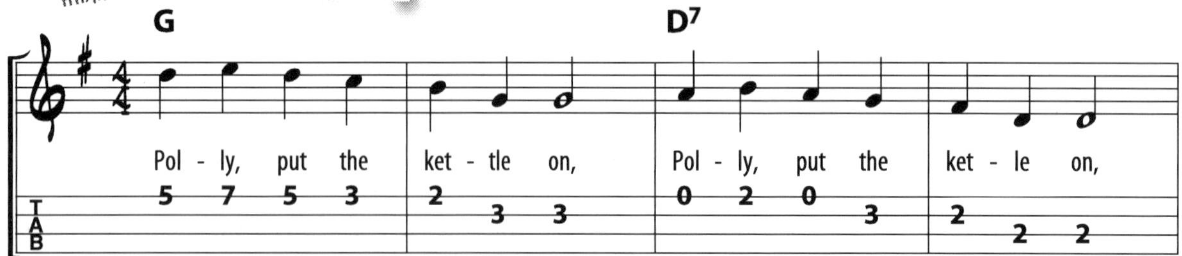

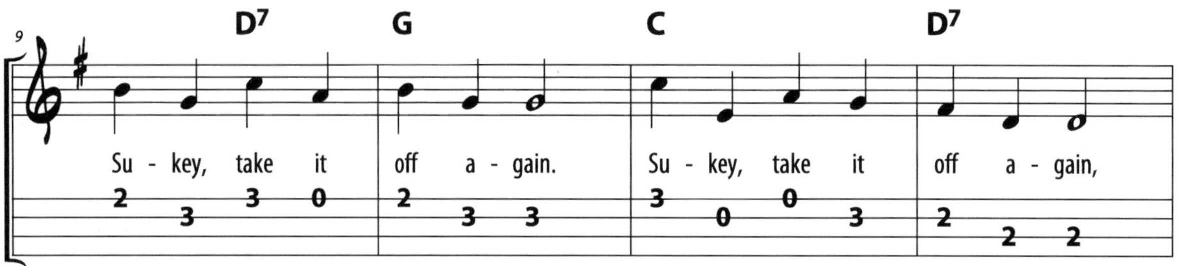

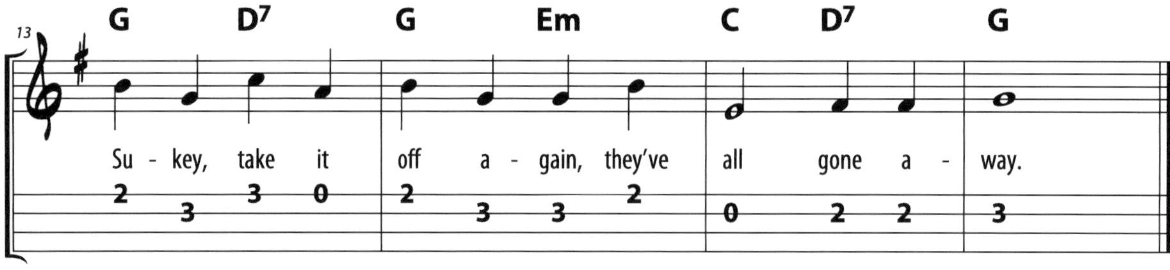

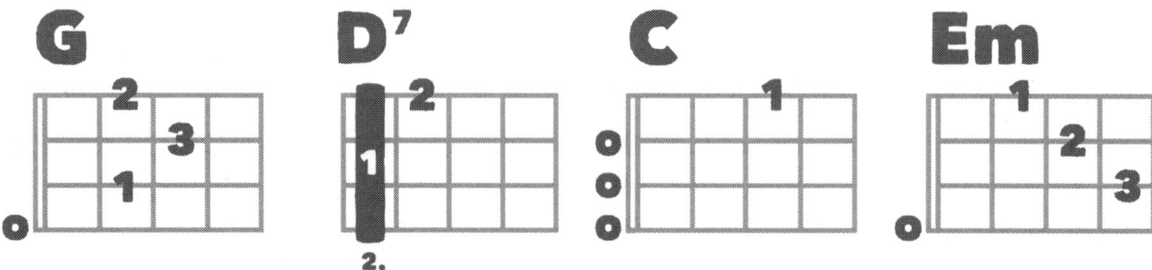

Away in a manger

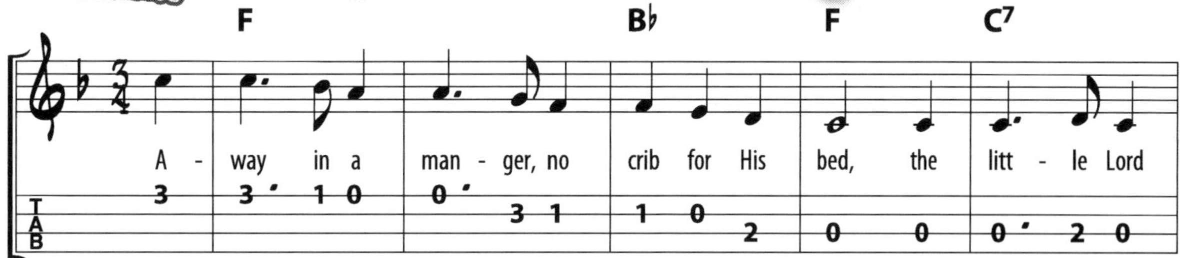
F
B♭
F
C7
A - way in a man - ger, no crib for His bed, the litt - le Lord
3 3 1 0 0 3 1 1 0 2 0 0 0 2 0

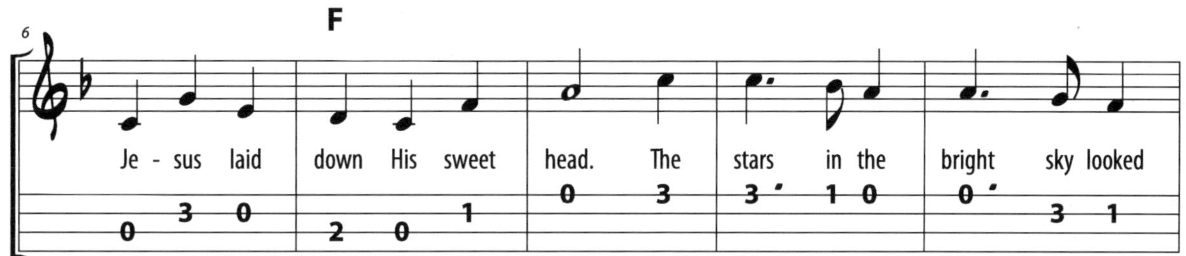
6
F
Je - sus laid down His sweet head. The stars in the bright sky looked
0 3 0 2 0 1 0 3 3 1 0 0 3 1

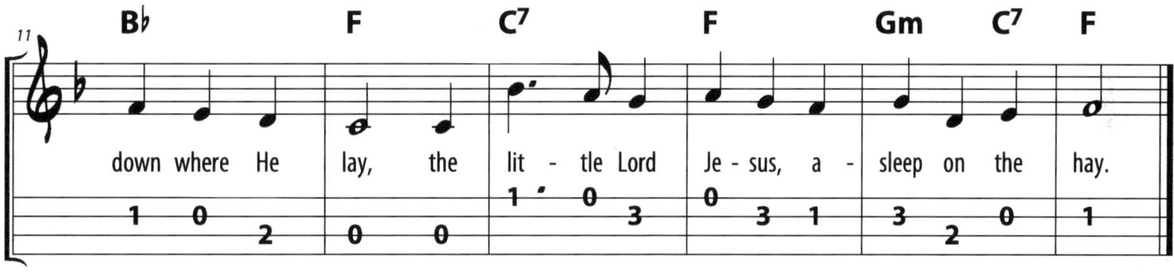
11
B♭
F
C7
F
Gm
C7
F
down where He lay, the lit - tle Lord Je - sus, a - sleep on the hay.
1 0 2 0 0 1 0 3 0 3 1 3 2 0 1

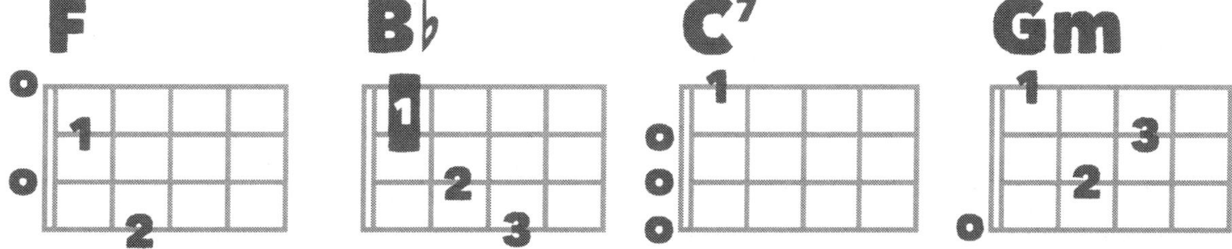
F
B♭
C7
Gm

Good King Wenceslas

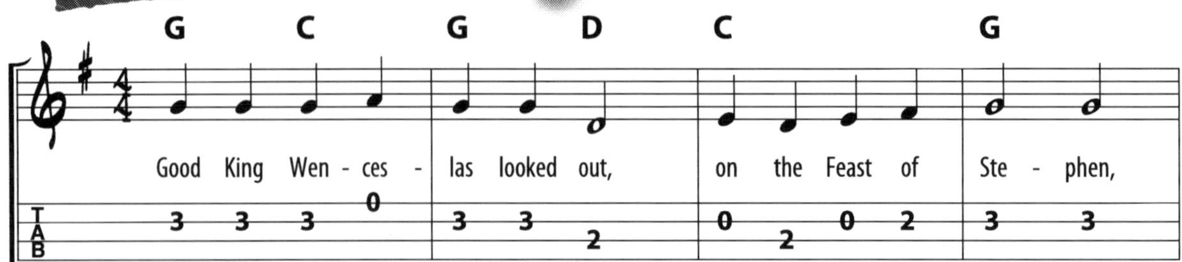

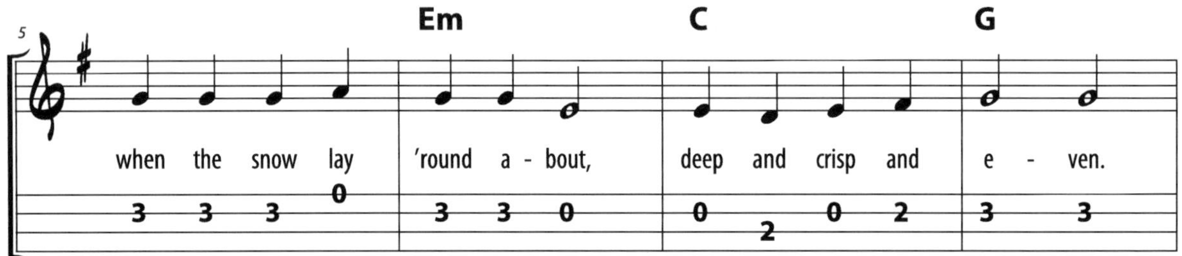

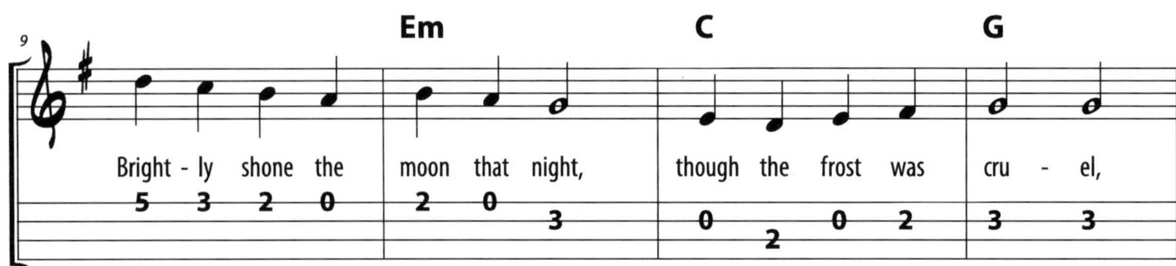

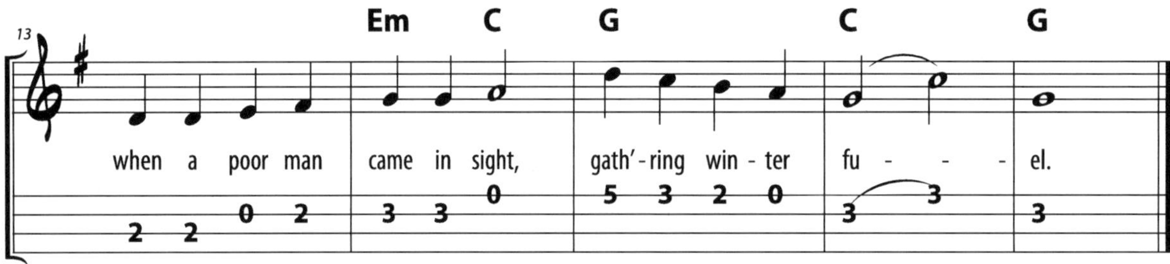

2. "Hither, page, and stand by me, if thou know'st it, telling;
Yonder peasant, who is he? Where and what his dwelling?"
"Sire, he lives a good league hence, underneath the mountain;
Right against the forest fence, by Saint Agnes' fountain."

3. "Bring me flesh, and bring me wine, bring me pine logs hither:
Thou and I shall see him dine, when we bear them thither."
Page and monarch, forth they went, forth they went together;
Through the rude wind's wild lament and the bitter weather.

4. "Sire, the night is darker now, and the wind blows stronger;
Fails my heart, I know not how; I can go no longer."
"Mark my footsteps, good my page. Tread thou in them boldly
Thou shalt find the winter's rage freeze thy blood less coldly."

5. In his master's steps he trod, where the snow lay dinted;
Heat was in the very sod which the saint had printed.
Therefore, Christian men, be sure, wealth or rank possessing,
Ye who now will bless the poor, shall yourselves find blessing.

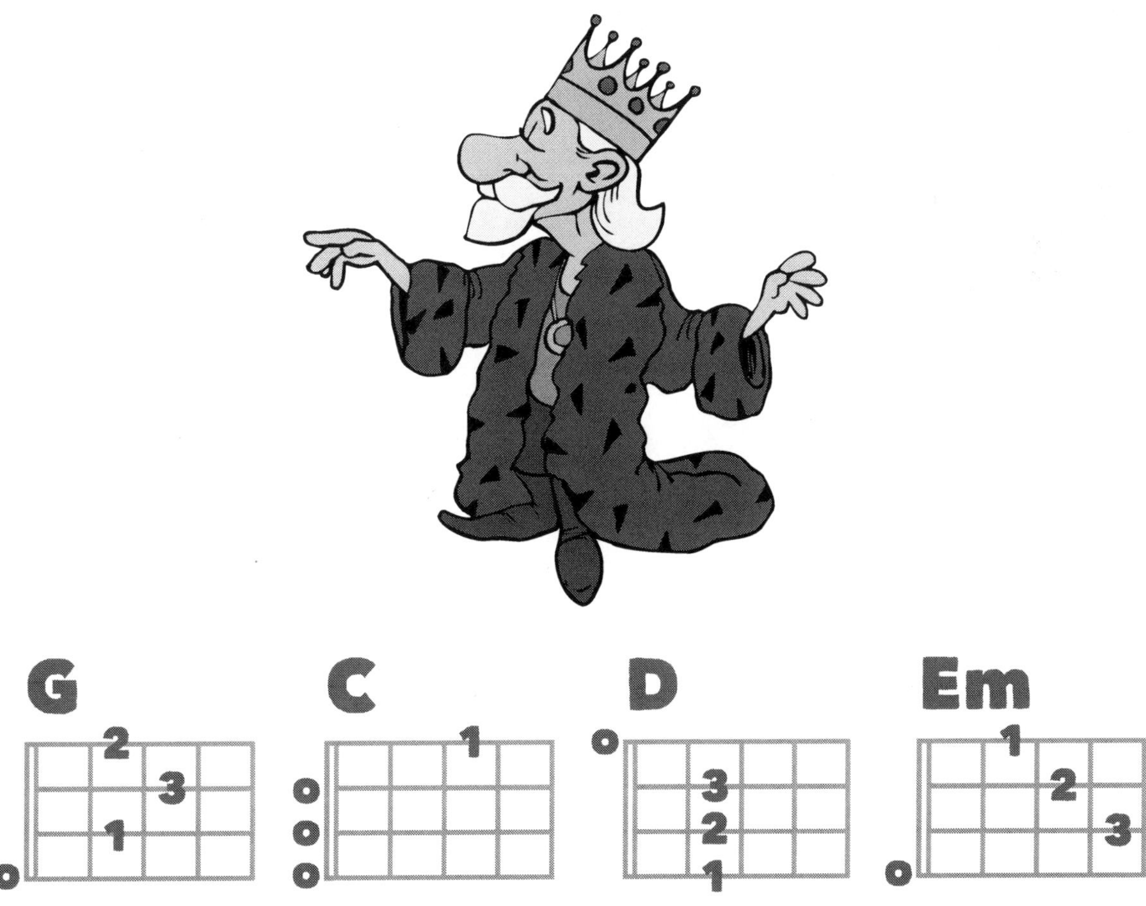

ark! The herald angels sing

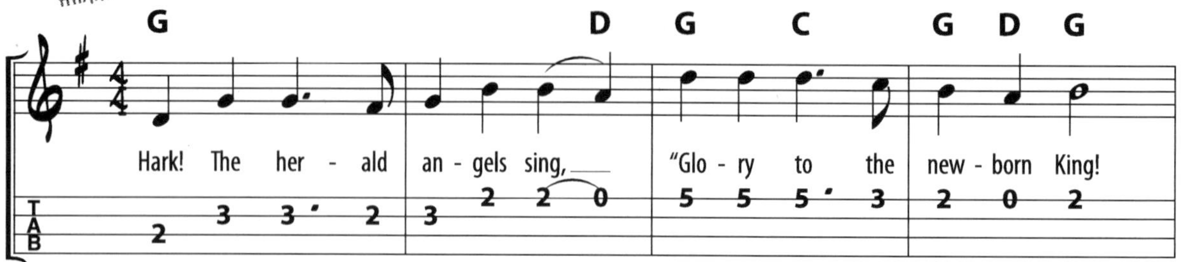

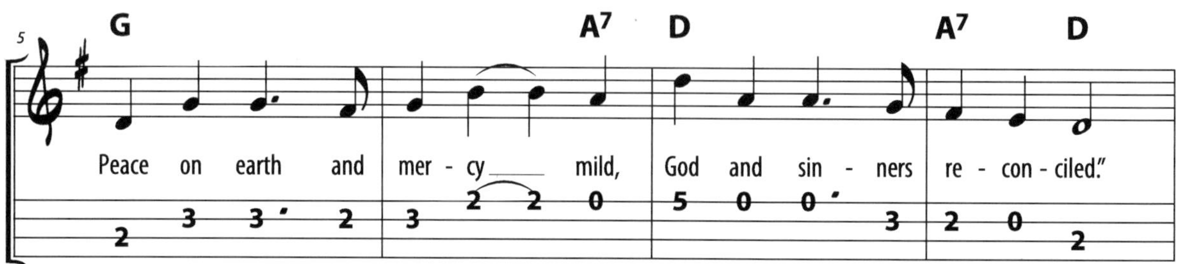

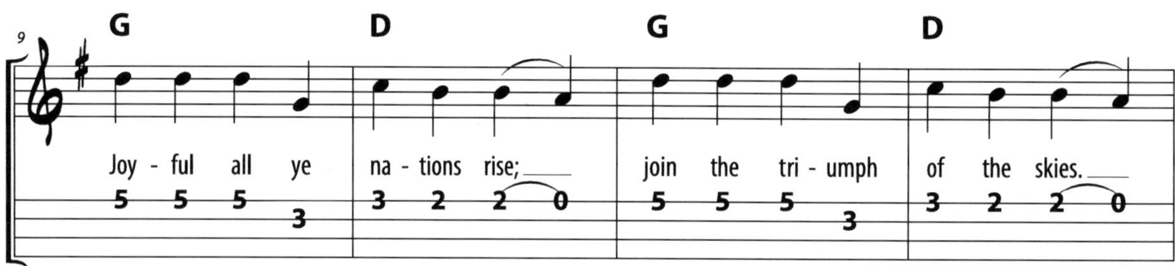

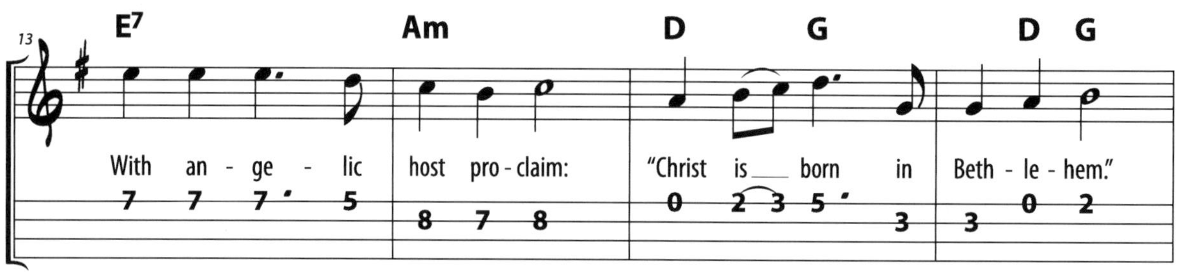

2. *Christ by highest heav'n adored,*
Christ the everlasting Lord!
Late in time behold Him come,
Offspring of a Virgin's womb.
Veiled in flesh the Godhead see
Hail the incarnate Deity!
Pleased as man with man to dwell,
Jesus, our Emmanuel.
Hark! The herald angels sing
"Glory to the newborn King!"

3. *Hail the heav'n-born Prince of Peace!*
Hail the Son of Righteousness!
Light and life to all He brings,
Ris'n with healing in His wings.
Mild He lays His glory by
Born that man no more may die.
Born to raise the sons of earth,
Born to give them second birth.
Hark! The herald angels sing
"Glory to the newborn King!"

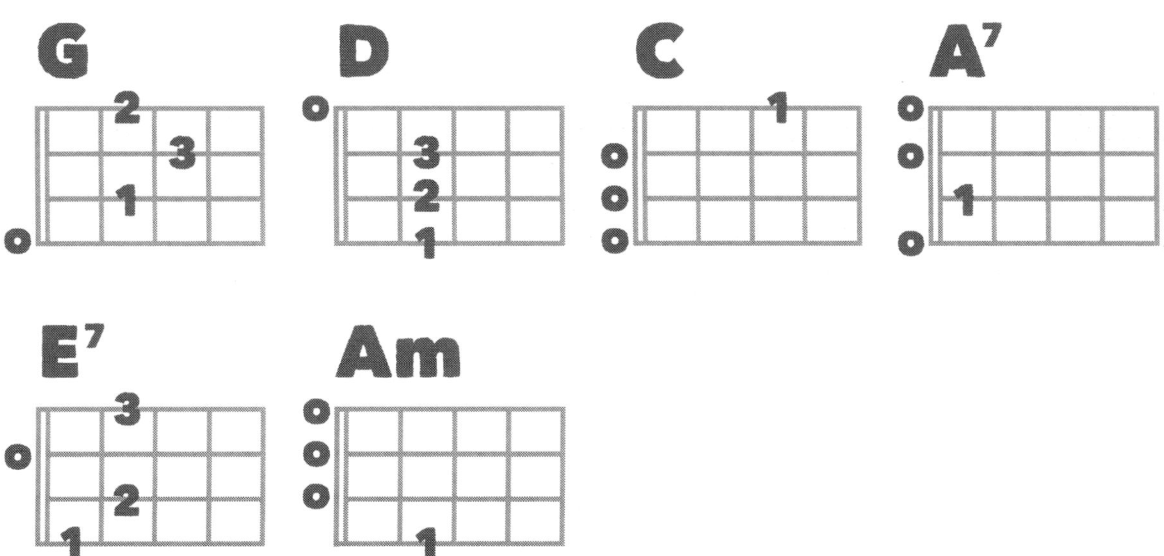

O holy night

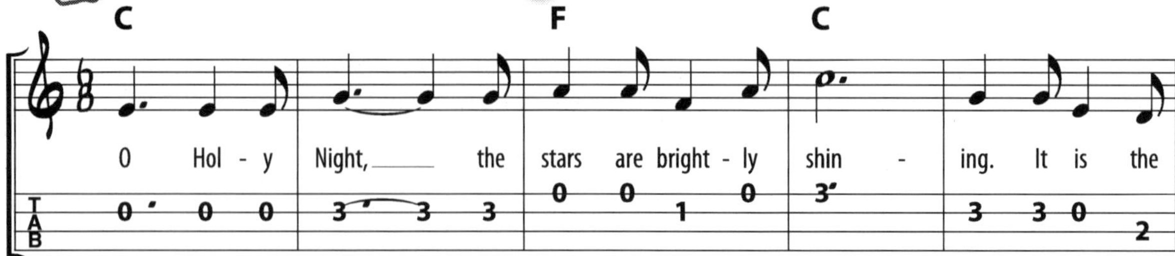
C F C
O Hol - y Night, the stars are bright - ly shin - ing. It is the

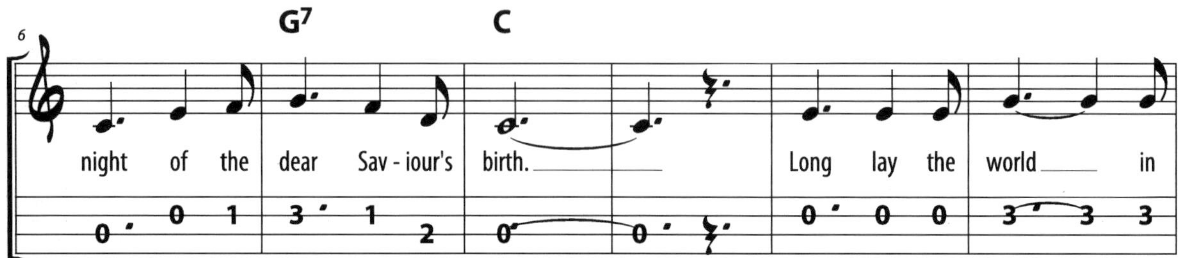
G7 C
night of the dear Sav - iour's birth. Long lay the world in

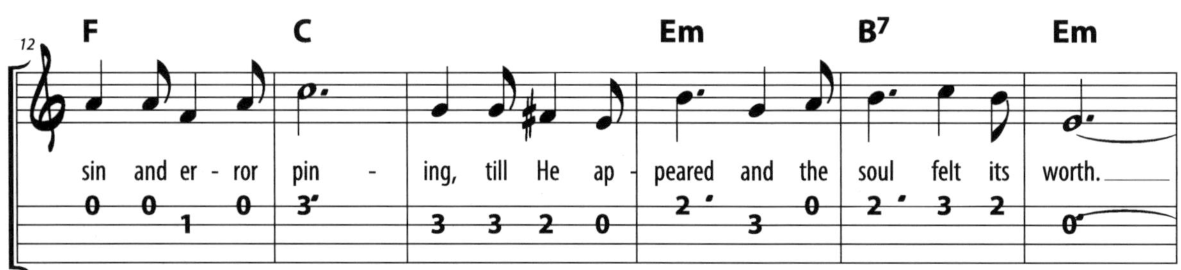
F C Em B7 Em
sin and er - ror pin - ing, till He ap - peared and the soul felt its worth.

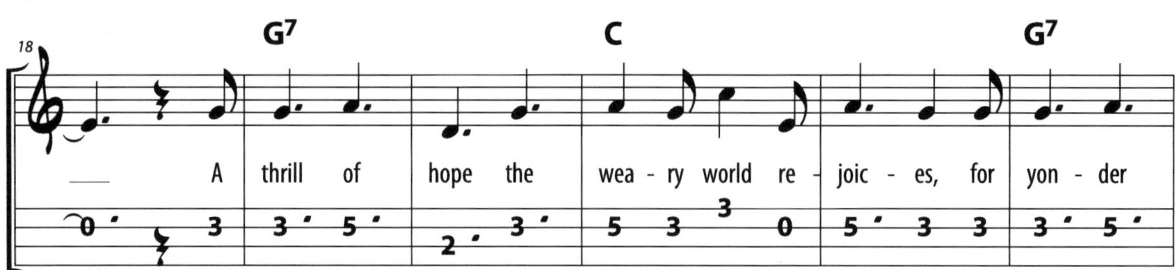
G7 C G7
A thrill of hope the wea - ry world re - joic - es, for yon - der

C Am Em
breaks a new and glo - rious morn. Fall on your knees!

Dm Am C G7 C
O, hear the an - gel voic - es! O night di - vine,

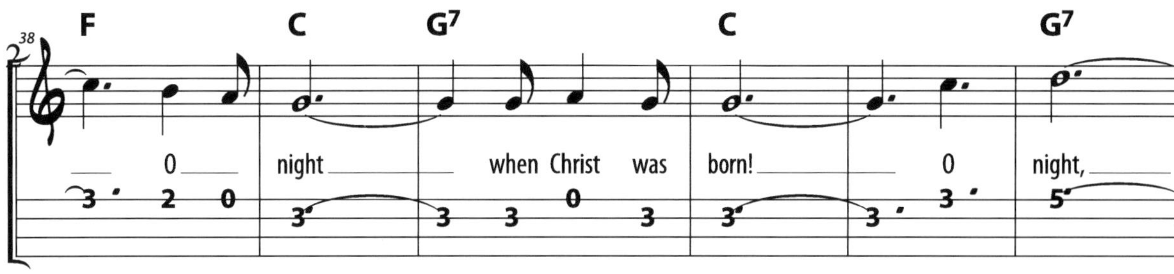

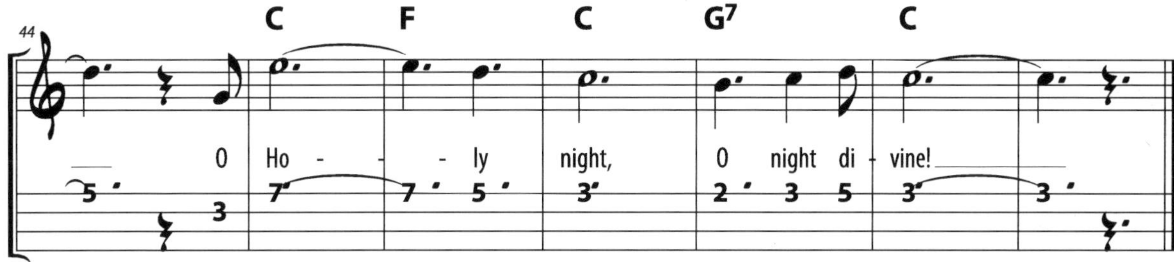

2. *Led by the light of faith serenely beaming,*
   with glowing hearts by His cradle we stand.
   O'er the world a star is sweetly gleaming,
   now come the wisemen from out of the Orient land.
   The King of kings lay thus lowly manger;
   In all our trials born to be our friends.
   He knows our need, our weakness is no stranger,
   behold your King! Before him lowly bend!

3. *Truly He taught us to love one another,*
   His law is love and His gospel is peace.
   Chains he shall break, for the slave is our brother.
   And in his name all oppression shall cease.
   Sweet hymns of joy in grateful chorus raise we,
   with all our hearts we praise His holy name.
   Christ is the Lord! Then ever, ever praise we,
   His power and glory ever more proclaim!

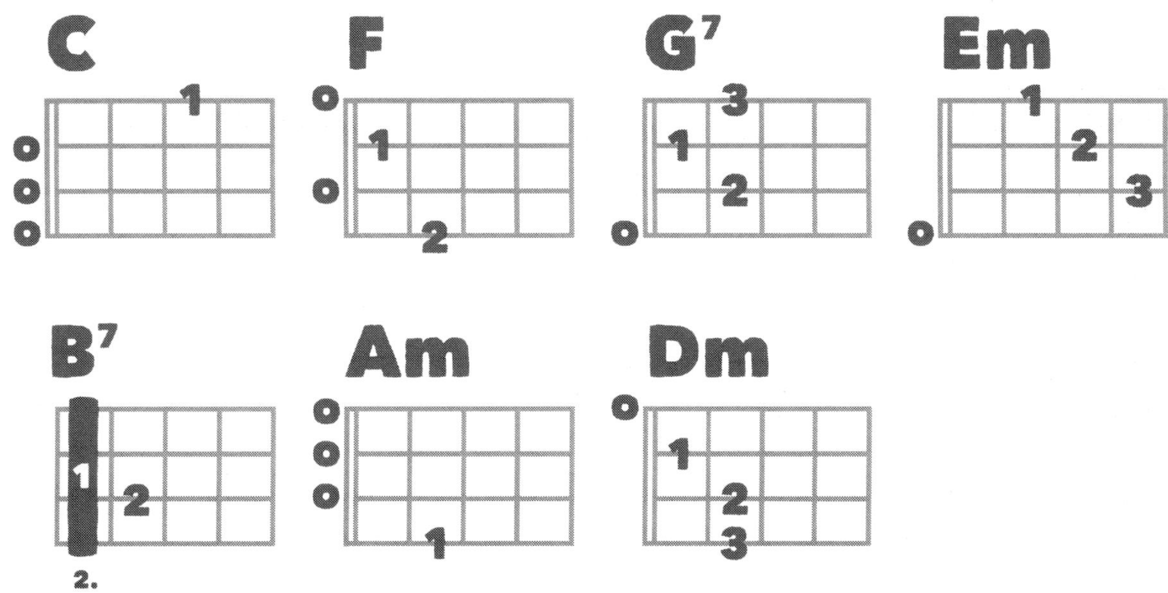

Toyland

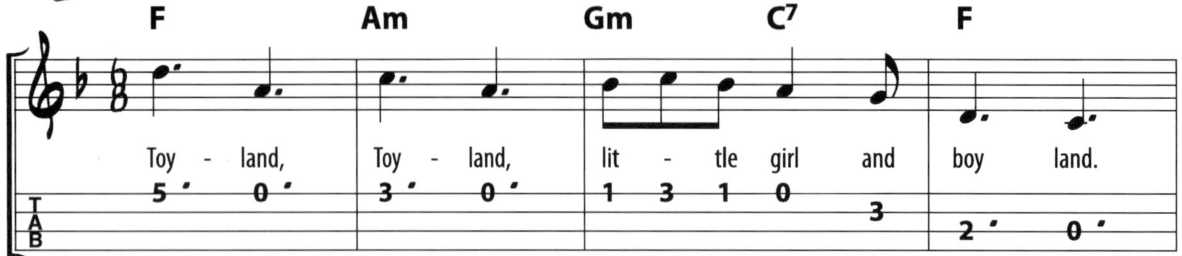
F Am Gm C7 F
Toy - land, Toy - land, lit - tle girl and boy land.
T
A
B

5
B♭ B♭m F Dm G7 C7
While you dwell with - in it, you are ev - er hap - py there!

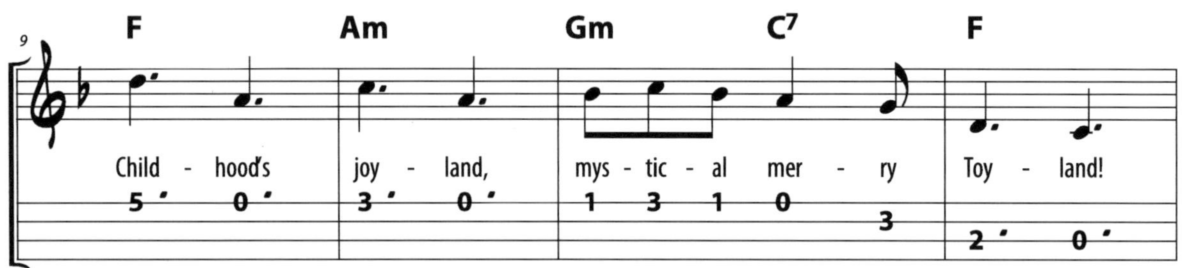
9
F Am Gm C7 F
Child - hood's joy - land, mys - tic - al mer - ry Toy - land!

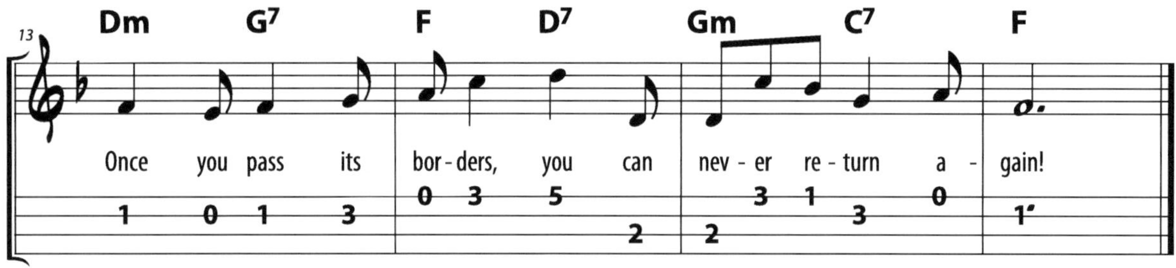
13
Dm G7 F D7 Gm C7 F
Once you pass its bor - ders, you can nev - er re - turn a - gain!

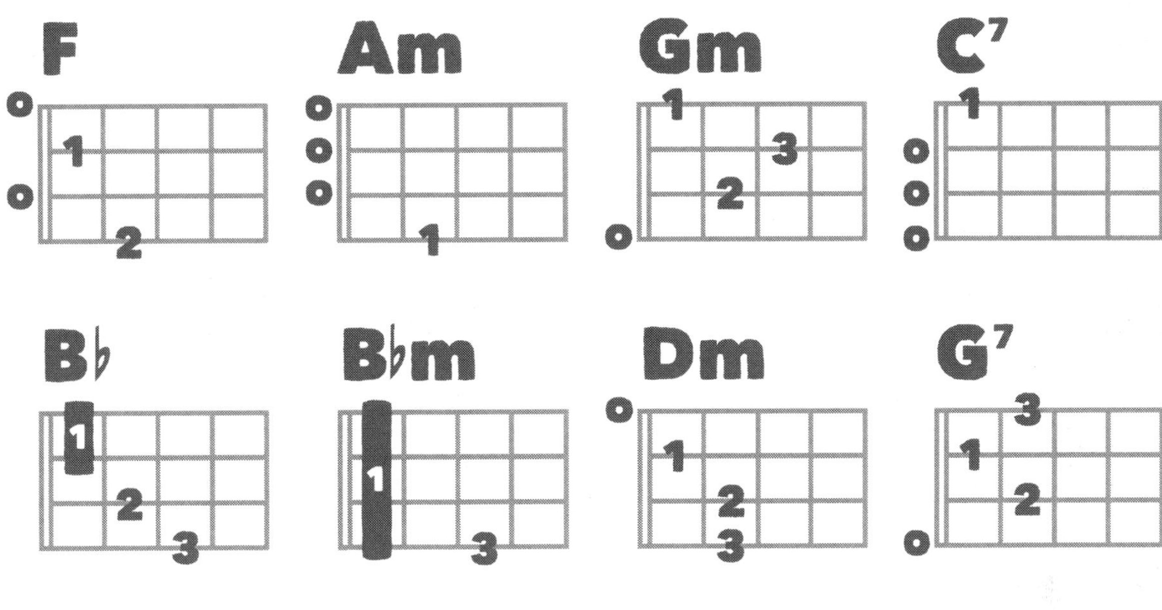

D7

2.

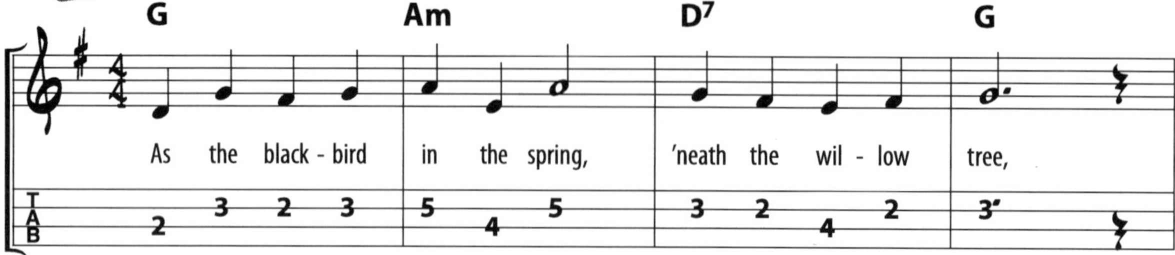

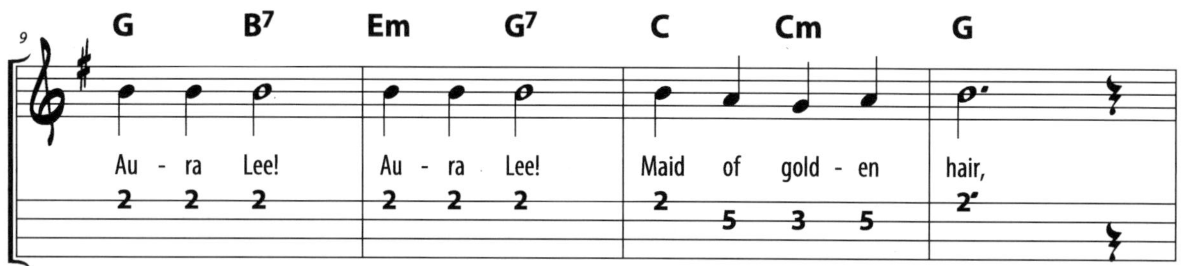

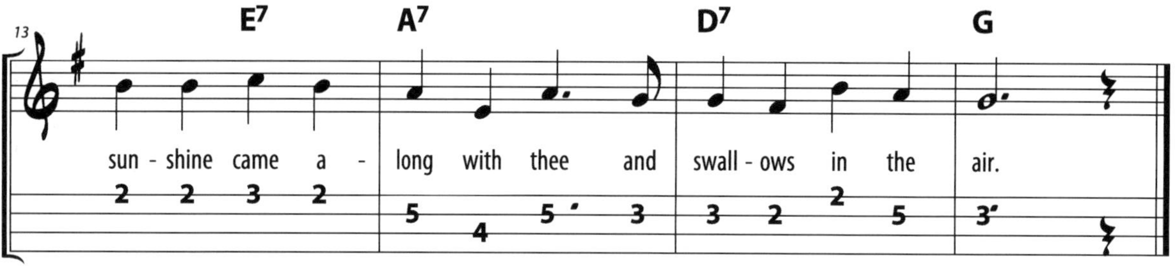

2. *In thy blush the rose was born,*
   music, when you spake.
   Through thine azure eye the morn,
   sparkling seemed to break.
   Aura Lea, Aura Lea,
   birds of crimson wing,
   never song have sung to me,
   as in that sweet spring.
   Aura Lee! Aura Lee! ...

3. *Aura Lea! The bird may flee,*
   the willow's golden hair
   swing through winter fitfully,
   on the stormy air.
   Yet if thy blue eyes I see,
   gloom will soon depart;
   For to me, sweet Aura Lea
   is sunshine through the heart.
   Aura Lee! Aura Lee! ...

4. *When the mistletoe was green,*
Midst the winter's snows,
Sunshine in thy face was seen,
Kissing lips of rose.
Aura Lea, Aura Lea,
Take my golden ring;
Love and light return with thee,
And swallows with the spring.
Aura Lee! Aura Lee! ...

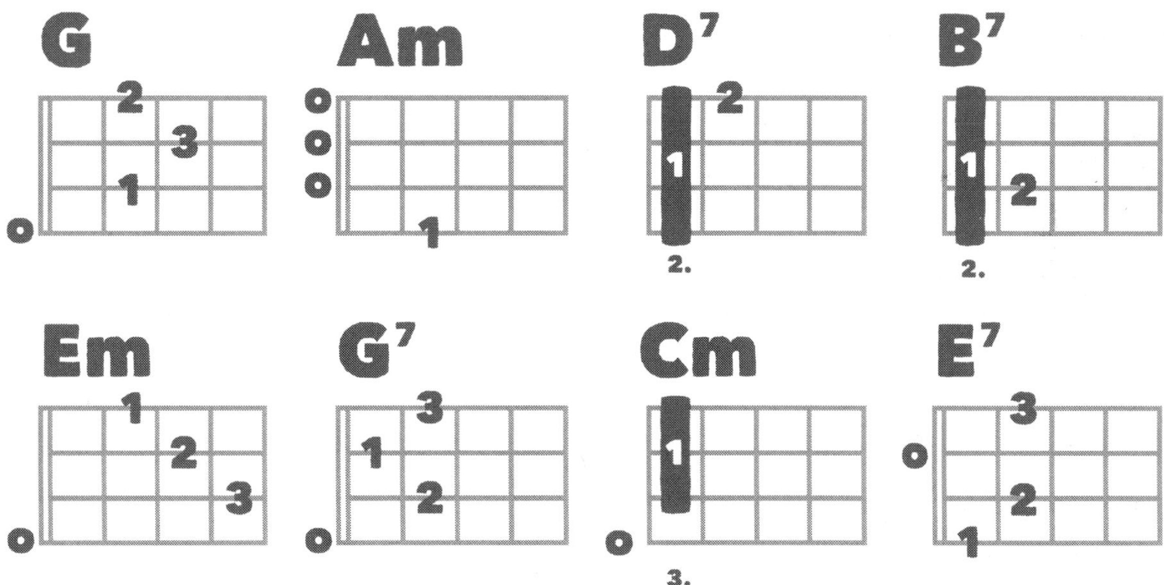

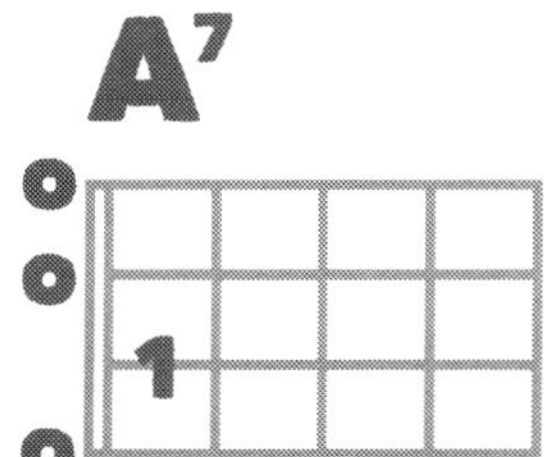

Down by the station

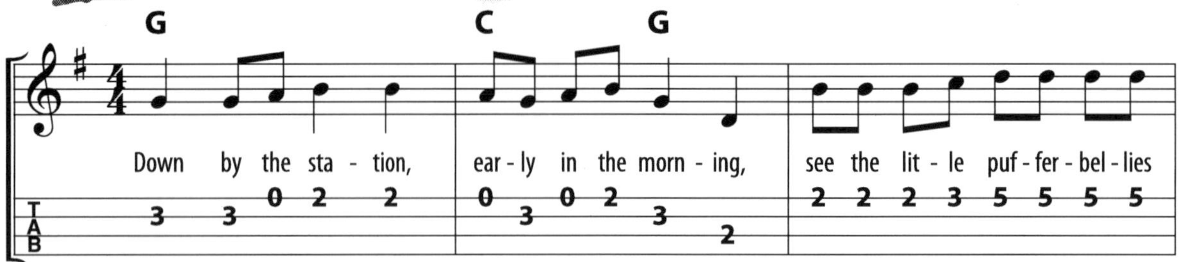

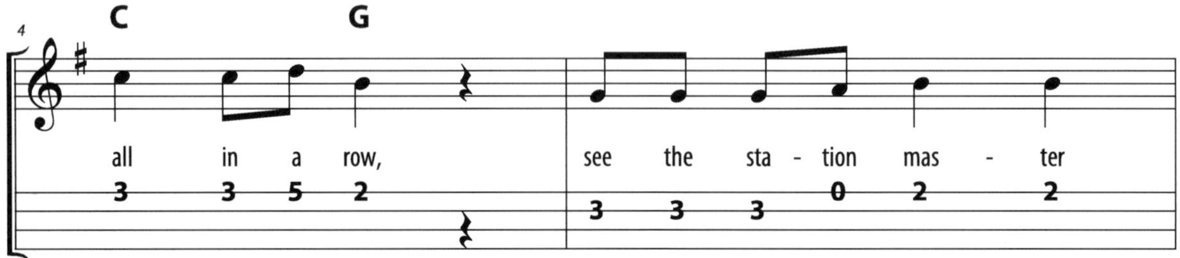

e's got the whole world in his hands

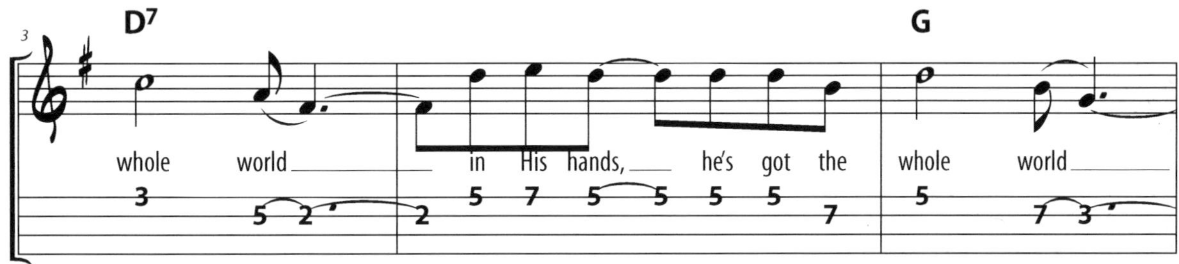

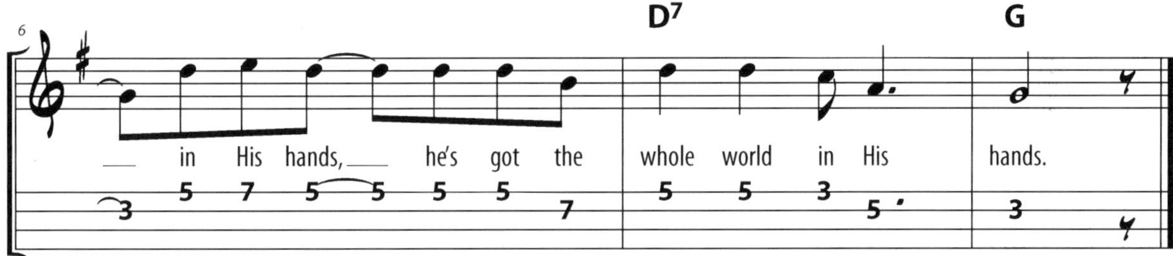

2. *He's got the tiny little baby in his hands.*
3. *He's got you and me brother in his hands.*
4. *He's got the son and the father in his hands.*
5. *He's got the mother and her daughter in his hands.*
6. *He's got everybody here in his hands.*
7. *He's got the sun and the moon in his hands.*
8. *He's got the whole world in his hands.*

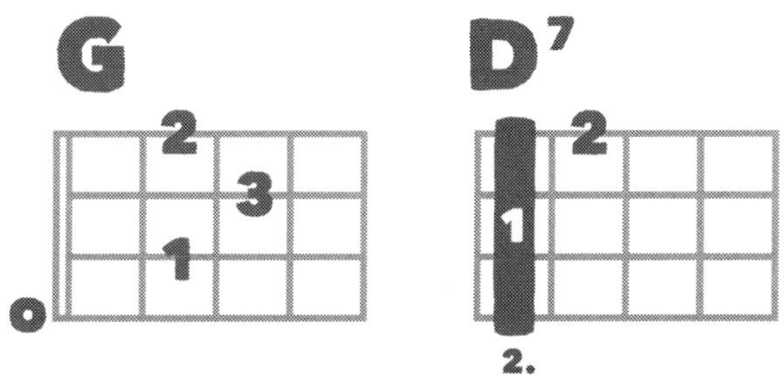

Joshua fit the battle of Jericho

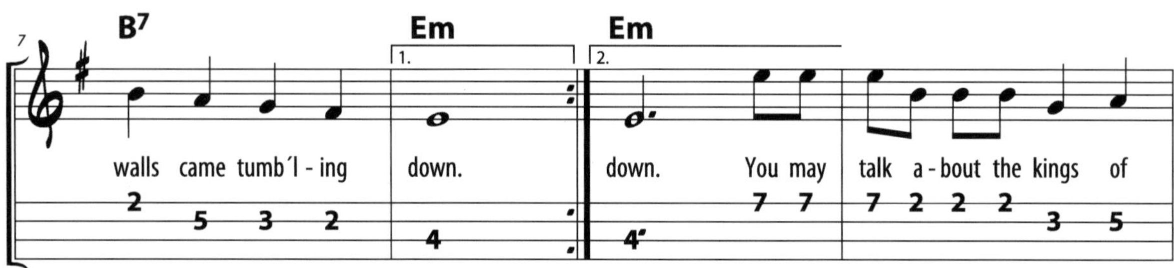

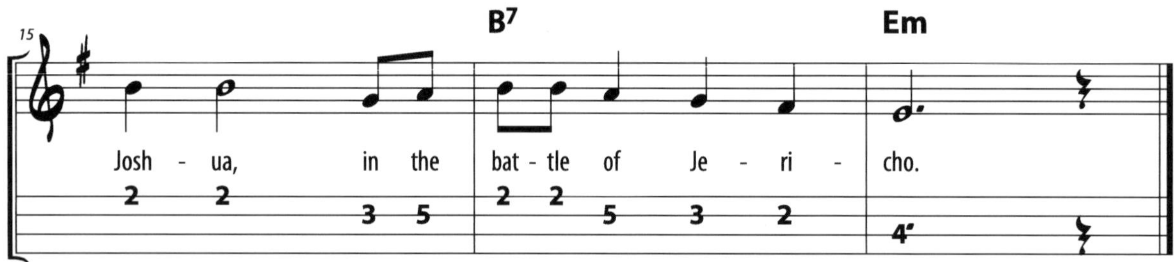

2. *Right up to the walls of Jericho,*
he marched with spear in Hand.
Go, blow dat ram's horn, Joshua cried,
'cause de battle am in my hand.

3. *Then de lamb ram sheep horns begin a blow.*
Trumpets begin to sound.
Joshua commanded de children to shout,
and de walls came tumbling down.

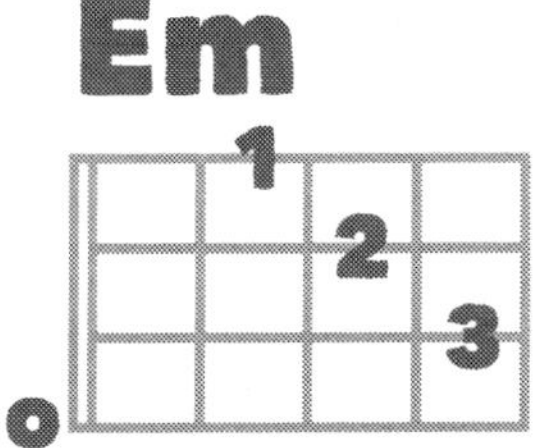

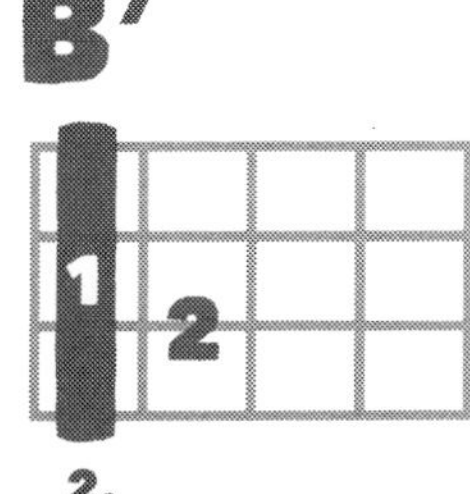

ittle brown jug

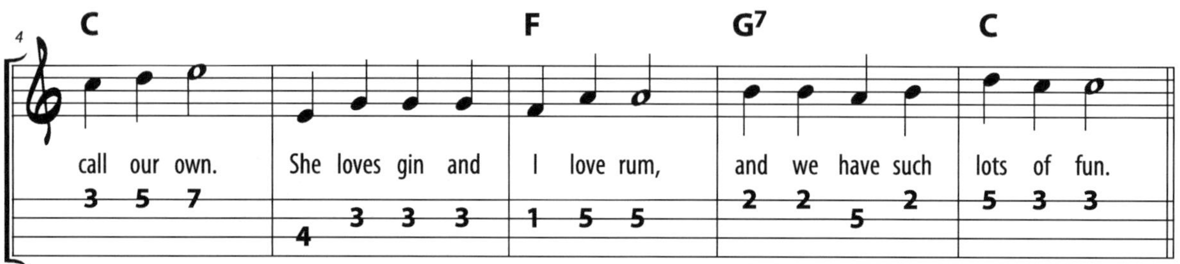

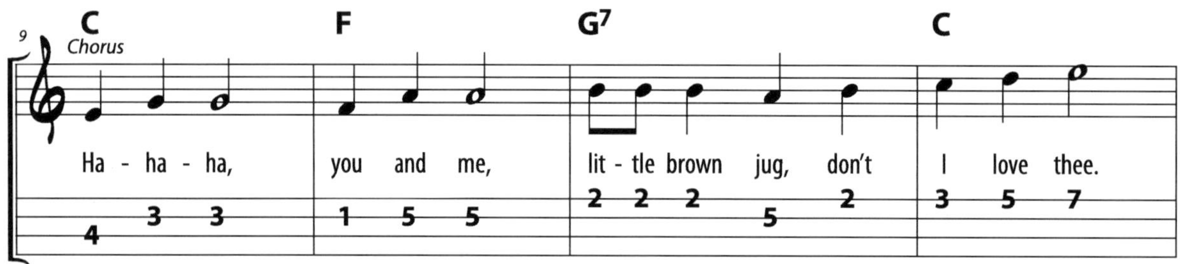

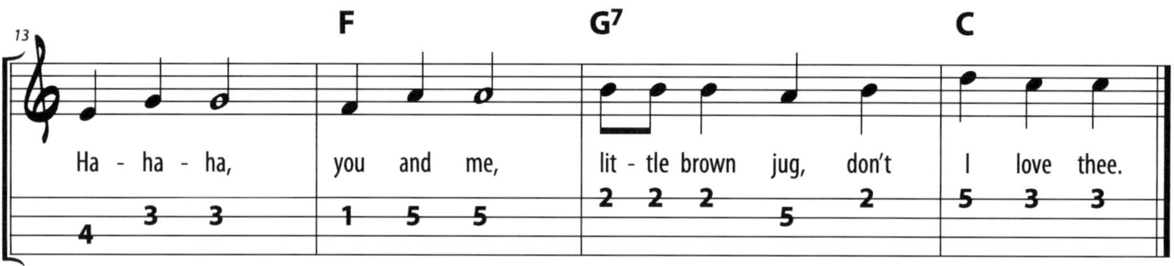

2. When I go toiling on the farm
I take the little jug under my arm;
Place it under a shady tree,
Little brown jug, 'tis you and me.

3. 'Tis you that makes me friends and foes,
'Tis you that makes me wear old clothes;
But, seeing you're so near my nose,
Tip her up and down she goes.

4. If all the folks in Adam's race
Were gathered together in one place,
I'd let them go without a tear
Before I'd part from you, my dear.

5. If I'd a cow that gave such milk,
I'd dress her in the finest silk;
Feed her up on oats and hay,
And milk her twenty times a day.

6. I bought a cow from Farmer Jones,
And she was nothing but skin and bones;
I fed her up as fine as silk,
She jumped the fence and strained her milk.

7. And when I die don't bury me at all,
Just pickle my bones in alcohol;
Put a bottle o' booze at my head and feet
And then I know that I will keep.

8. The rose is red, my nose is too,
The violet's blue and so are you;
And yet, I guess, before I stop,
We'd better take another drop.

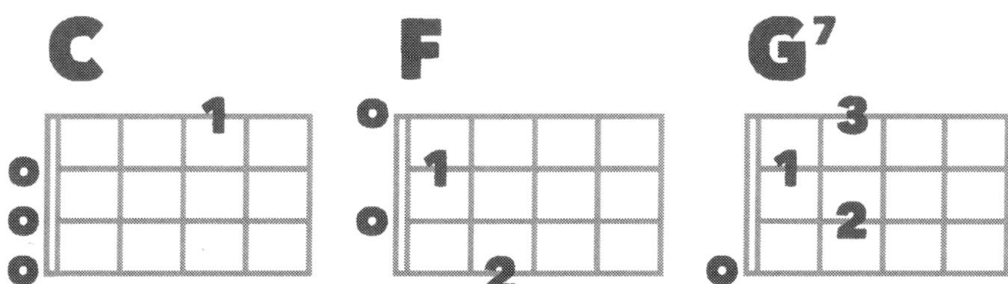

Alouette

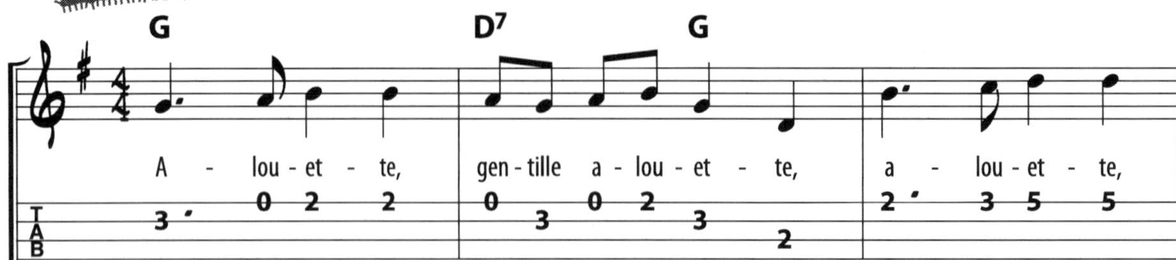
G
D7
G
A - lou - et - te,
gen - tille a - lou - et - te,
a - lou - et - te,

D7
G
D7
G
je te plu - me - rai.
Je te plu - me - rai la tête,
je te plu - me - rai la tête.

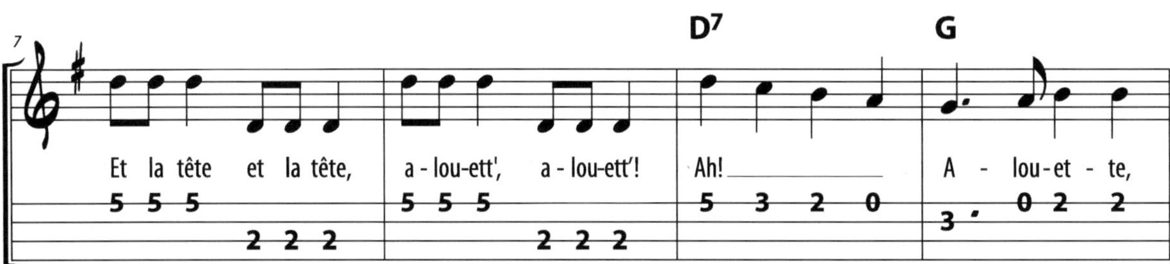
D7
G
Et la tête et la tête,
a - lou-ett', a - lou-ett'!
Ah!
A - lou - et - te,

D7
G
D7
G
gen - tille a - lou - et - te,
a - lou - et - te,
je te plu - me - rai.

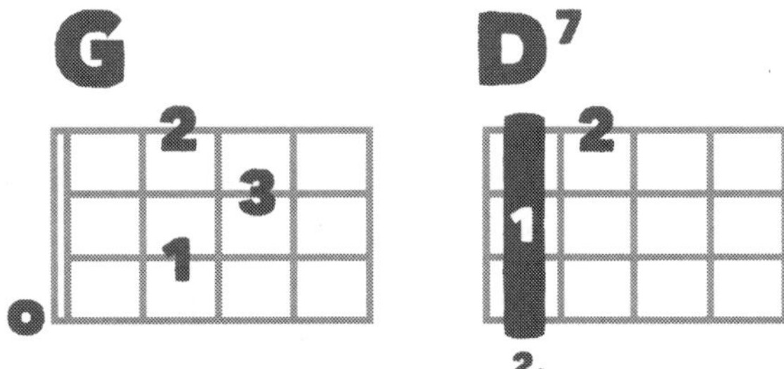
G
D7

ichael, row the boat ashore

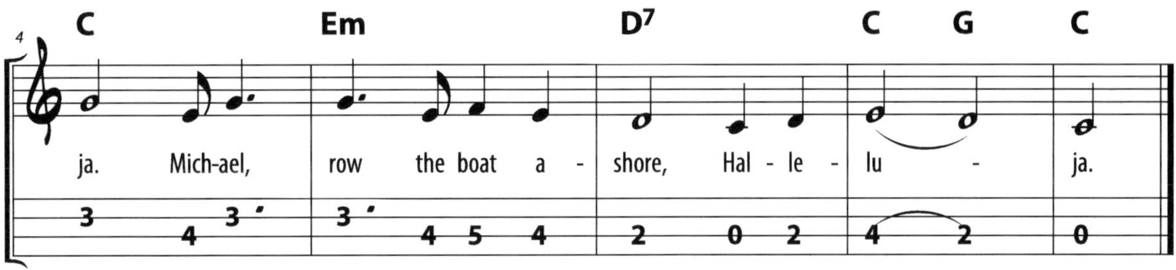

2. *Michael boat a gospelboat, Halleluja ...*
3. *Brother lend a helping hand, Halleluja ...*
4. *Sister help to trim the sail, Halleluja ...*
5. *Boasting talk will sink your soul, Halleluja ...*
6. *Jordan-stream is deep and wide, Halleluja ...*
7. *Jesus stand on the other side, Halleluja ...*

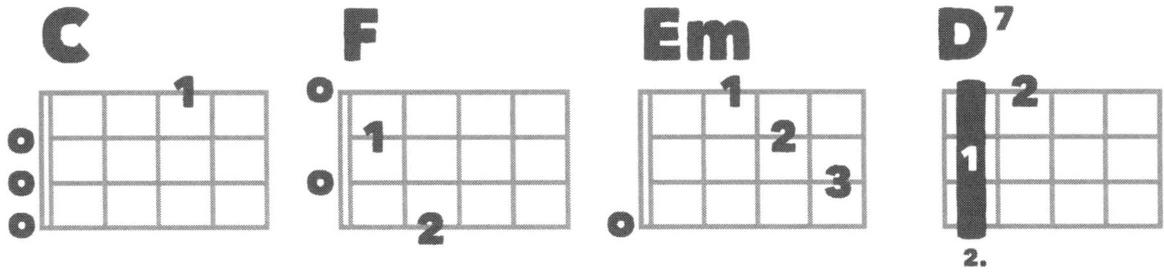

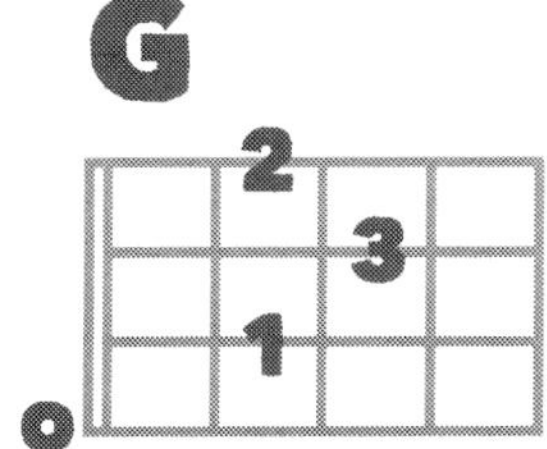

Scarborough Fair

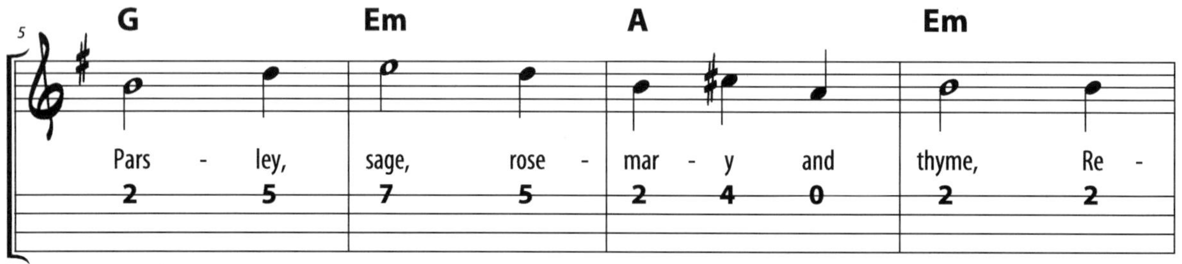

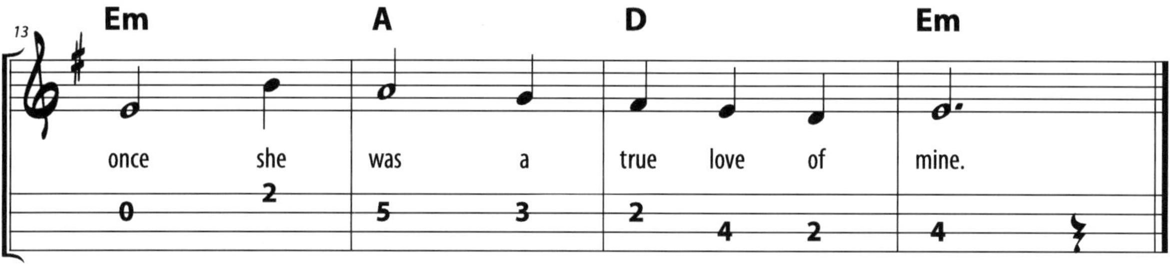

Tell her to make me a cambric shirt,
Parsley, sage, rosemary, and thyme;
Without a seam or needlework,
Then she shall be a true lover of mine.

Tell her to wash it in yonder well,
Parsley, sage, rosemary, and thyme;
Where never spring water or rain ever fell,
And she shall be a true lover of mine.

Tell her to dry it on yonder thorn,
Parsley, sage, rosemary, and thyme;
Which never bore blossom since Adam was born,
Then she shall be a true lover of mine.

Now he has asked me questions three,
Parsley, sage, rosemary, and thyme;
I hope he'll answer as many for me
Before he shall be a true lover of mine.

Tell him to buy me an acre of land,
Parsley, sage, rosemary, and thyme;
Between the salt water and the sea sand,
Then he shall be a true lover of mine.

Tell him to plough it with a ram's horn,
Parsley, sage, rosemary, and thyme;
And sow it all over with one pepper corn,
And he shall be a true lover of mine.

Tell him to sheer't with a sickle of leather,
Parsley, sage, rosemary, and thyme;
And bind it up with a peacock feather.
And he shall be a true lover of mine.

Tell him to thrash it on yonder wall,
Parsley, sage, rosemary, and thyme,
And never let one corn of it fall,
Then he shall be a true lover of mine.

When he has done and finished his work.
Parsley, sage, rosemary, and thyme:
Oh, tell him to come and he'll have his shirt,
And he shall be a true lover of mine.

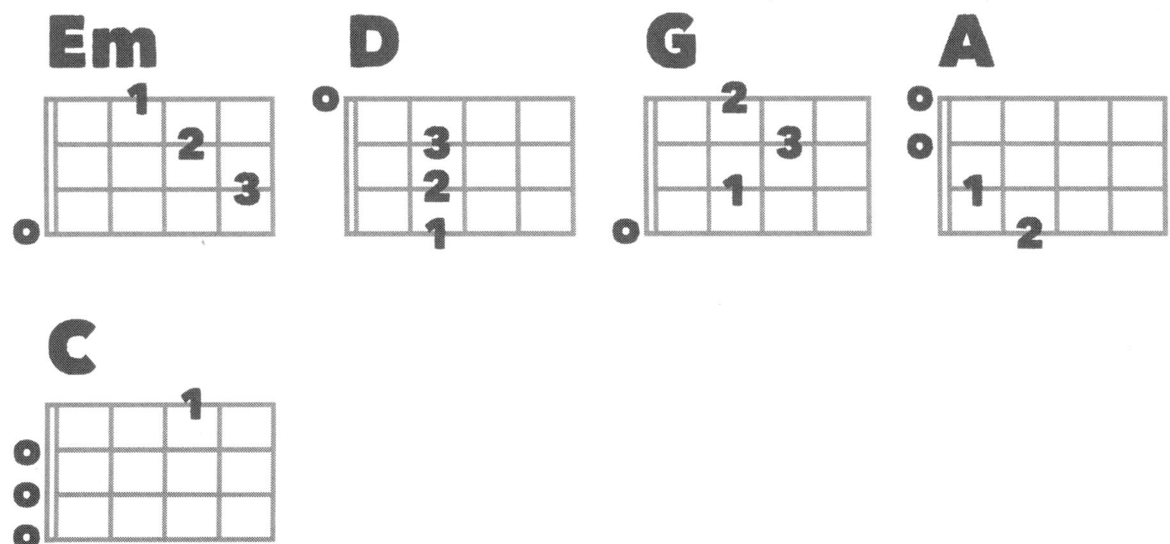

There was an old woman

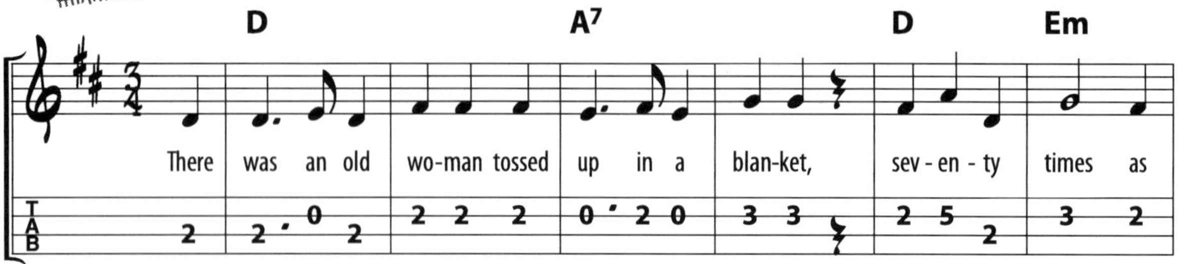

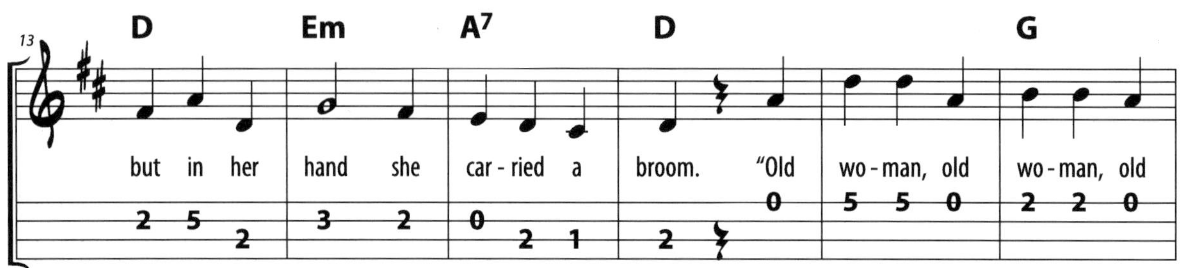

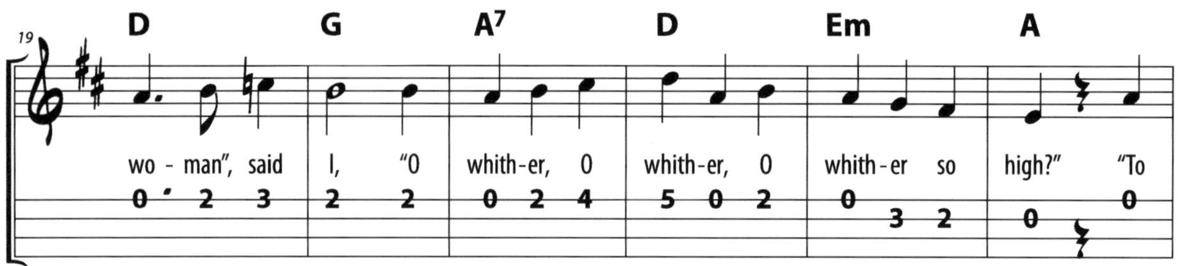

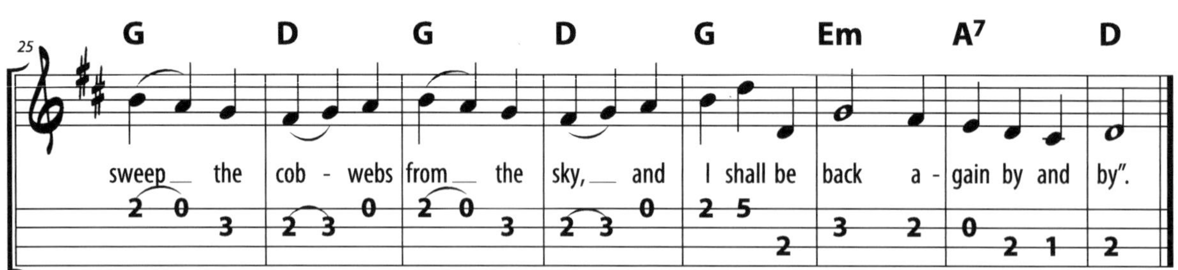

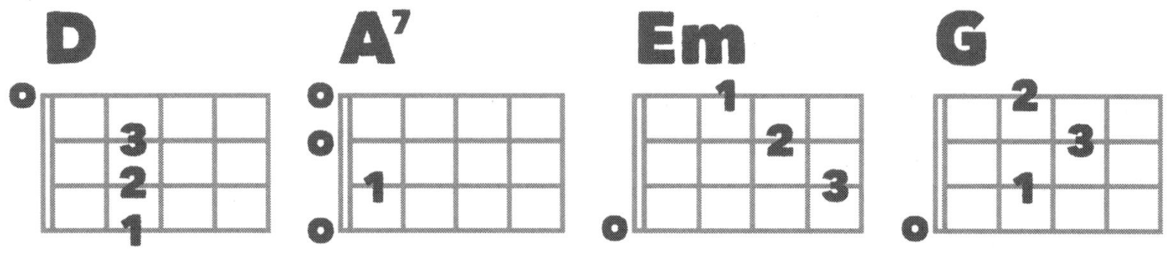

Do your ears hang low?

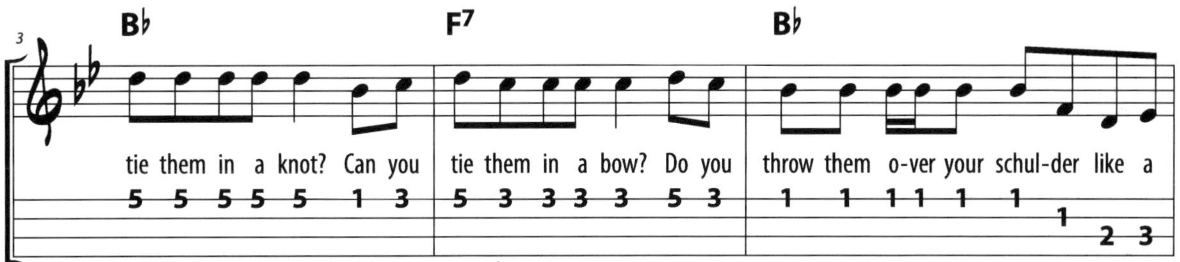

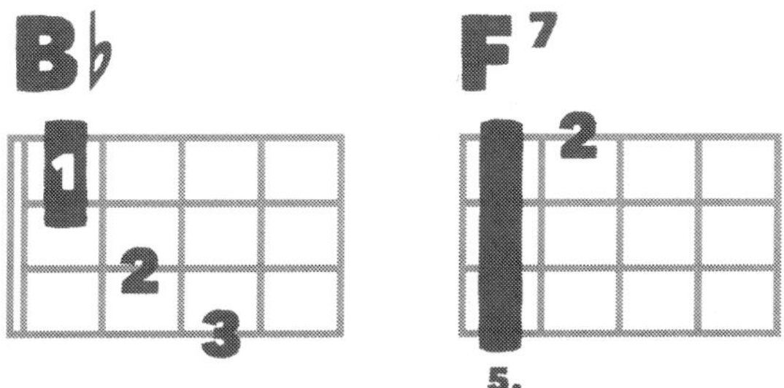

The riddle song

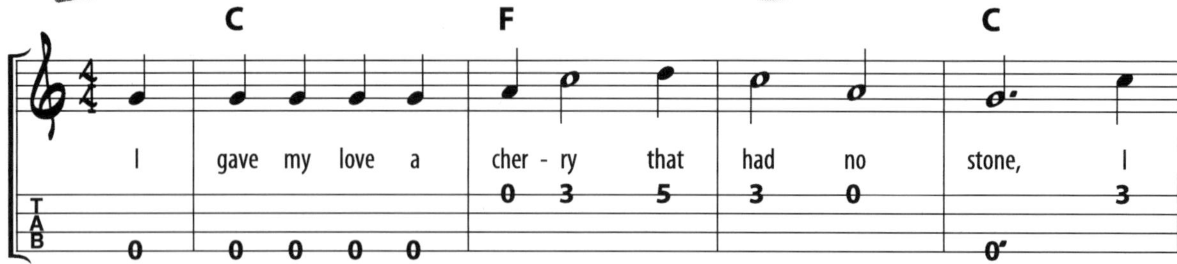

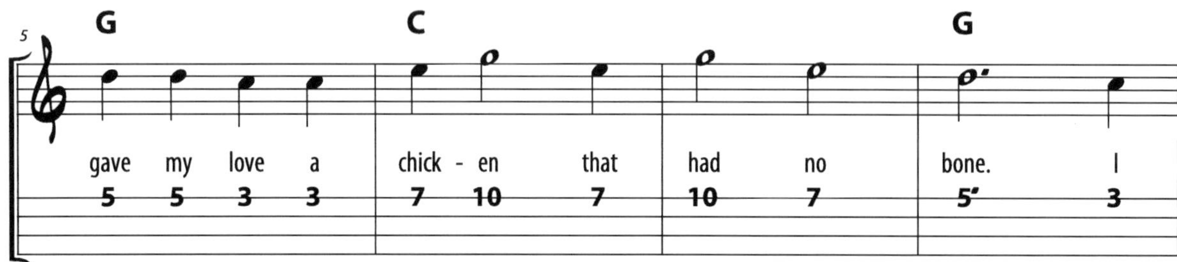

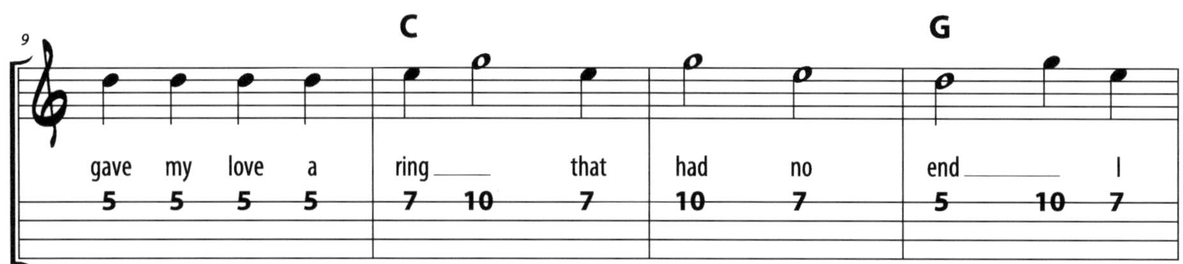

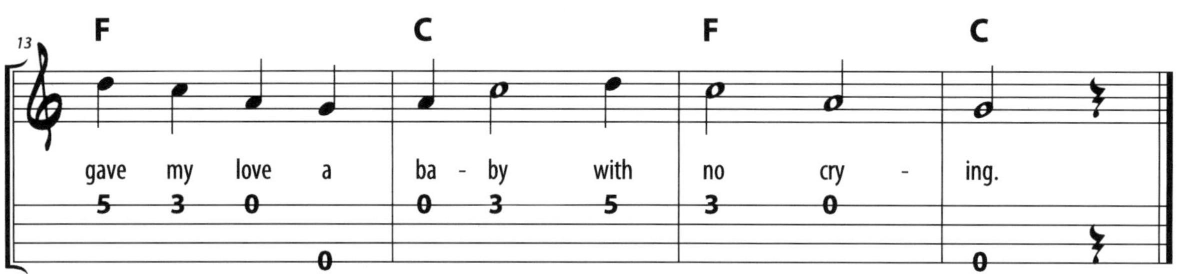

2. *How can there be a cherry*
That has no stone?
And how can there be a chicken
That has no bone?
And how can there be a story
That has no end?
And how can there be a baby
With no crying?

3. *A cherry when it's blooming*
It has no stone
A chicken when it's piping
It has no bone
The story that I love you
It has no end
A baby when it's sleeping
It's no crying.

(How to read) Chord diagrams

Horizontal lines represent the strings of the Ukulele, vertical lines the frets.

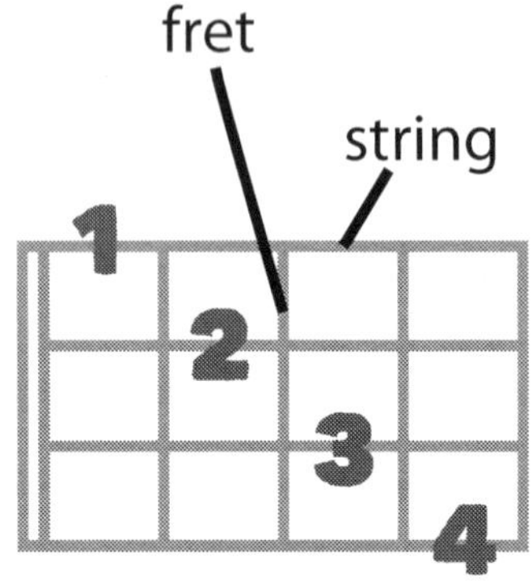

The fingers of the fretting hand are numbered 1-4:
1 = Index finger
2 = Middle finger
3 = Ringfinger
4 = Little finger (pinky)

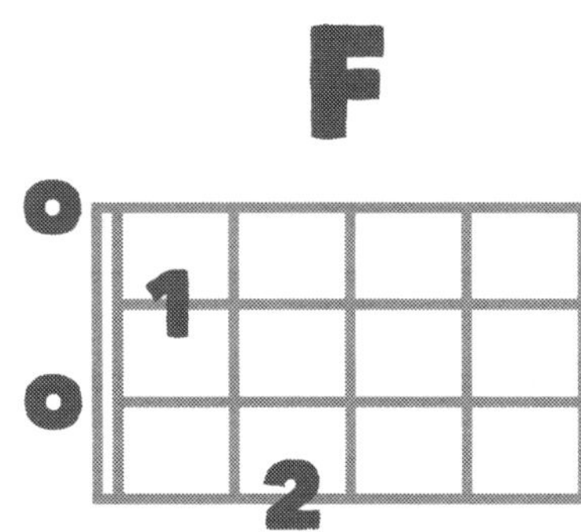

The chord symbol is given above the chord.

Open strings are indicated by an "0" to the left of the diagram, muted strings (strings that are not played or damped) by an "x".

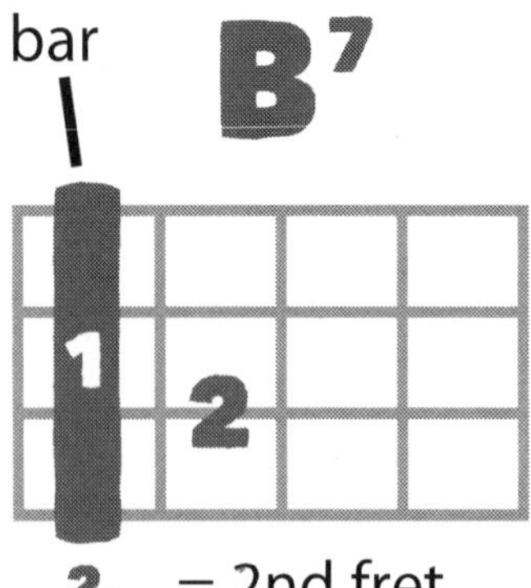

2. = 2nd fret

Fretboard positions are indicated below the chord. If a chord is to be played as a so-called bar chord (i.e. fretting more than one string with the same finger) this is indicated by a black bar. The number inside the bar indicates the recommended fretting finger.

Tuning the Ukulele

The strings of the Ukulele are numbered 1-4 (starting with the one next to the floor).

1st string	=	A
2nd string	=	E
3rd string	=	C
4th string	=	G

In contrast to most other string instruments, the strings of the Ukulele are tuned in what is called a reentrant tuning (meaning the lowest tuned string of the instrument is not the bottom string). This can make tuning the instrument slightly confusing, especially for beginners.
There are lots of ways to tune your Ukulele, one of which is shown below in graphical form.

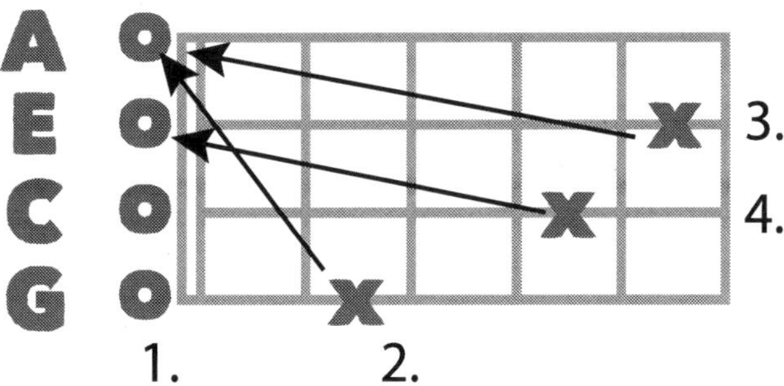

This reads as follows:

1. First tune the G string using a reference tone from another instrument (like a piano) or a tuner.
2. Fret the G string at the 2. fret. Play and compare to the open (not fretted) A string. Tune the A string until both pitches match exactly.
3. Fret the E string at the 5. Fret. Play and compare to the open A string. Tune the E string until both pitches match.
4. Finally, fret the C string at the 4. Fret. Play and compare to the open E string.

Tune the E string until both pitches match.

PS. Of course, using an (electronic) tuner is a great way to tune tour Ukulele, too.

Strumming patterns

The following is a selection of basic strumming pattern which you can use for song accompaniment. These are just for starters - you'll soon use other, more elaborate pattern or invent your own. Feel free to use a pick or your finger(s) for strumming – basically whatever feels best.

Here's how they're read:

- The horizontal lines represent the strings of your Ukulele.
  Downstroke (strumming in the direction of the floor): arrow upward
  Upstroke: arrow downward.
- The length of the arrows indicates which strings to strum.
- Each of these pattern shows a whole measure.

For song accompaniment you can choose (and also combine) whatever pattern feels best to you, but keep in mind to match the pattern's time to the time of the song, e.g. for a song in 4/4 time only use strumming patterns in 4/4 time.
Songs in 2/2 time can be played using strumming patterns in 4/4 time.

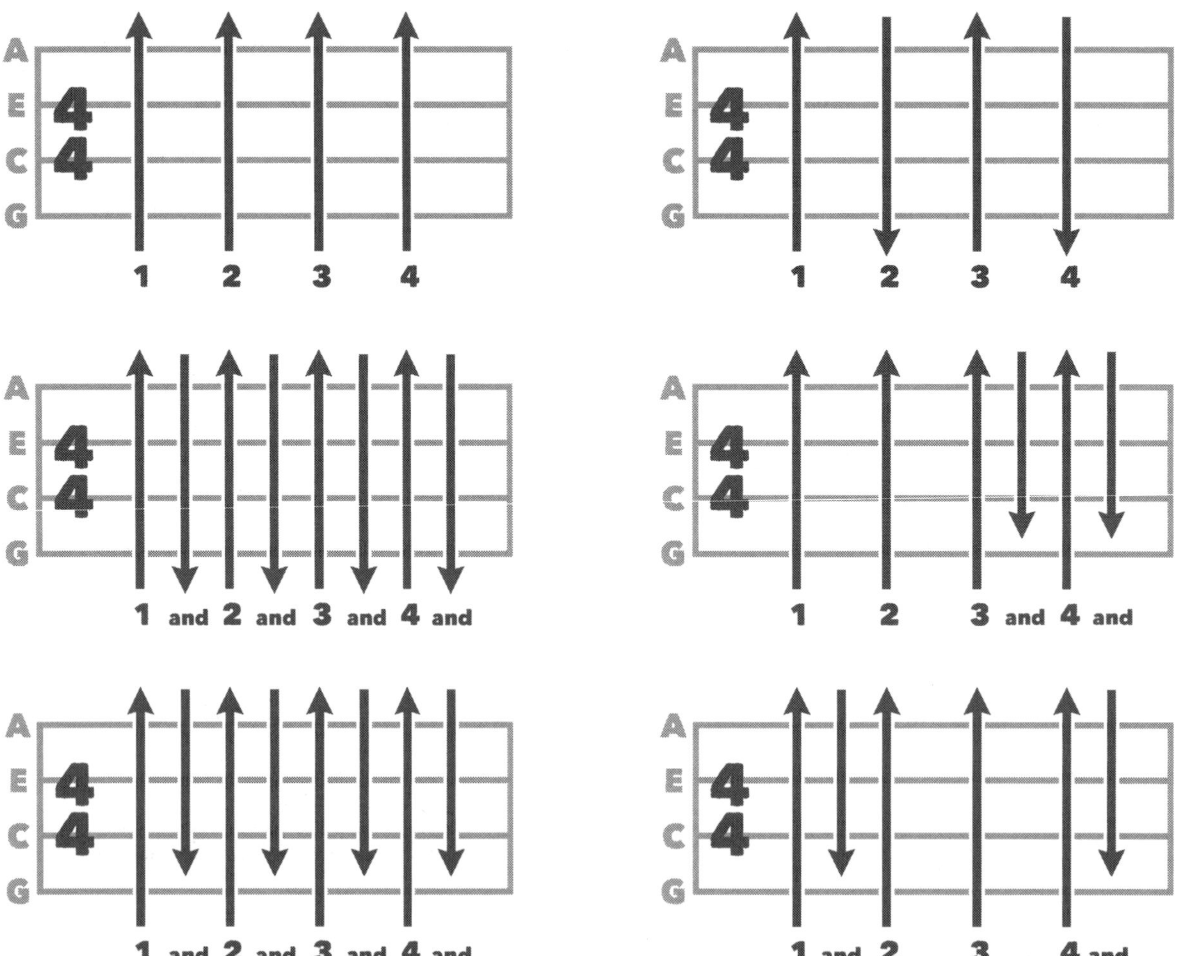

Strumming patterns

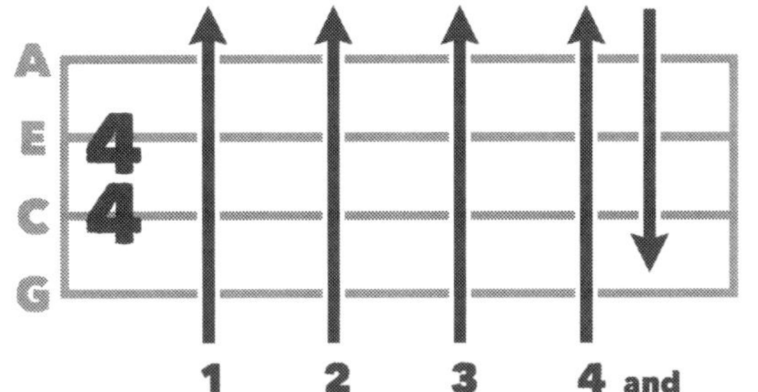

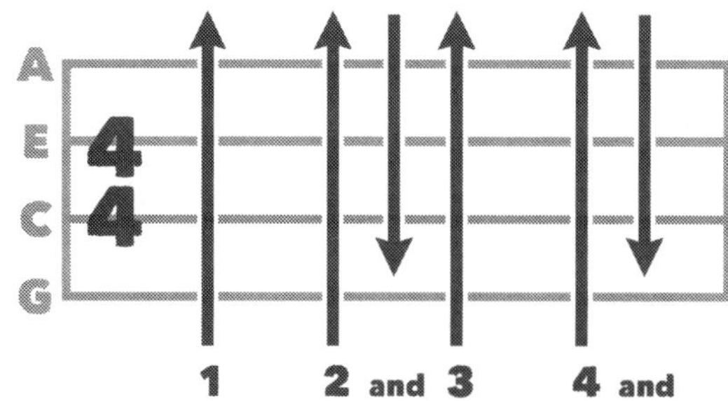

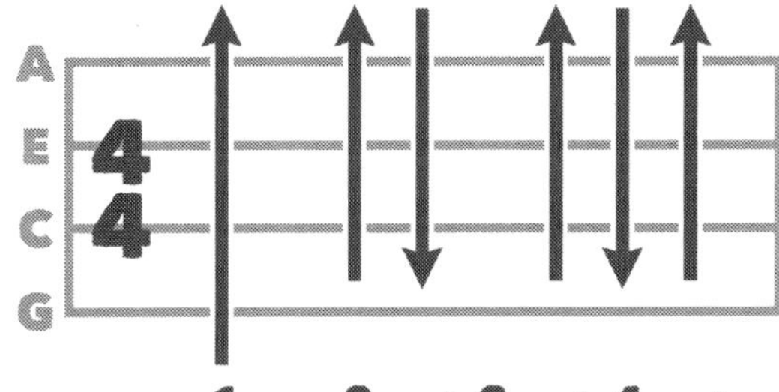

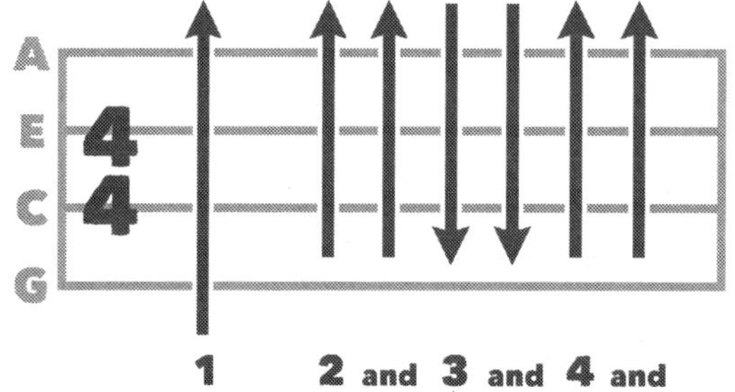

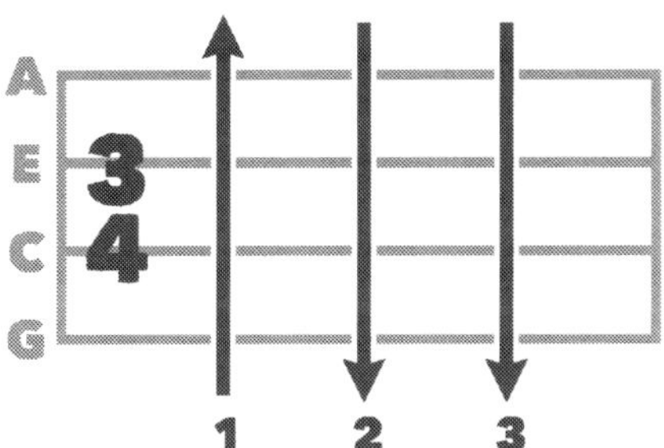

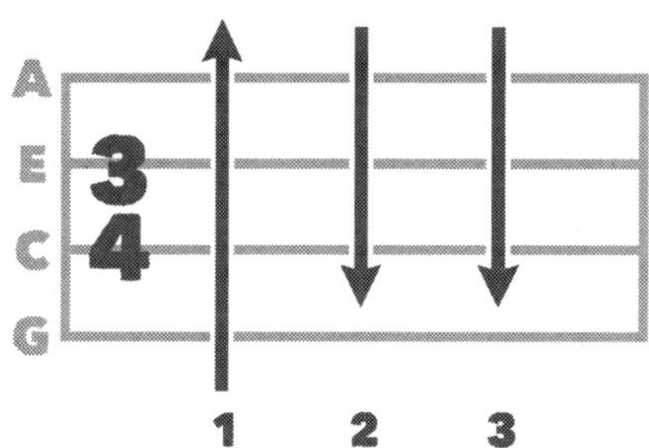

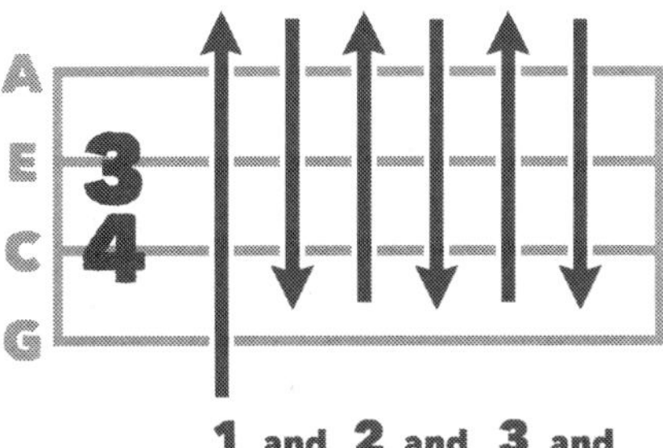

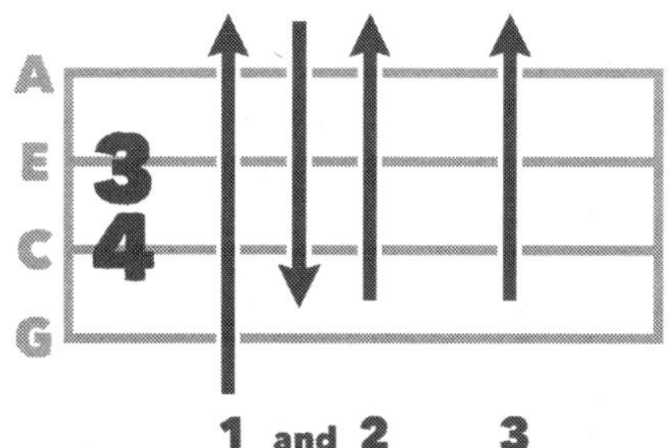

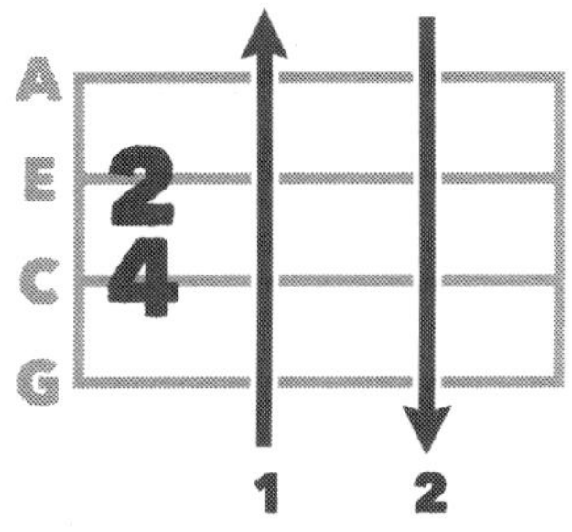

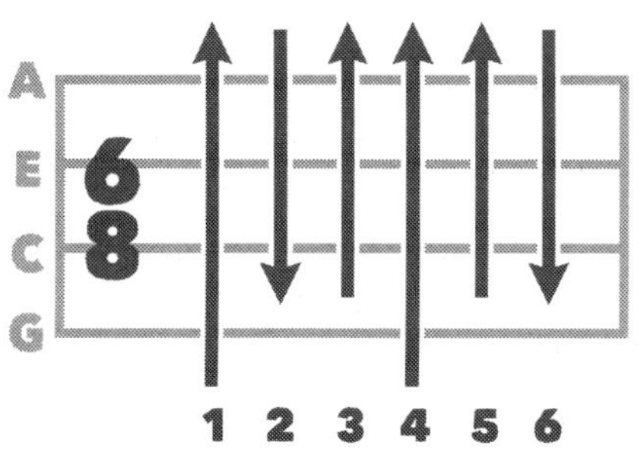

Picking patterns

A lot of songs sound particularly good when played using a picking pattern. Here's the basic idea: instead of picking all the notes of a chord simultaneously with you finger(s) or a pick, you play them successively, one after the other. Picking patterns are commonly used for longer musical sections (or even whole songs) and adapted to the chord changes if necessary. Here's an example, using the G major chord:

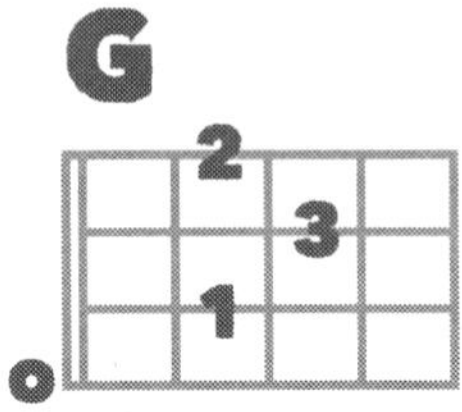

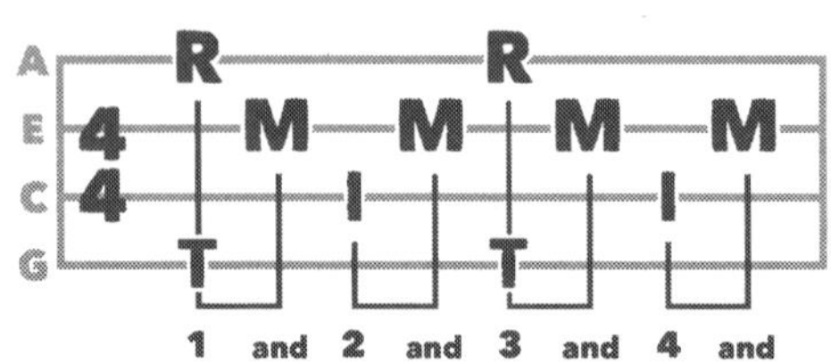

T = thumb
I = index finger
M = middle finger
R = ring finger

As in tablature, horizontal lines represent the strings of your Ukulele. The time signature is notated at the beginning of the pattern as a fraction (here: 4/4; this is a pattern for songs in 4/4 time). The letters T, I, M and R indicate the fingers of the picking hand. Below the pattern I've notated how to count it. Here's a step-by-step explanation of the above example:
- on the first beat ("1") thumb and ring finger simultaneously pick the G string and the A string.
- on the second half of the first beat ("1and") the middle finger picks the E string.
- on the second beat ("2") the index finger picks the C string.
- on the second half of the second beat ("2and") the middle finger picks the E string once again.
This pattern is repeated for the second half of the bar (this isn't always the case).

There are a few basic things to keep in mind when using picking patterns:
Obviously, the pattern's time signature has to match that of the song. In some cases, the pattern has to be adapted to a certain chord or a chord change, but most of the time you can use the following simple rule:

- pick the G string with your thumb,
- the C string with your index finger,
- the E string with your middle finger and
- the A string with your ring finger.

One of the best ways to practise picking patterns is to play them on open strings until the movement of your fingers becomes second nature – practicing this way ensures you'll be able to concentrate on more important things when it's time to play the song.
When the picking pattern has been "automized" to a certain degree it's time to add chords and chord changes. Take your time because nothing sounds worse than a "stuttering" picking pattern interfering with a smooth chord change.
On the following pages you'll find some basic picking patterns to choose from. Of course, this is just a small selection from the multitude of possible patterns, meant to whet your appetite – you'll soon find varying patterns and inventing new ones of your own can be lots of fun!

For a start, you may want to try:

- Combining different picking patterns (e. g. one for the verse and one for the chorus).
- Combining picking patterns with strumming patterns.
- Mixing picking patterns with melody lines and damping techniques.
- Playing some of your favorites "backwards".

Sometimes you'll encounter indications in Spanish:
P (pulgar) = thumb
I (indice) = index finger
M (medio) = middle finger
A (anular) = ring finger

Picking patterns

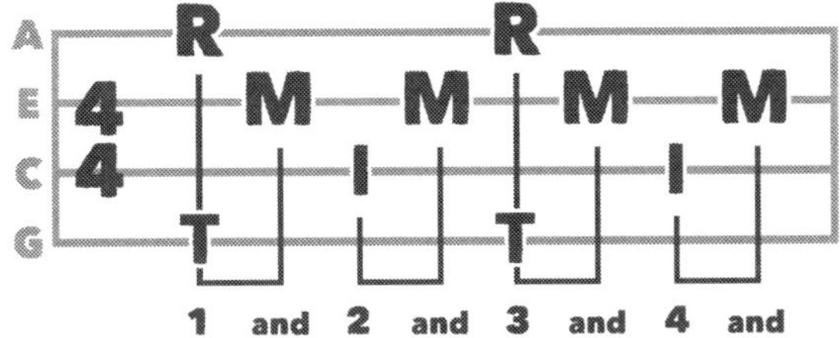

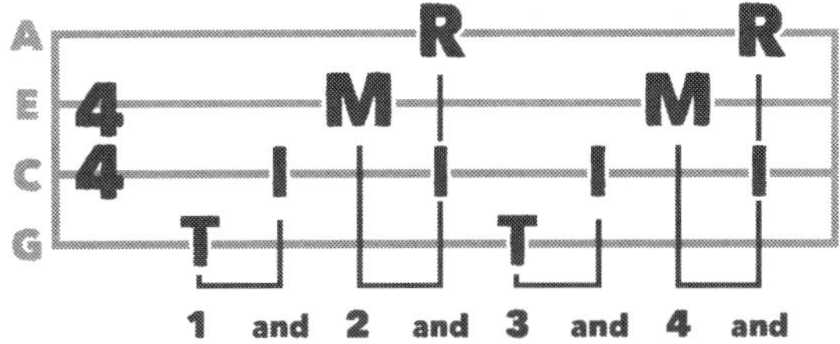

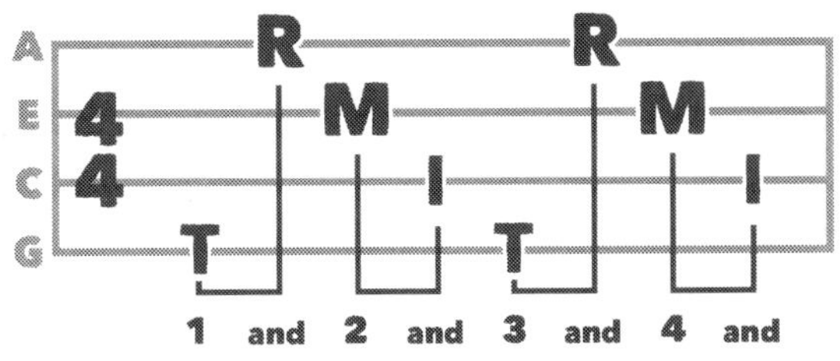

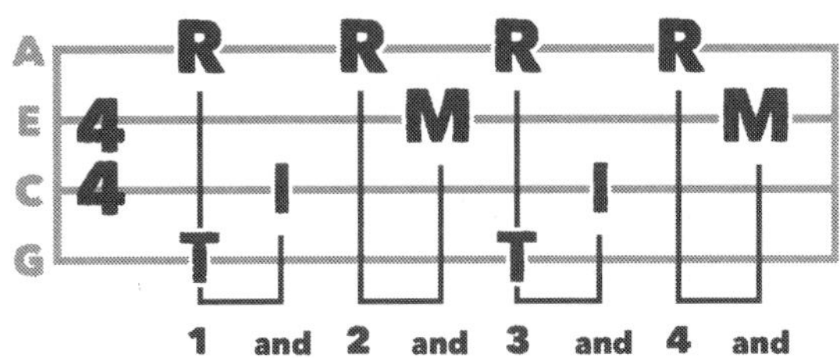

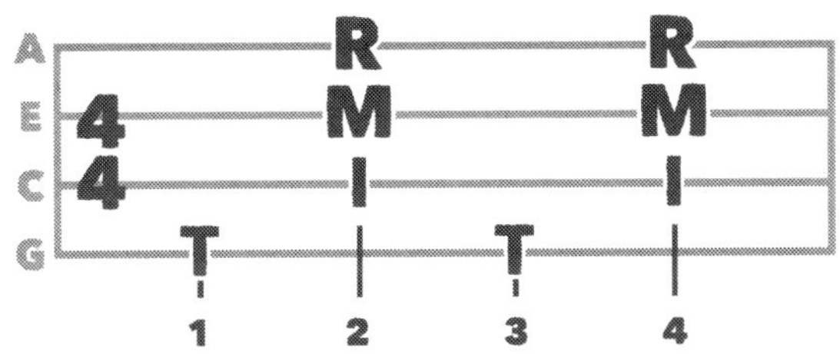

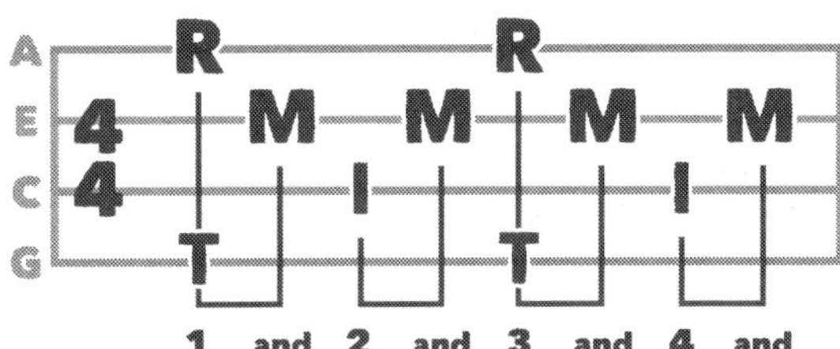

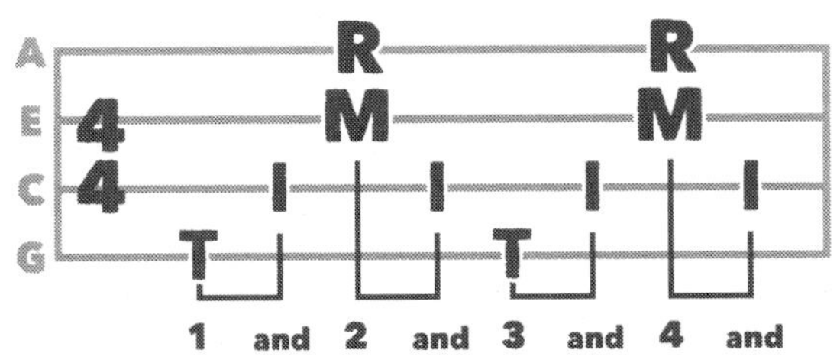

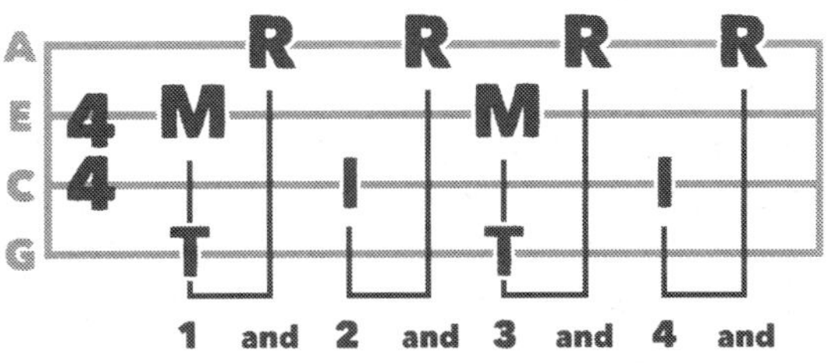

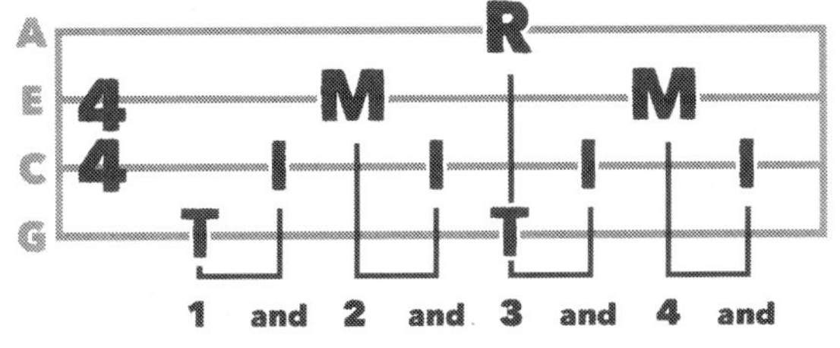

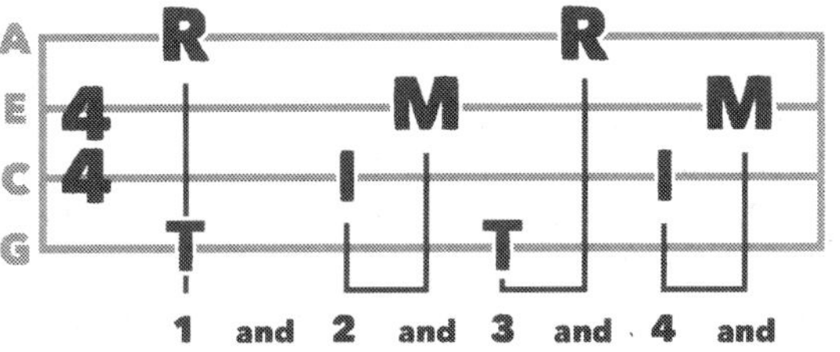

Picking Patterns

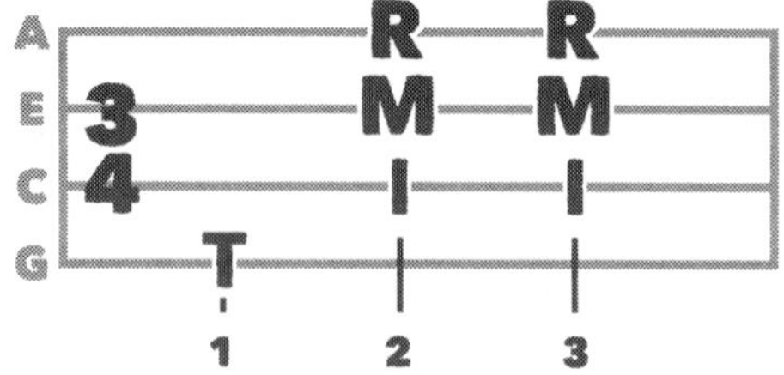

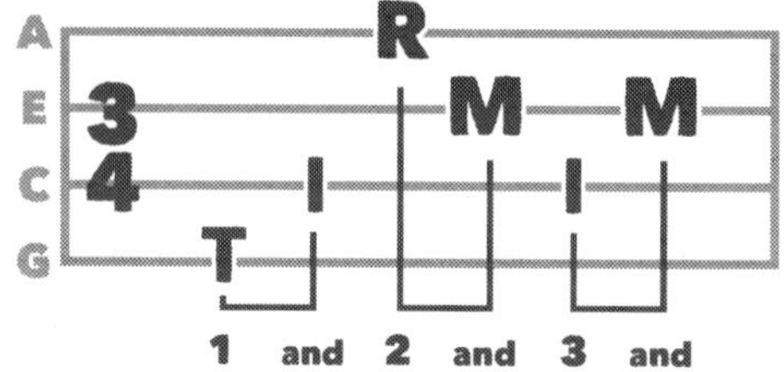

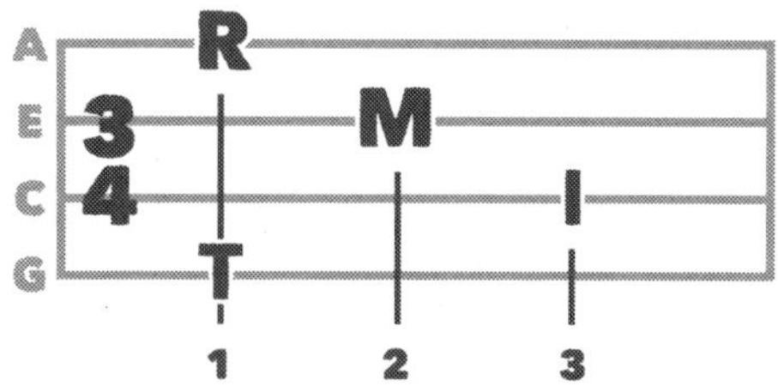

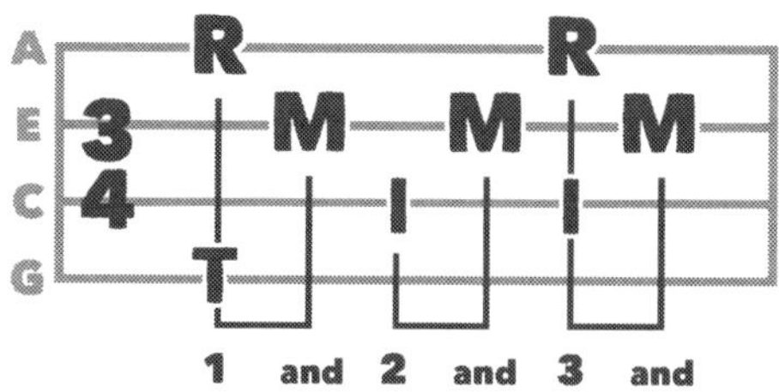

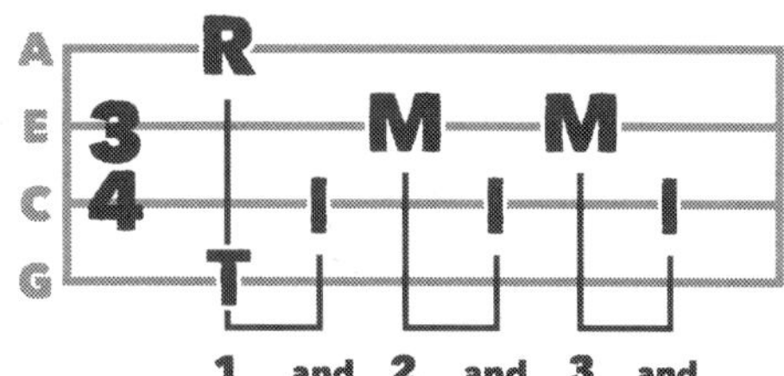

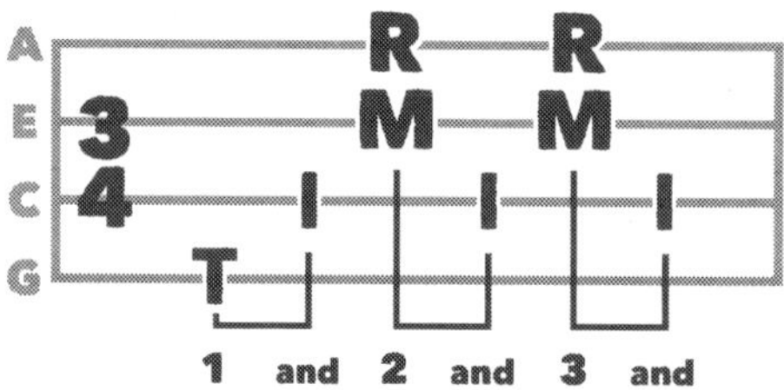

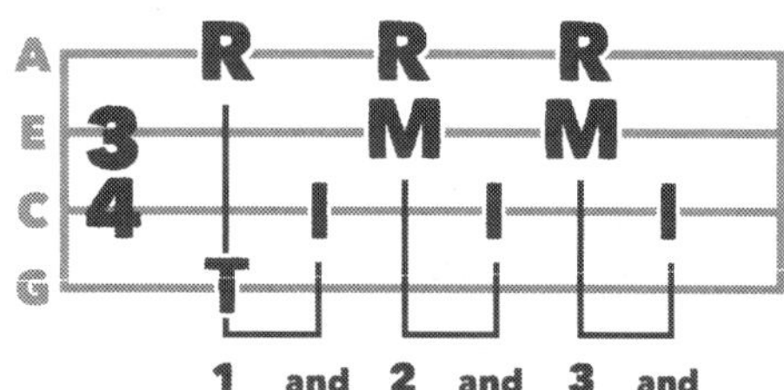

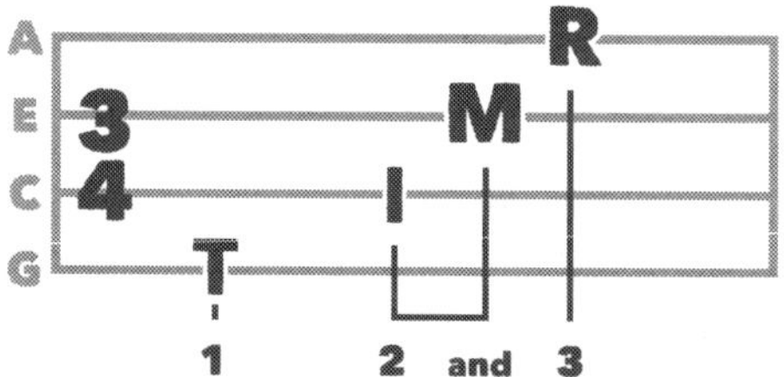

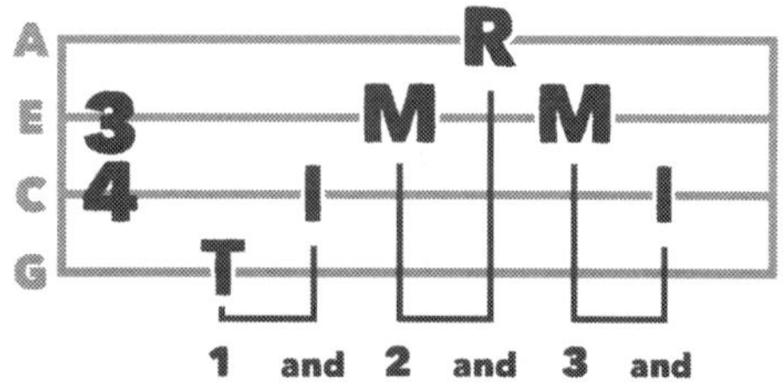

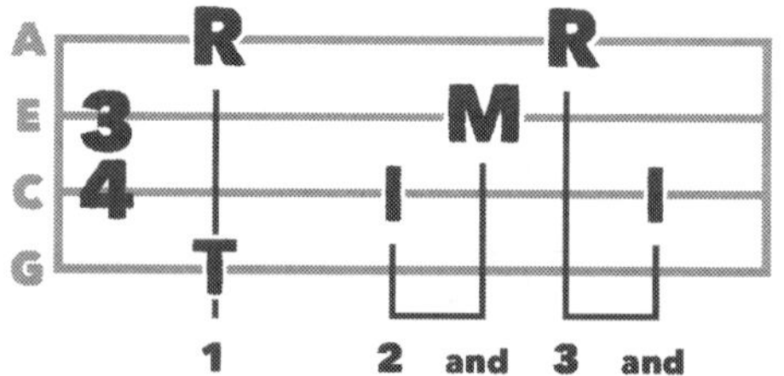

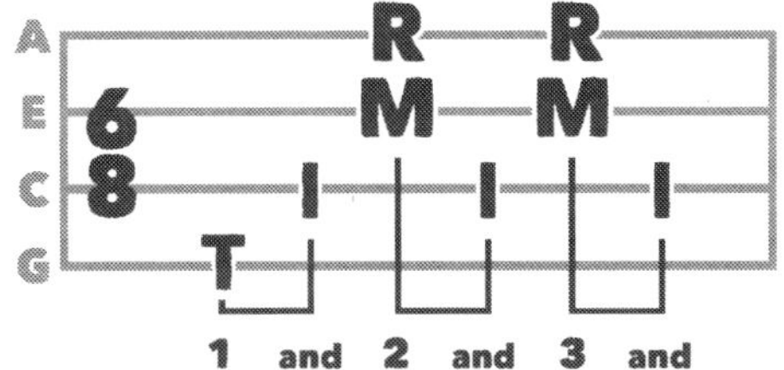
A
E
C
G
6
8
R R
M M
T I I I
1 and 2 and 3 and

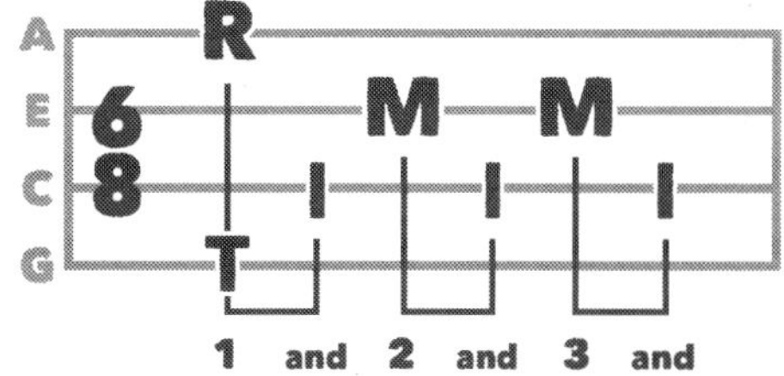
A
E
C
G
6
8
R
M M
T I I I
1 and 2 and 3 and

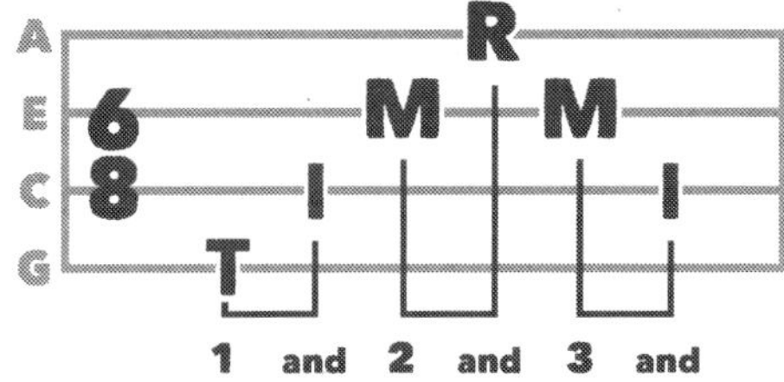
A
E
C
G
6
8
R
M M
T I I
1 and 2 and 3 and

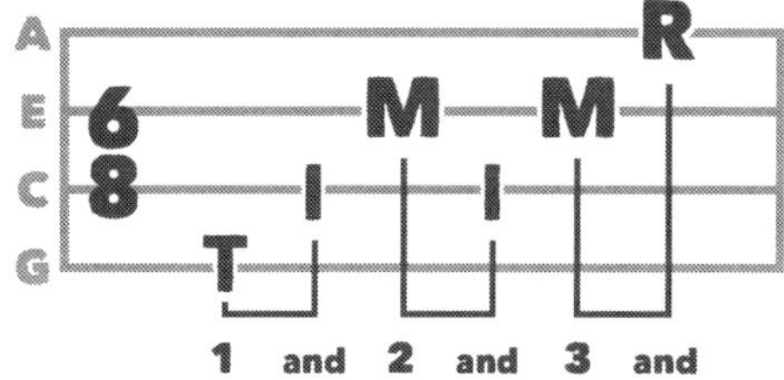
A
E
C
G
6
8
R
M M
T I I
1 and 2 and 3 and

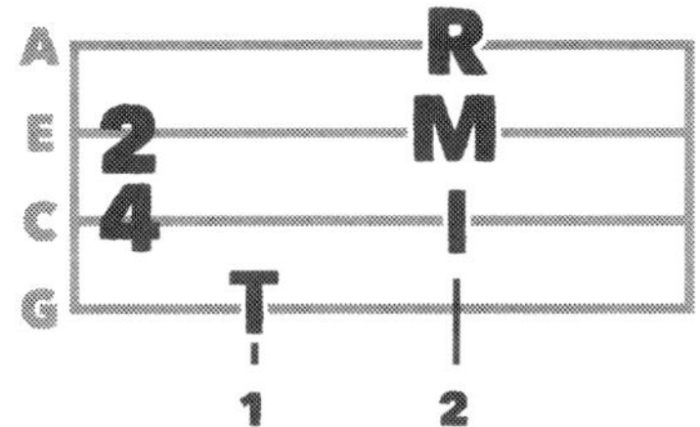
A
E
C
G
2
4
R
M
T I
1 2

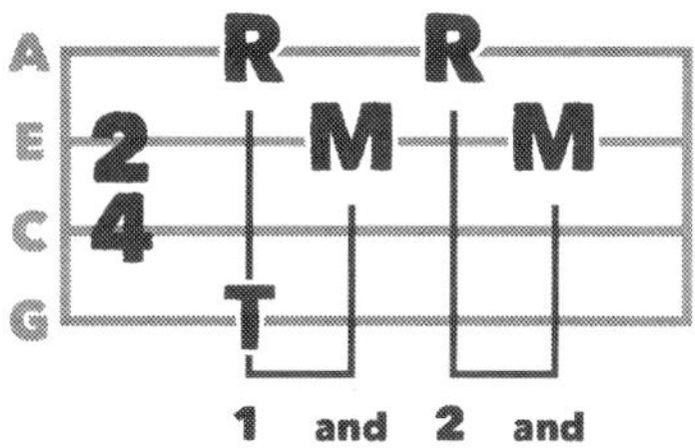
A
E
C
G
2
4
R R
M M
T
1 and 2 and

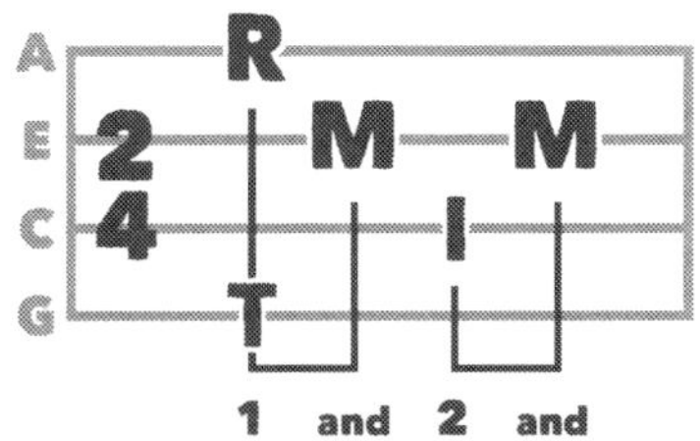
A
E
C
G
2
4
R
M M
T I
1 and 2 and

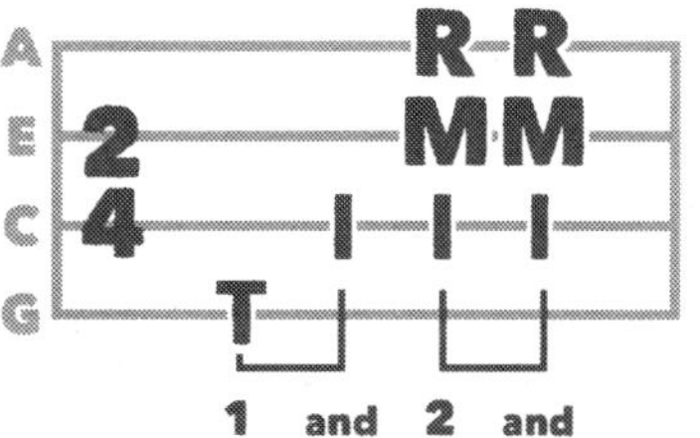
A
E
C
G
2
4
R R
MM
T I I I
1 and 2 and

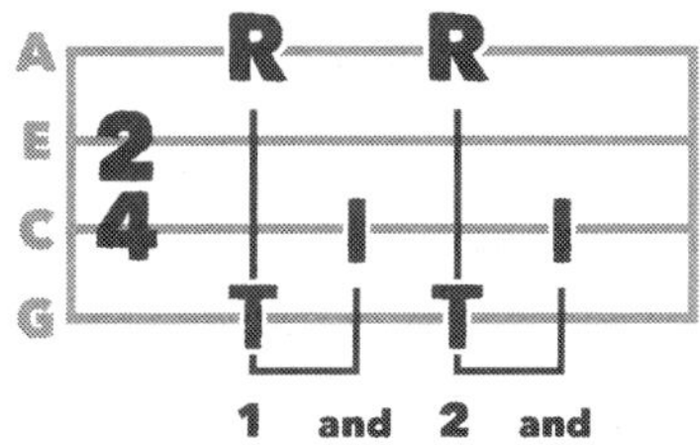
A
E
C
G
2
4
R R
T I T I
1 and 2 and

Basic chords

On the following pages I've compiled the chords used in this book. I've also included some chords you'll probably encounter in other books. Naturally, this chord collection is far from complete – there are literally thousands of Ukulele chords (some common, some pretty obscure). If you want to expand your chord repertoire (or simply look up a chord you don't know), a chord chart is always a wise investment, and of course you can find almost any Ukulele chord on the internet.
Depending on the musical context, some chords may have more than one name:

C♯ = D♭, D♯ = E♭, F♯ = G♭, G♯ = A♭ und A♯ = B♭

For Ukulele players this simply means: C♯ and D♭ are played the same and they sound the same. If, for example, you happen to stumble upon a G♯m (G sharp minor) chord, don't worry: just play A♭m.

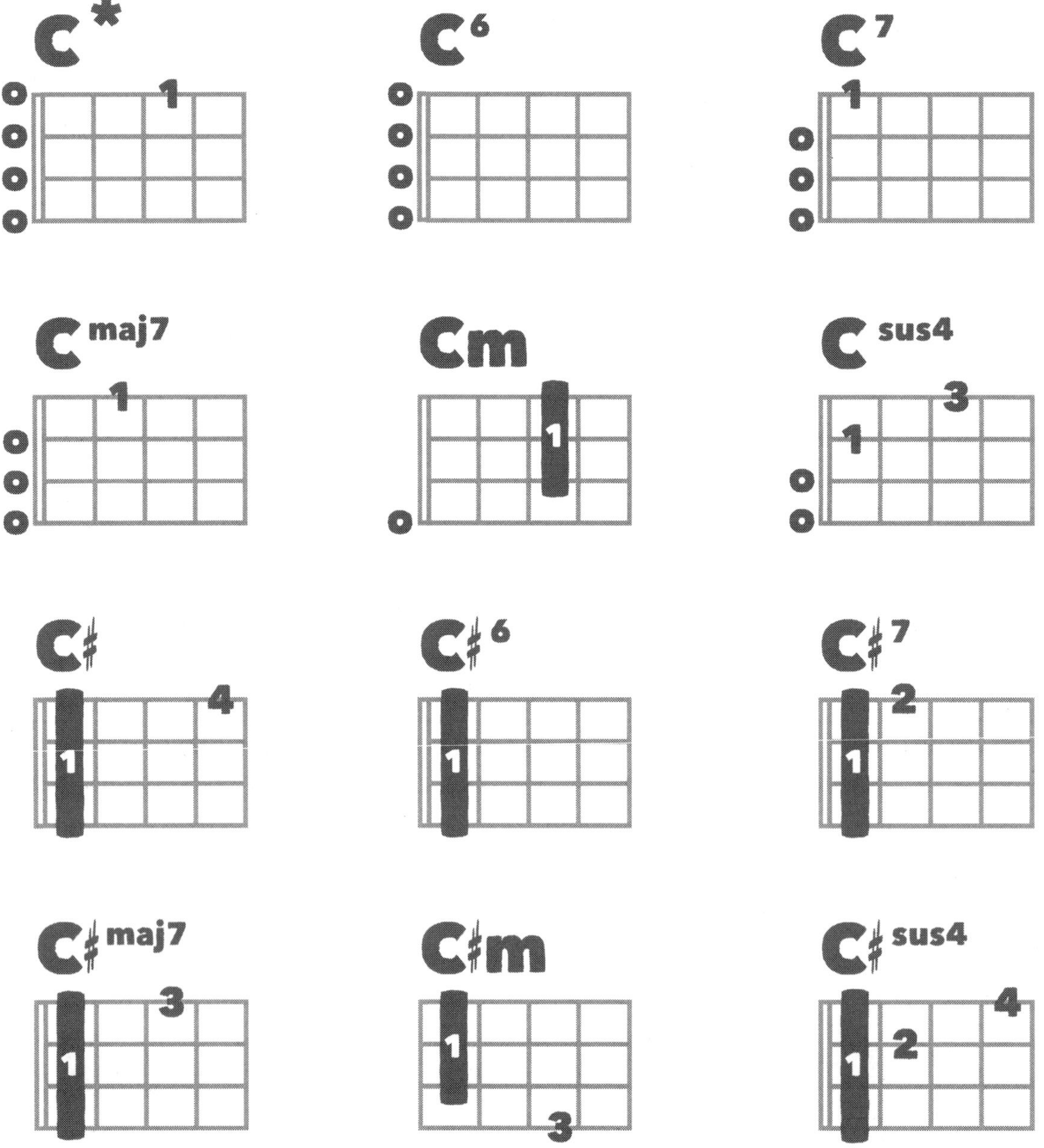

* = Alternate fingering for this chord: ring finger (3)

D

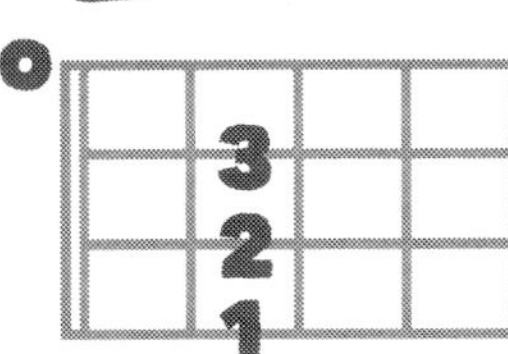

D^{6}

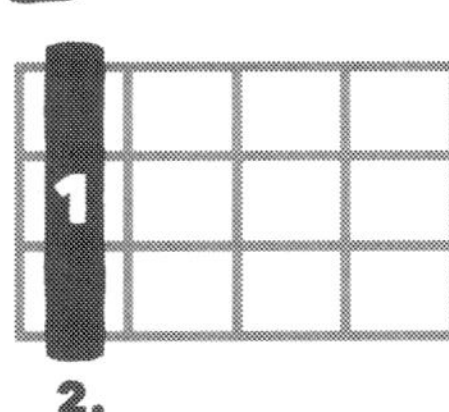

D^{7}

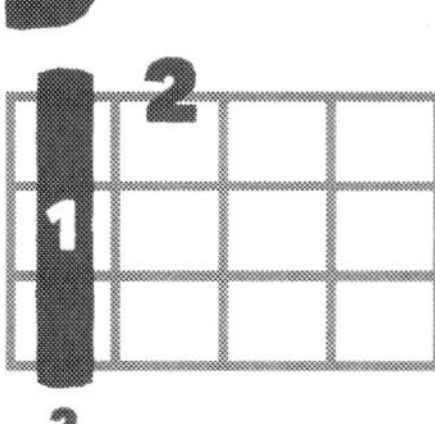

D^{maj7}

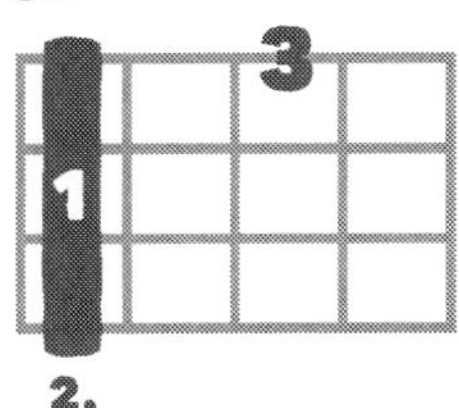

Dm

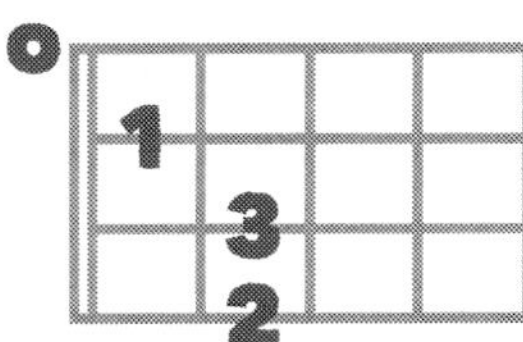

D^{sus4}

E♭

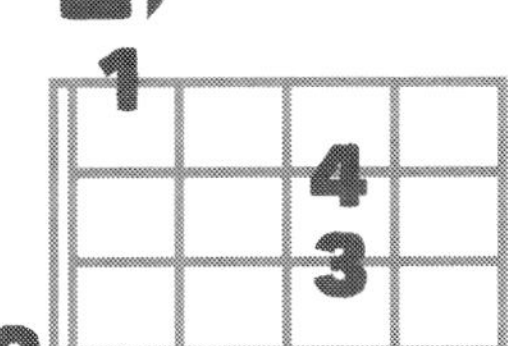

E♭^{6}

E♭^{7}

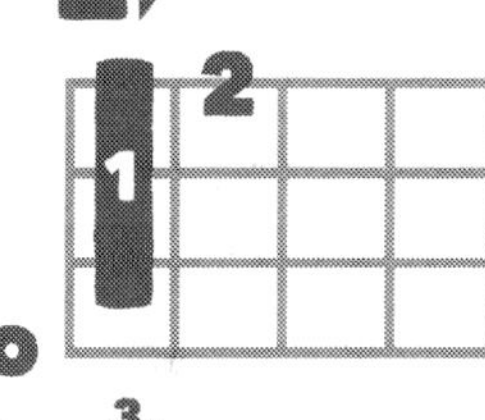

E♭^{maj7}

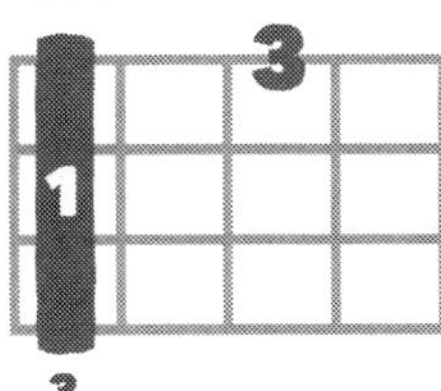

E♭m

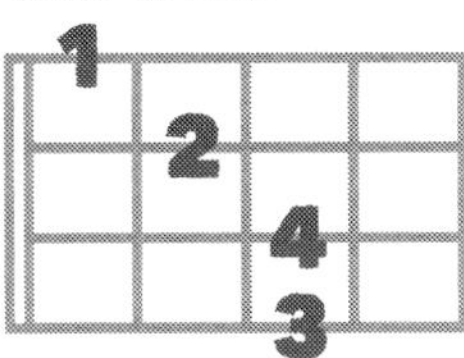

E♭$^{7/sus4}$

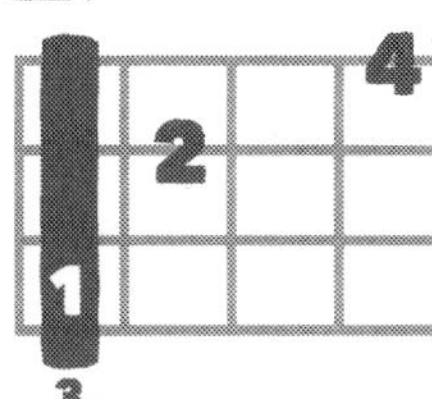

E

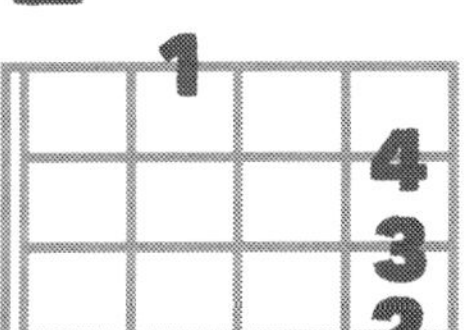

E^{6}

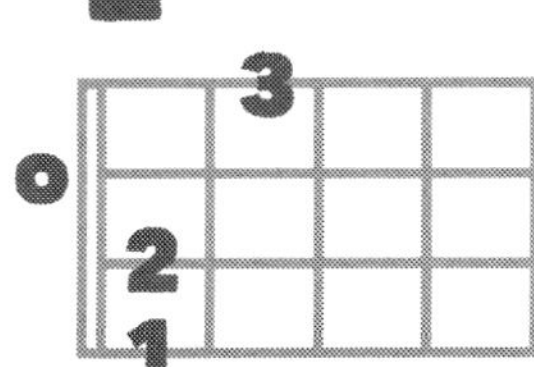

E^{7}

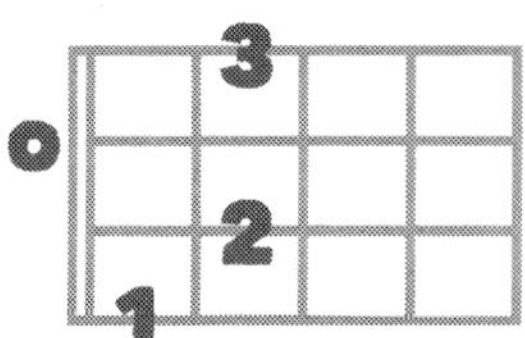

Basic chords

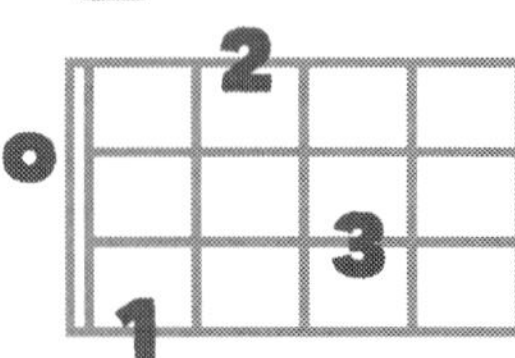

Em

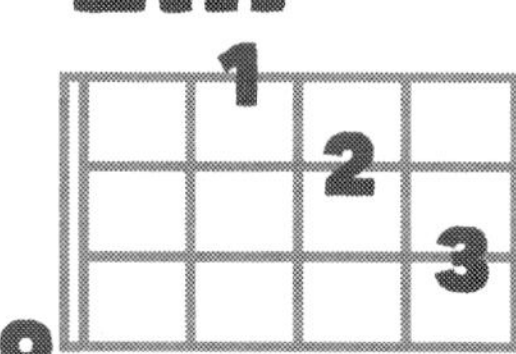

E sus4

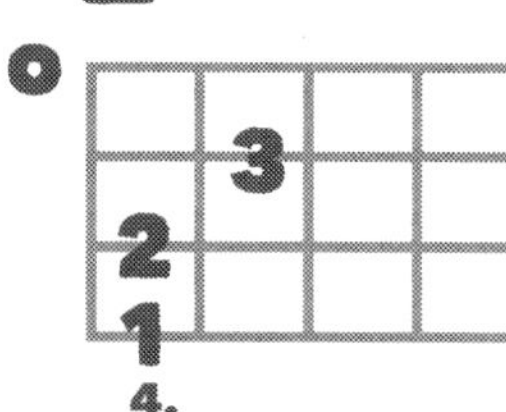

F

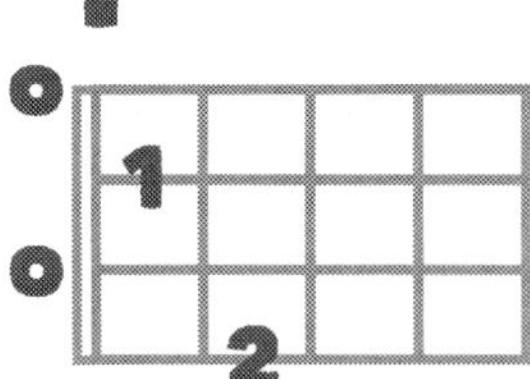

F 6

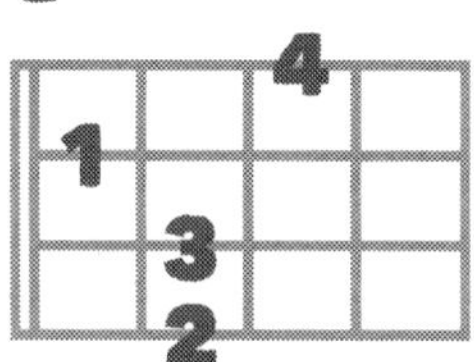

F 7

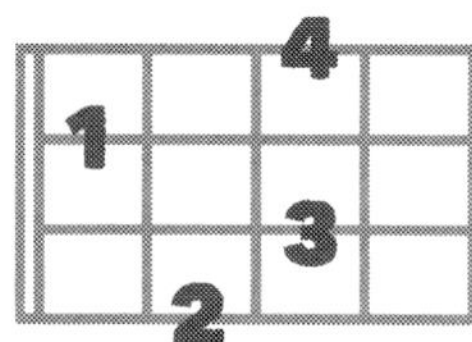

F maj7

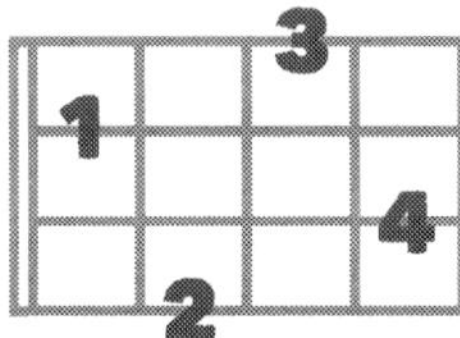

Fm

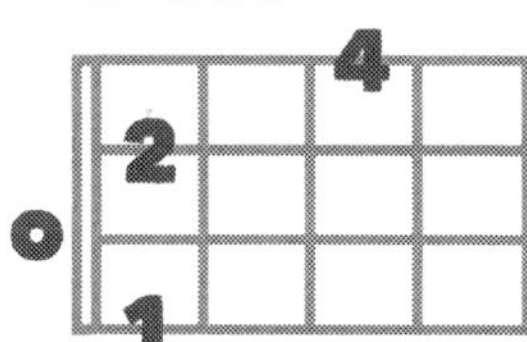

F sus4

F♯ *

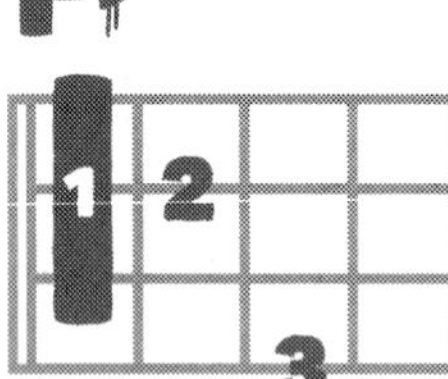

F♯ 6

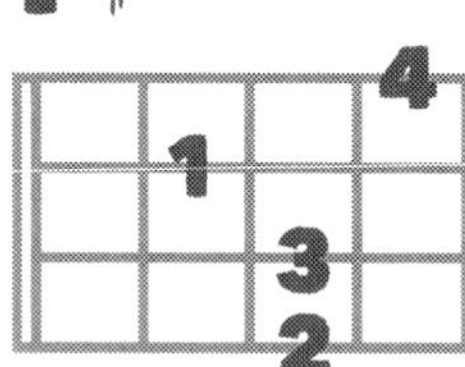

F♯ 7

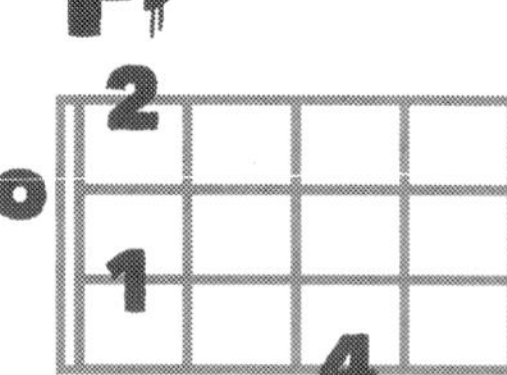

F♯ maj7

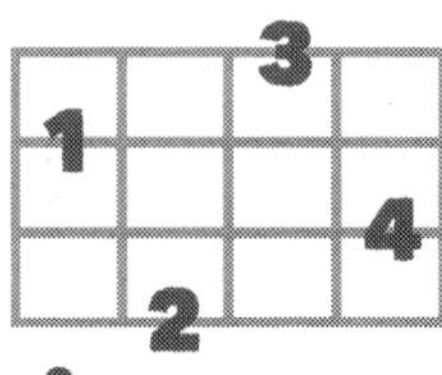

F♯m

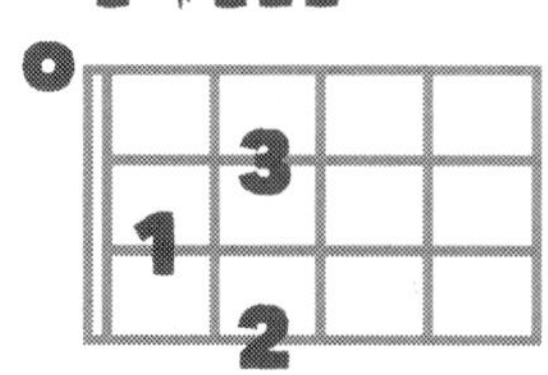

F♯ sus4

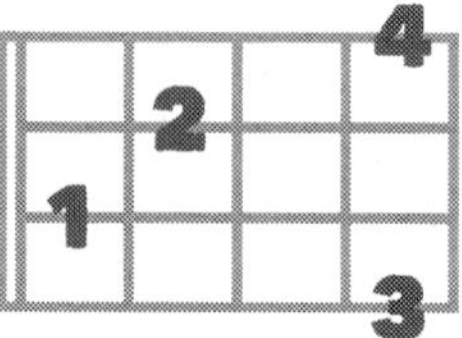

* = This chord can also be played as a full bar chord.

Basic chords

G

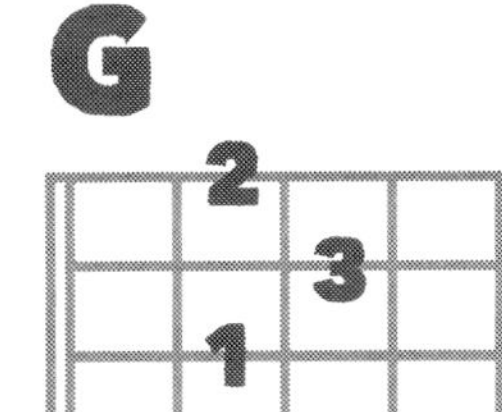

G6

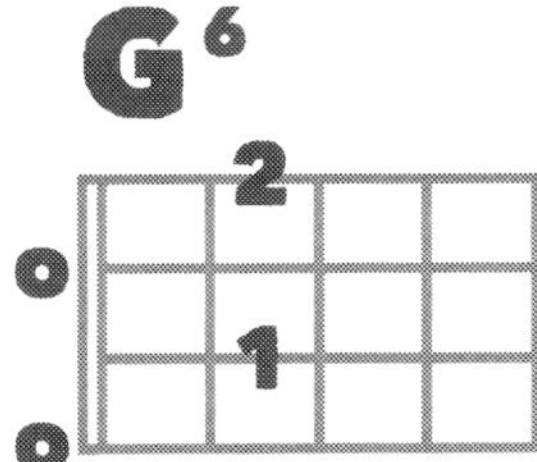

G7

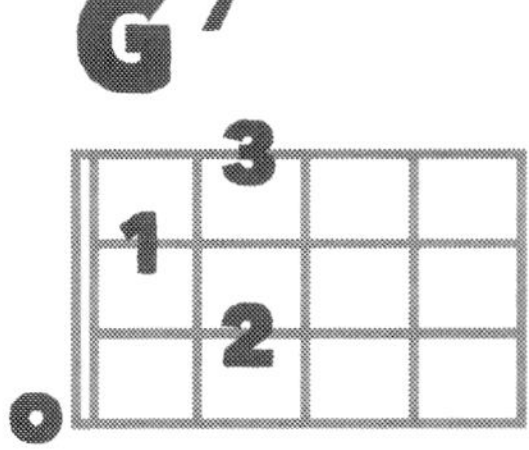

Gmaj7

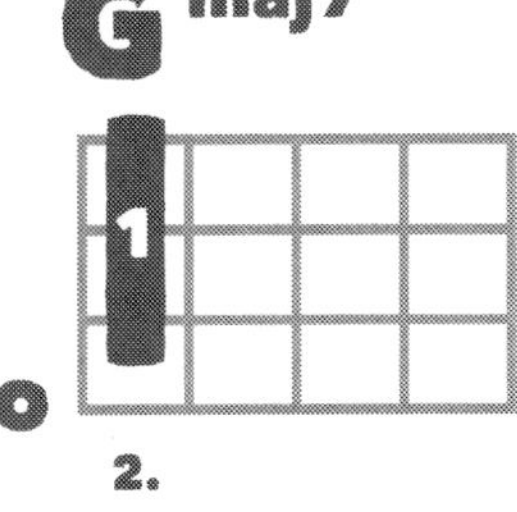

Gm

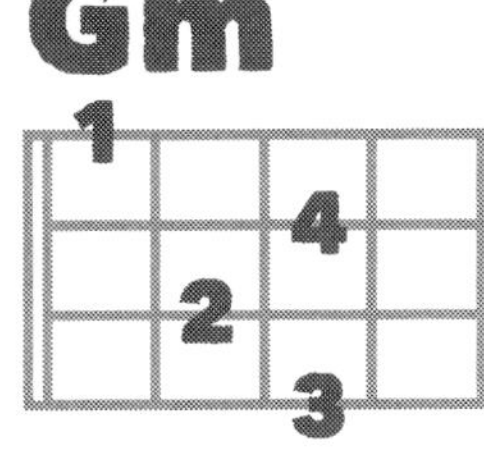

Gsus4

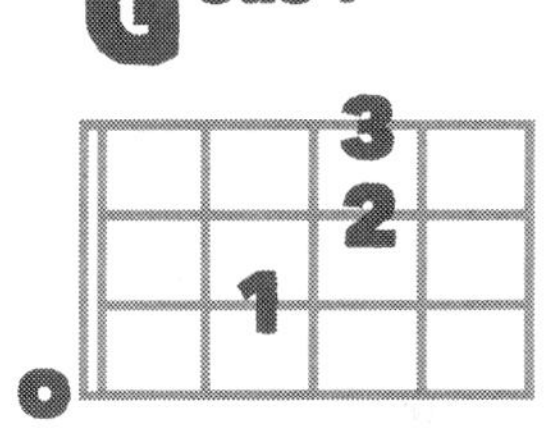

A♭

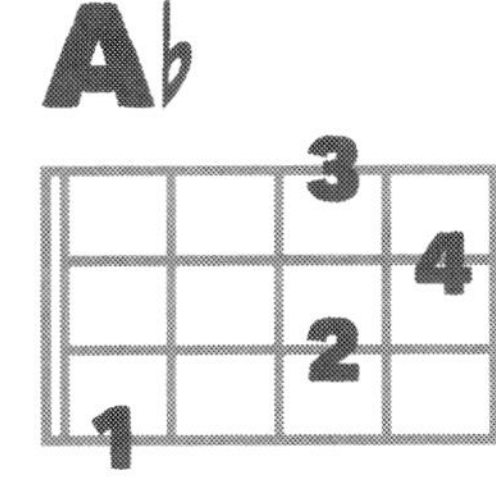

A♭6

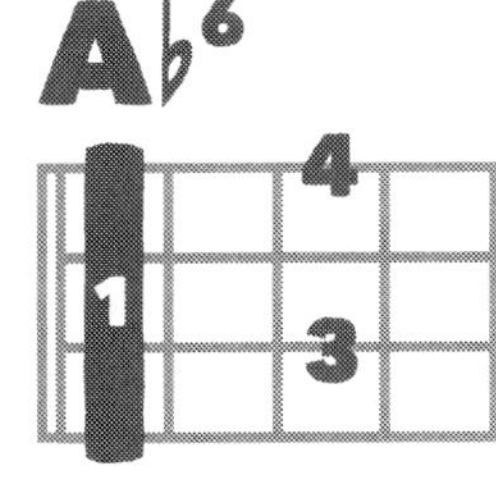

A♭7

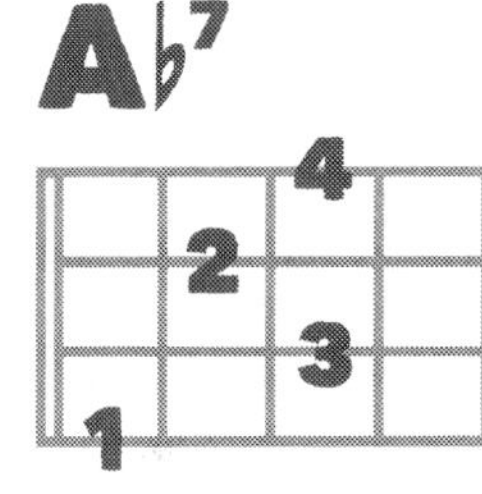

A♭maj7

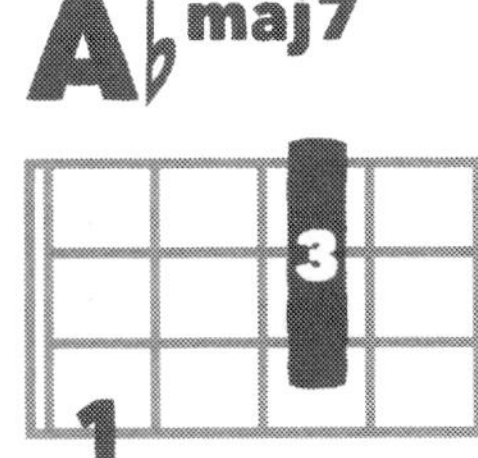

A♭m

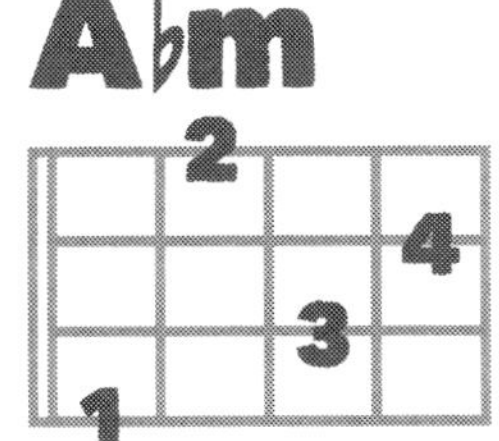

A♭sus4

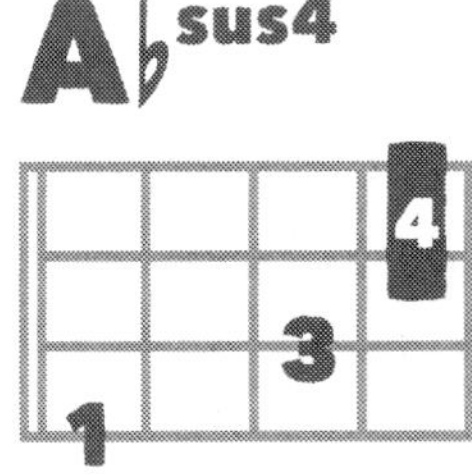

A

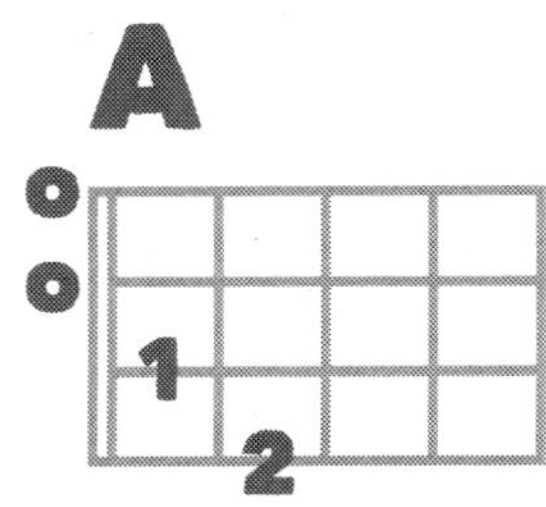

A6

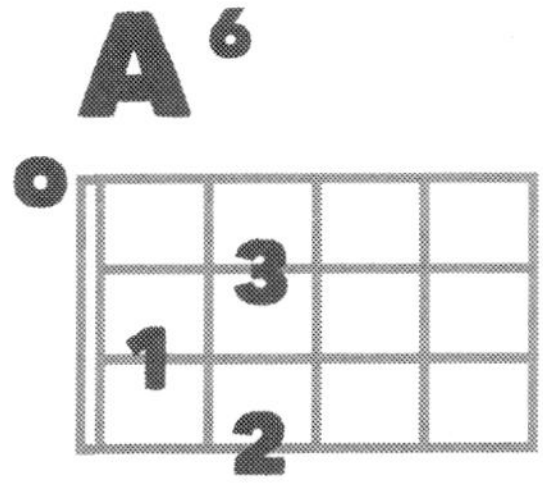

A7

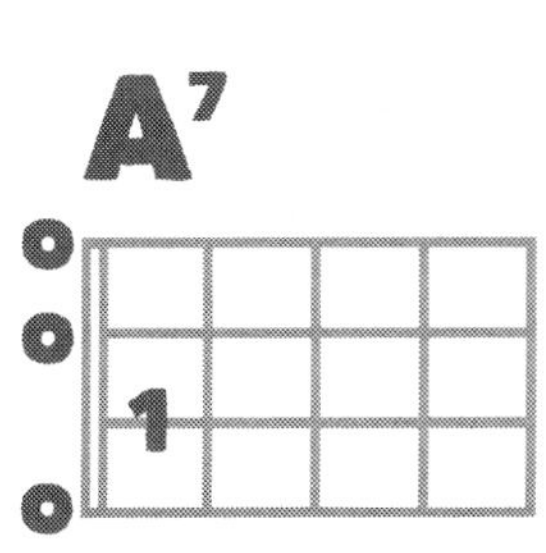

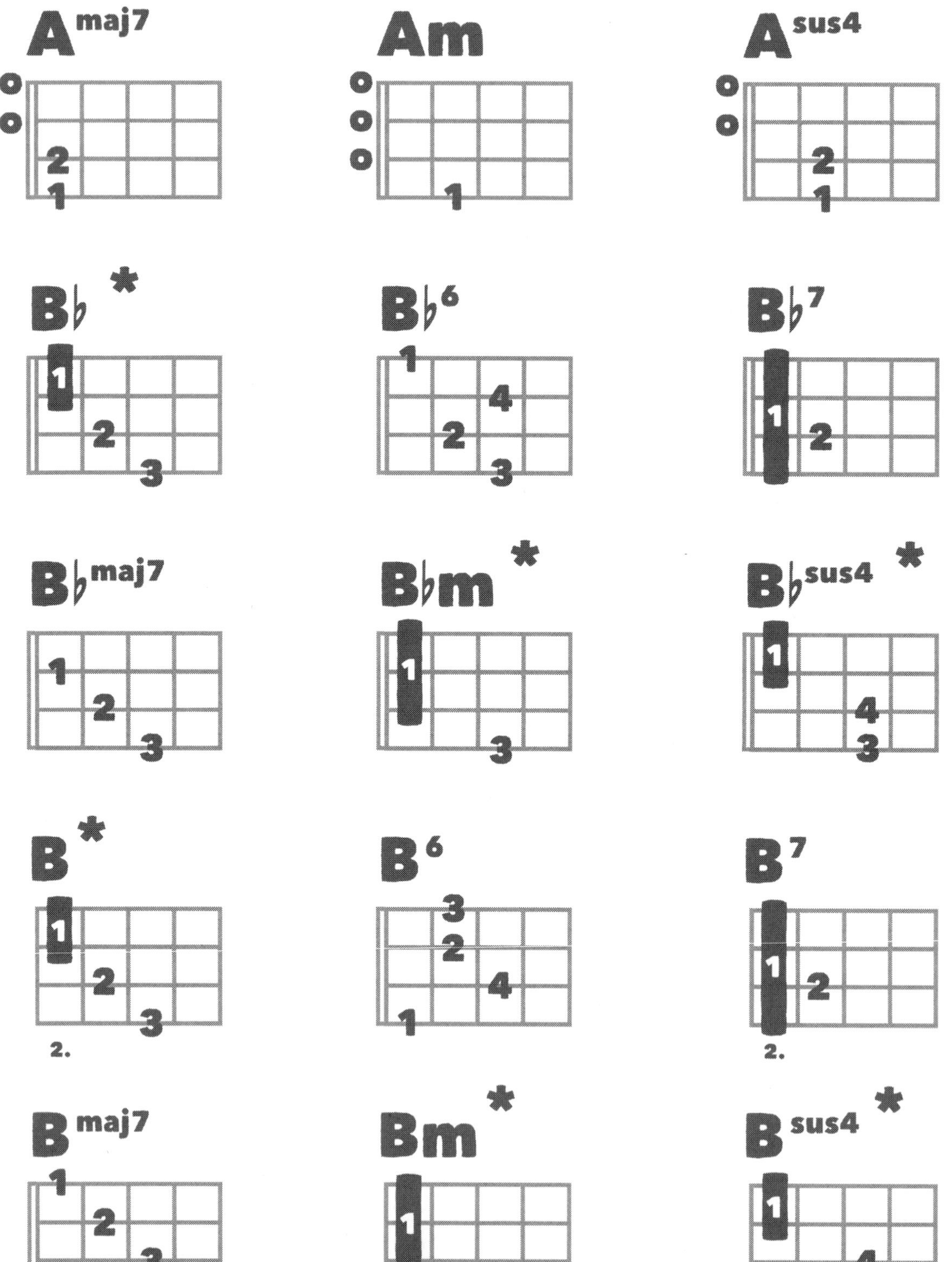

* = These chords can also be played as full bar chords.

Made in the USA
Columbia, SC
17 April 2018